Into the Shadows Furious

Into the
Shadows Furious
The Brutal Battle for New Georgia

Brian Altobello

★

PRESIDIO

Published by Presidio Press
505 B San Marin Drive, Suite 160
Novato, CA 94945-1340

Library of Congress Cataloging-in-Publication Data

Altobello, Brian.
    Into the shadows furious : the World War II assault on New Geor-
gia / by Brian Altobello.
        p. cm.
    Includes bibliographical references and index.
    ISBN 0-89141-717-6
    1. World War, 1939–1945—Campaigns—Solomon Islands—
Munda (Soloman Islands)—History, Military—20th century. I.
Title.
D767.98 .A48 2000
940.54'26—dc21

                              00-042766

All photos courtesy National Archives unless otherwise noted.
Printed in the United States of America

Contents

Acknowledgments

I received assistance from dozens of veterans who helped me locate personal accounts of the assault. Bob Schwolsky of the 169th Infantry Regiment and Norvil Wilson of the 37th Infantry Division Veterans Association arranged important interviews. Howard Brown of the 43rd Infantry Division Veterans Association, whose newsletter and website were most helpful. John McCarthy of the U.S. Marine Raider Association happily provided his collection of *Raider Patch* newsletters. Marine Raider Al Caraega, whose memory of the events that occurred over a half-century ago remain amazingly unblemished, was unselfish with his time.

The only published oral history of New Georgia is the work of Bob Conrad, whose series in the *Hartford Courant* on the 169th Regiment is an example of the very best in reporting. He was kind enough to share his research with me. My thanks go to Charles Henne, who publishes the *Buckeye Star News*, the 37th Infantry Division's Lone Star Chapter. Frank Guidone, a Marine Raider, and Frank Giliberto of the 169th Infantry, provided me with their exceptional memoirs of the battle.

Thanks to Tim Neinger, of the National Archives, Germain Pavlova-O'Neill of the Donovan Technical Library at Fort Benning, Georgia, and Mary Dennis, Office of the Clerk of Court, U.S. Army Judiciary, for their help. I am indebted to the interlibrary loan division of the Jefferson Parish East Bank Regional Library in Metairie, Louisiana. Ewan Stevenson, a Guadalcanal native, kept me supplied with important documents and photos. Technical assistance was provided by Cheryl Mire. Finally, I want to express my appreciation to Denise Hudson for her skillful editing and unfailing encouragement.

Introduction

Any discussion of the Southwest Pacific and South Pacific Areas in World War II must begin with the mighty Japanese stronghold at Rabaul on the extreme northeastern tip of New Britain in the Bismarck Islands. In January 1942, an insignificant Australian garrison was overwhelmed there, and the Japanese quickly began construction of three more airdromes, adding to the two that were already in place. Blessed with one of the best harbors in this vast region, it was rapidly stocked with thousands of tons of the finest ships in the Imperial Navy. Its five airfields soon accommodated hundreds of fighters and bombers in support of the more than one hundred thousand infantry who were with a large surplus of tanks and artillery. Possession of Rabaul gave the Japanese access to and domination over the Solomon Islands to the southeast and New Guinea to the southwest. Even more menacing, Rabaul was only 436 miles from Port Moresby on the southern coast of Papua New Guinea, the Allied base that was the protective shield for Australia. If Port Moresby were lost, the Japanese would be only three hundred short miles from the vulnerable Australian coast. Rabaul thus became a threatening fist waving in the direction of Darwin, Townsville, Brisbane, and points farther south.

So many ships and warplanes were sent to Rabaul that by May 1942 it rivaled Truk as the principal citadel of Japanese military power in the Pacific. Australian prime minister John Curtin was understandably anxious, for his best divisions were away fighting in the Middle East. President Franklin D. Roosevelt responded by ordering the 32nd and 41st Infantry Divisions to Australia. Additional Allied troops were sent to the Fijis, New Zealand, New Caledonia, the New

Hebrides, and Samoa despite the Allies' priority being the defeat of Germany.

The formidable outpost at Rabaul presented problems for the Japanese as well. In order to shield their prized enclave from naval or air assaults, they were forced to overextend themselves by establishing a protective umbrella to the south. Lae and Salamaua on the northern coast of New Guinea were taken, and by May 1942 they had completed the occupation of the Bismarck Archipelago. Landing strips were built at Buka in the northern Solomons, in the Treasury Islands, the Shortlands, and on Tulagi and Guadalcanal farther down the Solomon ladder. There was another purpose for these moves: If the Imperial government was to strike Australia, the Japanese first had to successfully interdict communication and supply lines into Australia from the United States. These bases would allow them the opportunity to attempt such a maneuver. The question was, did Japan have the resources to hold its far-reaching outposts in the face of its improving adversary?

Japanese strategy early in the war was to seize as many islands as quickly as possible and strengthen them in order to insulate the homeland. The attack on Pearl Harbor was designed to buy time to carry this out. The guess was that the United States would eventually become discouraged at the daunting task of uprooting the Japanese from their strongholds, and, fearing an intolerable loss of life, finally settle on a negotiated peace favorable to Japan. This strategy never included an ambition to conquer the United States. The Japanese simply wanted to deny the United States' air and naval bases from which its forces could disrupt their ultimate goal of creating a Greater East Asia Co-Prosperity Sphere.

Allied forces were in disarray in early 1942 after Pearl Harbor. Like the navy, the Japanese army had been undefeated as well. Save for the continuing struggle in China, it had conquered Hong Kong, Singapore, Malaya, the Dutch East Indies, and Burma, inflicting more than 175,000 Allied casualties. The Japanese also conquered the Philippines, the bastion of American presence in the Pacific and the scene of the collapse and surrender of more than a hundred thousand American and Filipino troops—the worst defeat in U.S. history. All was not what it seemed, however. Japan was the victim of a fatal illness: the so-called victory disease, which inflicted the Imperial government with a dementia of unrelenting optimism and a distorted self-image of invincibility. The destruction of the Japanese empire and the horrible suffering that the Japanese people endured was the responsibility of the decision makers in Tokyo who blindly spoke of victory even as late as 1944, when it was plainly out of their grasp. In this regard, Japan was much akin to its Axis partner, Germany.

A closer look should have revealed a Japan much weaker than was apparent. Japanese forces were being stretched desperately thin. They were forced to garrison dozens of islands; hold Malaya, Thailand, and Indochina; defend against the constant threat of their old nemesis, Russia, and continue the fight in China. Japan entered the war with only fifty-one divisions, and in December 1941 twenty-seven of them were in China—leaving only about a quarter of a million ground troops for any Pacific offensive. Moreover, as Adm. Isoroku Yamamoto, commander of the Japanese fleet, had foreseen, the sleeping giant had awakened.

America's industrial superiority was beginning to quickly narrow the gap with Japan. For example, three damaged battleships and three cruisers were available for action within three months of Pearl Harbor. By March 1942, the Pacific Fleet was able to muster seven battleships, five carriers, twenty-five cruisers, ninety-two destroyers, and sixty-one submarines. This growth occurred during a time when Japan's forces were hardly growing at all. Later, the United States would build three more battleships, ten more carriers, six cruisers, forty-four destroyers, and thirteen subs. Also crucial was the introduction of two planes into combat in 1943 that would prove to be more than a match for the celebrated Japanese Zero: the P-38 Lightning and the F4U Corsair. The twin-engine Lightning had great range and an impressive diving capability which its pilots used to pick off the lower-flying Zeros. The powerful Corsair became the fastest fighter in the Pacific in 1943. Japan would no longer rule the skies. In addition, it could no longer rely upon the element of surprise, which helped to explain why its early successes came with relative ease. Audacity is perhaps the best explanation for its stunning success on 7 December 1941 and in subsequent operations. But by 1943 that trump card had already been played.

Japan's most serious handicap was, arguably, its underestimation of America's nerve and determination. Most Japanese leaders were convinced that Americans lacked the stomach to endure a protracted, bloody conflict and would eventually opt for negotiation. On this point they were badly misinformed. It was this critical miscalculation that ultimately decided Japan's fate. The U.S. Joint Chiefs of Staff, rather than patiently awaiting the production of more resources and displaying caution, from the beginning looked to the offense. Admiral Ernest J. King, the chief of naval operations, ordered Adm. Chester W. Nimitz, the commander in chief of the Pacific Fleet, to defend the area east of 160 degrees longitude (later changed to 159 degrees longitude) for the purpose of protecting America's vital sea lanes to Australia. General Douglas MacArthur was subsequently given command of Allied forces west of that meridian in what became known as the Southwest Pacific Area (SWPA). At King's urging, Allied forces were given the okay at the Arcadia Conference in Washington in January 1942 to conduct a limited offensive against Japan to seize "vantage points" for subsequent offensive operations. This permission was given despite a reconfirmation of the Allied commitment to defeat Germany first and the relative weakness of the American strike force at that time.

Evidence of America's enragement over the Pearl Harbor and Philippines debacles was revealed when, in April 1942, Lt. Col. Jimmy Doolittle struck Tokyo and a handful of other major Japanese cities with a surprise bomber raid. Launched from the carrier *Hornet,* the raid proved that Japan had no monopoly on audacity, and while the damage inflicted was minimal, the surprise attack significantly altered Japanese thinking about their homeland's security. Admiral Yamamoto, consequently extended his country's defensive perimeter beyond his capacity to adequately secure it. Plans were made for three offensives to that end. First, Yamamoto envisioned an invasion of Hawaii via Midway Island with a diversionary move against the Aleutians. Second, he would launch an ambitious thrust at Port Moresby, giving him access to northern Australia. Third, the Solomons, New Hebrides, New Caledonia, Fiji Islands, and Samoa would be seized. Planes would then be able to meet Allied attacks by shuttling between airfields that would be constructed in those locations.

Early in the war there was conflict in Tokyo between the army and navy—just as there was in Washington. The Japanese army preferred to emphasize the war in China with an eye on Russia, whereas the navy argued successfully that vital raw materials, especially oil from the Dutch East Indies, needed to be safeguarded. Military assets were therefore directed to protect the sea lanes that carried these crucial materials, which meant strengthening and protecting Rabaul.

The first two enemy offensives were stymied in the spring of 1942 in the battles of the Coral Sea and Midway, in which Japan lost five carriers and hundreds of its most experienced pilots. Despite these staggering defeats, Admiral Yamamoto was not dissuaded. His third offensive, which was in reality an aggressive defensive operation, aimed to build airstrips close enough to threaten the Allied sea routes to Australia. These bases could also provide air cover for a hoped-for overland assault against Port Moresby. To accomplish this, airstrips would be built first in the Solomons, a constellation of islands ranging from two hundred fifty to six hundred miles from Rabaul. Unlike the New Hebrides, Samoa, and New Caledonia, there was no Allied presence in the Solomons. The inaugural site for the attack would be the tiny island of Tulagi, which possessed an excellent anchorage. A small Japanese force took control there on 4 May 1942. One month later, a construction crew landed on neighboring Guadalcanal and began building an airstrip.

Meanwhile, in Washington, Admiral King conceived of an operation to distract Japan from an invasion of Australia by occupying the Imperial Fleet. However, before such an offensive could be mounted, Rabaul had to be reckoned with. King planned to strengthen the garrisons in the New Hebrides, Fijis, New Caledonia, and Samoa. These would be the bases from which an eventual assault would be launched against that fortress.[1] Shortly after the Midway victory, on 2 July 1942, the Joint Chiefs decided to capitalize on their gain by devising a three-phase plan to take Rabaul. Because the United States had only seven fleet carriers, a step-by-step approach was necessary so that land-based planes could cover the operation from bases captured or built along the way. Airpower in the Pacific thus dictated strategy. The first phase called for the navy to seize Tulagi and the partially completed airfield on Guadalcanal. This would not only provide a base from which to catapult Allied forces toward Rabaul, but also halt any further eastern advance by the Japanese. Phase two called for army forces under General MacArthur to secure Lae and Salamaua in Papua New Guinea, while the navy began to climb up the ladder of the Solomons so fighters could cover the entire Bismarck Archipelago and Papua, and isolate Rabaul. On a map the two-pronged pincers attack looked like an inverted V, with Rabaul at the vertex—the cork at the top of the bottle—with the army moving from southwest to northeast and the navy from southeast to northwest. Phase three would be the actual assault on fortress Rabaul itself. The complex three-part plan was code-named Operation Cartwheel.

Guadalcanal was the site of one of the hardest fought campaigns of the war. Never before had American troops witnessed the savagery of the Japanese infantryman, who, despite almost always being out-gunned, continued to attack relentlessly. Tokyo clearly considered the Solomons a "vital buttress" to its defenses. Troops were even diverted to Guadalcanal from the overland assault being conducted on Port Moresby.[2]

General Alexander A. Vandegrift's 1st Marine Division learned quickly about its mysterious enemy when the adversaries first clashed on Tulagi on 7 August 1942. In thirty-one hours of fierce combat, members of the small Japanese garrison lunged at Marine positions with suicidal fury. Others clung stubbornly to their bunkers, conducting a stingy defense that cost the marines dearly. The marines met similar resistance on two other nearby islands: Gavutu and Tanambogo. One hundred and forty-four novice marines were killed in these engagements versus seven hundred Japanese killed in action (KIA). Only twenty-three enemy soldiers were captured, including twenty who were too badly wounded to kill themselves. Death was preferable to the eternal dishonor of surrender or even capture. This fanaticism, so foreign to the American fighting man, was to be demonstrated again and again in the impending struggle for the airfield on Guadalcanal and elsewhere.

When Vandegrift's men reached Guadalcanal's palm-studded shores, neither they nor the Japanese, who only lamely defended the island at the time of the landings, were aware they would be engaged in a violent struggle that would last for six months. Between August 1942 and January 1943, when the Japanese finally abandoned the island, there were two carrier battles, twelve major surface fleet battles (including the debacle off Savo Island, the worst defeat suffered by the U.S. Navy since 1812), more than a dozen bloody land battles, and hundreds of air raids and engagements. The Americans eventually needed two marine and two army divisions to secure "the 'Canal." The U.S. Navy lost 126,000 tons of shipping, including two fleet carriers, nine cruisers, and ten destroyers. The Imperial Fleet suffered the loss of 135,000 tons, including an escort carrier, two battleships, three cruisers, and thirteen destroyers. Even more significant, however, the Japanese lost more than eight hundred planes and hundreds of pilots—losses that occurred at a time when only 221 Zeros were being produced each month in Japan.[3] It was this loss of air superiority over Guadalcanal that caused Tokyo to conclude its Herculean effort to wrest the island from the tougher-than-expected Americans. Despite their unquestionable valor, tenacity, and courage, the Japanese were turned back in assault after assault. Despite their expert night-fighting capabilities on the seas and the excellent account they gave of themselves in each engagement, the attrition rate worked inexorably against them. The United States had the capability of replacing men, planes, pilots, ships, and materiel much more readily.

A Japanese pilot who flew missions in the Solomons lamented: "The interval between the time of our occupation of the Solomons and the enemy's return should have allowed us to hurl a wall of fire and steel at the invading forces; instead, our planes disappeared in the open sea from lack of fuel, our pilots became exhausted from overextended missions, we encountered severe difficulties in replacement of men, materiel, and aircraft, and we watched helplessly as enemy strength inexorably increased."[4]

One story even had Prime Minister Tojo instructing his technical experts to "devise some way to fly planes without gas, suggesting they use 'something like air.' They laughed until they realized that he was serious."[5] A long war favored the Americans, and it was evident to the regime in Tokyo by mid to late 1943 that their initial strategy for a quick war and hoped-for American negotiations was not to be.

The myth of Japan's invincibility died on Guadalcanal. Japanese soldiers' willingness to fight to the death, their unsurpassed aggressiveness, both on the offense and the defense, and their excellent combat skills went only so far against America's growing manpower and materiel superiority. At a New Year's Eve conclave in Tokyo, in the presence of the Emperor, someone asked why the Americans were able to create air bases so quickly. Admiral Osami Nagano, chief of the navy's general staff, replied that while his men built the airstrips with their crude tools, the enemy had machines.[6]

If American materiel could prevail over the Japanese Samurai warrior ethos on Guadalcanal, then it could do so elsewhere. With Henderson Field in U.S. hands, the entire Solomons chain was open to the Americans—and control over the Solomons meant that Rabaul was in jeopardy. America's industrial might, coupled with the great courage of its young men in combat, was rapidly eclipsing Japan's limited capabilities. Japanese leaders for far too long refused to evaluate realistically the increasingly gloomy scenario. Instead of husbanding its still formidable military assets after Midway and abandoning outposts too distant to defend adequately, much less use to mount offensives, the Imperial government, dominated for years by the military and infected with the Bushido code of the Samurai, continued to hallucinate. "Guadalcanal was a very fierce battle," wrote Admiral Yamamoto in a letter to Adm. Mitsumi Shimizu soon after the evacuation of the island. "At this moment I would like to borrow some knowledge from a wise man."[7]

Tokyo's Information Bureau issued a judiciously worded statement to the public as the withdrawal was taking place. It called the abandonment of the island a "deployment" by using Japanese characters never before seen.[8] At the same time that the Japanese were eating crow, however, there was a subtle suggestion of an offensive brewing. "Deployment" rhetorically meant aggression. It would be totally contrary to their nature for the officers in Imperial Headquarters to think otherwise. There was even the hint of a brewing counterblow to avenge Guadalcanal in the imperial rescript issued after the withdrawal. Emperor Hirohito's statement, written in the third person, read: "The Emperor is troubled by the great difficulties of the present war situation. The darkness is very deep, but dawn is about to break in the eastern sky. Today the finest of the Japanese Empire's army, navy, and air units are gathering. Sooner or later they will head toward the Solomon Islands where a decisive battle is being fought."[9]

Farther west and at roughly the same time that the Japanese admitted defeat on Guadalcanal, MacArthur and the Australians had conquered eastern New Guinea. The double loss stunned military planners in Tokyo, for they had thrown their best at the Allies. The proud Japanese were faced with the difficult task of defending what they still controlled. Their grandiose plan to capture New Caledonia, the Fijis, Samoa, and the New Hebrides was abandoned, as was any discussion about invading Australia. The Imperial Army was responsible for defending the remainder of New Guinea still in its hands, while the navy was given the mission of protecting the rest of the Solomons. Rabaul would continue to be both the strategic headquarters for the Japanese in the South Pacific and the target of Allied forces.

For the victorious Americans, the end of the Guadalcanal campaign meant the completion of phase one and the beginning of the second phase of the offensive, or "Task Two." Administrative command of both Task Two and Task Three (the final assault on Rabaul) was assigned to General MacArthur, who also maintained operational control over New Guinea. Seizing the remainder of the Japanese-held central and northern Solomons (as far as southern Bougainville) was left to the navy and Adm. William F. "Bull" Halsey Jr., one of America's most aggressive and admired commanders. Halsey, then, would serve under two bosses: MacArthur, his tactical commander, and Admiral Nimitz, his superior in the naval chain of command. This unwieldy, complex arrangement was a consequence more of the delicacies of awarding command responsibilities when huge egos abound than out of good judgement. It worked surprisingly well, however, simply because MacArthur and Nimitz never interfered with Halsey. He would not disappoint them.

In the midst of the struggle to regain control of Guadalcanal, the Japanese surreptitiously began construction of an airstrip in November 1942 at a place called Munda Point, approximately 180 miles northwest of Guadalcanal's Henderson Field. Labor battalions began clearing the grounds of an Australian Methodist mission at Munda on New Georgia, a companion island to Guadalcanal in the Solomons chain. The new base was to be stocked with Japanese fighters to help pound the marines defending Guadalcanal. It could therefore assist in its recapture or, at least, slow the Allied drive toward Rabaul. Admiral Halsey was not made aware of the base construction until 3 December because the work crews were successfully hidden from aerial photoreconnaissance. By 15 December the runway was complete. The next day the Japanese began building another airfield at Vila, just twenty miles northwest on the island of Kolombangara, the next rung in the Solomons ladder. These two fields, it was widely believed, had to be secured, for they threatened Halsey's drive to Bougainville, which itself boasted five enemy airfields. Their possession would preclude moving the navy's precious carriers toward Rabaul up "the Slot," the narrow and dangerous slice of ocean dividing the two strings of roughly parallel islands in the Solomons chain. Land-based aircraft could then be used to support Halsey's ground operations, flying from these newly built vantage points. Munda lay only 135 short miles from Kahili and Buin, the principal targets for the Allies on Bougainville. Moreover, Allied fighters, because of their limited range, would require bases closer to Bougainville or Rabaul in order to fly escort for bombing raids that originated farther away.

Preparation for Operation Toenails, the code name for the assault on Munda field, began on 28 March 1943. Historians of the Pacific War have neglected this operation, perhaps because the titanic conflict on Guadalcanal five months before upstaged it. In any event, the month-long campaign on the island of New Georgia possessed its own, unique drama.

Combat, more than any other human experience, has the unique power to strip from a man any pretense that masks his character, not only from others, but more importantly from himself. True self-discovery is achieved because every mortal emotion is played out and embellished on the battlefield. Hate, love, sadness, joy, indifference, excitement—emotions that are dulled by the routines of peace, are each so amplified in battle that noncombatants never comprehend and soldiers forever struggle to articulate. But more than anything else it is the litmus test from which to gauge a man's doubts about his courage, his essence. This is the *sine qua non* of the infantryman. In June 1943, the novice National Guard troops ordered to New Georgia were about to join this exclusive fraternity of self-discovery. But theirs would be a distinct kind of hell from the one that the marines on Guadalcanal endured, and, sadly, one that likely could have been avoided.

1 Blood Against Fire

For most Americans in early 1942, the South Pacific was a huge, mostly unexplored universe of breezy, palm-studded tropical islands, congenial natives, abundant flora, and eternal, blue waters that caressed pristine, unending beaches. But this image would begin to unravel with the battle that raged on Guadalcanal in August 1942. Eden, Americans learned, was not always the seductive paradise of legend.

Guadalcanal is located in the Solomons, a heavily jungled, mostly unpopulated stretch of coral islands that form a double chain roughly five hundred miles east of New Guinea. Situated between the only latitudes in the world where evaporation over land is greater than it is over water, the islands exist in a climate that produces as much as two hundred inches of rain annually, with temperatures rivaling the hottest on earth. Humming with angry mosquitoes, the islands harbor anonymous viruses [that few could escape] and frightful mangrove swamps. They were, as one observer remarked, "A queasy mixture of superabundant vegetation, swift to rot, on a bed of primeval slime."[1] Jack London, in his book *The Cruise of the Shark,* added this observation: "If I were a king, the worst punishment I could inflict on my enemies would be to banish them to the Solomons.—On second thought, I don't think I'd have the heart to do it."

The Solomons consist of fifteen large islands, four groups of smaller ones, and numerous islets that form a necklace stretching from northwest to southeast for approximately seven hundred miles but encompass acreage that equals only about the state of West Virginia. The sixth largest of these is seahorse-shaped New Georgia, located 180 miles northwest of Guadalcanal. Only about fifty miles long and ten to twelve miles wide, in the summer of 1943 the island was the scene of another clash between the Imperial Army and U.S. troops. The object of their contention was an airstrip that the Japanese built at Munda Point on the island's southeastern tip.

The native Melanesians in the Solomons experienced few changes after the Spanish explorer Don Alvaro de Mendaña sailed there from Peru in 1567, inspired by tales of gold told to him by the Incas. He named the islands after the fabled king's rich mines—presumably prior to making landfall, as there was no gold to be found there. Although the people had been under the British Solomon Islands Protectorate since 1893, they were administered by only a commissioner and his tiny staff ensconced on an island more than a hundred miles away. The only real contact the people had with Europeans was through missions staffed by Methodists, Seventh Day Adventists, and Catholics who attended to the spiritual needs of the few thousand inhabitants there. Aside from that, the natives were left to eke out a minimal existence by fishing, tending small gardens, and traveling by canoe to trade with the tiny posts scattered intermittently along the coast.

The rugged, inhospitable interior of the island was foreign even to its inhabitants, for it was dominated by several breached volcanoes whose craters radiated outward, forming huge, bladelike ridges ribboned with forbidding, tropical rivers. The people seldom ventured much beyond the bounds of their tiny hamlets, which were kept free of the ever-encroaching tentacles of the jungle only through constant vigilance lest they be swallowed by its virulent growth. They moved along the coast from lagoon to lagoon by canoe, trading and fishing, thus producing superb seamen. Although there were no good maps of the island, the people knew the location of every inlet, reef, and current—knowledge that the Allies would take advantage of in the approaching conflict. They could navigate with near precision using primitive but effective methods taught to them by their ancestors. At night they used *kavenga* or "star paths" that marked the location of an island. Overcast nights required the use of *te lapa* or "underwater lightning"—tiny flashes of light a few feet below the water's surface that indicated the direction of islands as much as a hundred miles away. The most unusual method of navigation involved a canoeist submerging himself naked in the sea and, using his bare testicles as a kind of seismograph, appraising the pulse of the waves that reflected back from an island to determine its approximate distance.[2]

Coastwatchers Fill the Void

When news of the Japanese conquest of Rabaul in January 1942 reached the Solomons, there was little that British authorities could do to provide protection for the native population. Most European residents—planters, merchants, civil employees, and missionaries—had been evacuated to Australia or New Zealand by February, and the commissioner went into hiding on the island of Mailaita. Nonetheless, an enormous contribution to the defense of the islands would be made when members of the Island Coastwatchers Service were brought in. Established in 1919 by the Royal Australian Navy's intelligence division, the service was composed mostly of European volunteers, many from the British protectorate staff, who elected to remain and resist the Japanese encroachment.

The coastwatchers' primary job was to observe enemy activity and report it to the Allies. They did this with a cumbersome but durable three-hundred-pound combination telegraph–voice radio called the 3-B-Z "teleradio." It performed well in the tropics and was simple to operate and maintain. However, it was so heavy that it had to be broken down into parts for transport: receiver, transmitter, two vibrators, speaker, six-volt batteries, battery charger, and its companion chemicals and supplies such as tools, benzene gas, and oil. It required a crew of ten or so men to carry it in dugout canoes through difficult currents or over the treacherous, steep ridges so common in the islands. At its best, the voice radio could reach four hundred miles, extending to a maximum effective range of six hundred miles when employed in the telegraph mode. A simple cipher system was used that, although not very secure, was easy for amateurs to learn. Other items vital to their mission, such as binoculars and medical supplies, were delivered to them by airdrops or, on occasion, by submarine. The coastwatchers were given strict orders to avoid contact with the Japanese. To underscore this, the radio net was given the code name "Ferdinand" after the well-known cartoon bull that would rather sniff flowers all day than fight a matador.

By mid-1941 there were about a thousand coastwatchers manning a hundred stations ranging from Papua New Guinea to the New Hebrides and covering an area of about twenty-five hundred miles—all supported by the Royal Australian Air Force. There were eight stations in the Solomons, one of which was on New Georgia under the direction of perhaps the most famous coastwatcher in the South Pacific: Maj. Donald G. Kennedy. Kennedy was a hard-drinking, womanizing New Zealander of Scottish descent who had been a district officer in the protectorate government before the war. Aided by a group of trusted native runners and scouts, he set up his New Georgia station in June 1942 on a strategic point called Segi. Located on the southeastern tip of the island, Segi sits on the western edge of Morovo Lagoon, the largest land-locked lagoon in the world. It was a locale so peaceful and secluded that the coastwatchers there were able to live a surprisingly polite existence. Kennedy's tin-roofed headquarters, which he shared with his seventeen-year-old Melanesian mistress, was an abandoned coconut plantation home appointed with china and clean linen that sat high atop a hill near the beach.[3] When he entertained the rare visitor, he indulged him with dinner followed by a drink of scotch on his wide, wrap-around veranda, his every need attended to by white-jacketed servants.

But this pocket of civility was no retreat from the war. Kennedy expected much from himself and his men and was gravely serious about his role as a coastwatcher. From his location he and his team could give a thirty-five-minute early warning to Guadalcanal's Henderson Field when they spotted enemy planes headed there. That was just enough time for the Americans to scramble their fighters, climb to altitude, and then swoop down on the incoming Japanese bombers. It was imperative that Kennedy and his men perform their job well—especially in the summer of 1942, when Allied planes were at a premium in the war zone. Kennedy himself attested to this in 1945, when he explained that the marines "had sometimes as few as six planes able to go up at one time, and that had it not been for the timely reports from Segi, they would not have been able to hold Guadalcanal."[4]

Bombers from Rabaul could make the roundtrip flight to Guadalcanal, but they had to risk it without fighter escorts. Other bases would have to be built closer to Guadalcanal or the Japanese would have to concede control of the skies to their enemy—something they were unwilling to do. A radio intercept of a Japanese transmission to Rabaul in December 1942 reads: "It will be difficult to realize a glorious victory [in the Solomons] except by planning to maintain *absolute air superiority*."[5]

In late 1942 the Japanese began improving the existing facilities on Rabaul and building new airstrips much closer to Guadalcanal. New bases at Buin-Faisi in the Shortland Islands, Kahili, and Ballale—all on or near the island of Bougainville—shortened the distance from 420 to 290 miles. On the southern coast of Kolombangara Island, an airdrome under construction at Vila was a step farther down the ladder. Closer still was the new base at Munda on New Georgia. Its proximity to Henderson (less than two hours) made it a crucial vantage point in the Japanese plan to interdict Allied naval and air activity in the Solomons, inhibit the expected Allied drive toward fortress Rabaul, and perhaps even provide a staging area for another offensive against Guadalcanal. Munda was one of the few places in the Solomons where the turf was stable enough to accommodate a landing strip for heavy bombers.

The Japanese Occupy Munda

On the moonless night of 13 November 1942, a swift Japanese destroyer, the *Hakazi*, cut through the Kula Gulf undetected and successfully landed three companies of the Japanese 6th Sasebo Special Naval Landing Force at Munda Point on New Georgia's west coast. Later, a rifle battalion was ferried to the island, followed closely by two crudely equipped engineer units. Their orders were to seize the mission located there and determine the suitability of the soil at Munda Point for a landing strip. They quickly determined that it would be an excellent location for a base. Aircraft there would have greatly increased loitering time in the Guadalcanal battle zone, and, because it was so well protected by reefs and barrier islets, it would be difficult for the Allies to conduct an amphibious assault.

One of Kennedy's assistants, Henry Wickham, first heard that the Japanese might be meddling in New Georgia on 18 November, when two excited native boys reported they had seen Japanese work crews unload heavy equipment from barges near Munda Point under the cover of darkness. Later, the Japanese prepared defensive positions along the beach and placed reserve positions in the hills surrounding the airstrip. It was evident from the initial Japanese plan that they believed it more likely any attack on their new facility would come from the sea rather than from the jungled interior.

Wickham hastily radioed the news to Guadalcanal. Despite the ongoing battle there, an air reconnaissance mission was quickly dispatched to Munda, but the pilots reported they could see nothing but the tops of trees. However, subsequent aerial photos confirmed the appearance of new buildings and a strange white line obscured by the jungle canopy. A second white strip was barely detectable in a later photo. Photo interpreters determined that the lines were made of crushed coral, the material of choice for surfacing roads and airstrips in the Solomons. On 9 December Adm. William Halsey, commander in chief of Allied forces in the South Pacific Area (SPA), became convinced that the Japanese were indeed building an airfield at Munda. The engineers had cleverly camouflaged their construction work for two weeks by working mostly at night and by tying wire cables to the treetops, cutting the trunks, and allowing the trees to hang free from the cables, thus providing natural cover from Allied photo missions. When they finally removed the tree cover to reveal their new creation, it was 1,094 yards long, forty-four yards wide, and could accommodate thirty-three fighters in concealed revetments. Powerful antiaircraft guns were emplaced along with an additional rifle battalion to complete the installation's defenses. On 23 December the field was christened when thirty-three Zeros from the 252nd Kokutai set down on the freshly ground coral.

In just one month the Japanese had tilted the balance of power in the central Solomons, not dramatically, but enough to concern Halsey. If Rabaul were to be taken, the island of Bougainville would first have to be reduced and secured. The formidable Japanese garrison there blocked the northwestern path up the Solomons toward Rabaul. Now, Munda's airfield—and another airstrip being built twenty miles to the northwest on neighboring Kolombangara's Vila River—hindered the passage to Bougainville.

It did not take long before the Japanese intruders became acquainted with Air Command Solomons (AirSols), commanded by RAdm. Aubrey W. Fitch, or the Cactus Air Force, the collective name for the Allied planes at Guadalcanal. (Later, when American troops landed on New Georgia, a subcommand called Air New Georgia—led by a marine, Brig. Gen. Francis P. Mulcahy—was created to control the island's air-cover and ground-support missions.)

Just hours after the enemy's planes landed at Munda, a squadron of Allied P-39 Airacobra and F4F Wildcat fighters appeared intending to strafe the new installation. As they closed in on the airfield at close to three hundred miles per hour, flying just over the island's treetops, they discovered Zeros sitting on the airstrip. Bursts from their 37mm and 20mm cannon and .50-caliber machine guns claimed seven of the newly arrived planes. Dogfights followed, and in those contests, two Zeros were flamed at a cost of two Grumman F4Fs and a P-39. The very next morning, twenty-six of Fitch's planes (nine SBD Dauntless dive-bombers, nine P-39s, four P-38s, and four F4Fs) struck again and scored two more kills and damaged eleven aircraft on the ground. Flying one of the P-39s was Maj. Paul Bechtel, an engineering graduate of the University of Wyoming. He described what happened on that cloudless Christmas Eve:

When we came in toward Munda from the east at about 0800, we discovered the Zero fighters were taking off. . . . They kicked up quite a cloud of dust. The SBDs immediately went into their dives from about 10,000 feet and raised Cain with those taking off and those that were around the field, starting their engines. The four F4Fs followed them down and had a field day shooting down Zeros, mainly in the traffic pattern. I could not see the individual planes from up high where I was, but I could see flamers as the Marines went around the traffic patterns with the Zeros, which were in their take-off and gathering pattern. They were burning up, one after another.[6]

On the twenty-sixth, five more Zeros flew in from Buin, 135 miles away on Bougainville, to beef up Munda's strength, but those five merely replaced five that were left burning on the ground by an air strike earlier that day. The attacks were incessant, and, despite impressive efforts to replenish the new airstrip with more planes, the Japanese were unable to keep pace with the attrition rate. The situation became so desperate for the Japanese that by 27 December, just four days after the first Zeros landed, it became evident to VAdm. Jinichi Kusaka of the Southeastern Fleet that the base was far too dangerous a place for an advanced outpost. Kusaka, who shared command of the area with the Eighth Army's Gen. Hitoshi Imamura, ordered Munda's surviving pilots back to Rabaul with the 252nd Kokutai's three remaining Zeros. The evacuation itself was a problem, for one of the Japanese Nell bombers sent to pick up the valuable pilots was shot down on the twenty-eighth while on its landing approach to Munda. The forsaken airfield was left to the infantry, who must have wondered why they were forced to defend a collection of mangled aircraft scattered about the shell-pocked airstrip. Hiroshi Ito recorded in his diary:

Under the threat of the enemy planes we closed the old year and opened the new one. . . . But due to the aggressive enemy attacks, it was impossible to give him a fight. . . . The enemy air attacks became so intense that I am not able to describe it by mouth or pen. I will remember this new year under the title of "American New Year!" The unceasing Boeings, North Americans, and Airacobras.

Still, the tough and determined soldier quietly endured and remained hopeful:

I celebrate my 25th birthday on a quiet and lonely island in the South Pacific. Be Happy! Be Happy! New Year. My one big objective is only the capture of Guadalcanal!!
I vow to an oath
Walking on danger,
I have crossed over the flowerbeds and cliffs.[7]

The Japanese again had underestimated Allied airpower, and the hope that Munda would serve as a permanent staging area for a counteroffensive on Guadalcanal now seemed quite naive. From now on the persecuted airfield would simply be used as an emergency strip for damaged aircraft or to temporarily refuel planes on missions farther down the Slot.[8] It was a huge misuse of men, equipment, and time.

Although reeling from the punishment delivered by the aircrews at Henderson, the airstrip at Munda was always quickly repaired and ready for use within hours of the air attacks. So Halsey pushed the envelope even further. On 4 January, after unloading reinforcements from the army's 25th Division on Guadalcanal, RAdm. Walden L. "Pug" Ainsworth was ordered to introduce the Japanese at Munda to the American surface fleet. Three cruisers and two destroyers from Task Force (TF) 67, escorted by radar-equipped Catalina scouts and spotters to adjust gunfire, turned northwestward at a brisk twenty-six knots and sped toward the tormented airstrip. An hour after midnight, the cruiser *Nashville* reached the Blanche Channel, turned to display a broadside to the unwary defenders, and unleashed salvo after salvo from its lethal guns.[9] Joining in the beating were the other four ships, which took turns with their five- and six-inch guns. Fifty minutes later, the navy had baptized little Munda Point with four thousand rounds. The shelling destroyed ten buildings and caused thirty-two casualties.[10] On the twenty-fourth, another naval bombardment group was sent into New Georgia waters, this time to shell the Japanese airstrip at Vila. Foster Hailey, a navy war correspondent on the destroyer *O'Bannon,* witnessed the 2 A.M. show: "There was a great flash of light, then the red-hot shells arched across the sky toward the Japanese positions. After a ranging shot or two . . . , all the bombarding ships began rapid fire. The shells were pouring across the sky like fire balls from a battery of Roman candles."[11]

In the awesome fury it seemed as though a new weapon had been introduced: a six-inch "machine gun." Then, after fifteen minutes of chaos, there was an abrupt stillness. In that short period, 405,000 pounds of shells hammered the helpless base, the equivalent of fifty B-17s dropping four tons of bombs each.

Fires started by the ships' gunfire lit up the night as they turned away, but again, the resourceful Japanese wasted no time in readying the airstrip for action. Admiral Ainsworth concluded, "The only real answer is to take the field away from them." Admiral Halsey reluctantly agreed.[12]

The decision to pull out all the remaining aircraft at Munda posed a major difficulty for the Japanese Seventeenth Army troops defending the Solomons, for it forced the cancellation of shipments of tons of much-needed food. Without protection from aircraft flying from airstrips like the one at Munda, surface shipments would be doomed. Even attempts to airdrop food and ammunition at night from Betty bombers were no longer possible. So the Japanese began using submarines to resupply the beleaguered, famished soldiers still resisting on Guadalcanal.[13]

It was an unsuccessful act of desperation. Tokyo, left with no other choice, ordered an "advance by turning" in early February 1943. The remaining eleven thousand starving, malaria-plagued Japanese troops, pursued from two sides by Americans eager for the final kill, were surreptitiously extracted from the island after six brutal months of combat. It was an ignoble end for the once-undefeated Japanese, but at least they could take consolation in the execution of the evacuation. In three nocturnal rescue missions performed by sixty fast destroyers operating just a few miles from Henderson Field and Allied aerial surveillance, the vanquished warriors were spirited away to either the Shortland Islands or Rabaul, where they would recover to fight again.

Sixty thousand U.S. marines and soldiers fought on Guadalcanal, losing 1,600 dead or missing. Of the 36,000 Japanese who were committed to battle during the campaign, 15,000 were killed or missing in action and 10,000 died from disease or sickness. The navies that collided in the battle's forty surface engagements endured the loss of approximately four times the number of casualties suffered by the ground troops and airmen.

Guadalcanal was the Gettysburg of the Pacific War. Although the earlier battle of Midway was a watershed *naval* victory for the Americans, Guadalcanal was the scene of the first major *land* encounter with the previously undefeated Japanese Imperial Army. It proved to the Allies that Japan could be beaten after its surprisingly easy victories at Hong Kong, the British citadel of Singapore, the Dutch East Indies, the Philippines, and Burma. Perhaps the Japanese were a victim of their own success, just as Gen. Robert E. Lee's undefeated Army of Northern Virginia had been when it boldly crossed the Potomac into Maryland and then Pennsylvania nearly eighty years before.

After the evacuation, a Japanese report found on the island certified the significance of the battle to the Japanese. It said, in part, that their success or failure in expelling the Allies from Guadalcanal would be "the fork in the road that leads to victory for them or for us."[14] The observation was prophetic. This epic encounter was the early litmus test between the two rivals. What would prevail in future battles in the bloody, tortured trail to Tokyo: Allied firepower or the code of Bushido? Guadalcanal provided some answers.

Coastwatchers to the Rescue

The coastwatchers understood how important their mission was to the Allies, as lives were saved with each positive sighting of enemy planes or ships. As air combat increased in the skies over the islands, however, these men found themselves in another lifesaving role: the rescue of downed pilots. In the Solomons, coastwatchers recovered over a hundred airmen from the surrounding waters. Whenever word reached Allied headquarters that a plane was down, the coastwatcher network would be notified and given the approximate location of the missing pilot or crew. Occasionally someone would spot a parachute or a signal flare or a rubber dinghy in the water. Whichever the case, eager natives would rush to their canoes, retrieve the aviators, and bring them back to their hideout—where a bag of rice and a case of canned meat awaited the rescuers as a reward. A similar reward was offered for downed Japanese pilots brought to Segi. Each airman in Halsey's command carried with him an officious message, written in pidgin, to give to any native who might assist him. The following is a translation:

The white man holding this paper is a friend of the Government. His plane has crashed and you must look after him so that he reaches safety. He is not able to ask in pidgin for everything he needs, so you must anticipate his wants. Bring drinking water and drinking coconuts. Give him food, such as fowls, eggs, bananas, pawpaws, and other suitable foods. If the Japanese come, hide the white man and give them false information. If anyone has a mosquito net, give it to the white man. If there is no resthouse in the village, allot him a newly built house to sleep in. Make a bush bed for him. If he is unable to walk, make a stretcher and carry him. The village medical orderly should attend to any wounds or sores. Some natives are to travel with him, to carry his effects and to guide him to a Government officer or to our lines or to other whites. Later you will be paid for these services. Get a pencil and paper from your mission teacher, and the white man will write you a note to leave with you. When a Government officer visits you, show him this, and he will pay you. If the Japanese come to your village, do not let them see this note.

These are the instructions of the Government, and you must obey them.[15]

When an aviator was rescued and brought to Segi, the lucky fellow would enjoy Kennedy's largess. Hot tea, English crackers, and jam, a shower and a shave, fresh clothes, and a mattress on the floor of a private bedroom draped with mosquito netting commonly greeted him. A decent inventory of medical supplies allowed for advanced first aid. In the morning, they ate a proper English breakfast of fresh eggs, bacon, and coffee. Incredibly, given the circumstances, Kennedy even provided morning and afternoon tea between lunch and dinner for his guests. The only thing wanting, it seemed, was a copy of the London *Times*.

Meanwhile, Kennedy had his men crank up the radio at exactly 4 P.M. and broadcast news of the recovery. The message was always exceptionally brief in order to prevent the enemy from getting a fix on their transmission. If a message had been reported to Kennedy informing him of a downed plane, the radio operator would read the code number of the original message to him, followed by the words, *Now here.* This simple routine allowed headquarters to identify rescued aviators who were ready for delivery. The next available floatplane would be sent to a predesignated rendezvous point several miles from Segi to transfer the men back to their squadrons, to a hospital, or, if they were Japanese and unhurt, to an interrogation officer. The PBY Catalina making the pickup would fly very low for the last half-hour before arriving in order to elude enemy radar. Then, its engines still humming, the crew would take aboard the rescued airman. Before the plane left, its crew would pass out wooden cases of food, medical supplies, and good whiskey for delivery to Kennedy.[16] He did not work on the cheap.

Twenty-two American and twenty Japanese aviators were plucked from the water and held for delivery to Guadalcanal by Kennedy and his alert crew.[17] This system of retrieval was so efficient that it bolstered the morale of the Allied airmen. Coastwatcher D. C. Horton, who was directly responsible for saving hundreds of lives, was typically modest. He was effusive in his praise of the unselfish natives who worked for him and Kennedy:

> Words are pallid things with which to try to express the feelings we had for the wholehearted courage and devotion of the island people under conditions of extreme difficulty. They gave of their own meager resources; they used their precious canoes; they were bold in hoodwinking the enemy and they never gave away any of us whose lives depended on them. The debt we owe them could only be paid back in some slight measure but—to paraphrase Churchill—in the history of the islands never have so many done so much for so few.[18]

The coastwatchers seemed to have no difficulty recruiting natives to perform these dangerous tasks, despite the obvious risks. Word spread quickly through the Solomons of the cruel slaying by the Japanese of four beloved Roman Catholic missionary priests ruthlessly bayoneted in the neck at Ruacatu on Guadalcanal, or the nuns who were raped for forty-eight hours on that same island before their throats were slit.[19] No doubt they also had knowledge of the fate of seven Australian men and women, members of a missionary family captured at Buna, New Guinea, in September 1942. The victims were forced to kneel on the beach and were beheaded one by one. After watching in horror as her parents were butchered, the sixteen-year-old daughter struggled hysterically with her captors, causing her executioner to miss her neck when he swung his sword. The soldiers were forced to hold her down while the macabre scene was repeated. At least one Japanese soldier who witnessed this heinous crime related that it was more than he could stand.[20]

Solomon islanders were also victimized. When the Japanese encroached upon their homeland in the spring of 1942, churches were looted and desecrated, canoes smashed, property stolen, homes commandeered, and women threatened. Their vegetable gardens of yams and taro roots were senselessly destroyed. Food was demanded at gunpoint. Most unpardonable, by all rules of Melanesian conduct, was the slaughter of the pigs and chickens in the villages. The invaders also invoked Japan's thirty-day workforce order, which obligated a native population to work for them. Manpower was needed to build airstrips, military warehouses, and housing, so the work order was often enforced. The Japanese would pay the conscripts with tobacco, food, and other gifts, but the Melanesians were nonetheless embittered by the experience.

For a variety of reasons, however, the enemy was sometimes successful in getting the voluntary cooperation of a village. Information of this magnitude would inevitably reach area commanders by way of loyal islanders, and soon thereafter American fighters and bombers would visit the village. The mission would immediately be followed by the dropping of leaflets written in pidgin warning the residents of neighboring hamlets of the consequences of collaboration with the Japanese. Clearly, the Allies wanted to convey the message that they were gaining the upper hand in the Solomons.

A kinship between the Americans and the natives quickly developed when they came into contact with each other. Americans were good about making restitution for accidentally damaging native villages or possessions. They taught the curious natives to play checkers and cards, brought them into their tents, and exchanged gifts with them. They played catch together and laughed together. The youthful GIs and marines truly enjoyed the company of their wooly-haired hosts. Sharing food is symbolic of trust and intimacy in

Melanesian culture, and the smiling Yanks were more than willing to hand them packages of their rations, endearing them to their new comrades. One marine, remembering the natives' love for candy, said: "We distributed cigarettes and ration chocolate, which the natives puffed and gulped hungrily. We had been warned to consume the highly concentrated chocolate bars slowly, and I was later to learn from experience that too much, too quickly, can make a man deathly sick. But the black men wolfed it down, and I still wonder if there was not an epidemic of bellyaches among them that night."[21]

Isaac Gafu, a local employed by the Allies in the wartime Labour Corps, talked about the "loving" way the Americans treated the islanders: "They outnumbered us, but there was not a feeling of white versus black among us. We all stayed together as if we were one race. . . . They treated us that way and it was really good. . . . We all ate together."[22]

Soldiers invited the islanders to sit at their mess tables, where they ate together as equals. This demonstration of kindness went a long way in forging more than just an alliance. It served to change attitudes. Hatred for the Japanese, along with the genuine friendliness of the young GIs, brought about a remarkable, mutual accommodation.

Interestingly, a nascent drive for self-determination for the Solomon islanders was attributed to the Americans, for during their years in the islands, soldiers denounced the sins of colonialism and encouraged the natives to consider ignoring their government taskmasters. Nori, one of the early leaders of the movement, was said to have been inspired by an American general. According to the story, the officer advised Nori that his people's poverty would continue unless they somehow achieved self-government.[23] Laborers who returned to their villages as the need for their services diminished refused to take orders from government-appointed headmen. On the island of Mailaita, where the natives were known to be particularly ruthless, a magistrate named Bell and seven of his constabulary were clubbed and hacked to death while collecting taxes. When Bell's body was recovered, it was discovered his killers had eaten his hand.[24] The nationalistic crusade that came to be called "Marching Rule" slowly spread from island to island, even before the war's end.

But Marching Rule became more of a quest for cultural rather than political liberty. According to one Solomon islander:

> We wanted to follow our customs, not those of the white man. For 50 years Church and State had been trying to make us as British as possible. We wanted to be Melanesian and follow the Melanesian way of life, of song, dancing, and feasting, not the dull British ideal of hard work to gain what we might need. . . .
>
> We were very much attracted by the Americans. . . . The Americans did not know what to do with their pay and paid absurd prices for trivial things. . . . They seemed to be a very generous people, much richer and far more generous than the British. Add to this that the Americans talked to us continually of the wickedness of colonialism, the Americans naively imagining that if you gave a race of headhunters immediate independence they would at once become a good democratic people. . . . The Americans often told us that the British government had done nothing for us, which was far from true.[25]

Not all islanders were convinced that fighting alongside their new American friends against the Japanese was wise. George Maclalo was a young laborer when the Japanese invaded the Solomons, working for Lever Brothers on one of their copra plantations. When the fighting began on Guadalcanal, he volunteered to be a soldier without really having a clear understanding of what that meant.

> Many times I saw Japanese in the bush, some very young soldiers, and I would think to myself, "My word . . . that man has the same heart as mine. Why will he not talk to me and I to him so that we will just become friends? You come so we can smoke together and afterwards, uhh, you go back to your line and I will go back to my line." Would it not be better if we did that? Why all this hatred? How about sharing a cigarette? But no. Instead I would say to myself, "I must kill him because if I don't, it will be me who will be killed." So I would fire at him.[26]

When asked in 1987 why so many had risked their lives in a war that was not directly theirs, he explained that the British were viewed as people who were not to be refused, and the natives' help, though never coerced, was expected of them.[27]

Scouts from the Fiji Islands, many of whom were police officers before the war, complemented Kennedy's growing band of men. Most were shirtless and shoeless, their broad, flat, incredibly tough feet perpetually wrinkled from constant exposure to moisture but immune from the sores that plagued the Americans. Many wore no headgear and sported traditional wrap-around, colorfully printed calico skirts called *lap-laps*. Others donned khakis and were issued captured Japanese helmets. They were armed and could be fierce jungle fighters. The Fiji scouts were preferred over the native New Georgians, who were known to "go bush" when things got sticky. But even the Fijis were sometimes unreliable in combat. They were apt to give incorrect information when not accompanied by British or New Zealand officers, and they did not always follow orders. One report complained that they were "unnerved, restless, and afraid and gradually retired to islands in the rear areas to await the outcome of the battle."[28] After the Allied landings they proved most useful as guides and in assisting with the transport of the wounded to rear areas for treatment. In return, they received an average daily payment of two Australian shillings, two sticks of tobacco, a pound of rice, and some tea.[29] One hundred and twenty Fiji scouts participated in the New Georgia operation. They lost eleven killed and twenty wounded, a casualty rate not unlike that suffered by their Allied partners, and accounted for well over a hundred Japanese dead and as many as eighty-three prisoners.[30] Their deeds of bravery were not overlooked. In a simple ceremony at Munda after the island was cleared of enemy forces, the Allies awarded two U.S. Silver Stars, two Australian Military Crosses, and one posthumous Victoria Cross to Fijian volunteers who proudly received their decorations alongside their uniformed colleagues from the United States and Australia.[31]

Undoubtedly the most famous of the island warriors was Jacob Vouza, a native of Guadalcanal. Vouza was once captured by the Japanese, tied to a tree, and tortured because he refused to divulge information of use against the Allies. They beat him, stabbed him repeatedly with bayonets, and then slashed his throat with a sword. Left for dead, he managed to bite through and wiggle free from the rope, then crawled three miles back to American positions. From this incredulous episode he developed quite a reputation among marines, soldiers, and fellow islanders alike. While recovering from his wounds, he told his admirers: "When I was a police-boy before the war, I often was naughty and caused plenty trouble for the government. So I told myself to do something good for King George to pay him back for all that trouble."[32]

In another documented account, Vouza was offered a bounty to track down a pair of enemy stragglers who had been seen near food supply stores dressed in khakis similar to the type worn by Allied scouts. Declining assistance, the muscular islander left alone and returned that same day, strolling into the bivouac area clinging to the severed head of one of the Japanese. He dropped the head at the feet of a group of men and announced indifferently to his startled audience that although the other straggler had gotten away, he would eventually get him, too.[33]

The Japanese were certainly aware of Kennedy's operation, and he knew the time would come when he would have to move or even leave New Georgia altogether. In the meantime, he was determined to continue to operate his radio and service the war effort until the enemy located him or the Allies no longer required his services. Japanese patrols were becoming distressingly more numerous, and his men's lives were becoming increasingly endangered. As long as the patrols stayed a comfortable distance away from his enclave, however, Kennedy let them roam through the jungle while concealing his den. His men carefully surveyed their moves, ready to strike if a hostile patrol wandered too close to the camp's perimeter, or, as Kennedy called it, the "forbidden zone." If that happened, they had orders to wipe out the patrol. No one could be permitted to escape. The heavy clutter of jungle growth made ambushes easy, for it channeled patrols onto narrow trails that could be lined with riflemen waiting to jump them. According to Billy Bennett, one of Kennedy's most trusted lieutenants:

When we started our own army, I was the sergeant. I was the one who always went out and investigated where the Japanese were. Every time a report came, Kennedy and I would sit down at a table and plan what to do and how to do it. . . . We only

picked those that we knew we could kill. You know, if a Japanese patrol was beyond our capacity to kill, we just left them
alone. We just hid from them. But, if we saw a patrol which we
knew we could easily attack, we would have to kill all the men
so that not a trace would be left behind. Not a thing.[34]

Frankie Talassasa, considered one of the most lethal assassins of
the bunch, was about five feet three or four inches tall and possessed
a fine, dignified face, alert eyes, and a lust for killing Japanese. Clad
only in a red *lap-lap* and a GI helmet, the modest scout was coaxed
into telling a marine officer how he once put away a handful Japs
while on patrol: "He had seen a Japanese patrol of five men and he
had followed the patrol, stalking it through the jungle for several
days. Finally he had caught the five Japs where he wanted them, all
of them sitting down on the trail, bunched up, jabbering and argu-
ing while they ate pickled fish. He had set his Owen gun on automatic and shot into them. 'Kill finish,' he said, his eyes lighting up
with pleasure."[35]

Total annihilation of the enemy patrols intimidated the enemy
and helped solve the chronic problem of finding food. Kennedy
and his "army" were normally sustained by the gardens from surrounding villages. One village would supply them enough food for
a week, and then the obligation would rotate to the next village so
as to spread the burden equally. This hardship was accepted without complaint, but the villagers balked at feeding Japanese prisoners. Kennedy was given full warning: "Either you can give them
to us and let us deal with them, or you can get rid of them."[36] The
situation was mitigated in December 1942 when Allied aircraft destroyed a Japanese destroyer and three cargo ships at Wickham Anchorage on nearby Vangunu. Kennedy's scouts were alerted and
they plundered about ten tons of rice and dry rations from the
wreckage of the four ships, bringing an end to their food worries
for a long time.

As the air war intensified, so too did the number of enemy pilots
recovered by Kennedy's band. The Segi stockade sometimes became
overcrowded while they awaited a PBY to ferry the prisoners to
Guadalcanal for interrogation. This required a large detail of guards

who could have been better utilized elsewhere. Kennedy solved the security problem by placing a constable inside the stockade with the prisoners, along with the normal perimeter guard, so that any escape effort would be quickly detected. The Japanese also became quite a nuisance, often complaining about rations, inadequate shelter, and even the quality of the toilet paper. The guards quickly grew tired of their whining, so one day they gathered bags of especially soft leaves, which they told the prisoners would better accommodate their sensitive backsides. However, the obliging natives failed to mention that the leaves were covered with invisible, sharp, poisonous spines. The badly blistered prisoners never again complained about the paper.[37]

Haughty and nonchalant despite his increasingly dangerous gambit, Kennedy was confident that his scouts could handle most Japanese threats. Alert sentries guarded all approaches to his compound twenty-four hours a day. Food, ammunition, and native canoes were cleverly hidden along the coast in case of emergency. "Getaway roads" through the jungle were cut. The New Zealander had even developed a system of signal fires that would allow him to determine the approximate course of the enemy's night patrols. Within minutes he could fill twenty large war canoes with his armed warriors to counter most threats. Nonetheless, Kennedy trusted almost no one, and therefore kept his most precious commodity, his teleradio, hidden in a camouflaged shack in the bush about a half-mile from his villa—its location known only to his most trusted agents. However, his arrogance made those less sure of the situation quite nervous.

One day the major was visited by an Englishman named Harold Cooper, a writer living in Suva in the Fijis. Cooper had heard about Kennedy and wanted to do a story about him and his operation. The Englishman was immediately impressed with his host, who pranced up to him as he stepped onto the beach. Kennedy displayed dark, penetrating eyes, a robust nose, and the remarkably wide grin of a man who hadn't seen a white face in some time. Although he was dressed in starchless khaki shorts, an Australian bush jacket, and wore no rank, he carried his medium frame in a commanding way. Perched atop his head was a Royal Australian Air Force bush hat adorned with a scarlet band and a gilded coat-of-arms badge. His sleeves were rolled up over his elbows, revealing muscular, hairy arms that quickly extended out to shake hands. Cooper guessed that he was about thirty-two.

Inside the villa the two were immediately refreshed with tea presented by one of Kennedy's scouts. After a suitable period of pleasantries, Cooper tried to steer the conversation to the coastwatcher's activities on the island, but Kennedy modestly preferred to talk about Suva, where he had been a schoolteacher before the war. Just then, Billy Bennett burst in and told Kennedy a Japanese patrol was within five miles of a village. According to Cooper, "Kennedy listened to the report with no great interest, and then said: 'Tell the boys to wait until they're sure they can kill all of them.'"

When Bennett left the room, Kennedy resumed the conversation as they nibbled on dried fish and sipped more tea. Bennett returned periodically to update his commander on the patrol's whereabouts, each time reporting that it was getting closer to the village. Finally, when the Japanese were within two miles and closing, Cooper asked where the village was. Kennedy, forgetting that Cooper was ignorant of the local geography, replied that it was the village they were in. Cooper, aghast at the revelation, later wrote:

> I should be lying if I tried to pretend that his reply did not set me puffing a little nervously at my half-finished Camel. If the Japanese were only two miles away, they were altogether too close for me, and for a moment I pondered the idea of suggesting to Kennedy that we should either douse the light or move to the other side of the veranda, so that our heads would not be so clearly visible to all and sundry outside. But Kennedy's serene indifference to the fate of the patrol (or perhaps his confidence that "the boys" would handle this situation with their customary skill) shamed me into silence.

After another hour of conversation, they retired for the night. Much to Cooper's relief, they shared the same room. However, when Kennedy handed him a Thompson submachine gun for self-protection, he lost his composure.

"Better keep this handy," Kennedy said. "Inside your mosquito net, perhaps. These Japanese are funny folks. You never know where they're going to pop up next."

Two short minutes later, Kennedy's heavy breathing indicated that he was already asleep.

The next morning, Bennett came into the room and asked Cooper if he wanted a souvenir. It was a canteen that had belonged to a member of the Japanese patrol. "The boys" apparently had done their job well.[38]

Buildup on New Georgia

During and after the Munda airstrip construction, the Japanese high command at Rabaul had slowly moved troops into New Georgia. The senior army officer at Rabaul was Lt. Gen. Hitoshi Imamura, the Eighth Army commander. Imamura ordered Maj. Gen. Noboru Sasaki of the 38th Division to Munda in early June to assume control of all ground operations. Under his command were the 13th and 229th Infantry Regiments. Overall responsibility for New Georgia's defense remained with the navy, however. The American command structure in the coming struggle was identical.

Assessment of the enemy's strength on the island was based in part on reports from the coastwatchers and from refugees who had escaped after the Japanese landings. Among the refugees was Jack Pratt, an African American fluent in native languages. Pratt lived on a small island just off the New Georgia coast and was helpful when questions arose about area geography.[39] Another was a Munda missionary nurse, thirty-six-year-old Merle Farland, who had been ordered off the island because her presence violated restrictions on white women in the Protectorate. She provided excellent information concerning the natives, vegetation, and the location of reefs and swamps in the area around Munda.[40] Some of the best intelligence prior to the American landings came from Japanese prisoners of war (POWs) and from documents captured by the natives and forwarded to the Allied command by seaplane.[41] Each division's intelligence staff (G2) was assigned a Japanese language section of two officers and ten enlisted men to translate these documents and interrogate POWs. It was concluded that on 30 June, on the eve of the American landings, roughly 10,500 troops, evenly divided between the army and navy, were on New Georgia and nearby Kolombangara, with 30,000 (the actual figure was closer to 15,000) in position to reinforce.[42] Additionally, the Japanese had 590 planes, although most of them were based at Rabaul and engaged primarily in the New Guinea campaign farther west. Save for a couple of days at the outset of the operation, Japanese bombing missions were thereafter confined to a few inconsequential harassment raids. Admiral Kusaka had at his disposal eight cruisers, eight submarines, sixteen destroyers, and a number of smaller vessels.

The twenty-five hundred men of the 229th Infantry Regiment (later reinforced by men from the 13th Regiment) left Rabaul for New Georgia in eleven transports on 12 November 1942 in the midst of the fighting on Guadalcanal. Their odyssey was indicative of the growing Allied air and sea strength in the Solomons by late 1942. The Allies called the continual Japanese effort to resupply Guadalcanal and other islands in the Solomons chain the "Tokyo Express," and sent planes, ships, and subs out regularly to intercept the convoys. Allied bombers and submarines surprised the 229th's convoy near Bougainville several hours after its departure from Rabaul, and eight of the eleven transports were sunk. Most of the dazed troops managed to swim ashore, where they were later rescued and reorganized. The other three transports continued on to Munda, thankful for their good fortune. Just a few hours after they had eluded the bomber ambush, U.S. submarines attacked the three undamaged vessels. Two more were sunk, including the ship carrying the regiment's artillery. The lone remaining transport staggered into New Georgia waters with a crew fearful they might never make it back to Rabaul. The men of the 229th finally boarded barges carrying twenty-five days' rations for the trip to shore. The ship's captain was so fearful of another sub attack that he gave the men only one hour to debark. When the hour was up, the ship raised anchor and sped off with men still aboard. Not until the next day did it return to complete the disembarkation. In the meantime, the men left behind, desperate for artillery of some kind, salvaged the transport's three antiaircraft guns and ferried them ashore, where they were positioned for direct-fire support within Munda's defensive perimeter.[43]

The Japanese Eighth Fleet was responsible for the defense of the central Solomons, but the army was never pleased with this arrangement. Its leaders preferred instead to husband forces to secure what they considered the more important island of New Guinea. Only reluctantly did they send troops to New Georgia and Kolombangara. When it became clear from the growing Allied presence in the area that more men would be needed to defend the forward airfields at Vila and Munda, the army balked, claiming that resupply and reinforcement were too dangerous now that the skies belonged to the enemy.[44] So, from late January until the end of April, the navy dispatched the 8th Combined Special Landing Force under RAdm. Minoru Ota to help reinforce the army units already there. Originally earmarked to reinforce the troops on Guadalcanal, these men were part of a naval ground force sometimes identified as Japanese marines. This combined army-navy force could have presented major conflicts for the defenders, for interservice rivalry in Japan was even greater than it was in the United States. But on New Georgia the relationship between General Sasaki and Admiral Ota was "extremely harmonious," according to RAdm. Tomoshige Samejima.[45]

General Sasaki's orders for the shoreline defense were explicit: "Repulse any landing. If a beachhead is established, the invader should be engaged on shore."[46] Gun emplacements (140mm, 120mm, and 80mm) were dug on the hills surrounding the field, and bunkers for automatic weapons were constructed on the beach itself and back from it, creating an effective defense in depth. In January an unnamed Japanese soldier betrayed considerable optimism in his diary: "We dream of the joy of reducing Guadalcanal. Moreover, the airfield is finished and friendly planes will come over and in large numbers."[47] In neither case were his dreams fulfilled. It was simply too dangerous to house planes at Munda with Guadalcanal's Henderson Field just 180 miles away.

Meanwhile, the hardships for the garrison on New Georgia multiplied. Virtually all supplies had to be brought by ship from Rabaul, which became increasingly perilous for Japan's overextended navy. It meant that ships would be traveling through Kula Gulf off the island's west coast, an area patrolled regularly by destroyers, PT boats, and reconnaissance planes. When supply vessels were sunk, the garrison had to make do without. The soldiers' initial foraging efforts produced nothing but coconuts, so the more resourceful troops discovered other food sources. The island's numerous inlets and lagoons provided seafood, and the troops maintained small vegetable gardens to supplement dwindling supplies of canned dehydrated fish and vegetables and polished rice rations. A diary entry found on the body of a Japanese soldier after a native ambush read: "Even in the face of the enemy, the men's minds are entirely occupied with thoughts of eating. We are waiting for the spring sprouts to come up."[48]

Fishing and agriculture also served to occupy the soldiers' time. Boredom can be a difficult adversary for troops in an indefinitely long defensive composure. The arduous routine of repair work, patrolling, physical training, and evening political lectures (on such topics as "the War Between the White and Yellow Races") was an exercise in endurance. Rations of saki on special days helped to relieve the boredom.

"We drank in celebration of the emperor's birthday—Sake," the rifleman killed in the native ambush recorded in his diary. "At 0700 we bowed toward the Imperial Palace on a mountain in the rain. We were stirred deeply, anew." His 21 March entry read: "Today is spring festival and I drank about 2 go (two-thirds of a pint) of sake and felt fine. As I lay drunk in the village, enemy planes flew noisily overhead, but I was not the least afraid. I must acknowledge the great power of sake."[49]

The Fight above the Jungle

Allied air raids at Munda became an almost daily event for the Japanese garrison, particularly after February, when the last of the Japanese escaped Guadalcanal and planes were freed for other missions. From his hidden perch in the jungle undergrowth overlooking Munda, Henry Wickham assisted the aviators by identifying enemy gun emplacements for them to target. South across Blanche Channel on nearby Rendova Island was coastwatcher D. C. Horton and four native scouts. Armed with captured Japanese ten-power, battery-operated artillery binoculars, Horton helped direct dozens of Allied dive-bomber attacks from his concealed position on a high hip of the island's towering volcano. His tiny station was nearly ideal. Living space for the crew, a kitchen, and shelter for their teleradio was located in a cavity between two rocky spurs on a ridge that afforded a great view of the enemy airfield across Blanche Channel. Horton mounted his binoculars on a tripod situated on a sturdy platform built over the crotch of a tree that had a tight weave of thick, leafy branches. The observer could sit back and relax in an easy chair while spying on the enemy encampment through an aperture cut through the leaves. The crew was more than satisfied with the spot. All shipping headed toward Munda Point in daylight was duly noted and reported, as were other enemy activities. Horton and his men also promptly sent in post-strike damage reports.[50]

The vigilant coastwatchers were a real boon to the Allies. Nonetheless, the airmen could expect to encounter determined Japanese in the skies above their island targets. Some of the most gripping air battles in history were fought in the first half of 1943 over the Solomon Sea. One such affair occured when Maj. Gregory J Weissenberger, while on a routine patrol over Rendova, ran into some unfriendly company:

We went down and broke out of the clouds into the fight, at about 6,000 feet over Blanche Channel. I saw a Jap Zero dead ahead on the tail of an F4F and pulled behind him and shot him down. Immediately on my left wing another F4F went by with a Zero getting into position on his tail. I shot down that Zero, as I did the first. Both Zeros went down burning. A third Zero started a head-on pass at me and I started to turn into him, but just before I could bear on him, he opened fire and hit my left wing stud underside of the engine, and the engine and the left side of the fuselage forward of the cockpit commenced to smoke heavily. Just after my plane was hit I got my sights on him and got in a good burst and he passed under my left wing, burning. I was in the fight not more than 60 seconds, I figure. I tried to get out of the plane, but was under a thousand feet before

I could make it [out of the plane]. The [plane's] tail hit me in the chest, when I jumped. The parachute functioned perfectly, but I was so low that the chute opened fully when I was only about a hundred feet from the water.

A destroyer plucked him from the ocean and returned Weissenberger to Guadalcanal, where he undoubtedly heard the following story from Wilbur J. Thomas, who flew a Corsair on that same mission:

We dove down to the attack. The first thing I saw, the Major made a quick turn to the right and got on the tail of a Zero. At the same time . . . I saw another Zero to my left and below me. All I had to do was chop down on the throttle and dive down on this second Zero's tail. I gave him a short burst, and he exploded. I turned to the left and right to look for the Major, but couldn't see him, but in my turn I saw three Zeros practically abreast to my left and below me. I made a diving turn on the Zero nearest me and came down on top of him, giving him a good burst at close range. He burst into flames, turned . . . and went into a steep spin. I could see my bullets going right into his cockpit.

When I pulled up I started looking for other Zeros when all of a sudden I saw tracers passing me. I dove and made a right turn. I was about 7,000 feet. I tried to see what was firing at me, but could see nothing, so I started after one of the other Zeros which I had located and was able to overtake him and gave him a good burst directly from his rear. I saw the bullets spray all through his cockpit and around the root of his wings. I could see ragged edges on his wings, but dove off . . . before I could see whether he burned or not.

My back was to his when I saw another Zero above me and crossing in front of me from the left. I climbed up to him and fired, hitting the plane around the cockpit. He exploded in the air.

I climbed again to about 10,000 feet and saw what appeared to be a Grumman. They were above me, so I pulled up and gave a burst at the Zero, but I was out of range. He peeled off to the right and dove straight down. I followed him in his dive, closing the distance between us all the time, firing bursts periodically at him. He did not explode or burst into flames but gave off a lot of smoke. I saw him crash into the water. When I pulled out of my dive, I was right down on the water. The spray from the ocean covered my windshield.

I was getting low on gas, so I told the other F4U . . . that I was going home. We returned together, pancaking about 1725. . . . The crew that refilled my plane said that I couldn't have had more than 5 gallons [of fuel left]. My plane performed wonderfully, receiving one 7.7 bullet hole in the glass enclosure of the cockpit just behind my head.[51]

B-25 Mitchell twin-engine bombers got in their licks, too, hammering Munda with thousand-pound bombs. Captain John Abney, a marine intelligence officer, thumbed a ride on one "milk run" to see for himself what a raid looked like from above. As the plane approached its target it lost altitude, and Abney observed:

Everything is very clear and gradually grows until you reach it. Then it seems to leap at the plane and melts into the same mass of blurs and tracers with the spectacular blossoms of fire, smoke, and wreckage to climax the run. One of the most realistic pictures of destruction to be seen is that of huge geysers of smoke, dirt, and debris belching skyward from a mass of flame and thunder and . . . little planes darting along spitting tracers at the world in general. There was a perfectly clear tropical sky and a lush, green island that were a picture of paradise, untouched and unaffected by the small spot of rocking, twisted, torn, exploding hell in the midst of it all. I looked out . . . and thought that once war comes, it really comes to stay.[52]

From ground level, the bombing runs did not usually inspire such effusive portraits. The violence and regularity of the attacks were such that even if spared from the sizzling shell fragments that eviscerated flesh and bone, many Japanese suffered from various stages of dementia. Nevertheless, on 6 June at least one Japanese gunner was almost enchanted by the sight of an attack as he and his comrades blasted away at their antagonists: "A total of 48 bombers and fighters dive-bombed us. The sight of the planes . . . after breaking out of formation was truly magnificent, even though they were the enemy. However, we kept up a concentrated fire without flinching. When a 250-kg bomb fell 40 meters away from our position, I thought that finally my end had come, but fortunately the bomb did not explode. Out of the total of 6 planes shot down, 2 were shot by our company. We are becoming more and more skillful and will some day be [remembered as] the best gunners of Imperial Japan."[53]

When SSgt. William I. Coffeen, a marine sergeant pilot, flopped into the cockpit of his Corsair and settled into his parachute harness, he never imagined that it would be nearly three months before he returned to Guadalcanal, bearded and bent. After plugging in his throat mike and earphones and inspecting the plane's two magnetos to determine if each engine was at full power, his plane leaped into the wind before dawn on 13 April 1943 from Henderson Field on a routine "milk run" to bomb Munda. When he reached altitude and began charging and test-firing his six .50-caliber wing guns, he was reminded of the danger he always faced. This time Coffeen and fifteen other fighters were heading west to New Georgia, escorting twelve dive-bombers, each loaded for bear.

Thirty minutes later, he beheld through the dawn's silver vapor the shadowy profile of New Georgia and its companion islets clustered together. In the early Solomon sun, they looked like carelessly discarded, darkened stepping stones protruding from an exquisitely serene universe of melted turquoise. Stunning. It was the last tranquil moment he would enjoy for some time.

As he climbed through twelve thousand feet, Coffeen's Corsair began to belch menacing smoke from its complaining engine and the oil pressure gauge rapidly plunged to zero. He was in real trouble. He turned the disabled plane around and tried to head for home, but it was no use. Losing speed, he dropped rapidly down to three thousand feet. With no time to curse the machine, the sergeant cut his switches, took a deep breath, climbed out of his cockpit, and jumped clear of the dying aircraft. His chute opened just a few seconds before he hit the water. While floating down the last few feet, Coffeen watched as his Corsair quietly sank beneath the waves. He hit the cold water moments later, scared and alone.

Trying to ignore two sharks that swam dangerously by him, he inflated his rubber raft and began to hand-paddle toward the nearest land he could see. Twice during the day he spotted friendly aircraft flying overhead. The flares and matches in the boat were wet, so he fired his pistol a few times and waved frantically. No luck.

Soon after the last flight of planes disappeared, a turbulent rainstorm blew up. Coffeen struggled to stay afloat, but the seas easily pushed over the rim of his boat and capsized it in the heaving swells. The mishap cost him almost all of his gear. Even worse, the tempest had pushed him farther out into open water. Never had he felt so utterly helpless and alone.

As darkness fell, the wind subsided and he was able to climb back into the raft. He tried to sleep, but it was impossible. In the black void of the Solomon Sea, the sky and ocean became one and the dark pressed hard against him like a heavy blanket. Fragile starlight momentarily strained to illuminate the downed pilot's world, but lingering cumulus soon cut it off. There was no use paddling blind. Better to save his strength for daylight. He fell back into the raft and surrendered to the waves, which lifted and dropped him with a rhythmic, heaving monotony.

Day two dawned over unruffled water and brought out a fierce white sun. His lips and face were soon badly burned. Thirst and hunger clawed at him. It had been thirty-six hours since he last had something to drink, and he was weakening by the hour. He knew he must make landfall, and it had to be that day or he would perish in his black rubber coffin. With the determination of a man facing death, he began to paddle through the glossy sea. His only companions were a school of bonita that slid playfully under him and an occasional kingfisher that rocketed from the water eight feet into the sky only to vanish again in a splash of silver. Above him, the midafternoon sun had lost its contour. The haze and humidity did little to shield him from the numbing heat. Nevertheless, he ignored the pain from his throbbing shoulders and pushed himself to the limit of his endurance, propelling the raft toward an island about three miles away. He reached it at dusk, exhausted and dehydrated, but alive. After refreshing himself with the milk and meat of a few coconuts, Coffeen collapsed in his raft to sleep. To protect himself from the virulent mosquitoes, he wrapped his feet in the sail, covered his head with a dampened undershirt, and curled under his poncho. Maybe, he thought, his luck was changing.

For the next two days he explored his new home looking for signs of life, but there was nothing to be found. He set out on his raft for another island just a few miles away. He paddled the entire day until he reached it and found abundant wildlife there, but no humans. Coffeen's struggle for survival was complex. He was searching for assistance from natives who were helpful to Allied pilots. But he also knew that these islands were in a Japanese-held area. If they found him he would be quickly dispatched. Still, he had to take his chances, so he set out for what appeared to be a much larger island to the north.

Spending each evening on small islands along the way, the resourceful pilot made steady progress. One night was particularly terrifying, however. He was awakened by what sounded like someone walking on the beach toward him. He kept very still, gripped his knife tightly in his right hand, and held his breath so as not to make a sound. Suddenly, he felt the weight of a heavy body jump on his chest. He pushed the thing off and sprinted into the water with his raft. Then he saw what menaced him: A huge monitor lizard stood on the beach hissing at him as he paddled quickly away. On other islands his sleep was interrupted by giant swamp rats that scampered over him at night and by smaller rodents that nibbled at his toes. These simply became nuisances in his increasingly weakened, malnourished condition. He was living almost entirely on coconuts and was weary from his island-to-island trek. Once a fierce storm forced him to seek shelter under a ledge on a hillside. For five days he ate no food as the wind and rain hammered his sanctuary relentlessly. Semicomatose with a malarial fever, he drifted in and out of consciousness while his spent, aching body screamed for mercy after fifteen days and nights of hell.

Nearing his mental and physical breaking point, he summoned the strength to make for a larger island that was close to Choiseul.

When he reached its shore he was so feeble that he could hardly crawl out of his raft. However, he found plenty of coconuts and rested for three days, regaining some of his strength. Then he spotted a small house on an island across a lagoon and decided he was strong enough to cross over to inspect it, even though it might be enemy-occupied.

Eight hours later, he dragged his raft ashore. Thin, covered with infected sores, and totally depleted, he had survived twenty days of wandering and hardship. If the Japanese captured him, so be it. Cautiously he approached the house. It squatted impassively in the sand just a few yards from the beach, covered with palm leaves and apparently unoccupied. It was. He found a few precious limes, squeezed their juice into some water, and drank the marvelous mixture from a coconut shell. In a crumbling chicken house he came across an old hen that was too quick for him to snare but had abandoned her nest, which contained a dozen or so eggs. He hungrily broke one of the eggs and swallowed it in one gulp. Although the eggs were rotten, he consumed two a day until they were all gone.

Three or four days later he made it to an island he thought was Choiseul. Once again he encountered no humans, although he did find fresh water and wildlife. By this time his teeth were so loose that he had to struggle to eat even coconut meat. Several Japanese planes flew overhead while he was in the open, and Coffeen was sure that they had seen him, but he was indifferent to them. The war had become indistinct and irrelevant.

Aimlessly, he paddled from island to island. Another storm tormented him and forced him to a deserted shore, where he labored to empty his raft of water. But his struggle had come to an end. A low cry of delirium escaped his swollen, bloody lips and he collapsed in his raft.

Then Coffeen caught a break. A native named Lukeana, passing by in a canoe, heard Coffeen wailing and watched him tumble into the raft, now adrift in the water. The islander paddled alongside him, established eye contact, and asked if he was an American. Coffeen managed a simple: "Me American." That was enough. The Good Samaritan hauled the pilot's limp body into his canoe and delivered him to a Methodist village on Choiseul, where they fed him yams, sugar cane, and fish. As soon as he was strong enough, the villagers brought him to a wonderfully cool waterfall to bathe, using lime for soap, Coffeen was slowly beginning to remember what it was like to be human. In three days he felt capable of making an overland trip to the district chief to make the proper connections for his return.

This should have been the conclusion of the story, but Coffeen's bad luck returned. Japanese troop-carrying barges had landed just a few miles from the village with a full complement of soldiers. In order to evade their new neighbors, Coffeen and his rescuers traveled only at night. Often they skirted so close to Japanese encampments that they could see their fires. They kept moving until they found a suitable sanctuary: a village five miles inland, where Coffeen remained for a month. There, on a diet of Spam, Vienna sausages, and yams, he gained twenty pounds. His health was returning and he was out of danger. Finally, on 25 June, Guadalcanal was notified of his location through the island grapevine of natives and coastwatchers. A PBY was dispatched to pick him up and whisk him back to a rear-area hospital.

After being away for nearly three months, Sergeant Coffeen's unforgettable ordeal was over. A month later he was released from the hospital and reunited with his squadron, which had just completed an enormously enjoyable leave in sunny Australia with its adoring female population. One of his buddies assured him that while they were there, they remembered to tell all the pretty Aussie girls about him.[54]

The relentless pounding from the bombing, the ponderous, tropical heat, and the anticipation of what Japanese soldiers knew was an inevitable ground assault created a feeling of stress in them that few men ever experience. In the three months that followed the discovery of the airfield at Munda in early December 1943, Japanese targets in the New Georgia area were spared from Allied air attacks only fourteen days. In February, targets were struck every day. The number of planes involved in the attacks on Munda averaged twenty in December, twenty-six in January, and forty-five in February.[55] By early May Allied aviators had hit the airfield 120 times. Pilots joked that they knew the area so intimately that they could direct their strafing runs at the Japanese commander's hut.[56] A Japanese naval doctor on Rendova noted the ominous threat of Allied airpower in his diary, comparing himself to "a lonely candle standing in the midst of a fierce wind."[57]

Another unfortunate Japanese soldier wrote in his diary on 5 April: "Upon landing at Munda, I noticed that the faces of the troops to be pale. I was surprised. Then again, frequent squalls, the jungle, bad roads, and frequent air raids. Labor battalions are working every day [to repair the airstrip]."

Three months later, on 4 July, he observed: "We are doing our utmost in laboring for the cause of the Greater East Asia Co-Prosperity Sphere. When I think of the time I was in Truk, why, it's exactly the opposite here."[58]

Navy PBY Catalina floatplanes that had been painted black, known as the "Black Cats," were used to fly psychological warfare missions. Besides their usual mission of rescuing downed pilots, they also dispatched to Munda and other Japanese strongholds in the islands each night to disrupt the enemy's sleep. A routine mission over Munda took about eight hours, including two to four hours in the vicinity of the airfield. Once over the target, they would drop a mix of fragmentation and incendiary bombs. They would also drop items that would make noise upon impact, such as empty beer bottles, hand grenades, doorknobs, and chains. Sometimes they would score a lucky hit and start a fire or damage the airstrip, but they undoubtedly contributed to the general stress and weariness of the defenders.[59]

Major Kennedy's War

There was little General Sasaki could do to counter the bruising punishment the Japanese sustained from the sky and sea. However, he could take action against another torment. The bulk of his troops were at Munda, the site of his headquarters, but he also maintained a 235-man outpost in eastern New Georgia at Viru Harbor. Their primary mission was to defend the harbor, but they also conducted regular patrols searching for Donald Kennedy, who they were sure was in the area. Even though Lieutenant Tagaki and his men far outgunned Kennedy and his charges, his patrols often sustained heavy casualties in their search for the elusive coastwatcher. It was not long, however, before Tagaki's men became more than a little reluctant to continue the patrols because of fear of Kennedy's adept warriors.[60] What Sasaki had begun to realize was that Kennedy had gone far beyond the role of a passive intelligence agent for the Allies, he had developed a small but superb guerrilla force. Kennedy had escalated the war in his sector despite knowing that his enemy had to be aware of his general whereabouts. Enemy activity in his sector had intensified, with barges probing coastal inlets uncomfortably close to Segi and reconnaissance patrols becoming bolder and more numerous. There was thus no reason to continue to avoid a firefight when the odds were in his favor. Kennedy later defended his aggressive style, noting:

> The Japanese had . . . been ordered to make friends with the natives, but they couldn't make friends with these natives while they were trusting me. Had I had one defeat from the Japanese, the thing would have been completely different. Had I taken the advice of this "Ferdinand" thing of don't fight—let them do this and you keep out of the way—then it would have been different. But these people realized that while I was able to fight and was able to lead them and to win in the little skirmishes we had . . . they were on the right side.[61]

As the exploits of the brash New Zealander's men began to grow, other islanders volunteered, bringing the total number of men under his command to roughly seventy. Most of the new recruits had no military training and had never fired a rifle, so Kennedy, or "Kenti" as the natives called him, provided them with some fundamental skills and discipline. After a bugler played reveille to begin their day, he ran them through the manual of arms and close-order drill on a field he had cleared for just that purpose. Marksmanship was continually stressed, so rifle, pistol, and hand-grenade ranges were built in the nearby jungle for instruction and practice. Each of his men could operate and jerry-rig a variety of weapons from the U.S.-manufactured 20mm cannon to the standard Japanese .25-caliber rifle—most of which were scavenged from wrecked planes or sea craft, or pilfered from enemy patrols. To improve their skills, Kennedy organized competitive events in which his men were timed disassembling and assembling the various weapons.

The training was rigorous at the very least, and even Kennedy's most trusted subordinates described his methods of discipline as unreasonably overzealous. Billy Bennett, a native of mixed heritage who knew him as well as anyone, explained that Kennedy was a "hard man" who rarely laughed and was quick to punish the slightest rules infraction or hesitation in executing an order. Because of his uncontrollable jealousy, Kennedy confined his young mistress, Magiko Sogo, to their house, never allowing her to speak with anyone other than himself. She described him as kind and sensitive early in the war, but as the conflict raged, so too did his temper.[62] This condition was further inflamed by his reliance on alcohol and caused his men to fear him more than the Japanese.

The major's preferred method of punishment was to tie the offender to a forty-four-gallon drum and have him brutally whipped with rattan by one of his strongest scouts. One unfortunate soul died after such a beating.[63] Higher crimes, such as not reporting a Japanese patrol or falling asleep on guard duty, merited the death penalty. Big, strong, and cursed with a constant expression of anger, he was not to be ignored, even by his top assistant, Billy Bennett, who eventually came to despise him.

On one occasion, before moving to Segi, Kennedy was told that the union jack that flew in front of a government building on the island of Gizo had been torn down. When he arrived to investigate the matter, he saw that someone had defecated on the flag and that the homes of Europeans who had evacuated the island had been looted. Furious, he angrily gave the order to burn down half of the homes in three neighboring villages.[64]

As the Kennedy legend grew, so too did his cache of weapons. Pilfered Japanese Arisaka rifles, booty from successful clashes with enemy patrols, began to outnumber American Springfields and M1s. For a good while there were only enough weapons to arm about half of his men, a problem that was remedied by a few meetings with the Japanese, who were becoming a better source of firearms than the

Allies. When Kennedy finally closed shop at Segi in late June 1943, he had accumulated an arsenal that included a 20mm cannon, eight machine guns, two submachine guns, twelve pistols, and sixty rifles. Kennedy even boasted an immodest fleet of six stolen Japanese *Daihatsu* troop-carrying barges on which he was able to mount powerful .50-caliber machine guns his men removed from a disabled B-24 Liberator bomber. Among these fifty-seven footers was one stolen from under the noses of the Japanese while they were ashore searching for food.

An amusing episode involved the Kennedy band and a Japanese reconnaissance patrol discovered on a barrier island thirty miles west of the Segi station. Seven unarmed scouts under the leadership of Ngatu, an elderly, almost blind chief, skillfully circled the island, grounded and camouflaged their canoe, and hid in the bush until nightfall. After a few hours they crept to the Japanese camp where they found all the enemy troops sleeping soundly. Stealing through the small encampment, they began stripping the camp clean of its weapons, food, and other valuables. A noise awakened one of the slumbering soldiers, who yelped when he saw a guerrilla standing over him. The rest of the enemy troops sat up and found themselves starring down the wrong ends of their own rifles. The next thing they knew, they were being hurriedly led away to the prisoner stockade at Segi. Not a shot was fired, and Kennedy's arms room increased its inventory.[65]

The coastwatcher's charges were most resourceful, routinely outwitting the hapless Japanese. Kennedy later described a *ruse de guerre* that occurred not far from his hideout:

We signaled some fighting planes to shoot up a couple of barges which we saw nosing the beach. Water flowed in and submerged the sterns sufficiently to cover the starting batteries. The Japs, about 50 of them, returned to find that they could not ride home that night; so they set off along the shore on a weary walk back to their headquarters. We plugged up the bullet holes, pumped out the water, and took the barges away during the night. Two days later, another barge came along with a spare engine in a crate, to replace an engine in one of the damaged barges. They put the engine ashore on the beach while they went off to look for the barge. During the night we lifted the engine and added it to our collection of trophies. It was a new Swedish diesel. . . .

The boys referred to these incidents as "good fella palay. Japan him he cross too much me fella win 'im. Me fella happy too much."[66]

On 11 December 1942, a vigilant Fiji scout observed two Japanese barges crawling slowly along the desolate shoreline in the serene waters of Morovo Lagoon, investigating every niche as they searched for Kennedy's well-concealed hideout. The camp sprang to life as Kennedy and Billy Bennett began making preparations to hit the interlopers hard.

Although only twenty-two years old, Bennett had acquired a legion of skills that Kennedy admired and put to good use. In addition to being an excellent sailor, mechanic, and radioman, he had proven himself to be fearless in tight situations. After gathering the men selected for a mission together for a briefing, he would give them a "fighting speech" to prepare them for the task ahead. Then, once the operation commenced, Bennett always placed himself in the most hazardous position, appearing undaunted by the obvious peril.

Twenty-three of the most experienced warriors, including two American pilots who had been rescued and were awaiting evacuation, were selected for the mission. After several hours of movement through some of the most inhospitable jungle terrain on earth, the raiders sighted the barges anchored in shallow water just five miles from Segi and surrounded them both. At about 7 A.M. Kennedy gave the order to open fire. The scouts attacked with grenades and small arms in a furious, effective fusillade. Japanese soldiers were dropping everywhere. Seconds later, Bennett, without awaiting orders, hopped on board one of the barges and quickly dispatched another of the enemy by sinking his bayonet in the man's belly. He then tore a grenade from his belt, pulled the safety pin, and shoveled it into the barge's open engine hatch as fluidly as a major league shortstop shuffles a double play ball to second base. He then grabbed the hatch, slammed it closed, and jumped on it. A muffled explosion lifted Bennett's 175-pound frame from the hatch and killed the enemy soldiers inside. The few Japanese taken prisoner were marched into the bush and shot. Kennedy then ordered his men to scavenge the barges and corpses for anything useful, especially weapons and fuel. The barges were then moved to deeper waters and sunk, leaving no trace of the enemy's presence. The victorious band returned to Segi with no casualties, a new supply of weapons, and a renewed sense of confidence. Morale soared and there was no shortage of recruits for Segi's proud militia.

One convert to the cause was a village headman named Seni, who brought with him a few of his best men to join Kennedy. To prove their worth to their new commander, Seni and two others set out on a canoe patrol to procure more weapons from their adversaries. The three skilled oarsmen silently skirted the New Georgia coast, their keen eyes piercing the jungle thicket for signs of the enemy. Suddenly, as they rounded a point knotted with vine-covered mangroves, they found themselves in a close-range face-off with a canoe transporting five Japanese soldiers. After a brief exchange of rifle fire, Seni, outgunned, turned his canoe and began to paddle away furiously. The islanders changed speeds, reversed their course, tacked, and positioned themselves to fire back at the other canoe, whose crew struggled to maneuver in the open water. One by one the enemy's numbers were reduced until they were all killed. Seni and company were back at Segi before dusk sporting five more rifles and toothy grins. Before the New Georgia campaign ended, this bold warrior was in command of thirty-two veteran guerrillas, each armed with a captured Japanese rifle.[67]

Another encounter validated Kennedy's reputation for impudence and nerve. In his possession was the five-ton schooner *Dundavata*, camouflaged with branches to look like a small islet. Once belonging to the Seventh Day Adventist mission on neighboring Choiseul, his men had commandeered the old two-master and converted it into a crude gunboat by fixing a salvaged .50-caliber machine gun to its bow. Adding to the craft's arsenal were two light machine guns pirated from a couple of crashed enemy Zeros. On 18 May 1943, a ten-man Japanese patrol on board a conscripted whaleboat was spotted prowling precariously close to Kennedy's base camp on the edge of Morovo Lagoon. The coastwatcher promptly gave orders to ready his transformed vessel for battle. Shortly thereafter, he and a dozen of his eager men were underway, with the major at the helm and two canoes of riflemen in tow. A scout party went ahead by canoe to help search for the enemy in the shadowy lagoon.

When dawn broke a few hours later, the scouts spotted the Japanese on a small, palm-studded island just ahead. They hurried back to report their discovery and Kennedy immediately turned behind a nearby island to mask their presence. He positioned a lookout with binoculars on top of a coconut palm and sent a volunteer to reconnoiter the island where the Japanese had been sighted. He then calmly settled back with a bottle of scotch to await his adversary's next move.

It was nearly midnight when one of Kennedy's men awakened him with a report that the enemy was on the move. He issued the order to pursue, and his little band quickly and skillfully edged out into the somber, shallow waters of the lagoon from behind their island shield. The sharp-eyed natives spotted the shadowed hull of the enemy whaleboat. Kennedy responded to the report by turning the old schooner, still camouflaged with palm and coconut branches, in the direction of his prey.

As soon as the enemy saw the *Dundavata*, however, they pivoted and fled. Kennedy turned the helm over to Billy Bennett, manned the boat's .50 caliber, and began raking the enemy vessel with gunfire at five hundred yards. The Japanese returned fire, but Kennedy kept his aim steady and continued blasting away along with his mates as they gained on the slower whaleboat. The major caught a bullet in his thigh during the furious exchange and was momentarily stunned, but he quickly recovered and returned to his smoking weapon. After expending almost four belts of ammo, the .50 caliber jammed. Cursing violently, the bloodied commander limped to one of the other machine guns, roughly shoved away its operator, and angrily began firing it himself.

Only a hundred yards away now, the wounded Japanese craft lay virtually dead in the water, so the skipper shouted out the command to ram it. Bouncing through the water at seven knots, the schooner struck the Japanese boat and threw its crew into the murky lagoon. At the moment of collision, the *Dundavata*'s crew christened the helpless boat with a cascade of grenades, and within minutes the crippled vessel capsized and slowly began to slip below the surface. All ten Japanese on board were killed. Several of the guerrillas collected, stripped, and buried the bodies on a nearby islet while others scoured the wreck for anything of use. The triumphant schooner sailed back to Segi with only a few slightly wounded aboard, including Kennedy. Again their magnificent audacity had helped the guerrillas to prevail.[68]

The coastwatcher's wound healed quickly enough, but it fueled his profound hatred for the Japanese. However, Kennedy never learned the real truth of that encounter. Just months before Billy Bennett's death in 1988, he confessed that his hatred for his commander had grown so intense that he attempted to kill Kennedy that day. It was he, not a Japanese soldier, who had fired the shot that wounded Kennedy.[69]

Seizing the Russells

During the Guadalcanal campaign the Japanese had used the tiny Russell Islands as a staging center for a portion of their *Daihatsu* fleet. A mere twenty minutes from Henderson Field by air and roughly a third of the way from Guadalcanal to New Georgia, Allied planners believed that they must be taken before an assault on Munda could be accomplished. Possession of the Russells would give Admiral Halsey an anchorage large enough for a PT-boat base to be used against Japanese reinforcements headed for New Georgia and a place to install radar to furnish protection for Henderson Field. Most importantly, an airbase could be constructed there to support the nearby ground operation on New Georgia—a luxury that the marines landing on Guadalcanal had not enjoyed. A large landing in the Russells would also serve as a dress rehearsal for the assault on New Georgia. Commanded by a Regular Army officer and West Point graduate Maj. Gen. John H. Hester, the 43rd Infantry Division, a green National Guard unit made up of three regiments from New England, was selected to be the vanguard of the central Solomons offensive. Their meager role in the last stages of the mop-up of the few remaining enemy stragglers on Guadalcanal was the extent of their combat experience. An invasion of the Russells was just the type of training they would need to prepare them for what was to come later. Accompanying Hester would be the 3rd Marine Raider Battalion and other army and marine units, for a total of nine thousand troops. Coastwatchers accurately reported that enemy troops had evacuated the islands early in February as the fighting on Guadalcanal drew to a close. Despite this report, Halsey warned RAdm. Richmond Kelly Turner, commander of the invasion force, to expect some resistance.

On the morning of 17 February a convoy of transports and six destroyers carrying the Americans from New Caledonia to the Russells via Guadalcanal was discovered by Japanese air scouts who reported the find to their headquarters at Rabaul. Within hours a formation of twin-engine Betty bombers, flying at low altitude and armed with deadly torpedoes, was headed in the direction of Turner's unsuspecting ships. It was after dark when they made contact, so the Japanese fired flares and ignited float lights, brightening the Solomons' sky and illuminating the ships for the hunters. Turner's destroyers took corrective action by circling the vulnerable troop carriers and preparing to engage the bombers when they made their torpedo runs. Meanwhile, orders were given for the ships to begin zigzagging in an effort to elude the approaching enemy. When the planes were within range of the destroyers' five-inch guns, the orchestra of heavy artillery commenced, followed soon after by staccato bursts from the vessels' 40mm and 20mm antiaircraft guns. The barrage produced a din that the men in the 43rd had never experienced before.

Luckily, the aerial attack was poorly staged. The seven bombers separated too quickly, providing individual targets for the anxious gunners. At least five of the Bettys were shot down. None of the ships in the convoy was hit, and no casualties were sustained. However, there were several tense moments. The captain of the transport *President Adams,* whose hold was teeming with frightened soldiers, reported seeing a bomber release a torpedo just off his bow. The USS *Maury,* a fifteen-hundred-ton single-stack destroyer, had an even closer call:

> Suddenly we spotted a single plane coming in on the port beam. I shifted the director to this new target and opened fire

with the five-inch battery, but the range was very short. [Seaman Jeff] Gilmore spotted the blue exhaust from the plane's engines in the hazy moonlight and opened up at about 1500 yards. The other two port 20-mm gunners followed his tracers to the target and joined in. A full-throated rat-tat-tat-tat of the 20s joined in the blasting of the five-inch.

My eyes followed the red tracers to a black shadow roaring in. It was a twin-engine Betty with her bomb bay doors open, flying at bridge level and heading directly for me personally! At about 500 yards its torpedo dropped out and splashed into the water. If that torpedo hit, I was going to be blown vertically out of the control officer's hatch and the coaming would rip my arms off. I braced my forearms against the inside rim of the hatch so I would be blown clear. All port 20-mm gunners kept their triggers closed and three streams of tracers intersected the target.

The plane skimmed over the forecastle lower than the director. From my elevated perch, I could look into the cockpit and see the two pilots in the green glare of their instruments. The big plane was burning and, with a huge burst of spray, smeared into the water a few hundred yards to starboard. . . . The torpedo must have passed under the ship. It had probably been dropped too close to arm and rise to a running depth.[70]

Nearby torpedo explosions rocked the transports and terrified the prayerful soldiers, who huddled below deck. Louisianan Louis Burton, a 1941 graduate of Louisiana State University, who was on the transport *President Jackson* with the rest of B Company, 169th Infantry's mortar platoon, recalls:

The sky exploded with flares and sirens and antiaircraft fire. They made us go down below—down to where our bunks were—which is not where anyone would want to be. You'd want to be on the deck, even though it was dangerous. It was certainly memorable. Explosions. Ship shaking. Dark. Just a little red light shining. Every time there'd be a tremendous explosion, I thought it was a torpedo. But it probably was one of our guns.

It separated the guys according to bravery in my head. The most frightened ones were at the top of the steps. Crying. The next bravest were sitting on the steps. The next bravest were at the bottom of the steps. The next bravest were the ones who stood beside their bunks but wouldn't lie down. That's where I was. Then there were those who laid down. The bravest of all were the ones who played dice by the little red light. The attack was repelled after about two hours (actually, it was over in fifteen minutes) and they allowed us to move up to the deck.[71]

Technical Sergeant Sal LaMagna, a member of F Company, 169th Infantry, ignored orders to descend to his bunk so he could watch the fireworks until a naval officer came by and screamed at him to follow orders. "Boy, was he pissed off!" LaMagna recalled. "He slammed the hatch door shut behind me. The hold was dark except for a red light. Every near miss shook the ship like jelly. Everyone was quiet, waiting for the worst. Then Norby Senio, our platoon sergeant, yells out: 'Anybody wanna buy a watch?' That broke the tension and we all laughed."[72]

Although the 21 February landings on the Russells were made with great bravado, they were entirely unopposed. The marines' 3rd Raider Battalion seized the beach on Pavuvu Island, and a regimental combat team from the 43rd Infantry Division captured neighboring Banika. Storming from their Higgins landing craft with rifles at the ready, the soldiers were met by two smiling Aussie coastwatchers who offered the slightly embarrassed men a spot of tea.

On board the *Maury,* three hundred uneasy National Guardsmen from Maine's 103rd Infantry Regiment awaited their turn to land. The regimental commander and his staff headed for shore in the first Higgins boat. However, when the other landing craft pulled alongside to shuttle the rest of the soldiers to shore, the troops balked and refused to board them. One of the ship's officers, Lt. Warren Armstrong, saw what was happening and intervened. He ordered the men in the first wave to get into the remaining boats. Still nobody budged. Armstrong then questioned some of them individually, presumably the noncommissioned officers, to determine who was assigned to which wave, but he received nothing but evasive answers. No one would admit he had been assigned to the first wave. Either the men were not properly informed of their order in the assault, or they were reluctant to board without direct orders from their own officers. Whichever the case, their hesitation was a clear indication that there was a leadership and discipline problem among the men that would loom large once they were engaged in combat. Finally, Armstrong took matters into his own hands. He pulled out his .45-caliber pistol and, in a firm, controlled voice, ordered a few at a time to board the waiting boats. The men complied, many muttering profane complaints as they began to inch forward, but there was no resistance.[73]

Elsewhere there was more fumbling. Sergeant Herman Martocci of Middletown, Connecticut, struggled in the pitch darkness with the rest of the men in the 169th Infantry. "We had so much stuff on us we looked like a bunch of jackasses," he said later. "The lieutenant was ahead of me. He stepped off the boat and he must have hit a hole because he went down and disappeared. But he just kept walking toward the beach and finally his head came out. I said, 'Jesus, I ain't going to get off there. I'm going to get off over here.'"[74]

Jim Lucas, a marine who participated in the invasion, recalled the fear he felt during the final approach to the beach: "My knees began to tremble, and I sat down, bitterly ashamed of myself. The suspense, I found later, is always harder than real combat. When would the firing start?" Later, as the dim light of dawn allowed Lucas and his companions a glimpse of the beach where they might die, he described seeing "the outline of trees on the islands, and I saw a Jap back on every one of them. Suddenly there was a plane overhead. I wilted. It was ours, but the discovery came too late to save me a nervous breakdown."

After what seemed an eternity, they hit the beach:

We made three futile tries before we found a break in the coral. . . . As our boat nudged the sand, the first Marines were on the beach, ready for trouble. Still burdened with too much gear, I struggled to the side of the boat, balancing myself precariously. As I stepped into the water to wade ashore, my automatic lifebelt inflated, giving me the appearance of an outraged toad.

Our assault waves moved inland fifty yards and spread out in defensive formation. Others searched out the nineteen wharf buildings fronting the bay with drawn bayonets. Not a Jap. . . . We began to feel an unreasonable, angry disappointment. We deserved more than this! Where were the 700 Japs we had been promised?[75]

Four short days after the landings, patrol boats were operating out of their new base at Wernham Cove on the island of Pavuvu. Within three weeks the first of two airstrips was built on Banika Island, transforming the Russells into a formidable Allied stronghold. Banika also became perhaps the most popular strip for the pilots of Marine Air Group (MAG) 21, who nicknamed it "boomtown." Eventually it included a free hamburger stand and a steam laundry among other amenities.[76] While the sailors in the navy's Construction Battalions (Seabees) were busy with these projects, the soldiers and marines continued to train during their four-month stay in the Russells. However, the islands' mostly gentle terrain with its pleasant, relatively cleared coconut groves was nothing like what they would encounter on New Georgia. Consequently, their training was only marginally profitable.

When not on duty, the men played volleyball or softball and swam in the pristine waters that embraced their peaceful sanctuary. There were also open-air theaters with coconut log seats for viewing popular movies. Occasionally the men would put on shows themselves, usually of the musical-comedy variety. One especially memorable performer was an out-of-the-closet homosexual clerk-typist the men affectionately nicknamed "Mary." A female impersonator in civilian life, the GI enjoyed coming out on stage wearing an evening gown with half of a coconut shell stuffed inside over each breast. He looked and even sounded like Jenny Simms, and he was a huge favorite with the rollicking crowd of servicemen.[77]

The Russells amazingly were mosquito-free, although every other island in the area was swarming with them. It was such a welcome relief that it became a routine practice for pilots on their way back to Guadalcanal to develop some form of "mechanical trouble" so they could land and enjoy an hour or so of tropical luxury while their planes were being serviced.[78] Fresh food was scarce, however, and the situation deteriorated to the point where food supplies had to be guarded around the clock to discourage theft. Jim Lucas tells the story of a group of hungry marines who approached the guard posted outside an army food dump. "Okay, boys," the marines said. "You're relieved. You can eat now." The GIs happily left their posts hours before they were supposed to be spelled. When they returned, the food was gone, and so, too, was their marine "relief."[79]

Raymond "Slim" Winialski from Hartford, Connecticut, a rifleman in the 169th Infantry, dispelled a common notion:

> Our ration supply was terrible. We were undernourished until about two weeks before we went into combat.
>
> You get a bunch of men together, especially GIs, and there's no women around, and the talk is always about women. But over there, we were so hungry that we forgot about women. All we'd talk about in our free time is what we would eat when we would get home, and we would listen to guys tell how their mothers would prepare certain meals. One guy would explain how she would roast a leg of lamb, how she would slit it and put the garlic in. Your tongue would be hanging out just thinking about it.[80]

To satisfy their thirst, a few enterprising Alabamans produced a mash made of raisins, papayas, and coconut milk, a sort of mongrelized Polynesian beer that tasted like a malignant peach brandy. As he gagged on the foul brew that someone labeled "Pavuvu Paralyzer," one GI complained that he had unloaded from his ship cases of Black and White Label Scotch stamped "For Medicinal Use" that was earmarked for the officers' club. Resigned to their fate, the men endured the noxious mixture and either suffered through the next morning's physical training exercise or checked themselves into the infirmary for sick call.

Their revelry was muted, however, by thoughts of the impending contest with the enemy. Lieutenant James Chase of Maine remembers one unmistakable index: "We used to say that you could tell how hard the next campaign was going to be by how many bottles of beer they gave to each soldier. I think we got two bottles of lager when we were in the Russells and when we were set to go to New Georgia, they gave us five or six bottles.[81]

By then they all had heard stories from the marines about the enemy on Guadalcanal—some true, some exaggerated, and some invention. They were told that the Japs would sneak into foxholes at night, or strap themselves into trees for days, waiting to shoot the first unsuspecting GI who came along, or that they were able to scamper smoothly through the jungle like monkeys. There were also the inevitable feelings of self-doubt that every untested soldier experiences. James Wilcox, a Trinity College graduate from Hartford and an officer in the 169th Infantry, wondered just how those long months of training for infantry assaults with tank support on fields uncluttered by jungle growth would benefit them in the Solomons.[82]

Not until 6 March, nearly two weeks after the occupation, did the Japanese dare to attack the new American staging area. On that day, five Zeros killed eight marines on the ground. The attack was the beginning of what was to be four months of almost daily harassing raids. Planes were dispatched from Guadalcanal to provide protection until the airstrip in the Russells was completed. Each day there were dogfights—thrilling, deadly duels forgotten by all but the participants.

Just as they had underestimated Allied strength at Guadalcanal, the Japanese, slow to realize the magnitude of the buildup in the Russells, reacted much too sluggishly to it. This delayed response can partially be explained by the simple fact that the Imperial government was struggling to fight a two-front war in the South Pacific. Simultaneous to Halsey's offensive up the Solomons ladder from the southeast was another assault moving toward Rabaul from the southwest as General MacArthur and the Australians threatened to expand their foothold on the northern coast of New Guinea. General Imamura and Admiral Kusaka had no choice but to defend fortress Rabaul from two directions, depleting their already dwindling resources.

In the spring of 1943, military planners in Tokyo, stung by the loss of Papua New Guinea and Guadalcanal, recognized that they had completely overextended themselves. Now they sought to husband their assets until the spring of the following year. By then, they were assured, the Imperial Fleet would be built back to its prewar strength and aircraft production levels trebled. In the interim, there would be a moratorium on offensive operations and a partial pullback of their perimeter to create a defense in depth the Japanese prayed would slow the Allied advance and allow them time to lick their wounds. Within that new perimeter was New Georgia. Consequently, the Japanese began preparing to hold on to the Munda and Vila airfields and inflict as many casualties as possible on the Americans. Reluctantly, the Japanese increased the size of the garrison on New Georgia and Kolombangara to more than ten thousand men.

In contrast to Tokyo's mindset at the end of 1942, when it had been unthinkable to expect anything less than the recapture of Guadalcanal and the conquest of Port Moresby, Imperial Headquarters in Tokyo had clearly set its sights much lower. Admiral Halsey had a force of three hundred combat-ready aircraft on Guadalcanal, and air superiority was gradually shifting to the Allies. Now it was Allied aircraft that came to bomb Japanese airfields just like they had done to Henderson Field in mid-1942. The new bases in the Russells moved the Allies eighty miles closer to Japanese installations on New Georgia and Kolombangara, tightening the grip significantly. In addition, six naval task forces were ready to blunt any Japanese move. The new Japanese strategy was born of defeat, but it was the only option left to them. However, this alteration in strategy would have no effect on the tenacity of the fighting. The killing would continue unabated.

2 First Communion

Tokyo's strategic turnabout was hardly a sign of despair in the Imperial high command. While their forces would suspend ambitious offensive campaigns for the moment, the Allied drive could be harnessed, Japanese leaders believed, by an active defense of the geography still within Hirohito's realm. First, no new airstrips would be built in the Solomons, but those currently in operation would be improved and defended, and strikes against Allied outposts would be intensified. Farther west, New Guinea's defenses would be fortified to deter MacArthur's quest for control of its strategic northern coast. However, more men and machines were needed to accomplish these goals. Rabaul was therefore strengthened, and a hundred thousand fresh troops—some pulled from as far away as Korea and China—were dispatched to reinforce those already in New Guinea and the Solomons. In addition, Admiral Yamamoto, commander in chief of the Combined Fleet, sent two hundred planes borrowed from Third Fleet carriers stationed at Truk, his great naval base in the Caroline Islands, to Rabaul and several airstrips in the northern Solomons to augment the three hundred already there.

Both moves failed. On 3 March 1943, eight Japanese troop transports attended by an equal number of destroyers sailed into a rude wind toward New Guinea's Huon Peninsula with 6,912 men of the 51st Division. The convoy was struck in broad daylight by dozens of Australian and American warplanes, including B-25 light and A-20 attack bombers, which skip-bombed the enemy ships from mast-top altitude. All eight transports and half of the destroyers were sunk, and sixty-one of the covering force's planes were shot down. A total

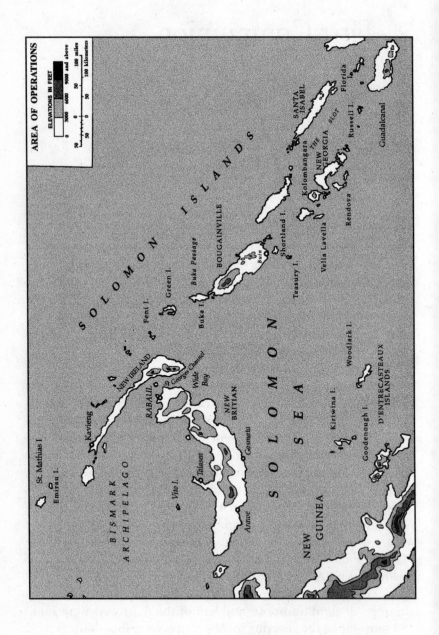

of 3,664 of the 51st Division's men were drowned or burned to death in the wreckage-filled waters. When the Battle of the Bismarck Sea ended, the victorious Allies discovered they had suffered only thirteen men killed and four planes lost. It proved to be one of the most pivotal battles in the Pacific theater. It not only underscored Allied intelligence advantages, such as Ultra (the code name for monitoring, intercepting, and decoding enemy radio communications) and aerial photography, but it also provided yet another illustration of the tilt the war had been taking toward the Allies since the Japanese debacle at Midway a year before.

There would be other lessons for Yamamoto's stunned forces. Kolombangara had become a key island in the enemy's system of supply and reinforcements for its troops at Munda. Fast Tokyo Express destroyers or submarines would slip through the Blackett Strait to Vila, where troop-carrying barges would complete the transport of men and cargo to New Georgia. Halsey successfully intercepted these missions during daylight hours, but the Japanese still owned the night. Thus was born Operation Fifth Avenue, a scheme to mine the approaches to Vila. On the night of 6–7 May, four converted destroyers covered by a cruiser-destroyer force planted 250 mines in long, straight rows across the Blackett Strait's sea-lanes. Moving slowly through the black water at fifteen knots, the ships laid mines at the rate of twelve per second. Their mission completed, they doubled their speed and continued west into Vella Gulf and then headed south through Gizo Strait. The Japanese were aware of the activity, but there were so few minesweepers left in the Imperial Navy that Tokyo could spare no more for the Solomons. These rather defenseless vessels could work only during daylight hours, when they were mugged again and again by American fighters based on Guadalcanal.

It was a dangerous mission, for these waters separated two enemy-fortified islands and were teeming with Japanese naval activity. But the payoff turned out to be worth the risk. In a few short hours, a four-ship division of unsuspecting Japanese destroyers closed in on Blackett at full steam. The ships unloaded their cargo at Vila without incident and headed west back up the strait. Suddenly, the *Kuroshio* exploded in a golden ball and slipped below the choppy water, steaming and spitting fire. Two other ships also hit mines but managed to survive. However, an alert Australian coastwatcher on Kolombangara reported the explosions to Guadalcanal, and the next day nineteen Allied planes finished off the last two. The Japanese lost 192 sailors killed and 104 wounded. By the end of the day, however, the avenue had been swept clean of the remaining mines.[1]

In April, Admiral Yamamoto, agonizing over the loss of Guadalcanal and the recent defeat in the Bismarck Sea, launched the I Operation to regain air supremacy over eastern New Guinea and the Solomons. The admiral ordered his land-based force of 86 fighters and more than 100 bombers, newly reinforced with 96 fighters, 65 dive-bombers, and a few torpedo bombers from the Third Fleet, to hit Allied positions in New Guinea, the Russells, and Guadalcanal, as well as U.S. surface vessels near their anchorages. It was the largest Japanese naval air operation since Midway. Yet despite the numerous attractive targets available to these enemy planes, the massive effort was a failure. Not only did Yamamoto's pilots fail to regain air superiority in the theater, their losses were devastating. In three major strikes on 7, 12, and 16 April, the new Allied air commander in the Solomons, RAdm. Marc A. Mitscher, threw 76 planes at Yamamoto's intruders and exacted between 40 and 60 kills while suffering the loss of only 21 aircraft. One American destroyer was sunk, along with a tanker, a New Zealand corvette, and two Dutch merchant ships. Boastful Japanese pilots returned to Rabaul with bogus reports of the operation's success, but the truth was that inexperienced Japanese pilots flying inferior warplanes against growing numbers of Allied aircraft could no longer expect victory in the air. If the Allies controlled the skies, they could dictate the pace and direction of the war. The failure of the I Operation, Yamamoto's last (the admiral was killed when his plane was ambushed over Bougainville on 13 April), gave evidence that Japan was approaching the apocalypse.

As the Japanese were withdrawing their claws, Bull Halsey met with MacArthur for three days in April at the general's headquarters in Brisbane, Australia, to finalize details for the beginning of Operation Cartwheel, the assault on Rabaul. In keeping with the strategy of advancing toward the stronghold on a two-pronged axis, Halsey was authorized to begin the invasion of New Georgia, called Operation Toenails, on 15 May to coincide with amphibious landings in the Trobriands and at Nassau Bay, New Guinea, both in MacArthur's SWPA command. The date was later pushed back to 30 June by mutual agreement. MacArthur characteristically conceived of Toenails as simply a diversionary attack to drain the Japanese of their assets. This would allow him, driving up the western axis of advance toward Rabaul, to conquer New Guinea more easily.

Halsey was relieved. Hungry as always for action, he feared that the four months of relative idleness since the Russells were occupied might impact morale and spirit. Besides, he just was not one for sitting still, particularly when the enemy was backpedaling. The admiral's reputation began to develop soon after he assumed command of the South Pacific Area from Adm. Robert L. Ghormley during the Guadalcanal campaign. When reporters questioned the new SPA commander about his strategy for victory, Halsey responded: "Kill Japs, kill Japs, kill more Japs." Then, in a speech delivered in late August 1942 to the midshipmen at the Naval Academy, he elicited wild cheers from his well-starched and heretofore motionless audience when he confessed, "Missing the Battle of Midway [he had been hospitalized for a debilitating skin disease] has been the greatest disappointment of my life. But I am going back to the Pacific [voice rising] where I intend *personally* to have a crack at those yellow-bellied sons of bitches and their carriers."[2]

After the war, General MacArthur wrote of Halsey: "He was the same, aggressive type as John Paul Jones, David Farragut, and George Dewey. His one thought was to close with the enemy and fight him to the death. The bugaboo of many sailors, the fear of losing ships, was completely alien to his conception of sea action."[3]

When news of Halsey's appointment as SPA commander reached the ranks, one officer, recalling the reaction on Guadalcanal, said: "One minute we were too limp with malaria to crawl out of our foxholes; the next we were running around whooping like kids."[4] He was their type of officer—never supercilious or self-affected, he enjoyed the company of junior officers and enlisted men for meals, drank heartily himself, and flagrantly ignored the navy's prohibition against alcohol aboard ships.

Once, two sailors were ambling down a passageway talking admiringly about him. "I'd go to hell for that old SOB," one of them said. He immediately felt someone's finger jab into his back. It was Halsey himself. "Young man," he corrected, "I'm not so old."[5] The admiral often appeared in wrinkled khakis, sucking on an unfiltered cigarette and barking out graveled-voice commands from under a sweat-stained, long-billed, navy-issue baseball cap. Wiry, profane, quick-witted, and confrontational, he was a sailor's sailor: a blue collar, muddied, tattooed, sea dog who simplified the sometimes multifarious Allied strategy in the Pacific into a simple aphorism: attack, attack, and then attack again. "The only good Jap is a Jap who's been dead six months," he once remarked. "When we get through with them, the Japanese language will be spoken only in hell."[6] On 10 August 1945, when he received word of the impending Japanese surrender, he bristled, "Have we got enough fuel to turn around and hit the bastards once more before they quit?"[7] Five days later, when Admiral Nimitz broadcast the cease-fire order, Halsey still was wary of the treacherous Japanese. He ordered the Combat Air Patrol that flew cover over his fleet to "Investigate and shoot down all snoopers—not vindictively, but in a friendly sort of way."[8]

Sometimes his impetuosity became a liability, as was the case in the battle of Leyte Gulf when his overzealousness could have been costly. But to most Americans, especially those who served under him, he was the epitome of a combat leader. His thinly veiled disdain for the enemy was a refreshing change from most other poker-faced military and civilian leaders, and it closely duplicated the public's sentiment toward the Japanese.

Selection of a beach on which to land his troops was now foremost in Halsey's mind. A direct assault against Munda itself was never considered, for it was well protected by forbidding coral shoals, unmarked reefs, and barrier islets rendering it unsuitable for an amphibious operation of this magnitude. Besides, the Japanese had set up shore guns, assuring that an amphibious landing there would be most costly. Finally, there were an estimated eleven thousand Japanese defenders in the New Georgia group, three thousand of whom defended Munda itself. Halsey's war plans officer suggested early on that Segi might be the best spot for the initial landing, for it was occupied by friendlies and, although its beach was inadequate for a large landing force, landings there would be unopposed. Segi, however, was also on the opposite end of the island, about fifty miles from the objective. Another staff officer proposed a combined airborne-waterborne assault using the 2nd and 3rd Marine Parachute Battalions, then in New Zealand, to target either Munda Point or a nearby beachhead.[9] The most attractive option, however, was to locate a channel with safe sea approaches to a beach both near the airstrip and large enough to accommodate a division-size force. New Georgia, however, was mostly unmapped and the charts of its waters too old to be reliable. Aerial photography proved useless because of the thick canopy of trees blanketing the island. Patrols would have to be sent to walk the terrain and visually map trails, inlets, and anchorages, and otherwise evaluate the geography—a dangerous proposition. Luckily, Halsey had Donald Kennedy and his network of native scouts at Segi to guide them.

On 3 March, almost a full month before Toenails was approved, a small reconnaissance party under the command of Lt. William Coultas, a naval intelligence officer on Halsey's staff was ordered to Segi to collect information on New Georgia's terrain, enemy disposition, beach sites, and the like. A pilot, Coultas had been to the Solomons before the war on a scientific expedition, knew the native culture, was a magnificent bushman, and could even speak pidgin. He was accompanied by Capt. Clay Boyd and three enlisted men from the 1st Marine Raider Battalion, all chosen because of their ruggedness and experience in guerrilla-like operations in the jungle. The men flew in a PBY Catalina to Kennedy's headquarters. Coultas was impressed with the sophistication of what he saw. There were sentries manning observation platforms in the palms and patrolling the tiny harbor on foot with stolen Japanese weapons. Everywhere there were camouflaged canoes and a system of escape roads that disappeared in several directions into the jungle. And, of course, there was Kennedy himself, appearing to the visitors more like an aloof, gentrified landlord than a ruthless jungle warrior.

At 4 P.M. the following day, the recon team, after studying maps of the area with Kennedy, set out in two large canoes with twenty natives to explore the island. Paddling northwest all night at about a three-knot per hour pace, which the muscular natives could keep for as much as fourteen hours straight, they reached an inlet on the northern coast where they hid their canoes. They then traversed the island overland, heading southwest until they reached Roviana Lagoon, just a few miles from Munda and a possible landing site. It took them three days to travel the twenty miles across the rugged hinterland. So dense was the vegetation that they felt comfortable enough to build fires even though they were near Japanese encampments.[10] Their arduous trek did not please the natives, who knew the trip could have been made by canoe in twelve hours. The natives missed the point, however. Their orders were to traverse the island's spine to determine how difficult it was to navigate through the New Georgia interior.

Although they accomplished that mission, they were unable to get a look at Munda. Coultas did not want to return without fresh intelligence on the airstrip, so he split the party in two. One group would head back by canoe to Kennedy's compound by way of Viru Harbor, about eleven miles west of Segi. That group was instructed to carefully observe a Japanese encampment there because Viru was a possible target for the main assault. Coultas and Boyd decided to travel by canoe in the darkness southward across Blanche Channel to Rendova, the island where Dick Horton's coastwatching station was located. This was no easy task, for the Japanese had placed about a hundred of their soldiers and marines on the island to secure it and establish observation posts there. Their patrols kept an especially watchful eye on Rendova's northern shore. Luckily, the two officers' adroit native paddlers eluded the enemy pickets.

They spent two days with Horton, viewing the activities in and around the base from the coastwatcher's excellent mountain lookout ten miles from the main enemy camp. Coultas and Boyd, using Horton's powerful mounted telescope, took turns observing the movement of barges in and out of Munda and counting the planes sitting on the airstrip. They also gleaned information about Japanese traffic patterns, habits of operation, and potential avenues of approach to Munda from Horton and his native staff. They sketched maps and made estimates of the enemy's strength and morale, his ability to resupply and reinforce, and the positions of his heavier weapons. Finally, on 13 March, they left for Segi to reunite with the other half of their patrol. Within a week they were back at Admiral Halsey's headquarters in Nouméa, New Caledonia, reporting their valuable findings to naval intelligence.

The day after Coultas returned, four more daring marine recon patrols were ordered to Segi to expand upon the intelligence already collected. For the next three weeks, traveling only at night in native-guided canoes, these three-man parties sketched and photographed the coasts of New Georgia's two large sister islands, Kolombangara and Vangunu. They also gathered hydrographic information on Roviana Lagoon, through which the main landings would be made, and reexamined potential beachheads on New Georgia's southern and eastern coasts. The patrols also observed the enemy and submitted updated reports on the strength and location of enemy forces, including one report that described the Japanese infantry as "husky and apparently well fed."[11] As Coultas and Boyd had done before them, they sketched maps and learned the names of the natives they encountered along the way. They also confirmed the hazards and difficulties of movement through the island's heavily vegetated, tangled interior.

Sometimes the recon patrols would unexpectedly encounter the enemy, and although their mission was collecting intelligence, they did not avoid a chance to hurt their foes if the situation presented itself. Such was the case when Bill Werden, a marine Raider assigned to his company's scout and sniper platoon, happened upon a thirty-man party of Japanese infantry making camp eight miles from Segi at dusk.

Werden, always focused and intense, was not only considered a little nuts by his comrades, he also was probably the best jungle warrior in the 4th Raider Battalion. His reputation was won during training, when he would amuse himself by crawling within a few feet behind someone on guard and run his hand across the guard's throat. He also would sneak up on fellow marines involved in a nightly card game, appearing out of nowhere. "We never heard his approach," recalled John McCormick, one of Werden's men, "he would simply be there. He had powers of emanation a ghost or banshee would have been proud of. . . . At one time or another, we all had to stand guard, and many of us had had this uncanny experience. Several times while on guard, peering into the darkness, I suddenly felt his hand on my shoulder."[12]

While scouting on New Georgia, Werden silently slithered up to an unsuspecting Japanese patrol through the gaggle of undergrowth, calculating his next move. The soldiers were passing around a bottle of sake, so he decided to use a technique on them that he had been practicing. He pulled the pins from two grenades and held them both in his left hand. Then he armed a third and held it tightly in his right. Werden waited patiently for just the right moment, then rose to one knee and released the arming "spoon" from the grenade in his right hand and let it fly. He quickly shuffled the others one at a time to his right hand and threw them into the enemy's midst before the first exploded. As he dropped flat on the ground, he could feel the concussion from the three blasts not twenty yards away. Werden, not wanting to give the survivors a chance to react, jumped up with his Thompson submachine gun and fired several bursts. He again plopped down, rolled over a few times, got up in a crouch, and sped away. Later, the bodies of fourteen Japanese were discovered on the trail. The survivors never knew what hit them.[13]

Perhaps the most important of the recon patrols was one sent by Admiral Mitscher's AirSols to determine if there was a suitable site for an airbase on the island other than Munda. The command's operations officer, Stephen Jurika, and another staff officer, civil engineer Bill Painter, led the mission. The two were secretly implanted on the island by a PBY with a fighter escort in what had become standard procedure. First the floatplane touched down in an isolated spot in Morovo Lagoon a good distance from Segi Point. Next, a team of Kennedy's men met them and led them overland to Kennedy's base camp. After they spent a few days acclimating themselves to the environment, the coastwatcher provided them with six of his best tribesmen as escorts. Besides taking another look at Munda, they were to inspect potential airfield sites Kennedy had identified from the air several weeks before. Dressed in fatigues soaked in coffee to darken them, the survey team evaded Japanese recon patrols and climbed a hill just a few miles from the enemy airfield. From that spot they were able to study the garrison's routines, sketch the layout of the entire bivouac area around the airstrip, and determine that it was capable of handling bombers once it was captured. Based upon the information they gathered, it was decided that Segi was the only possible location for another airstrip.

Hundreds of pieces of information poured into Halsey's intelligence staff's office in the weeks prior to D day. Native islanders throughout the Solomons brought information about Japanese troop, naval, air strength, and disposition to coastwatcher radio stations for relay to higher headquarters. After the completion of combat or reconnaissance missions, pilots and PT boat skippers confirmed enemy barge concentrations, naval activity, and shore-gun emplacements. Captured documents, POW interrogations, and information provided by the Raider patrols also helped to provide an excellent picture of what the GIs were about to confront on New Georgia's unforgiving terrain. From this cornucopia of sometimes conflicting material, an intelligence picture had to be developed so that the assault would be successful without being costly. New Georgia, after all, was just another rung in the ladder to Bougainville, the center of Japanese strength in the Solomons.

Based on the information gathered, particularly by the Segi patrols, Admiral Turner, the officer responsible for amphibious operations, decided to conduct five landings. Rendova Island, just south of New Georgia across Blanche Channel, would serve as a staging area for the principal landing on a yet-to-be determined undefended beach somewhere east of the airfield. This battle would be the reverse of Guadalcanal: An infantry division would traverse the island after landing on a hidden beach and assault the enemy airdrome. There would be secondary landings as well, each planned for 30 June. More troops would be released at Rice Anchorage on the island's northeast coast to prevent enemy reinforcements on Kolombangara from reaching Munda. Much smaller forces would simultaneously secure Viru Harbor and Wickham Anchorage (on Vangunu Island's east coast). These two points would become staging centers for patrol boats and other craft that would shuttle supplies between the Russells and Rendova. Finally, Segi would be occupied and an auxiliary airstrip quickly built there to provide support for the final assault on Munda.[14]

The last recons were performed by patrols that left Segi on 13 June. Their mission was to locate artillery positions, bivouac areas, and routes for the invasion forces. Some of the team members remained with natives at each of these sites to guide the landing parties with lamps when they hit the beach on the night of 30 June. These missions were hazardous, for the men were lightly armed and no match for the Japanese actively patrolling the island.

Sergeant Frank Guidone and two fellow marines, operating from a base camp just a few miles from Munda, were moving quietly up a hill when they heard pots clanging and the sound of Japanese voices coming from just over the crest, about fifty feet away. They immediately froze and, after a few agonizing moments, dropped quietly to the moist ground, where they remained absolutely motionless for the rest of the evening. They were simply too close to chance making a getaway. A cloud of mosquitoes made them pay for their unlucky encounter as they endured Japanese songs and laughter throughout that miserable night. Once, out of boredom, Guidone aimed his rifle at the head of an enemy soldier squatting in a puddle of water relieving his bowels. He could easily have made his first kill, but he was too smart to give in to the temptation. By morning, both the mosquitoes and the Japanese were gone, and Guidone, who boxed for the Corps, was thankful that he had made it through alive. "If they hadn't been washing the dishes," he admitted later, "we would have been caught."[15]

Gunnery Sergeant Joseph Sciarra accompanied Guidone on another mission in which they wandered too close to an enemy outpost. As they carefully crept forward to peer at their antagonists, a shadowy contour abruptly materialized through the foliage just a few yards ahead. It was a Japanese sentry who had heard or seen something move. "*Tomare!* [halt]," the man cried out fearfully. The two marines froze, then, without breathing, skated backward a few steps and quietly covered themselves with leaves and vines. The sentry probed through the underbrush for a few minutes, inching closer and closer to the pair, who clenched their K-Bar knives, ready to silence him if he approached any closer. The man gave up the hunt rather quickly, however, perhaps doubting his own senses in surroundings that were equally alien to him. When he was a comfortable distance away, the two marines scrambled back to their camp armed both with some good intelligence and an even better war story.[16]

General Sasaki was aware that an Allied landing somewhere in the New Georgia group (Kolombangara, Vangunu, Rendova, or New Georgia proper) was imminent. He had received reports of large numbers of troop transports collecting at Guadalcanal, and aerial activity of all types was steadily increasing. The Japanese commander also obtained physical evidence that Americans were prowling on his island when C-ration cans were discovered in a makeshift shelter not far from his headquarters. Scraps of a letter written to a marine by his girlfriend were also found on a jungle trail only a half-mile from the base.[17] More and more of Sasaki's patrols failed to return—particularly those in the domain of his nemesis, Donald Kennedy. The general knew that the crafty New Zealander, a likely liaison with the probing recon teams, was in the region of Segi Point. Determined to overpower Kennedy's scouts and locate him, Sasaki in mid-June ordered elements of the 229th Infantry to settle the matter. He dispatched additional troops to the small outpost at Viru Harbor, bringing the strength there to about 225 men. Then the predators set off for Segi, hoping to trap their unsuspecting prey. Kennedy, however, had learned from his sentries that Viru had been reinforced, so he had his charges keep a watchful eye on the base.

An attack was not long in coming. Natives reported that a twenty-five-man Japanese recon patrol had begun slicing a trail through the jungle undergrowth roughly parallel to the coast from Viru to Nono, a village five miles from Segi. They stopped there for the night and set up camp, posting guards for perimeter security. Between their camp and the shoreline, however, were legions of twisted mangrove roots they thought would incapacitate any intruder, so they left that flank unprotected. It proved to be a costly mistake. Five canoes carrying Kennedy and his well-armed warriors silently approached the shore near the enemy camp through the darkness. When they were within a few feet of the beach, they slid out of their canoes, waded ashore, and, on signal, lobbed grenades into the midst of the sleeping soldiers. Then they emptied their rifles into the horrified, scattering survivors. The Japanese who escaped that fusillade retreated west toward Viru in confusion without firing a shot.

Again Kennedy had triumphed. The raid had been his largest and most successful, bringing the number of enemy killed in his zone of operation to fifty-four.[18] He knew that the situation had changed, however. He could no longer operate with such impunity, for contact with the Japanese was becoming much too frequent and their tactics more audacious. A captured map told him that the enemy knew his general whereabouts, so the anxious coastwatcher radioed for help. Admiral Turner had originally planned a landing at Segi on 30 June to coincide with the other D-day landings, but the sudden enemy move against Kennedy was unsettling. If Segi were lost, it would disrupt the planned construction of the airstrip there and threaten the entire mission. Something had to be done to protect the undermanned outpost. Turner's response was to order roughly eight hundred infantry to move immediately to the imperiled base.

Just before daybreak on 21 June, two American destroyer-transports, the *Dent* and *Waters,* stole into Panga Bay in search of Donald Kennedy's sequestered station. The ships carried the 4th Marine Raider Battalion's O and P companies and half of the headquarters company. As they approached Segi, the crews spotted signal fires Kennedy had started to serve as beacons for the landing force. When the coastwatcher's men detected the approaching ships, fourteen natives scurried to their canoes and swiftly paddled toward the two APDs to guide them safely through the shoals to a deepwater anchorage. That accomplished, the Raiders, who were making their first combat landing, climbed over the sides of the old ships and descended quietly into Higgins landing craft. Within thirty short minutes they had hit the shore and fanned out into a perimeter defense, ready for action. Two companies from the 43rd Division's 103rd Regiment landed the next day. Their job was to secure Segi while the marines conducted a raid on Viru Harbor.

As the men disembarked from the vessels and waded ashore on the tiny beach, Kennedy must have known that his service at Segi was drawing to a close. He was no longer the master of this realm. Hundreds of infantry now occupied every conceivable space in his camp, setting up perimeters, machine-gun emplacements, communication stations, and command posts. Soon a busy airstrip would be built on what was now a peaceful coconut grove fronting his comfortable residence, inviting even more activity. On 30 June the 47th Seabee Battalion, led by Comdr. J. S. Lyles of Oklahoma, began work on the fighter airstrip. Halsey wanted it done in two weeks. Working twenty-four-hour days (floodlights were strung in spite of the tactical situation), the engineers cleared coconut trees, hauled coral, and graded the strip despite being lashed by tropical rains that dumped fourteen inches while they toiled. On the morning of 11 July, a navy Corsair that had been crippled over Munda became the first to land on the new seventy-five- by twenty-five-hundred-foot runway. It had taken the Seabees just under eleven days after the first landing boat ground ashore, something of a record for converting raw jungle into a landing strip.[19] Two days later it was home to thirty fighters. The strip was later expanded to accommodate bombers. In the meantime, whenever bombers came up from Guadalcanal to hit Munda or surrounding targets, fighters from Segi would climb up to escort them. It was an amazing accomplishment that the Seabees would repeat again and again in the Pacific War.

As soon as Munda was in Allied hands, Kennedy would pack his teleradio and leave his station for the island of Vangunu with his pregnant lover, Magiko. He continued coastwatching there until the completion of the Solomons campaign. Magiko had a baby girl on Vangunu, but the child died of malaria in 1945. Kennedy's contribution was huge. He had worked continuously in Japanese-held territory for a year, with no support and no promise of assistance. Acting not only as an effective coastwatcher and brilliant guerrilla leader, he also managed to convince the islanders that their government had not abandoned them during the Japanese occupation. It was people like Donald Kennedy who won the respect of the Solomon islanders and held them in the Allied camp during the pivotal years of 1942–43, when the balance of power in the South Pacific was still in question.

Viru Harbor

Admiral Turner selected the marine Raiders for the Viru operation for a very simple reason: They were perhaps the best outfit in the entire Marine Corps. The Raiders, modeled after the British Commandos and Chinese guerrillas, were a quasi-guerrilla force that infiltrated enemy territory by clandestine amphibious assaults. Their focus was reconnaissance and raids—special operations of various types relying on mobility and speed rather than firepower. In this regard, Col. Merritt A. "Red Mike" Edson, one of the Raider's founding fathers, envisioned the new organization as a sort of a seaborne version of a parachute unit.[20]

The man responsible for molding the men of the newly formed 4th Raider Battalion into the elite troops they had become was their commander, Lt. Col. James Roosevelt, the president's son. A recipient of the Navy Cross for heroism during the raid on Makin Island with the 2nd Raiders, he should never have even been in the armed services. Part of his stomach had been removed, and he had exceptionally poor vision. Without his glasses he was virtually blind. He also suffered from flat feet and was forced to wear tennis shoes instead of field boots. Despite these physical handicaps, he made it through the challenging training on sheer guts and later became one of the most respected Raider commanders. He never had an opportunity to lead his battalion into battle, however. Plagued by malaria, he had to be evacuated for treatment on the eve of the Segi landing.

Lieutenant Colonel Mickey Currin, a newly promoted thirty-two-year-old Californian, was chosen to replace the ailing Roosevelt. A marine's marine, he had worked his way up from private. Assisting the handsome, mustachioed Irishman were two outstanding company commanders: 1st Lt. Ray Luckel of O Company and Capt. Tony Walker of P Company. Luckel, like his commander, had been an enlisted man for most of his career. Big, strong, and intelligent, he was just the man to lead his neophyte marines into their first battle. Walker, a Yale graduate from Washington D.C., had played football first for his alma mater and then professionally. Like Luckel, he was extremely sturdy and athletic, quick on his feet, and a weapons expert. All three were dedicated warriors who commanded the highest respect from their men. They would need every ounce of that respect during the mission they were about to undertake.

Lieutenant Colonel Currin's instructions were to move from Segi to Viru Harbor on 30 June and seize it from the enemy garrison in time to welcome a seaborne force of 355 soldiers slated to land that

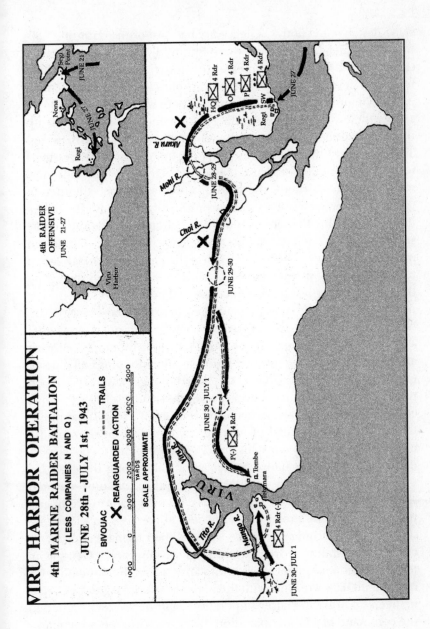

same day. The mission was necessary because of the daunting 130-foot-high cliffs enclosing the three-hundred-yard-wide harbor as it sliced inland. In the late nineteenth century, five coral and stone fortresses perched atop the cliffs had protected the harbor's inhabitants from unwelcome headhunters. There were no beaches. Consequently, any amphibious landing party would be forced to sail up the harbor under the guns of the waiting Japanese shore batteries. The guns were the Raiders' primary objective. Currin understood well that if he could not secure the hamlet before the Allied invaders arrived on the thirtieth, the landing force would be slaughtered.

Viru was some eleven air miles from Segi, but because the meandering trails the Raiders would follow circumvented unfordable streams and impassable swamps, the distance was closer to fourteen miles—miles that would be nothing like the forced marches they had trained for back in the states. Currin's men would be struggling through the toughest terrain encountered by U.S. forces in the entire Pacific. Although it was true that earlier reconnaissance patrols had covered the distance in two days, a few lightly armed men could slice through the jungle barrier much more easily than 375 officers and men in two fully equipped Raider companies plus half a headquarters company. Recognizing this, Currin sought and received permission to leave Segi on the twenty-seventh—a full twenty-four hours earlier than planned—so as to ensure reaching Viru on D-day morning. Additionally, instead of moving the entire distance overland, Currin was allowed to move his men west toward Viru on boats, paddling with Kennedy's native guides a few miles along the coast before debarking. Not only would that save a little more time, it would also conserve his men's strength. Three months prior to this operation, he had spent a total of twenty days in the area on reconnaissance patrols and was therefore well-qualified to make judgments concerning infantry movement through the murky New Georgia interior. Currin was one of the few who anticipated the difficulties his men would have wrestling with the island's unforgiving terrain. Had he been on Admiral Halsey's operations staff instead of assigned to the command of a Raider battalion the entire Viru operation might have been scrapped.

When darkness fell on the twenty-seventh, the order was given for the marines to "saddle up" and climb into the approximately fifty small, black rubber boats that would deliver them to a native village about a quarter of the way to Viru. Lieutenant Colonel Currin and his staff led the procession a few hundred yards offshore in two enormous New Georgian war canoes. The canoes, called *vouvas,* were propelled at a fast pace by two dozen of his muscular native guides. Also on board the canoes were mortar shells and other heavy equipment, such as radios.

Able to carry more than thirty men, the canoes were inlaid with mother of pearl and white cowrie shells and topped with wreaths of areca leaves for protection against "devil-devils." Most spectacular were the figureheads of gods called *nguzunguzus* (pronounced "noozoonoozoos") ornamenting their high prows near the water line. These were beautifully carved miniature creatures with doglike heads whose job was to scare away evil nautical spirits and generally ensure a safe and successful voyage. Native women were strictly forbidden to even touch the *vouvas* on penalty of decapitation, for if they did so, the vessel would lose its *mana* or supernatural powers.

If moonlight broke through the darkness, they hid in the still shadows cast by the many islets sprinkled throughout the tricky New Georgia channels. When clouds reappeared to eclipse the cool moonlight, the paddlers resumed their hushed, rhythmical rowing. In their wake was left only the whisper of dripping paddles and the warm gleam of phosphorescent light that melted away behind them. Once they slipped silently by a Japanese force of undetermined size that had occupied a coastal village. From several hundred yards off shore, their campfires were barely visible through the inky darkness.

An hour later, the moon's dim light shining on an islet created a silhouette that looked to the jittery Raiders like a Japanese destroyer. For a few intense minutes they halted their paddling to listen until they were sure it was a mirage. In case they did stumble into an enemy ship or barge, the plan was for everyone to go into the water and use their boats as shields. Fortunately, the voyage was uneventful. An hour after midnight the guides spotted the village of Regi, their first destination. Regi was nothing more than a tiny cluster of a few dozen or so grass huts built above the water on stilts. The natives there offered no resistance. Currin's tired men stepped ashore on the deserted beach, thankful to be free of the rubber boats after covering eight miles in four and a half hours. If the enemy attacked now, they could defend themselves. In the water, they would not have survived an ambush. After establishing a hasty perimeter defense and munching on chocolate bars for dinner, they tried to get some sleep—some of them inside the little village's huts. They tried to cover their tracks on the muddy beach, but without rain, it was almost impossible. Meanwhile, a few of Kennedy's scouts collected the boats and towed them back to Segi to preserve the mission's secrecy.

At 6:30 A.M., the marines and their remaining native guides began the overland trek to Viru on a narrow trail flanked by an impassable snarl of vines and protruding roots and creepers that entangled the interlopers. The going was so tough that even their guides argued among themselves about what route to take. Progress was measured in feet and yards rather than miles. Soon after they started out, the trail disappeared into a two-mile-wide mangrove swamp. For three hours the silence was broken only by the sound of sucking mud and whispered profanities. Unfortunately, higher ground brought no relief to the already weary men. Steep, muddy hills and swollen streams added to their woes, forcing them to move in a single, slow-moving column stretching about a half-mile. The men at the head of the column churned up a muddy ooze that made the footing difficult for those who followed, sometimes forcing them to ascend the steeper hills on all fours.[21] Sergeant Henry Berry, a machine gunner, recalled his frustration:

The jungle was indescribable—worst shithole you have ever seen! As I remember, we hiked through that stuff any way we could. At best we averaged a half-mile per hour, maybe less. The only good thing about the next three days was them chocolate bars. I think they were called D bars. They were real good. I just about lived on them for the rest of the time we were on New Georgia.

We started out with M-1s, BARs [Browning Automatic Rifles], machine guns, Thompsons, mortars, and .37mm antitank rifles. Hell, those .37s were impossible, you know, they're those big, long things. Every time you'd take a step, they'd get caught on some kind of a vine. Finally, we figured, what the hell, if the Japs have tanks, we'll just have to handle them one way or another. So we tossed the .37s into the bush. They're probably still there and would make one hell of a souvenir if someone wants to go get them. But you can have them as far as I'm concerned. What a waste! The only souvenir I wanted to get home was my own ass![22]

One of the major bothers the Raiders endured was keeping their weapons in good working order—a difficult task on swampy New Georgia. The muzzles would become clogged with mud, sand, and debris, and though daily cleaning and oiling helped, the problem persisted. Forty-two-year-old Capt. Paul Redmond finally remedied it. The Connecticut-born 4th Raider Catholic chaplain, a World War I veteran, gave the Raiders condoms and directed the men to stretch them over their muzzles, protecting the apertures from moisture and mud while still enabling the weapons to be fired immediately. The smiling marines promptly nicknamed the innovation "Redmond's Rifle Rubbers." The technique had been used on Guadalcanal the previous September, when General Vandegrift ordered a hundred gross for the same purpose. The priest later joked that a visiting navy chaplain threatened to have him excommunicated for promoting the use of contraceptives.[23]

Three hours later, just one and one-half tough miles from the beach, the Raiders made contact with a Japanese patrol one of the scouts reported had been shadowing them. Currin bit down hard on his unlit cigar and ordered the column's rear guard to set up an ambush. A platoon from P Company deployed on each side of the trail, blending into the heavy carpet of dark undergrowth smoldering over the jungle floor. They did not have to wait long. Five minutes later the Japanese point man came creeping down the trail. Currin related the details of what happened next to *Chicago Tribune* reporter Clay Gowran, who was accompanying the Raiders: "The [lead] Nip apparently thought we were miles ahead. He suddenly popped around that bend, and there were three Marines standing in the trail. The Jap stared at them, and they stared at him. Our boys started first. Before the Nip could raise his rifle, he was full of lead. Three others ran up to see what was going on and got it the same way."[24]

The rest of the estimated twenty-man enemy patrol escaped into the jungle. A few hours later, an enemy patrol (it could easily have been the same one) collided with Lt. DeVillo W. Brown's platoon, only to break contact after about an hour of combat. These two fire-fights, along with the exacting terrain, delayed the Raiders' drive to Viru considerably. In eleven draining hours of struggle they had moved less than three miles.[25] Fortunately, they had suffered no casualties.

When Brown's platoon joined the others, however, they discovered that Sgt. John Sudro and his four-man rifle team were missing. The men had been cut off during the firefight and were unaware that the rest of the platoon had moved to rejoin the main column. When Sudro finally realized that the others were gone, the Japanese patrol had begun to set up camp just a few yards away from the five marines, who listened and watched the enemy cook rice, boil tea, and shuttle sentries. Any movement or noise was sure to be noticed, so they settled in for a long, sleepless night. The unsuspecting Japanese broke camp at dawn and moved off into the jungle. Sudro decided it would be futile to attempt to reunite with his unit without a map or a native guide, so he and his men retraced their steps and two days later made it back to Segi.

Currin realized that even with the extra day he had been given to reach Viru, the Raiders did not have enough time. The village was still eleven miles away. To arrive there by the morning of the thirtieth as planned would mean making an arduous all-night march through the jungle. Even if they made it by morning, Currin could not have ordered his men to immediately make a combat assault. Adding to their misery, food was becoming a major worry. They had packed three days' jungle rations (mostly biscuits and six-by-three-inch chocolate bars) when they left Segi, but along the way the Raiders had shared their meager meals with the native scouts, thinking they would be resupplied when they secured Viru. Another day in the bush would mean two days on paltry half-rations. Hunger, however, was the more manageable problem. Currin decided to request a twenty-four-hour extension, but his radios failed him. Unable to reach Segi, he reluctantly ordered two native runners to go back to the base camp and inform Kennedy of the delays and tell him to radio their expected time of arrival in Viru: 1 July, one day after D day. But the messengers had difficulty getting to Segi, and Kennedy had trouble reaching the navy headquarters in the Russells. Consequently, the leader of the Viru invasion force, Comdr. Stanley Leith, did not receive Currin's urgent message until after his destroyers were underway on the morning of the invasion. Admiral Turner did not learn of Currin's message until a few hours *after* the scheduled assault.[26]

At roughly 5 P.M., the two spent Raider companies reached a wide, forbidding river that carved its way through the solid walls of the leafy jungle cathedral. Currin decided it was the best place to bivouac for the night. Clay Gowran recorded that they had forded ten jungle streams and four rather expansive rivers that day. After dining on cheese and pork paste, the men slept like the dead despite the unforgiving Solomon rain while Currin and his shivering staff huddled under their ponchos to discuss the next day's course of action. Twenty-one-year-old Sgt. Anthony P. Coulis of P Company remembered what it was like: "After machine guns were emplaced on a tight defensive line around the bivouac area, we dug in for the night. Rain, that damned rain, started to fall, tormenting us further. Miserably we started a silent cursing streak. Crouching under our ponchos, we ate scraps of cheese from our C rations. A few minutes later I was asleep, despite the rain which poured down on us all night. I was tired, dead tired, and I didn't give a damn if my throat was slit as I lay sleeping, half sitting among the roots."[27]

During the night, some of the men on watch heard the sounds of gunfire in the distance. Later they learned that the natives assigned the task of taking their rubber boats back to Segi had been surprised by a Japanese ambush and massacred. Even though the islanders were not members of their special fraternity, the loss was sorely felt. The Japanese had won a victory and at the same time gathered intelligence about their numbers based upon the number of boats that the natives were towing. The next time the enemy would be better prepared.

Father Redmond slid through the slush up to Clay Gowran, who was suffering with malaria, and secretly slipped him a two-ounce bottle of brandy to ease his discomfort. The jungle ordeal was perhaps most difficult for the good padre, who was twice the age of the rest of the Raiders. Yet he never complained or asked for assistance.[28]

As the rain continued to lash down on them, Redmond talked to the reporter about his work in the United States, his brother the pro golfer, his teaching days at Catholic University, and why he was there. Gowran, wrapped in his glistening poncho, just listened. Redmond was not at all like other clergymen he had known. The padre was always approachable, and the men adored him. No one understood their failings more or was so quick to forgive them their sins. He brought all of them closer to God. Even Redmond would admit, however, that in combat, God was a pretty easy sell.

Their tortuous advance was no easier on the morning of the second day. Three times they forded the same meandering twenty-yard-wide river, which had swollen to several times its usual size because of the recent heavy rains. They managed to cross it only by forming a human chain, locking wrists, and pulling each other through the murky current. Only those who were close to six feet tall made it across without going under at some point. The others were lifted up by their taller comrades. Weapons were hoisted above their heads to keep them dry. Everything else got wet except cigarettes, coffee, matches, and personal items like the photos and toilet paper they carried in sealed rubber pouches. It was slow going, but moving around the river's serpentine path would have burned up even more time. That day they would travel but seven exhausting miles in twelve hours. Sergeant Coulis described their progress:

> By midafternoon, we had reached the peak of physical exertion. We alternately crawled up and tobogganed down greasy ridges. We forded numerous jungle streams and swam three of them. The repeated torture of plunging into icy streams; the chopping away of endless underbrush and foliage; the continuous drizzle of rain; the days without hot food or drink; the mosquitoes tormenting us at night. It was sheer physical torture. The racking struggle of overtired muscles and empty bellies against the viciousness of the jungle itself. How I ever lived through that day, I'll never know. That night we didn't even

stand guard. We plunged into the brush next to the trail and fell asleep with a prayer for protection on our lips.[29]

A marine war correspondent traveling with the Raiders gave this account:

We never did take more than two steps without slipping, stumbling, climbing over rocks, over and under trails. At times we walked hundreds of yards by stepping from rock to rock. Again we would tread our way through the swamps by jumping from one patch of grass to another, from one root of a mangrove tree to another. We forded a half a dozen streams a day—once across a river which came up to the chins of Marines five feet ten in height. Many a shorter man swam from 20 to 50 yards with full equipment. We lived on rations—out of cans for two days and on chocolate bars the rest of the time.[30]

The first several hours of the march passed without incident. At about 2 P.M., however, Lieutenant Brown's P Company platoon, which had taken another trail toward the objective and was therefore separated from the rest of the battalion, stumbled onto some Japanese just after crossing the Choi River. The forty-five-man enemy force was dug in on the crest of a three-hundred-foot hill overlooking the trail. Private Milton "Cajun" Robert from Arabi, Louisiana, was on point about fifteen minutes ahead of the rest of the platoon with two other Raiders and a native guide. Suddenly, the guide jerked up his head as if he could smell the enemy nearby. Just then gunfire began popping from a position not forty yards away, raking the area around them. One of the Raiders was killed instantly when a bullet struck just below his left ear. The others made for a large banyan tree and fired back from behind its thick roots. Robert turned his BAR sideways so that it would "walk" laterally rather than up and emptied an entire twenty-round cartridge. A enemy machine gun continued to bark at them, however. They tried silencing it with grenades, holding onto them for three seconds before throwing them because the gun position was so close. Finally, it stopped firing. Then an enemy grenade exploded close enough to Robert to tear the camouflage fabric off his helmet. He shook off the effects of the blast and rose slowly to peek over a root. Spotting the head of an enemy soldier just opposite him on the other side of the same root system, he backed up a bit, carefully placed the barrel of his BAR on the root, and just about tore the man's head off with a short burst. Another head appeared but then ducked behind the roots. Robert's partner, a Raider named Harbord, was facedown directly in line with where the second man's head had appeared. Nevertheless, Robert fired three or four bursts over Harbord and blasted through the roots where the Japanese was located.

"I didn't care about shooting through Harbord as I thought he was dead," Robert recalled. "But when the battle was over, I almost had a heart attack when Harbord stood up and everything fell out of his pack. (Robert's BAR had ripped it apart as he lay there still). He said that they almost got me. I told him that it was me and for him to look on the other side of the roots."[31] When the rest of the platoon caught up to Robert and the others, fire from three Nambu machine guns and numerous small arms greeted them. The marines spread out and returned fire with rifles and machine guns, but this looked like a good time to employ their homemade concussion grenades. The smallest of these were made out of plastic explosives stuffed into empty ration cans. The larger ones, about the size of a cantaloupe, were made by binding four packages of TNT together with a tire chain. These deadly devices were better suited to New Georgia's entangled interior because the lighter fragmentation grenades would easily get caught in the innumerable vines and branches overhead and fall short of the mark. Besides, the concussion of these heavier, homemade explosives could kill a man fifteen feet away. Yelling "Marine mortar!" to mislead the Japanese into thinking they were being mortared, the Raiders hurled their "grenades" at the enemy positions on the hill. Then, in typical Raider fashion, the platoon fixed bayonets and charged toward the hillcrest.

"They had machine guns and the way they had us bore-sighted, there was nothing for us to do but go right up that ridge after them," recalled the battalion's operations officer. "As soon as they opened fire, two of my men were killed, then we got off of the trail into the bush. We didn't waste any time. I kept the 1st squad in position for covering fire and took the other two squads up the ridge by infiltration. I guess we must have taken a little over an hour to clean them out but I don't think that more than two or three got away."[32]

Another witness, twenty-year-old Willard Goodson, recalled:

We went right up that ridge into the muzzle of that damned gun. There wasn't any withdrawal, or second charge, or anything like that. Five of the boys died going up, but another, Steve M. Klos, kept right on going. . . . You should have seen that guy, sir. . . . A bullet tore into his left leg and smacked him down so hard it sprained his right ankle, but he kept on going on his hands and knees. He had . . . [a] homemade bomb in each fist and a lighted cigarette in his mouth. When he got within throwing distance he lit the fuses and heaved them. . . . With only sniper fire to heckle us, we went on up and over. There were 18 Jap bodies lying around the gun, sprawled out the way the bomb had tossed them.[33]

When they finally reached the crest, the Raiders counted forty-five backpacks along with the enemy dead. The survivors had obviously been in a hurry to make their getaway.

After clearing the hill, the Raiders continued their march. Steve Klos was in pain, but he refused to allow anyone to carry him. With the help of one of the native scouts, he followed his unit slowly from behind. Grimacing and exhausted, he staggered into the bivouac site four hours after the others. The next day he managed to stumble seven miles, then covered six more the day after in a remarkable display of strength and forbearance. When his fellow Raiders finally reached Viru, he was with them.

The Americans suffered their first casualties of the operation, and five young men were buried in the steamy jungle earth that day. Their deaths made the war a reality to the eighteen- and nineteen-year-olds who watched silently as Orra Gilbert, Marty Johnson, George Rossiter, Everett Tower, and Rase Warren were lowered into shallow holes. It was a numbing experience for these teenagers who had never before considered their own mortality. Nevertheless, they pushed the pain into an unreachable corner of their minds and focused on their task. They would grieve later, when they were not so preoccupied with their dirty mission. Never would they have guessed that the anguish would always return—even after a half-century had passed.

Meanwhile, aboard the destroyer escorts *Kilty, Hopkins,* and *Crosby,* two companies of the 43rd Division's 103rd Infantry and supporting units approached Viru Harbor on the morning of the thirtieth while Currin's harried unit was still at least a day away. Despite several unsuccessful attempts to radio the Raider commander from offshore, Commander Leith ordered his force to move through the rainsqualls into the harbor knowing that Currin probably had not yet arrived. The marines were to fire white parachute signal flares to mark their positions, and when these were not forthcoming, it was clear that Viru remained in enemy hands. However, there was no way to be sure without moving forward. Cautiously, the three destroyers eased toward the harbor's entrance, its menacing cliffs waiting like huge, open jaws for the unsuspecting soldiers who quietly awaited the order to embark on their landing craft. When the ships were within a thousand yards of the harbor's mouth, a Japanese three-inch gun that was supposed to have been either taken out or manned by Currin's Raiders, opened fire, its shells exploding near the slow-moving gray targets. Leith's crews spotted the gun flashes on a cliff, and returned fire while he withdrew his force out of range. Major Masao Hara, commander of the 1st Battalion, 229th Infantry, which was defending Viru, bragged to his superiors that he had repulsed an Allied landing when he saw the ships withdraw.[34]

A landing was now out of the question, but Leith was reluctant to leave the area while Currin's men were possibly imperiled. The ships steamed back and forth off the harbor entrance awaiting further instructions from RAdm. George H. Fort, who was responsible for the landings in that sector. After several more attempts to reach Currin by radio failed (his command set had been dead since the previous day), the decision was made to put the two 103rd Infantry assault companies ashore at the village of Nono, near Currin's original landing site. From there, they would be in a position to lend assistance to the Raiders if they were in jeopardy. Ironically, the GIs did not link up with Currin's Raiders until three days after the harbor was secured. They, too, had fallen prey to the treachery of the New Georgia landscape.

After another wretched, rainy night, the Raiders moved out at dawn on 30 June to within striking distance of Major Hara's three-hundred-man garrison. After advancing only four miles in twelve interminable hours the day before, the marines found the going tougher than ever. The fact that the Japanese chose to ignore Currin's progress was no accident of luck. The previous night Lieutenant Colonel Currin huddled with his scouts to determine if any of them had actually walked the trails they were taking. None of them had. The commander angrily unfolded his map and reconfigured their course. Even without enemy contact, the Raiders nevertheless made only a few more miles. Correspondent Gowran and the others were coming to realize that their true enemy was the unholy jungle they slaved to drive through:

[T]he rain which had dogged us since the start of the mission began again. It added to the misery of the march, to the days without hot food or drink, to the mosquitoes which tormented us at night. . . .

The nightmare of that 30 June 43 was not Jap-devised; it was the racking struggle of overtired muscles and empty bellies against the inanimate viciousness of the jungle itself. . . . Against the snake-like roots which reached out to trip us. Against the damnable mud which sucked us down. Against the million and one vines and creepers which clawed at a man and threw him off balance.

That day I heard men curse the jungle; curse it in hoarse, hysterical whispers in a way they had never cursed the enemy. As we tired it seemed to gain strength in its silent war against us. The smallest vine was enough to throw a man onto his face in the mud if it caught his foot. The tentacles took a vicious pleasure in sweeping our helmets from our heads, or snagging rifle barrels from our shoulders. It seems like a little thing, probably, to people back home. But too much of it could drive an exhausted, starving man mad.[35]

His remarks proved to be more prophetic than he could ever have imagined, for later in the campaign hundreds of men had to be hospitalized for a disorder that is best described as madness.

The marines eventually reached the junction of the trails to Tetemara and Tombe. Currin's native scouts assured him that Hara had men defending both villages, so the colonel split his haggard troops. He sent Captain Walker and two platoons from P Company numbering about a hundred men toward Tombe, which sat on a high cliff overlooking Viru Harbor's eastern shore. Currin and the remainder of his force, about two hundred seventy-five men, would assault Tetemara, located on the opposite shore of the narrow waterway, where the majority of Hara's force was stationed. Because of the impossible terrain and the radio problems they were experiencing, Currin did not try to coordinate the assaults. Walker would be on his own and would attack as soon as possible in the morning.

The colonel's larger force had the roughest go of it, for it was forced to ford three more swift-running rivers. To complicate matters further, it was late afternoon, and on cloudy days hardly any sunlight was able to break through the thick, triple-canopy foliage. When Currin finally reached the fifty-yard-wide Mango River, the last of the three, he and his bewildered men were cloaked in almost total darkness. The river toyed with the fatigued Raiders as they formed another human chain, squeezed the wrists of the men on either side of them, and prayed that their next step would find footing. Their weariness betrayed their failing eyes. Every tree stump became a deadly snake; every log looked like a hungry crocodile.

There was no respite when the last man finally emerged from the muddy torrent. They arose from the banks of the swollen Mango into the soggy air of a mosquito-infested mangrove swamp. There were still three more miles before they reached a high ridge Currin had spotted on his topographic map and on which he planned to bivouac for the night. That meant they would have to move through the treacherous swamp after dark. There was no other choice but to move on.

"Now began what could have been a scene from Dante's *Inferno*," recalled Roy Batterton. "The swamp was every bit as ghastly as we had been led to believe. The water was from knee to waist-deep. Under the surface were snake-like roots by the millions. Under the roots was bottomless black mud."[36]

After moving ahead a short distance in the rapidly dimming light, the exhausted column came to a halt. It was too dark to see. The chief scout approached Currin and began pointing off to the side, murmuring something in pidgin that none of the Raiders could understand. However, the natives set out with their machetes and began hacking away at the undergrowth to get at the trees that sprouted from the knee-deep water. After a few minutes they each brought back chunks of wood and leaves that glowed with a pale green, bioluminescent light that grew naturally in the fetid swamp on decaying wood. Some pieces glowed so brightly that one could see the outline of the hands of the man clutching them. The natives passed out a piece to every man in the column. Now they could move through the black wetness without losing contact with the rest of their stumbling comrades. Tiny, green-white lanterns lit their way as they moved out in a ghostly procession. If it had not been for the scouts, the Raiders might never have made it through those clammy waters that night.

Four seemingly eternal hours later, the beleaguered men emerged from the swamp and flopped exhausted onto dry ground, insects still loitering around their heads. Their legs ached from the hours of lifting them from the sticky paste on the swamp's bottom. Back and shoulder muscles screamed for relief. The men were so tired that no one talked or even bothered to open his fly to relieve himself. They simply urinated in their trousers. No one thought anything of it. No one thought at all. It took energy to think, and there was none to spare.

Mickey Currin plodded up and down the weary procession, encouraging the drained Raiders on, hiding his own struggle with fatigue as they moved farther into the unknown. He knew better than the rest how far they were from help. They were out of radio contact with headquarters, so for all his superiors knew, the enemy had destroyed them. They were low on ammunition as a result of the two unexpected firefights. They were almost out of food. Up ahead, the enemy lay waiting for them. He knew that each of his young marines had to dig deep within himself to find the motivation to push forward. Never in their short lives had they been so challenged. Currin had to keep them from surrendering to the jungle. He looked in each of their faces as they stumbled by him, asking them about injuries, sharing his own food, or simply patting them affectionately on their tired shoulders.

It was a mere half a mile to Tetemara, but it proved to be a cursed, half-mile climb up a steep, punishing mountain. Currin wanted to be in position to attack from the high ground at dawn the next morning, so he commanded his men to move out. Without a word they began the climb, the jungle's humidity hanging like heavy sacks on each of them. However, a powerful group dynamic helped pull them together to the top: No one wanted to embarrass himself by quitting as long as the rest were still driving forward.

It seemed like a thousand years since that day when they had returned home to announce that they had enlisted in the Corps. The laughter and love at family farewell dinners; the looks of admiration from friends; the adulation they received when they visited home after boot camp; fawning neighbors and girlfriends; going to church in a perfectly creased uniform adorned with crimson stripes and a rifle qualification badge—where had those moments gone? Where had that world gone? The nationalistic passion that just a few months before had burned hot within them had cooled, blurred by a new passion: their squads and platoons. The instinct to survive still remained, sharpened by the tumult of war, but even it had been dulled by the Raiders conditioned instinct to fight. It was a metamorphosis that every warrior since antiquity has experienced. But each man had had to struggle with the transformation in his own unique way. Now, with each unsteady step deeper into the seamless New Georgia jungle, these men, like their dead comrades before them, edged closer to self-actualization.

Slick and muddy from the constant rains, the men struggled to gain a foothold during the agonizingly slow ascent. With their rifles slung over their backs, they pulled on branches and roots as the trail became increasingly slippery for those in the rear. Even the relentless, powerful natives accompanying them balked—particularly those who carried the mortar ammunition. They refused to go any farther unless they were relieved. At that point, Jack Pratt, the chief guide, promised all that the terrain would soon become manageable if they could just conquer this one last ridge. Batterton recalled what happened during the final hundred yards of the tortuous climb, when the men were on their hands and knees trying to scale the slimy peak: "Time after time a few would get within yards of the crest, and then the leading man would hit a slick spot and tumble the whole lot to the bottom. Sliding men smashed against machine guns, rocks, and trees, and other men. Finally we crawled over the crest and fell exhausted on both sides of the trail."[37]

Sergeant Anthony P. Coulis, who was near the end of the column when they finally stopped about fifteen hundred yards from the village: "That night we crawled over the crest into the flat top of a ridge and fell exhausted into the mud. I didn't even try to eat. In fact, I found out, to my dismay, that I was also out of drinking water. We flopped in the goo and slept like dead men. Tomorrow we were to attack!"[38] The moon hung brightly above the Solomons, casting a preternatural glow over the island. Yet barely a glint of light seeped down through the jungle canopy to the depleted, hungry men of the 4th Raider Battalion. Apparently even the heavens had forsaken them. They collapsed on the dark, wet earth until morning. In sixteen painful hours, with only two twenty-minute rest periods, they had managed to make just seven miles.

At 9 A.M. on 1 July, Captain Walker and his men assaulted the tiny village of Tombe, engaging in a brief but furious battle. In a fortunate coincidence of the war, his attack coincided with an air strike by six American SBD Dauntless dive-bombers. Walker, as shocked by the first bomb's explosion as the Japanese, waited for the attack to end and then moved on the stunned enemy. Most defenders who died did so in the initial burst of fire from the marines, for the Japanese were too busy searching for a safe place to hide during the bombing to notice the Raiders who suddenly materialized in their midst.[39] Within twenty minutes the Japanese were completely overwhelmed. Thirteen enemy soldiers tried to escape on a palm-covered barge tied up near the village pier. But the marines, throwing grenades and peppering the barge with rifle and machine-gun fire, killed all of them.[40] About sixty enemy dead lay scattered throughout the little village. The remainder of the small force scattered into the jungle. Walker suffered no losses.[41]

As the victorious Raiders kicked through the killing ground, they saw the results of their textbook attack. In one still-smoking machine-gun nest near the edge of a high cliff lay a wounded Japanese defender who was discovered playing dead. Private Robert had just helped subdue the position with his BAR and did not fancy any of its occupants seeing another day, but just then Father Redmond walked up and asked what was going on. When the men told him the soldier was still alive, the priest made the sign of the cross, muttered, "May God have mercy on his soul," and kept on going. Robert and a buddy waited a minute or two and then picked up the Japanese soldier and heaved him over the cliff into the harbor. Elsewhere, a small group of Raiders stood above the form of a man on the ground. It was the first Japanese that Pfc. Roger C. Spaulding had ever seen. The man was lying on his back with his own bayonet firmly implanted in his stomach. He was still alive but he was suffering from shock, his yellow-green face frozen with a look of horror at what he had done to himself. In a final paradox, the dying man's fingers stretched from the bayonet's handle toward the bloody blade as though he was trying to remove it. But it was too late. Hirohito had his sacrifice.[42]

Once the village was secure, the Raiders began searching for food but found nothing except for some foul-tasting pickled rations. Later that morning, however, a party of Seabees landed with a field kitchen and fed the hungry men pancakes until they were stuffed. At noon a ship came into the harbor with two cans of beer for every marine.

Meanwhile, Currin's Raiders were stripping down and cleaning their M1s in preparation for their assault on Tetemara when they heard the fireworks across the harbor. The air attack, which had shifted its focus to Tetemara, forced the defenders there out of their positions and into the apparent safety of the jungle. Fifteen minutes after the bombing ceased, Currin's men made their first contact. The

surprised enemy outposts were easily overrun, but the resistance stiffened as they neared the village, for by then the enemy had returned
to their prepared bunkers. Japanese .51-caliber machine guns and
well-camouflaged positions did not open fire until the marine point
men came within ten yards of them. The majority of the Raider casualties that day resulted from this fire.[43] Two men fell in the initial
barrage, while the rest quickly scampered into the thick underbrush.
More would have died had not one of the enemy's machine guns
jammed.[44]

Clay Gowran's firsthand account of the battle was ripe with real-
ism:

> Slowly we moved forward. The advances were sporadic. Some-
> times we lay along the trail for 30 minutes at a time; then the
> order would be whispered back down along the line . . . "Mov-
> ing up. Let's go! Moving up!"
> We were fighting an unseen enemy. We never saw a Jap, but
> their bullets whined and echoed over our heads. I always imag-
> ined the roar of the guns never ceased once a battle had
> started. But it was not like that at all. This fight for Viru . . . was
> really a series of little battles lasting from a minute to 15 at the
> most, with long periods of silence in between. A machine gun
> would open fire somewhere ahead, and we would hug the
> ground. Other weapons would take it up, and the jungle would
> resound with their clattering roar. The sharper crack of rifles
> and pop of grenades, then the heavier, duller *wumph-wumph* of
> demolition bombs would punctuate the racket. For minutes all
> hell would break loose over and around us. Then, so suddenly
> you could not believe it, the guns would stop and the jungle
> would be still again. Not a sound but the dripping of the rain.
> Not a movement to be seen anywhere.[45]

The rain's intensity increased, and the men lay flat in the mud as
bullets whizzed above and around them, fired by snipers positioned
as high as fifty feet above them in trees. The snipers were perhaps a
greater concern to the men than the machine-gun fire, for the guns
could easily be located. Currin scampered to the head of his stalled

column, slid hard behind a wide tree stump, and began to plan for the battle ahead. For the time being, he was forced to ignore the sniper fire. He sent Lieutenant Luckel's platoon forward until it drew fire from a machine gun. Luckel's men hammered the bunker with a furious fire while five Raiders from the demolition platoon snaked around it on each side. Each man carried a homemade explosive in one hand and another strapped to his chest. Crawling slowly on their bellies in the mud, they edged toward the enemy gun emplacement until they were close enough to throw their deadly TNT charges. The huge explosions vaporized the position.

Two of these demo men, Donzel Harker and Billy Chance, eighteen and twenty-three years old respectively, crawled forward to take out another emplacement, but its gun was not firing and the two slithered past it. They continued on their bellies through the forward defense line, the rear positions, and finally into the village itself before they realized what they had done.

"Boy, by that time my knees were doing a rumba," Harker said afterward. "We decided to get the hell out of there and right now. Turning around we crawled back, and after 20 minutes managed to get back inside our own lines without getting shot. Oh yeah, on the way back we bagged a sniper. He was perched in a tree with his back to us, and he never knew what hit him. He came down like a shotgunned duck."[46]

Twenty-two-year-old Sgt. Loren Schofield of Omaha had been pinned down for almost thirty minutes under the raking fire from an enemy machine-gun nest seventy-five yards ahead of him. Bullets pecked closer and closer around him as he pressed against the wet earth. Thinking that he'd get the jump on the gun crew while they were changing ammo belts, and worried that his present location was untenable, he popped to his feet to run to a better position from which he could fire at them. Something hit him square in the chest and knocked him flat on his back. He was stunned but in no real pain. When his head cleared, he crawled behind a tree stump and looked at his chest. A bullet had smashed into the grenade he had been carrying in his left breast pocket, saving his life. Schofield, now with a couple of cracked ribs, grabbed the chipped grenade, moved forward a few yards, and lobbed it into the nest. The explosion finished off all four of the machine gun's crew.[47]

By early afternoon, Currin's men had gained control over a small ridge on the down slope of the mountain, forcing Hara's men to withdraw from their positions. However, the Raiders correctly guessed that the move was made in preparation for a Japanese counterblow. Silence replaced the sounds of battle. Forgotten for the moment was their monotonous suffering. They were too busy watching the wooded thickness ahead of them for signs of a counterattack. Three days before they had been youngsters eager to ply their trade. Now, as if caught in some accelerated time warp, they had become deadly killers. Seventy-five yards ahead, the Japanese began yelling. The Raiders knew from stories about the 1st Marine Division's experiences on Guadalcanal that what they heard was the ghostly preface to a suicidal banzai charge. *"Tenno Heika, Banzai!"* "Marine, you die!" Mortars soon added their awful chorus as they began coughing shells into the marines' new position. Currin reinforced the low ridge with two machine-gun squads just in time to repel the screaming Japanese who attacked as predicted.

"For three minutes they howled and shrieked and all the while the guns were still. Then, at the climax, they charged," wrote Clay Gowran. "The staccato chatter of one of our guns began, then another, and another, and another, swelling into a clamoring rush of sound as the Marines smashed lead into the onrushing Japanese."[48]

It was over in thirty seconds. The Japanese were repulsed and scattered into the jungle in disorder. Currin gave the order to fix bayonets, and the marines began a wild gallop into the village to clear it of any remaining enemy. As they stormed the outpost, they hollered in the way men do when overcome by blood lust. All memory of their aches and sore muscles, sleeplessness, and hunger vanished. Lieutenant Malcolm N. McCarthy's platoon rushed up to capture the three-inch naval gun that had blocked the harbor entrance so well. Other marines spent the next hour cleaning out Japanese from caves or flushing out lone riflemen from their hiding places in the immediate area. At least a half-dozen of the enemy chose to plunge to their death by jumping from atop the 150-foot cliffs that abutted the harbor.[49]

When the fighting stopped, Currin's exultant men scavenged the village and counted forty-eight enemy dead. Another group of nearly eighty men likely drowned when they tried to flee by swimming the mouth of the Mango River. Major Hara and 166 of his men withdrew into the safety of the jungle.[50] A diary found on the twisted body of the Japanese officer indicated that Hara's men had determined the exact location of Major Kennedy's camp and were preparing to mount an attack on it.[51] Of even greater value than the intelligence documents they discovered were the cases of tinned salmon several famished marines happened upon. At 4 P.M., after the perimeter had been secured, Currin allowed the men to feast on this delicacy. At about the same time, a navy schooner and two Landing Craft, Tank (LCT), having spotted the American flag flying, came skimming into the narrow harbor, bringing fresh stores of food, clean clothes, and mail. One of the letters was from the wife of 1st Sgt. Pete Kovisovic, who had been killed just hours before in the assault. Her jubilant message brought news of the birth of their son.

The next day, the Raiders bathed and put on dry socks and dungarees. This may seem like a trivial matter, but to the veterans of the Viru operation, it was a moment they would not forget. Two Hundred sixty-eight men and two officers reported for sick call in the morning, most suffering from foot ailments. Still, morale was never higher.[52] The men had stood up to the test of battle, answering questions about themselves that had plagued them since boot camp. Combat had given them a glimpse into their souls, an uncommon opportunity for anyone. They liked what they saw, and they quietly reveled in it. They were proud to be marine Raiders.

After the defeat at Viru, aware that an Allied offensive was about to commence, Rabaul ordered General Sasaki and Admiral Ota to hold New Georgia at all costs.[53] Consequently, Major Hara was ordered to move his beaten force back to Munda to aid in its defense. He, too, found the going tough, as the indifferent jungle punished all who entered it. The battered Japanese force took eighteen days to make the forty-mile trek to Munda, arriving just in time to take part in the airfield's final defense.

Although Currin's Raider battalion secured Viru a day late, the delay was not crucial. Tank landing ships (LSTs) moved into the harbor immediately and began unloading equipment for the construction of the PT boat base. Soon a construction battalion began work. In addition to capturing the three-inch gun, the marines took four 80mm guns, eight antiaircraft guns, and sixteen machine guns. The marines suffered 13 dead and 15 wounded, compared to Japanese losses of 61 dead and roughly 100 wounded.

Early in the evening on 1 July, the dead Raiders were buried in a tiny clearing on a bluff overlooking the harbor with Father Redmond officiating. The simple, dignified ceremony restored civility and pattern to their lives. The chaplain read the funeral rites from his Bible with the help of a flashlight. When it was over, the priest looked down at the freshly dug graves. "You men who have given your lives here in the jungles of Viru," he said sadly, "were of all races and religions. But you were comrades in life, and here in this spot you shall remain comrades."[54] Redmond then closed his remarks with a reference to their bravery, noting that they had made the ultimate sacrifice.

But were their deaths necessary? Construction of the PT boat base was never completed, for it was determined that the location was unsuitable for the navy's purposes. It never figured even remotely into the capture of the airfield at Munda. Currin's battalion had had its baptism of fire on New Georgia, but the operation was unnecessary. Important lessons were learned, however. Even a relatively small force like Currin's encountered great difficulty traversing New Georgia's forbidding interior, despite being lightly armed, not burdened with more than a few days' worth of field rations, and facing only light resistance from Japanese patrols along the way. Plans called for a large force to be landed on the island, requiring logistical trains to support an extended operation. Moreover, that force was expected to drive several miles through that same terrain, carry heavier weapons and more supplies, and, most significantly, confront well-camouflaged and well-protected Japanese defenders. The situation was apt to become precarious. Did the arduous trek to Viru and the subsequent postponement of the attack give Admiral Halsey and his planners pause? Perhaps, but the operation had already been set in motion.

Vangunu

Another target of the complex D-day operation was an anchorage on Vangunu, an island situated east of New Georgia in a position to allow the Japanese to interdict communication and transportation between New Georgia and the Russell Islands. The 2nd Battalion, 103rd Infantry Regiment, along with two companies from the 4th Raider Battalion, was ordered to seize Wickham Anchorage on the island's east coast. Intelligence reports indicated that the Japanese had roughly a hundred defenders located mostly in Kaeruka, a village adjacent to a seldom-used barge base near Wickham. The attack plan was much the same as the one employed at Viru Harbor, calling for a landing on an undefended beachhead followed by a relatively short movement to the enemy stronghold.

At about 3 A.M. on 30 June, in high winds and rain, the invaders moved in to secure Oloana Bay, located just a few miles from Kaeruka. The weather was so bad, in fact, that Admiral Fort, commander of the invasion force, decided to abort the landings until dawn. However, the two APDs carrying the landing force either did not receive or ignored the order and began debarking troops. The already confused situation became even more muddled when the two destroyer commanders discovered they were off course, relocated, and then continued unloading men.

Just moving people from the APDs into the waiting Higgins landing craft was a gamble. It was so dark, according to Irvin L. Cross, that "it was impossible to see the landing craft from the deck of the destroyer."[55] The men swung their legs over the rail, squeezing it tightly, and rolled their equipment-laden bodies over the side as the ship bounced beneath them. Steel helmets became cymbals in the lashing rain, muting the frantic orders being screamed at them from above and below. Once over the rail, they began their precarious descent downward, searching blindly with their boots for footing on the slippery cargo net, one hair-raising step at a time. The angry ocean tended to thrust the landing craft upward, knocking men off the net and on top of the men who had preceded them. Men cursed their misery above the din of the crashing sea.

Once they shoved off, the coxswains managing the Landing Craft Infantry (LCI) lost contact with each other and were forced to bounce toward the invisible shore individually or in pairs. Signal lights placed along the beach by prelanding search parties were blotted out by the squall. There was no talking inside the small boats. The men sat pasty-faced, vomiting into their helmets from the agony of seasickness. When they finally crawled ashore, they discovered they had been scattered for miles along the bay. Six boats capsized in the mistake-filled affair.[56] Fortunately, no men were lost.

Two boats, each ferrying a platoon of Raiders and managing to stay together in the howling storm and high seas, were turned around and headed *away* from the beachhead. The swell of one surge slammed both boats down on top of a reef several miles west of the landing site. Engines whined as they struggled to escape the reef. The rain continued its relentless pounding, accompanied by a strong wind. The nervous Raiders, most of whom could not swim well, were convinced that this was no place to die. One of the craft finally freed itself from the reef's grip, ripping its rudder off in the process. The coxswain screamed for the men to tie lines to several bailing buckets on board and ordered them to fling the buckets overboard into the churning water. He then piloted the beleaguered thirty-six-foot vessel with extraordinary resourcefulness to shore. The reef tore a hole in the bottom of the other boat and it rapidly took on water. There was nothing else to do except abandon it and take to the violent water, much to the dismay of the men.

Vangunu's silhouette lay before them like a giant sea creature in repose. Making sure to stay close together, they began to wade toward the island, thinking they were but a few hundred yards from shore. Actually, they were about two miles out. After several hours of struggling in the waves, they reached a sandy beach seven miles from Oloana Bay.[57]

At about 7:30 A.M., Lt. Col. Lester E. Brown, the ranking army officer on shore and commander of the operation, led a combined force of about five hundred soldiers and marines (only about seventy-five of the Raiders were on his beach) on a seven-mile trek to the enemy-held village of Kaeruka. The rain began to fall again, bringing with it more mud and misery. The radios failed, just as they had at Viru, leaving Brown and his men on their own, entirely cut off from the others. The going was easier than on New Georgia, and they made good progress, slowed only by two streams that had become shoulder-deep torrents because of the rain. The strongest swimmers plunged into the water to string ropes from the opposite banks so the rest of their force could cross hand-over-hand. By 1:20 P.M., all of the marines who had been scattered about during the horrific night managed to catch up with the main body. Brown now had his full contingent of men.

Six hours after departure, the raiding party neared its objective and assembled for an assault on the village. Without radios, Brown was unable to call for artillery support, so the men were forced to move in without the customary preparatory shelling. This would turn out to be costly.

When Brown and his men got within about fifty yards of the Kaeruka, they could hear the enemy engaged in the ritual of morning exercise. Surprise would have been complete had not a BAR discharged accidentally, forcing a premature assault on the stunned Japanese garrison. Firing their weapons from their hips, the attackers charged through thick jungle foliage, looking for live targets as bullets lanced through the air around them.

As the Americans tightened the noose on the camp, the defense stiffened. Enemy soldiers firing automatic weapons from well-concealed spider holes and two well-protected bunkers exacted a heavy toll. Roughly four hours later, the Japanese were subdued as the men moved through Kaeruka to the beach. The attacking force lost 22 dead and 43 wounded. The Japanese suffered 120 dead. Several surviving enemy troops retreated into the bush, however, and the exhausted Americans had to endure intermittent mortar and automatic-weapons fire well into the night.

The firing finally stopped shortly after midnight. Taking advantage of the unexpected luxury, some men not on duty inside the perimeter fell into a deep sleep in their muddy foxholes. Worn with fatigue, they had not slept in thirty-six hours. Then, at 2 A.M., a disturbing sound, barely audible at first but becoming more discernable by the moment, split the tenuous stillness. It was the dreadful diesel putter of Japanese troop-carrying barges, and they were headed directly for the village.

Brown ordered his weary men to scramble to the beach and form a hasty defense line. A skeletal force was left in place to protect the rear while the bulk of the men hustled to find a suitable place for cover behind the abundant, graceful palms lining the shore. The heavier weapons were quickly moved into position as well. Soon hundreds of Japanese infantry would be swarming onto the beach. There was no way of knowing how many barges were converging on them. It was one of the few times in the war that American troops were forced to repel a Japanese seaborne invasion. However, no one there was thinking about historical precedent of than.

Anxious eyes strained to see through the dark abyss, wondering how large a force they would have to face. Lieutenant Colonel Brown was certain the Japanese did not yet know the Americans had seized the village, and that they were instead ferrying reinforcements or supplies to their outpost. He was sure they were unaware of the surprise that awaited them.

Heavy, leaden clouds, still lingering from the day's showers, hid the moon, so it was not until the intruders were about a hundred yards from shore that Brown's men were able to detect the faint outline of three barges carrying 120 men. The hum of their motors had grown to an angry roar. It was the Americans' first brush with an unknown fear that grabbed at each man's stomach, which was relieved somewhat by the comfort each felt from his weapon.

When the Japanese were within seventy-five yards of the beach, Brown gave the order to open fire. Shouts could be heard from the barges, but the enemy did not return fire at first, apparently believing that their own men were mistakenly attacking them. The barges pressed onward, providing easy targets for the Americans, who raked the three craft mercilessly with BAR and Thompson submachine-gun fire and rifle grenades. One of the barges sank and the other two wallowed aimlessly in the surf. Several of the enemy jumped into the water and tried to swim ashore while Brown's troops continued to fire in their direction, indifferent to their screams. It was a turkey shoot. Some 109 of the unfortunates were killed in the debacle. Only eleven Japanese made it to shore. Five of those were quickly killed, but six others managed to escape the carnage. The next morning the victorious troops, less three of their buddies killed in the episode, enjoyed the spoils of their victory by cooking a sumptuous breakfast of fresh vegetables and chicken that had been recovered from the barges. Although they would continue to encounter machine-gun and 37mm fire, it was from a comfortable distance. The thirty or so Japanese remaining in the bush had no stomach for an organized attack. Brown and his men had effectively secured Wickham Anchorage for the Allies, and on 12 July they left Vangunu for good.

Meanwhile, the six Japanese survivors tried to make their way back to New Georgia. Traveling by foot and native canoe, they made their way for twenty miles along Vangunu's eastern coast and around to the western side of the island, where they crossed Marovo Lagoon and headed west for New Georgia on rafts made of palm logs. Eating roots, reptiles, and whatever else they could find in the jungle, they traversed the entire length of the island's northern coastline until they arrived at Rice Anchorage, where they hoped to link up with friendly units in the vicinity. But their tribulation was not over. Roughly a month after their escape from Vangunu, the six bearded, emaciated wayfarers were jumped by a marine patrol and five of them killed in a blistering burst of gunfire as they slowly paddled by in their canoe. Coincidentally, the patrol that ambushed them was from the 4th Raider Battalion, which had helped surprise those same Japanese in their barges at Vangunu. The only enemy soldier to survive was recovered from the canoe, wounded but lucid enough to recount for interrogators their four-week jungle ordeal.[58]

Much like Viru Harbor, the Vangunu operation was inconsequential. The small Japanese garrison there could arguably have been bypassed. Unless strengthened significantly, there was not much chance of the enemy intercepting Allied shipping headed up the Slot from Guadalcanal or the Russells. Moreover, once in friendly hands, it served only as a refresh point for small craft headed elsewhere. Yet no responsible commander could overlook an enemy force, however weak, in a position to disrupt his main supply line. Perhaps the Vangunu invasion was prudent. But for the families of the twenty-four Americans who died there, questions would remain.

3 Rising Shadows

A wretched, low sky enveloped the Solomon Sea at midnight on 29 June 1943 when the periscope of Japanese submarine RO-103 broke the surface during a routine reconnaissance patrol southeast of Vangunu. What the skipper saw through the dusty curtain of fog must have startled him. A destroyer force screening a column of six troop transports and two destroyer transports was moving hastily through the gray mist headed toward Blanche Channel. It was the first wave of an amphibious force transporting an entire army division to the New Georgia island group under the capable command of Admiral Turner. This first echelon was composed of the 43rd Division's 172nd and 103rd Infantry Regiments (the 169th would follow later in the week), on their maiden voyage into the combat zone, with various other smaller units that together totaled about six thousand men.

Reveille sounded at 2 A.M. aboard the transports, but the call was unnecessary, as most men had not been able to sleep. Smothered by the rainy gloom, they huddled together in their ships, quiet and withdrawn as the ships' stewards distributed sandwiches and hot coffee. A message from their commander was read to them on all ships: "You have got what it takes. Your path will not be easy. But your guts will make you carry on. God speed and God bless you."[1] Their destination was the island of Rendova, just eight miles across Blanche Channel from Munda. Much like its sister island, New Georgia, it had happily evaded civilization since Genesis. Besides a handful of native islanders, its only denizens were the 140 or so Japanese riflemen and their unknown neighbor, coastwatcher D. C. Horton, who had continued for months to relay excellent intelligence about the go-ings-on at Munda. The rabbit's foot–shaped island would not only offer a convenient launching area for the main assault on New Geor-gia, but also an ideal spot for artillery to zero in on Munda airfield.[2]

General Sasaki at Munda was alerted and apparently was "com-pletely baffled" by the sub's report.[3] He had been led to believe that he had nothing to fear but small Allied probes and patrols infiltrat-ing his zone. There was little that the stunned Admiral Kusaka, com-mander of the Southeastern Fleet at Rabaul, could do for the mo-ment. The Japanese Eighth Fleet had foolishly pulled planes from advance bases back to Truk, guessing that their I Operation con-ducted in April had thwarted Allied ambitions for the moment. They were also distracted by reports of General MacArthur's coincident invasion of Nassau Bay on New Guinea and Gen. Walter Kreuger's Sixth Army assault on Woodlark and Kiriwina—islands located just 325 miles south of Rabaul, well within range of American fighters.

The Japanese were in no shape to counter what appeared to be a major landing. Sasaki had roughly 10,500 men, but they were about evenly divided between Kolombangara and New Georgia. Although only a nine-mile stretch of the Kula Gulf separated the two islands, his troops at Kolombangara were there to defend the Vila airfield. Few could be spared to reinforce Sasaki. He had only two under-strength battalions and supporting units from the 229th Infantry Regiment and the 6th Kure Special Naval Landing Force. Rabaul could muster only one cruiser and eight destroyers, plus sixty-six bombers and eighty-three fighters.[4] These forces could be beefed up, but Kusaka knew that trying to play catch-up with the Americans was, after the debacle at Guadalcanal, a formula for failure. One worried Japanese soldier penned the following in his diary: "If the enemy comes to Rendova, our garrison of 72 men is certain to be killed. And I am one of those 72 men. Life is like a weak candle in a strong wind. It may go out at any moment."[5]

A somber procession of ships silently crept into Rendova Harbor at dawn on 30 June. Solemn soldiers from the 43rd Infantry Division and a marine antiaircraft battalion climbed from their transports' decks onto Higgins landing craft with the thirty-four-hundred-foot

Mount Rendova looming in front of them. A legion of shifting coconut palms lining the uneven shoreline bowed toward the ocean
as if bending under the pressure of the thick undergrowth that
leaned hard against them.

There was considerable disorder. Two companies of specially
trained troops from the 172nd Infantry called "Barracudas" were supposed to have landed at about 5 A.M., an hour before the first wave,
to silence the small enemy garrison Horton had reported was on the
island. In the awful weather and darkness, however, they missed the
markers placed for them in the harbor by Horton and a three-man
American reconnaissance party that had been inserted on the island
two weeks before. "Snowy" Rhoades, a veteran Australian coastwatcher from Guadalcanal and the former manager of the Lever
Brothers plantation that fronted the harbor where the landing was
to take place, led the Barracudas toward their target beach. Although
he knew every sandbar and shoal on the island, even he was unable
to locate the barrier islands that marked the harbor entrance or see
the flashlight that Horton and the recon team was using to signal
them.[6] They wound up landing at another beach four miles away and
had to reembark on their two APDs at dawn. They finally rejoined
the invasion force ten minutes after its arrival.

Leslie Gill had been the resident owner of the Lambeti plantation,
located a few miles east of Munda, before the Japanese moved onto
his island. Now he was with the Americans on Rendova, helping them
move into the neighborhood.

"The towering hulls of the transports came alive with organized
activity," Gill later recalled. "Magically, the sea swarmed with landing craft dropped from the ships. Troops in jungle suits, armed and
laden with equipment, swarmed over the gunwales and dropped
crablike down the nets into the plunging landing barges, far below.
Everyone went via the nets—general and staff, war correspondents,
officers and men. Everyone wanted to get the hell out of there before the Japs came over."[7]

The first wave of troops hit the beach at 7 A.M., and men sprayed
out into the cover of the jungle in a rainy downpour, ducking sporadic Japanese machine-gun fire. The greatest danger seemed to
come from their own guns, for coxswains on the incoming craft fired

promiscuously over the troops and into the coconut palms as men and equipment accumulated on the beach. This gunfire ceased only after an officer on the beach turned and angrily threatened to shoot back if it did not stop. Some seventy-five yards into the woods, a Japanese sniper in a tree was shot dead. Electrified by their first kill, the green troops rushed to the body and began searching for souvenirs, disrupting their unit's advance. It was not until the regiment's commanding officer came ashore that order was restored.[8]

Horton was watching it all, hardly impressed by the American effort. He attributed the landing's success not to the army's execution, but rather to the poor weather, for it had grounded the Japanese planes.

"With the light of dawn I ferried three U.S. officers to a convenient island from which we watched the incredible pile-up of troops and material on Rendova Beach," recalled Horton. "There was at first no discipline and no order, which reflected dismally on the planning of the operation. . . . I felt safer on one of the small islands offshore and withdrew thither with my scouts—appearing, when required, to provide information and answer as politely as I might the hundreds of foolish questions shot at me."[9]

When the Barracudas finally landed, Rhoades, a twice-wounded World War I veteran, elbowed his way through the troops already ashore and advanced boldly into the plantation. As he surveyed the situation, he accidentally flushed out two extremely frightened enemy soldiers who seemed undecided as to whether they should fire their weapons or run. Rhoades abruptly let loose a burst from his Owen submachine gun and dispatched them both without breaking stride.[10] There were less than a hundred leaderless defenders, their commander having been moved to Munda with malaria. Most were civilians who had been in nonessential jobs. Now employed by the navy, they were drawn from groups considered unfit for combat and made only a token effort to repel the intruders, losing about half their men in the process. Some of the survivors made their way in canoes across Blanche Channel to Munda to join the garrison there. Four were captured in the water pushing a raft made of two empty gasoline drums. The remainder scattered into the thick jungle.[11]

Rhoades, fearing that the coastwatcher's hideaway would be discovered by the enemy as they fled into the island's interior, asked for and received a patrol to protect the tiny sanctuary. Meanwhile, the Japanese had forced a native to lead them to the station at bayonet point, where they surprised 1st. Lt. Robbie Robinson, Horton's new assistant. With automatic weapons fire kicking up around his hut, he removed the codes and crystals from the radio, then stumbled quickly downhill toward the beach. The Japanese gave chase for a while, then doubled back to the campsite, where they smashed the radio, pilfered the premises, and shot the crew's pet dog. Fortunately, they overlooked Horton's tiny bush shack, which was hidden under a rocky outcropping and which housed the spare teleradio and other supplies.

Two days later, headquarters received a native report indicating that a party of about twenty Japanese was roaming near a village on the island's west coast, so Rhoades volunteered to lead a patrol there. Nineteen soldiers accompanied by ten locals traveled by barge to the mouth of a remote river where several villagers met them. Rhoades, who was unfamiliar with the area, relied on the sturdy locals to guide them to the Japanese camp. Before setting out, he ordered six of the natives accompanying his patrol to carry the unpleasantly heavy panniers of ammunition and sternly assured them that they would be shot if they abandoned their cargo.

After a short trek through the thickening wood they found the camp in a slight depression near the riverbank. The Japanese were cooking rice and chatting noisily. No guards were visible anywhere. Rhoades whispered to the army officer in charge of the patrol to have his men fire their rifle grenades, but the man refused until he could locate nine of his men who had been separated somewhere back along the trail. Seconds after he left, one of the Japanese appeared from behind a tree and stood just a few feet in front of Rhoades. Crouched low in the forest undergrowth, the Aussie stared at the man and prayed that he would not have to shoot. Except for a rather nervous native guide, he was alone and no more than twenty-five yards away from the unsuspecting Japanese. Suddenly, they made eye contact and the frightened soldier yelled. Rhoades chopped him in half with a short burst and scooted for better cover. He fired, moved, and fired again, hoping to give the impression that there were more men out there. The Japanese responded with grenades and machine-gun fire. Rhoades's guide lifted himself up to get a better look and was cut down.

By this time the nine "lost" men had returned. Rhoades called up a rifle grenadier and told him to aim for the base of a large banyan tree, where the coastwatcher guessed the machine gun was hidden. The man's first shot fell in the giant tree's root system and the firing abruptly ended.

"Thinking that the Nips might think that they were practically sur-rounded by a superior force, I now called out 'Ko San Sai' (surren-der), but the only result was a few quick shots over my head," Rhoades recalled. "Then two Nips tried to cross the river within my coverage but a burst sent them back. Then there was much splash-ing and then dead silence. I guessed . . . that they were escaping un-der the edge of the steep river bank. I called out to the Yanks to rush them, but they would not move."[12]

Alone, Rhoades walked up to the banyan tree. He found the badly wounded gunner lying near the mangled machine gun and impas-sively shot him dead.[13] Blood trails led to the river and Rhoades de-manded that the officer, who had reappeared, pursue them. When he protested that the danger of ambush was too great, an argument ensued. Rhoades insisted that the surviving Japanese were hobbled by wounds and could easily be overtaken. The officer refused to give in and ordered his troops back to the barge. The natives followed them, carrying the body of their fellow villager. The Aussie was fu-rious, but there was nothing more to do. Back on the coast they stayed only long enough to witness the guide's cremation ceremony on the beach and then departed.

"During the trip back . . . the U.S. troops spoke in no uncertain terms of their officer and what they would eventually do to him," re-called Rhoades. "They said we have seen you shoot it out with the little bastards and would follow you anywhere."[14]

Munda's three- and five-inch shore guns finally spoke up just min-utes after the landings commenced. The first salvo hit the engine room of the destroyer *Gwin*, killing three sailors. Two other destroyers answered with their five-inch guns, peppering the airfield with heavy, accurate gunfire. Within two hours of the landings, marine artillerymen from the 9th Defense Battalion joined in with their powerful "Long Tom" 155mm guns, cheered insanely on by exultant Seabees who stopped their road-building operation to watch the fun. It was the first time in the war that artillery fired on targets from an adjacent island. The Seabees had worked extra hard to provide a clearing for the huge guns, using TNT and tractors to remove trees. When that was done, they used their tractors to move the guns into place.

This proved to be no easy task, said Frank Chadwick, because the "guns and vehicles were up to their hubs in mud. We had tractors pull the artillery, but in the sludge they weren't enough. So we hooked up the tractors and had 40 guys help *push* the tractors [and guns] through the mud."[15]

Standing behind the batteries, the Seabees watched each projectile blast out of the guns' tubes and then stared in awe as the rounds soared toward their targets, screaming encouragement with every salvo. It was just the stimulant they needed to return reinvigorated to their work.

The ability to adjust artillery fire improved considerably when a 130-foot observation tower was erected on high ground near Mount Rendova soon after the landings. It was a big improvement over clutching binoculars atop a swaying palm. The tower allowed marine and army observers to radio corrections to the batteries once they observed shells strike their target. The system was further enhanced when planes taking photos of the target areas dropped their film near the tower—where it was retrieved, developed, and then studied to assess target damage shortly after the fire missions.[16]

From above, a perpetual thirty-two-plane patrol from Admiral Mitscher's AirSols circled Rendova to ward off Japanese predators. None were visible until 11:15 A.M., when twenty-seven Zeros, the only planes Kusaka had available, flew down to strafe the landing beaches. They were capably handled, however. What the enemy needed was a bombing raid on the vulnerable ships unloading in the harbor. Unfortunately for them, it came too late. It was not until after the unloading at Rendova was completed and the destroyers and transports had begun to make their way back to Guadalcanal that they encountered a strike force capable of doing any real harm. That meant that the day's amphibious landings, one of the most dangerous of all combat operations, had the luxury of eight hours of daylight without any real opposition from Japanese airmen. Why was this so? First, there was the bad weather. Second, the Japanese attack aircraft were based at faraway Rabaul to protect them from American air strikes. Finally, Kusaka's pilots were so inexperienced that they had not yet trained for night takeoffs.[17]

In the late afternoon on 1 July came the anticipated warning from the coastwatcher station on Vella Lavella: "Hear planes bearing northwest, course southeast!" Twenty-five torpedo-carrying Betty bombers and twenty-four Zero fighters finally appeared and spotted the convoy below. The covering force of Corsairs and Wildcats gave chase, but several of the bombers escaped and released their torpedoes. One hit Admiral Turner's 7,712-ton flagship *McCawley* amidships in the engine room, punching a twenty-foot hole in its side just as its gunners were downing two of the enemy planes. The ship quickly began taking water. Turner and the crew, less fifteen sailors killed in the explosion, transferred to other ships while a tug towed the stricken *McCawley* to safety. If the enemy attack had been just an hour earlier, the death toll would have been much higher, for the ship would have been caught in the middle of landing its cargo of twelve-hundred troops and hundreds of tons of supplies. At 8:23 P.M., three more torpedoes ripped into the *McCawley*'s hull, sending the ship to the bottom in just thirty seconds. Later it was discovered that American PT boats, thinking they were attacking an enemy convoy, had launched the last three torpedoes.[18]

For the men on Rendova, the real enemy—rain and mud—was making its presence felt. Heavy vehicle traffic ground the earth into a viscous brown paste hampering movement of all kinds. Hundreds of coconut logs were cut to corduroy roadbeds, but even that expedient often failed as the logs simply sank farther into the churned-up sludge. One bulldozer sank almost out of sight in the hellish muck.[19] Commander H. Roy Whittaker of Philadelphia, commander of the Seabees on Rendova—mostly construction and oil-field workers from Oklahoma and Texas—later recalled:

All day long we sweated and swore and worked to bring the heavy stuff ashore [from the supply ships] and hide it from the Jap bombers. Our mesh, designed to "snowshoe" vehicles over soft mud, failed miserably. The men ceased to look like men; they looked like slimy frogs working in some prehistoric ooze. As they sank to their knees they discarded their clothes. They slung water out of their eyes, cussed their mud-slickened hands, and somehow kept the stuff rolling.

When night came we had unloaded six ships, but the scene on the beach was dismal. More troops, Marines and Seabees had come in, but the mud was about to lick us. Foxholes filled with water as rapidly as they could be dug. . . . The men rolled their exhausted, mud-covered bodies in tents and slept in the mud.[20]

The next morning brought more bad weather, forcing home the air patrol orbiting the island and leaving the mud-encrusted troops without a screen of any sort. Compounding the problem, a search radar designed for use on beachheads broke down when someone filled its generator with diesel fuel instead of gasoline.[21] However, the threat of a pending storm eased their worries about an air raid.

More troops and supplies were introduced to the island on the second, including the 169th Infantry Regiment, which would provide a third of the troops for the forthcoming assault on Munda. Containers, vehicles, and equipment of all sorts and sizes were piled without pattern along the beach. Laced between them were lines of men—hundreds of them—unloading ships and loading trucks in bucket brigades, their shirts boiling on their backs in the tropical heat. After the beachhead was consolidated and all of the equipment properly placed, the men lined up for chow, just as they had been accustomed to doing during their training exercises. As they patiently waited their turn to be served, they heard the drone of aircraft engines and paused to look up at what they believed to be friendly aircraft. John Price and Will Mitchell of the 172nd Infantry, who had gone into the water for a brief break from their work, admired the beauty of the formation above as they stepped out of the water to put their clothes back on. The Japanese pilots looking down on the placid scene below savored their good luck. There was no antiaircraft fire, no American planes to evade, and nobody on the ground was scrambling for cover. Surprise was complete. Dive-bombers borrowed from a carrier for the attack, twin-engine bombers, and fighters all converged on the crowded beachhead. Flames and explosions punctuated the panic as the enemy planes had their way with the invaders, killing 59 men and wounding 77—the most casualties caused by a Japanese air strike in the South Pacific. Commander Whittaker's Seabees took the worst hits, losing 23 men.

"The first bombs knocked out two main fuel dumps, and we had to lie there in the mud and watch our supplies burn while the Japs strafed us," Whittaker said later. "One bomb landed under our largest bulldozer, and that big machine just reared up like a stallion and disintegrated. A five-ton cache of our dynamite went off, exploding the eardrums of the men nearest it. That soggy earth quivered like jelly under us."[22]

Corporal David Slater, a marine hunkered low in a watery foxhole, remembered looking up "at the approaching planes—death twinkling in the sunlight. The smaller guns clattered and spit . . . , but the deep coughs of the 90mm guns were missing. Diamond formations of four aircraft sailed over. . . . The world ripped apart. Fragments thunked into pale trunks; earth and coral pelted down. Then the heaving subsided."[23]

The planes began their approach while machine-gunner Anthony Wassel was on the open beach. It was too late to run for cover, so he piled scoops of coral on top of himself for protection. He survived, but an explosion welded the coral to his skin. Company F, 169th Infantry, was debarking from LCIs when the planes appeared. Sergeant Sal LaMagna was not thrilled: "F Company, with 170 men, couldn't get off fast enough. Some jumped over the side and swam. I took a swan dive off the ramp as soon as it hit the water. Some would fly if they could. Jap planes flew over and strafed the boat with bullets going through the hull, into the hold, and ricocheting like fire flies in a jar."[24]

Louis Burton, a clerk in the 43rd Division's headquarters, rushed for the nearest foxhole and collided with the division commander. He saw terror in the general's eyes, substantially increasing his own.[25]

Two days later, the Japanese mounted one of the most significant air strikes of the campaign. Sixty-six Zero fighters escorting seventeen army Aichi dive-bombers hit Rendova, but this time radar gave the defenders sufficient notice. Fighters intercepted the Zeros at eight thousand feet and quickly shot down four. While attempting a fighter sweep, twelve more were burned when they flew into a maelstrom of clattering 40mm and 90mm antiaircraft fire delivered by the 9th Marine Defense Battalion and .50-caliber fire from the LCIs and LSTs moored in the harbor. Leslie Gill recalled hearing

. . . the unsynchronized drone of the Jap planes, while we dug our noses and toes into the bottom of our foxholes and held our breath. Then it started. With the noise of a thunderclap, the first bomb exploded near us—growing to a shattering crescendo of hideous scrunching as plane after plane peeled off and added its "stick" to the pattern of bombs that was rocking us. From the islets and ships and from the whole area our flak roared into the sky. The ground shuddered and shook with monstrous reverberations. . . . The air palpitated with the prodigious pulsation of our flak. It was Hell.[26]

Sixteen Betty bombers flying in a low, tight V formation came in out of the sun over the crowded harbor, dropping their lethal payloads of high explosives. Their low altitude indicated that they did not expect much of a greeting. They were dead wrong. The log of one of the landing craft circling in the harbor below offers this blow-by-blow account of the action:

The planes approached in our direction and passed almost overhead. Our guns, four 20-mm Oerlikons and two .50 caliber Browning Navy-type machine guns fired steadily at the planes, and tracers could be seen hitting squarely in the fuselage, wings, and tail assembly. Some of the tracers from the .50 caliber could be seen passing through the wings.

The plane burst into flames near the right engine, the tail assembly and main fuselage were blown off by an explosion, and the wings and forward cockpit with one side flaming fluttered like a leaf down toward us. Our gunners, in the meantime, shifted their attention to the second plane from the outside on the left of the "V." Our other 20 mm and .50 caliber machine guns had been concentrating their fire on this plane and had it already limping when the additional fire was turned on it. One motor was smoking. With all six guns riddling back and forth, the plane suddenly exploded and fell in many blazing pieces into the harbor. In the meantime, the first plane we hit fell into the water about two to three hundred yards astern of us.

By then it was impossible to direct our guns to fire at any individual plane. Our tracers could be seen going into several other planes, and undoubtedly this assisted in the destruction of some more of the enemy bombers. By this time planes were falling so fast it was hard to keep track of them.[27]

An estimated thirteen of the sixteen bombers making the attack were destroyed by the gunfire from the landing craft flotilla in the harbor. It was the first time most of the gunners fired their weapons in combat. Six Americans were killed and thirteen wounded, but damage on the island was light, with no planes or vessels lost. Meanwhile, the returning Japanese pilots reported they had sunk five transports and burned fourteen Allied fighters.[28] Ten physically exhausted Seabees had to be evacuated to medical facilities for hysteria and nervous collapse after the attack, a condition that portended a major problem for the infantry on New Georgia.

After the losses suffered from this and other raids, the Japanese army would no longer contribute any of its aircraft to the defense of the Solomons.[29] The Japanese lost 101 planes compared to just seventeen U.S. aircraft by 2 July, and the campaign had just begun.[30] From then on the Imperial Fleet would have to go it alone if it hoped to offer some help to Sasaki's infantry. The Americans not only were launching more aircraft than the Japanese had available, but they were of better quality and flown by better pilots. Moreover, the two new airfields in the Russells put the fliers sixty miles closer to Rendova, and another was being readied at Segi just across Blanche Channel. What a difference it was from a year before, when the

Japanese had commanded the sea approaches to Guadalcanal and dominated the skies. Now the Allies held all the cards. Although vapor trails continued to score the skies over Rendova daily, subsequent Japanese attacks were mostly uninspired. The Japanese bombers and torpedo planes managed to hit only three U.S. ships during the entire five-week campaign, and only one horizontal bombing attack succeeded in reaching its objective during daylight.[31] Without the army's air help, Admiral Kusaka could mount no more major air attacks against U.S. forces in the central Solomons. Air action was restricted to occasional fighter sweeps and night harassment bombing raids. Thus ended the most active four-day period of the air war in the Solomons campaign.[32]

Fortune, General Sasaki believed, favored the bold. As a product of the Japanese Imperial Army and its offensive-mindedness, the stocky, mustachioed commander felt trapped in his defensive posture and preferred, even now, to attempt a gambler's throw of the dice. On 4 July, he huddled with his staff in his office on Kokengolo Hill, he stared at a map of Rendova and then, finger slashing across the chart, detailed to his staff officers what he had in mind. It did not much matter what they thought. He was pleased with the plan. It energized him. What he intended to propose to Kusaka was an immediate counterlanding on Rendova while the Americans were distracted with the buildup of men and equipment still in progress. His troops would board landing craft at Munda at night, quietly cross Blanche Channel, mingle discreetly with the American craft moored in Rendova Harbor, and then assault the beachhead on order.[33] The recommendation died on the admiral's desk, rejected because of an apparent shortage of boats to mount such an attack. No record exists of Sasaki's reaction to Rabaul's refusal, but it is easy to guess his great disappointment.

Did the plan have a chance? On 4 and 5 July, both the 172nd and the 169th regiments were being transported in increments to Zanana beach on New Georgia in preparation for their move on Munda. If Sasaki's gambit were to have any hope of success, he would have had to launch his operation either before the 43rd Division's force had been entirely assembled at Zanana, or at least before a significant number of troops were landed. The general had orders to defend the airfield, and if a sizable Allied force were in place on his island, he would have been forced to remain to counter it. If, however, he could have managed to execute a well-conducted invasion before the fourth, when Rendova was most vulnerable, he could have, at the very least, upset the timetable for a thrust against New Georgia and consequently the entire Solomons campaign.

In light of the deteriorating situation, Admiral Kusaka met with his army counterpart, General Imamura, and both agreed to immediately ship four thousand reinforcements to beleaguered New Georgia via Kolombangara. It was welcome news, to be sure, but scant consolation to Sasaki, who required more than twice that number to stop the Americans. Yet his disappointment was shared by commands all the way up to Tokyo.

The Tragedy of the USS *Strong*

By the Fourth of July General Hester was poised for the assault on the airfield. However, before he got the green light, a blocking force was needed to isolate Munda from resupply and reinforcement from Kolombangara, a stone's throw across the Kula Gulf. A force of twenty-six hundred marines from the 1st Raider Battalion and soldiers from the 37th Infantry Division's 3rd Battalion, 145th Infantry, and 3rd Battalion, 148th Infantry, was selected for the dangerous operation. It was dangerous because they would be inserted behind enemy lines without any regular support lifeline from Rendova. The Northern Landing Group (NLG), as it was called, would conduct a secret night landing at secluded Rice Anchorage, fourteen miles from Munda on New Georgia's northwest coast. It would then move south to interdict movement into Munda and, once the airfield was captured, block any escape attempts. The force would become, in other words, the northern appendage of a huge pincer. Hester's men coming from Zanana would close the claw. Seven transports carried the men of the NLG, which was commanded by a marine, Col. Harry Liversedge. Three light cruisers and four destroyers shielded the transports. The landing was set for the night of 5 July, the same night the four thousand Japanese reinforcements were being sent to Vila on Kolombangara. Both groups were headed for Kula Gulf.

At 11:23 P.M. on 4 July, the squadron commander, RAdm. Walden L. "Pug" Ainsworth, slowed his covering force from twenty-five to twenty knots. It was making its final approach into the gulf in column formation minutes ahead of the transports. The three old cruisers—the *Honolulu, Helena,* and *St. Louis*—were screened by the destroyers *O'Bannon, Chevalier, Nicholas,* and *Strong.* The seas were moderate, but squalls were beginning to kick up from the southwest. The stiffening breeze became sweet with the aroma of rain as the warships began to curl around Visuvisu Point and head into the gulf.

An hour later, Ainsworth's vessels were ordered to bombard Vila on Kolombangara. For the next ten minutes the seven ships fired three thousand high-explosive shells at its airfield. They then changed course and shifted their murderous fire to Bairoko Harbor, one of the objectives assigned to the NLG, which was just beginning to debark at Rice Anchorage. The ships pounded that target for six minutes, then turned north to check on the progress of the landing. If all were going well, the squadron would head back to Guadalcanal.

The destroyer *Strong* had been on combat operations for six months without once suffering a hit from an enemy projectile, and its crew was beginning to wonder how long their luck would hold. Shipfitter First Class Arthur W. English recalled that everyone aboard "seemed to lead a charmed life, and the ship itself always came out without a mark on her. Although we were good as a crew, we also were certain that Lady Luck had taken a hand in our game. No crew could be that good. As a consequence, it got so that every time we were under fire we got to wondering if this would be it."[34]

Ninety seconds after the destroyer completed its course change, Lt. James A. Curran, a gunnery officer, spotted what sailors in the combat zone dread most: a thin, phosphorescent wake bubbling through the inky water headed directly for the ship's port bow. Curran shouted out a warning, but it was too late. Moments later there was an explosion and crewmen throughout the ship were thrown violently to the deck. The *Strong*'s good fortune had finally ended. A Japanese torpedo had found its mark. Neither the *Strong* nor any other ship in the task force made radar contact with any enemy surface vessels prior to the torpedo's impact, leading to the initial belief that a submarine had launched it. Actually, the lethal weapon had been launched by a destroyer from the unthinkable distance of twenty-two thousand yards, about twelve miles, well out of reach of the ships' radar. Traveling at forty-nine knots, the "long-lance" torpedo's range was at least that distance. At thirty-six knots its maximum effective range was twenty-five miles, making the *Strong* an attainable target. It was later said to be the longest-range torpedo strike of the war.[35] Damage was extensive. Two major compartments on the ship were destroyed, a fire room along and the adjacent number-one engine room. All of the crewmembers in those compartments were killed. "The cries and moans of my men for a split second or two before their almost instant death haunted me for years," remembered the *Strong*'s captain, Lt. Comdr. Joseph H. Wellings.[36] The torpedo also blew a large hole in the port side of the ship and another in the main deck above the number-one fire room. The bulkhead between the destroyed engine room and the number-two fire room was cracked, allowing in still more water. Radiomen reported the hit to Admiral Ainsworth, who immediately dispatched two of the nearest destroyers to assist the helpless vessel.

Wellings attempted to save his ship by beaching it at Rice Anchorage, but the pilothouse wheel was limp when the first officer tried turning the ship hard left. The after steering section was then ordered to apply full left rudder from below. Again the ship failed to respond. The *Strong* listed 15 to 20 degrees to starboard almost immediately and gradually dipped to 30 degrees. The surviving crewmen felt a rumble somewhere in the ship's aft section and steam began to vent furiously from the after stack. Finally, the ravaged vessel buckled near its center. There was little more that could be done to keep the ship afloat. The list increased to 40 to 45 degrees just twenty minutes after impact, making it impossible to stand. The skipper therefore ordered all hands to cease damage control efforts, move to the port topside, and prepare to abandon ship.[37]

Meanwhile, the USS *Chevalier* raced to the scene while its crew feverishly prepared for the rescue. Quartermasters issued blankets, the galley crew cranked up the coffee urns, and cargo nets were dropped over the ship's side. Within thirty minutes after the torpedo hit, with the wind now gusting more angrily, the *Chevalier* was within a few hundred yards of the sinking ship. All around the *Strong* the

water erupted with explosions from the impact of high-explosive artillery shells coming from the Japanese-held village of Enogai, a few
miles down the New Georgia coast. That base's 140mm guns had begun to target the disabled vessel after the torpedo hit. It was no place
to linger, so the *Chevalier*'s skipper, Comdr. Eph McLean, decided to
maintain some speed and, while his gunners replied to the incoming fire, intentionally ram his ship's bow into the *Strong* to expedite
the rescue. It was a brazen maneuver, but it saved scores of lives. Six
minutes before impact, the *Chevalier*'s engines were backed two-
thirds. All hands on both ships braced themselves as the skipper
coasted his twenty-one-hundred-ton ship at ten knots on a 30-degree
angle into the *Strong*'s port side.

"I had decided that the *Chevalier* would have to take some damage
in that the bow would have to be put alongside with some force and
be held there by the engines until a line could be passed over by
hand," McLean later explained. "This was the quickest and most positive way of getting alongside in time to save as many as possible, as
the *Strong* was settling fast."[38] The collision caused the crippled ship
to list another 10 degrees, and Wellings feared that it might roll over.
But the *Strong* struggled to hang on a little longer. A two-by-ten-foot
hole was torn in the *Chevalier,* but it was well above the waterline.

In the heat of the night's confusion, another destroyer in the task
force, the *O'Bannon,* appeared on the scene to assist in the rescue.
However, because visibility was so poor, the two destroyers did not
spot each other until two minutes before the *Chevalier* rammed the
Strong. Blindfolded by the heavy rain and darkness, the *O'Bannon* was
just a few yards away and closing fast under the *Chevalier*'s stern,
roughly perpendicular to it. The *Chevalier*'s executive officer rushed
to the ship's annunciators and rang up "Emergency Full Ahead." Seconds later the *O'Bannon* scraped away the starboard depth-charge
rack and smoke-screen generator extending about eight inches outboard as it crossed just under the *Chevalier*'s stern. The hulls did not
collide, missing each other by less than a foot.[39]

Just after impact with the *Chevalier,* panic streaked through some
of the crew. In the unyielding darkness and rain, several of the men
were about to jump over the side without any specific order. Lieutenant (j.g.) O. Milton Hackett moved toward the trouble spot and

shouted that he would shoot the first man who attempted to jump. The officer was not armed, but his bluff worked in the darkness and the men held fast.[40]

Wellings gave the order for the *Strong*'s crew to abandon ship. Most of the men began jumping into the water and swimming to the cargo nets draped over the *Chevalier*'s side. Others chose to stay dry and grab hold of one of the six-inch manila lines secured to the *Strong*'s deck to keep the two destroyers together. Swinging in the wind, they climbed hand-over-hand across the chasm between the two rocking ships and into the waiting arms of the *Chevalier*'s sailors while shell blasts continued to mushroom closer and closer. In just seven minutes, seven officers and 234 men were rescued. There were still roughly fifty men waiting in the water to be rescued when the *Chevalier* was forced to shove off as hastily as it had arrived. Enemy submarines were in the area, making the two destroyers easy targets. Worse, the menacing shore batteries were illuminating the scene with star shells, and a few of the big guns were beginning to find their mark. A single 4.6-inch shell hit the spray shield of one of the *Strong*'s 40mm guns and tore it loose. Wellings, who remained until all was secured, was struck in the wrist and leg by fragments from another near miss. A stick of bombs dropped by an unseen enemy aircraft exploded not a hundred yards off the *Chevalier*'s fantail, causing several seams to open aft. It would have been reckless for McLean to wait any longer. According to Wellings:

As soon as *Chevalier* began to cast off from the *Strong*, I took a quick look fore and aft from both the starboard and port wings of the bridge. All personnel were clear of the topside of the ship. . . . The water was now almost up to the bridge level on the starboard side. I decided to take a last quick look along the main deck amidships, but I was blocked by water as I started down the incline ladder leading to the main deck. I quickly returned to the bridge and was shocked to see my leading quartermaster sitting in the chart house. I said, "Rodriques, why didn't you go to the forecastle and get aboard the *Chevalier* with the rest of the bridge personnel?" He replied, "I'm not leaving the ship until you do, captain."A quick glance outside the bridge area convinced me the ship was about to roll over to starboard. I then said, "There's no one topside and no one alive below decks. Let's get off right now before we're trapped inside when she rolls over." We both then stepped on top of the bridge wind screen, outboard of the starboard director. He stepped into the water, and I followed right after my loyal quartermaster.[41]

Wellings was wrong. His communications officer, Lt. Benjamin F. Jetton, and his assistant, Ens. William C. Hedrick, were still below decks stuffing classified radio codes into weighted bags and throwing them overboard. Despite the clear order to abandon ship, and in disregard of their own lives, they continued to perform their required duty. Both men were officially listed as missing, but they were almost certainly trapped inside their ship and were posthumously awarded the Silver Star for their heroism.

The Officer of the Deck that night, Lt. Donald A. Regan, recalled:

A mooring line was passed across at this time, and Mr. Hackett and I secured it by putting the loop over the edge of the 20mm [gun] shield. I told Hackett to watch that it did not slip off. Men were going across on this line. Another line was sent over and I held this while men went over. After awhile the Chevvy [*Chevalier*] began backing away. One man was midway across the line I was holding (Garrett). I instinctively held on to the line, and was pulled overboard with it as the Chevvy pulled away, striking the deck of the *Strong* with my right hip. On getting into the water, I still held on and got my arm in the loop of this line as my right leg was paralyzed. . . . Garrett yelled that he couldn't hold on, and he slid down.[42]

Forty-one minutes after the torpedo smashed into the *Strong*, it disappeared under the bouncing, oil-covered seas two and a half miles due west of Rice Anchorage.

Lieutenant Hugh Barr Miller, a lawyer from Tuscaloosa, Alabama, and the ship's machine-gun officer, was helping to clear the ship of all personnel minutes before the sinking. When the *Chevalier* pulled away, one of the mooring lines that had been used in the rescue had fouled alongside the submerging destroyer and pinned the legs of two men against the deck. Miller scrambled toward them and began to cut through the line with his knife. He could feel the ship lurching and settling beneath him, but he was determined that the two would not be strapped onto it when it went down. Just as he cut through, the ship sank beneath them. Now there was a new horror: The suction caused by the fast-sinking ship pulled the helpless men below the surface, deeper and deeper into the gruesome black underworld of the gulf. Fortunately, Miller was wearing his Kapok life jacket, and with his arms around the two men, all three somehow made it to the surface.[43]

Moments later the ocean suddenly and violently convulsed from the force of three or four underwater explosions. The dying ship's three-hundred-pound starboard depth charges had detonated. Their safeties probably were disabled by the shock of the torpedo blast, causing them to explode when the *Strong* reached the depth for which they had been calibrated. The explosions were so potent that the *Chevalier* began to flood from the impact of the bursts. Lieutenant Hackett, although shaken, was thankful that his heavy-weather gear saved him from a deadly saltwater enema, a common consequence of underwater explosions. Wellings, however, was knocked unconscious. When he came to, Quartermaster Rodriques was pulling him onto the floater net. Now suffering from stomach and back pain, he was of little help to Rodriques when they began paddling toward what they hoped was Rice Anchorage. Meanwhile, they were able to rescue three more of their shipmates. One was SN Robert F. Gregory, an eighteen-year-old from South Carolina, who was clinging to a rubber raft with ten others when the depth charges exploded. One of the two others died a few minutes later, and the second had an arm and leg nearly blown off. The concussion also knocked Lieutenant Miller unconscious. When he recovered, he was still holding up the heads of the two men he had saved. Soon he drifted to a floater net and the three were pulled to temporary safety, but Miller was seriously hurt. The pressure on his diaphragm was so intense that he could hardly breathe. Throughout the night they picked up more men, some injured and some not. When morning broke, the abandoned sailors had become a small party on two floater nets and two rafts.

Lieutenant Regan was somewhat luckier, despite the great pain he endured from his smashed right side. He managed to be picked up by the ship's gig (motorized boat), but discovered he "could not stand on my right leg," he later recalled. "The boat was covered with fuel oil. I made my way back to the after compartment and directed the coxswain in picking up men in the water, i.e., turning off the motor and listening for cries. I believe we picked up about a dozen men. My left eye was swollen shut caused by bumping into something while in the water."

As Regan and the others aboard the gig motored toward the New Georgia coast searching for Rice Anchorage, they heard machine-gun fire in the distance and headed for it.

We were underway about five minutes when a DD (destroyer) began firing in our direction. I ordered all hands down in the boat. My thought was that we had been picked up on the ship's radar screen and were mistaken for a sub. I changed course, and the tracers also seemed to change. I stopped the boat, and although the firing seemed directed at us with shells whistling overhead, firing soon ceased and we resumed our way. This made us very wary about showing lights. . . .

Meanwhile I had given morphine injections to four men suffering from blast injuries. Other first aid was impossible in the dark, because of oil, darkness, and the crowded condition of the boat.[44]

Instead of trying to find and approach one of the ships, they decided to wait until dawn, when Regan knew the transports would be heading back home. Positioning themselves somewhere north of Rice Anchorage, they spotted one of the destroyer-transports steaming toward Visuvisu Point. Regan pulled out the semaphore flags and sent "Survivors of *Strong*—please take us aboard." They were rescued and made the trip back to Guadalcanal with the squadron.[45]

About four hours after Lieutenant Commander Wellings was pulled onto the floater net, he lapsed into semiconsciousness and "wondered how my lovely wife and five-year-old daughter were in Dedham, Mass. I knew that our respective families would assist them in every way possible if I were killed by the Japanese, or captured and became a prisoner of war. Frankly, I had just about given up all hope of being rescued because I knew our ships would be clearing the gulf at maximum sustained speed to set course for Guadalcanal. It then being less than an hour before dawn."[46]

Then, a miracle: The destroyer *Gwin,* the last ship remaining in the lower gulf, changed course to clear the area. At 5:10 A.M. the lookouts saw the flashlight of the five survivors and hastened to retrieve them from their misery.

Meanwhile, on one of the other rafts, SN Robert Gregory and eleven others drifted at sea for two and a half days, shadowed by suspicious black frigate birds that glided effortlessly above them. They spent much of their time trying to calm their shipmate, Electrician's Mate Willard Langley, who had two limbs almost torn off by the depth-charge blasts. He was in great pain and begged them to throw him overboard and let him die. But they persevered, eluding Japanese planes that came even at night, playing searchlights over the water in search of survivors.

"We were all blind from the oil in the water, except Seaman First Class Richard Cody of Los Angeles," recalled Gregory. "Cody would tell us when he saw a plane coming and we would duck and lie as if we were dead to keep them from seeing us. We saw . . . our comrades [on other rafts] shot to death with machine guns [from an enemy boat], and could hear the Japs scream with laughter after they had got them. . . . I don't see how we escaped."[47]

They finally washed ashore on a narrow, deserted beach bordering a dense jungle, unaware that they were on Japanese-held Kolombangara. They hid their raft and made their way into the bush about a hundred yards, where they constructed a crude shelter. Someone found an aluminum can of gasoline, which they used to clean the oil from their bodies, and a few cans of food left by enemy soldiers, but it was spoiled. There was an abundance of coconuts and papayas, however. Their main worry was Langley. His condition had worsened. The flesh hung loosely from his wounded arm, and they were forced to use a sheath knife to cut it off. Gangrene was beginning to set in, so they decided to amputate his hand even though none of them had any medical training.

Gregory's eight-man party (four had since died) spent ten days on Kolombangara, taking turns going to the beach to search for anything useful. One of the men found a sea bag containing three pairs of shoes—a priceless discovery since all of them had discarded their shoes when they abandoned ship. Whoever went scouting for food wore them. On one such trip they came across the bloated, decomposed bodies of some of their comrades from the *Strong*, recognizable only by their uniforms.

With hope and strength slowly fading, some of the men began talking about searching for the Japanese and surrendering to them rather than face certain death from starvation and exposure. "We knew there were plenty of Japs on the island," said Gregory, "and we could hear constant firing."[48] The next day's foray to the beach convinced them of the recklessness of their plan when they discovered the mutilated torsos of two more Americans. Nearby lay their severed heads, hands, and feet. The hideous discovery had a telling effect on the defenseless sailors, who, confronted with the enemy's barbarity, wondered how they would ever get back alive. The Japanese owned the waters around Kolombangara, so the likelihood of the navy sending rescue craft in search of survivors was virtually nil. Nevertheless, they refused to concede defeat. Two of the men, W. J. Genner and George Hege, who had a wife and three children at home in North Carolina, volunteered to circle the island and search for some means of escape while they still had the strength. They promised to send help if they were successful.

The remainder of the party waited for two days, but Genner and Hege never returned. Langley's condition was worsening by the hour. Impatience with their predicament got the better of the men, including the semiconscious Langley, who reintroduced the idea of surrendering to the Japanese. Their discussion turned heated. Gregory and the two others who did most of the scouting were adamant. They said they would rather die in the jungle and insisted on remaining where they were. The trio did, however, vow to expand their search for help even farther down the beach. Their exhortations probably saved everyone's lives, for the very next day the determined explorers spotted a rubber surfboat bobbing in the waves and swam out to pull it ashore.

It was noon on their ninth day on the island when Gregory returned to their shelter with the good news. After talking over their plan to paddle east to New Georgia, where they knew there were Americans, they decided to wait one more day for Hege and Genner. When their comrades had not appeared by sunset the next day, the five men carried Langley and armfuls of coconuts to the beach, removed the surfboat from where they had hidden it, and slipped quietly away. They hand-paddled across the twenty-two-mile-wide Kula Gulf, reaching New Georgia before daybreak, exhausted and hungry.

They were sitting on the ground eating coconuts when they spotted a bronzed, muscular native with a mop of bushy hair and porpoise-teeth necklaces running toward them, waving his arms. The sailors, happy to see another human being, rose to greet him. The islander, who spoke fairly good English, was the former chief of a nearby village. He explained to them how the Japanese had driven his people from their home, raping and mutilating the women and killing some of the men. He gave them water and cigarettes and promised to return with help the next day. Around midnight, a small group of natives showed up to guide them to Enogai. A few hours later, they entered the American camp there bearing Langley on a litter. The next morning all six men were put aboard a floatplane and flown to Guadalcanal, where they were reunited with their crew.[49]

Somewhere in the middle of Kula Gulf, Lt. Hugh Miller was still suffering from the injuries he received in the underwater blasts. After being separated from his other shipmates, Miller collected two more broken rafts carrying survivors. Together, the battered sailors spent their first chilly night clinging to their float net as the cold sea pulsed beneath them. At dawn on 5 July, Miller sent three officers toward New Georgia on one of the rafts to seek help. None came. He tried the same with the other raft the next day, and again there was no word. Meanwhile, as they drifted at the whim of the wind and waves, several of the men died from internal injuries and were buried at sea. Only six remained alive when, in the middle of their third night in the gulf, Miller awoke to see the blurred contour of an island. They were only a hundred yards from land. Those who were able hand-paddled until they pulled themselves onto a crooked islet just north of Arundel Island. They had drifted east some ten miles from the site of the sinking.

The sailors rested for two days, nourishing themselves on coconuts. It was too little too late for Lt. (jg) A. E. Oberg, who finally succumbed to his injuries. The remaining five placed SN Eddie Deering, who was too injured to assist, in the center of their float net and set off across the half-mile-wide strait for Arundel. D. J. Mullane and Lloyd Lawrence on the front corners dug into the water with makeshift paddles. Miller was not able to use his upper body, so he sat on the back and kicked. Frank Armbruster, the best swimmer in the group, pulled the net. It took two hours of punishing work, but they managed to reach the larger island. There they found a gurgling, freshwater spring and a discarded Japanese army blanket, but only a few coconuts. A better source of food was needed, so they decided to keep moving. Meanwhile, their numbers again diminished when Deering died on the morning of the thirteenth.

After burying their shipmate, they slowly followed the eastern shoreline south. In the distance they spotted what appeared to be a cultivated plantation. They stumbled ahead, hoping to find fruit, water, and friendly natives. Miller used a cane to help him along but he was passing more blood from his rectum, and his strength was fading fast. The others took turns assisting him, but after three miles he could no longer move and was nearly unconscious. They had no choice but to bivouac there and decide what to do the next day. As dusk fell, the lieutenant prayed that he would regain his strength by morning. Unfortunately, when the morning of the fifteenth dawned, Miller realized he could not go on.

I made the men take what equipment we had and ordered them to leave me, which they did. Our equipment at that time consisted of only a sheath knife, a rainproof parka, and several tins of emergency rations. I gave my shoes to one of the men who was barefooted. All I had left was two Japanese beer bottles of water, a broken pocket knife and the small inch and a half blade which had been broken out of it, the Japanese blanket, and my staff. I was so uncomfortable that I didn't try to conserve my water and I exhausted my supply before the morning of the 16th of July; I thought I would be dead by then, but I rallied.

The day of the 16th I had no water, but I became determined to live. Late in the afternoon of the 17th I was still without water and quite uncomfortable and I prayed for rain and in my prayers promised that if I could get rain, I would get up and help myself. That night there was a very heavy rain, and I was able to catch enough water in one of the empty emergency tins to fill up my two beer bottles, to drink four tins, and then catch the tin full again.[50]

Miller awoke at dawn, drank the remaining tin of water, and began the trek back to the spring where his party had originally landed. It would be grueling, but he had a fierce will and a strong constitution. As a student at the University of Alabama he was on the golf squad, the baseball and track teams, and was named an All-America quarterback in 1930 when he led the Crimson Tide to victory over Washington State in the Rose Bowl. He moved slowly, covering only about half a mile that morning. As he crept across a salt flat at low tide, he heard the sound of an aircraft and froze. Within a few moments a Japanese Zero curled down from the low cloud ceiling, made a quick pass, and then returned to finish him off. The plane roared toward him, its wing guns blazing. Machine-gun rounds thudded all around, spraying him with mud. Then the fighter pulled up and disappeared into the clouds. One round splattered when it hit a rock, sending two tiny bits of sizzling steel into him, one lodging in his neck and the other in his wrist. Fortunately, they were flesh wounds. After extracting both slivers, Miller continued his treacherous journey.

Later that day he happened upon an excellent spring that was swollen from the previous night's rainstorm. Refreshed, the thirty-three-year-old lawyer hobbled around, still barefooted, until he found a coconut, broke it open, and consumed its meat. It was the first solid food that he was able to hold down since the sinking. With plenty of good drinking water and coconuts around, he decided to remain while his strength slowly returned. Moreover, he had cut his feet on the coral, making it difficult for him to walk. He knew he was likely on Arundel or some other island west of Kula Gulf in the Japanese sector, for the enemy was conducting almost daily patrols in the area, forcing him to move his camp from time to time. Nevertheless, Miller began to believe that he might make it back alive.

On 26 July he built a permanent camp a hundred yards from the freshwater spring in a tight cluster of mangrove trees. He found a natural shelter protected on all sides by underbrush under the loop of one of the great trees. Safe from the prying eyes of Japanese sea patrols, he fashioned a bunk and a pillow from palm fronds and settled in to what would be his home for the next three weeks.

He shared his tight quarters with a family of four gruesome-looking but otherwise inoffensive lizards, whose nest was just a foot or so from his makeshift pillow. They were surprisingly nonchalant about the disturbance caused by their new roommate and went about their daily routine as if he was not there.

On the first day in his new residence, Miller spotted what appeared to be a low-flying navy TBF Avenger torpedo bomber and attempted to attract the pilot's attention. With any luck the pilot would see that he was a stranded American and report his location. Although the odds were against him, Miller refused to be discouraged: "I never lost hope for my eventual rescue. This plane circled a dozen times very low and looked me over very carefully, often being so close that I could see the plane's crew well—so well that I could almost identify them if I saw them again.[51]

If the airmen reported the sighting, it fell on deaf ears. No rescue effort was mounted. At the end of his third week eluding death, Miller remained marooned and alone to contend with Arundel's increasingly active Japanese garrison.

Virtually every night the enemy was shuttling troop-carrying barges and small boats from Vila, their stronghold on Kolombangara, to a coconut plantation just a few miles from Miller's camp. They carried a cargo of reinforcements and supplies destined for New Georgia, where the assault on Munda was nearing its climax.

Miller never let his daily struggle to survive distract him from his duty. He was a naval officer, and he had been blessed with a unique opportunity to provide valuable intelligence information when he eventually escaped from his island prison. He watched the Japanese movements, made mental notes of patterns, times, and numbers, and carefully reconnoitered the area in the vicinity of his hidden camp.

On the night of 2 August, Miller heard the putter of what sounded like a navy PT boat and crawled to the beach to get a look. Its skipper cut the engines and drifted quietly to shore, where the boat finally stopped to hide under the sagging branches of a mangrove tree that grew near the breaking surf. Still not sure whether the mysterious vessel was friendly or not, Miller waited to see what would happen next. After an hour or so, the familiar rumble of Japanese barges could be heard in the distance. In a few minutes the rumble grew louder and the silhouettes of several of the enemy craft materialized in the dull moonlight. Suddenly, the hidden boat's machine guns erupted, its .50-calibers breaking the enemy barges, hacking them to pieces while Miller silently cheered from the sidelines. One of the crewmen aboard the PT boat began to spray the beach near Miller's hiding place with a tommy gun. He dove to the sand to avoid and the random gunfire. It also discouraged him from trying to make a move toward the boat, even though he knew it would soon be shoving off.

"When they went to leave," he recalled, "I tried to attract their attention, but I know you can't yell, 'Hey Marine' or 'Hey Navy' because the Japs have done so much of that when anybody hears it they shoot in that direction, so the only way I could hurriedly think of to identify myself was that I ran up a leaning tree, which I used for my lookout post, and sang the Marine hymn at the top of my voice. By that time they were so busy finishing off the Japs with their pistols as they moved to get back to Rice Anchorage that they could not hear me. Shortly after our boat left, Japanese boats came and picked up all the screaming, yelling Japanese survivors."[52]

Miller returned to the beach the next morning and spotted the body of a dead Japanese soldier rolling back and forth in the foamy surf. The man's uniform and gear were intact, and he still wore his leather boots. The temptation was irresistible. Despite the risk of being sighted, Miller ran out of the bush and stripped the dead man of his precious footwear, socks, bayonet, grenade carrier, two hand grenades, and uniform. Miller wore the uniform beneath his own oil-soaked clothing in order to protect his already irritated skin. He also pilfered five tins of barely edible Japanese beef, which he forced himself to eat at lunch every other day for its protein. That same afternoon, however, he spied a Japanese patrol lurking along the beach most likely looking for survivors. They found the nude body that Miller had scavenged. He immediately regretted not taking the time to hide the body. Now the enemy was alerted to his presence. He knew they would be looking for him.

The day continued uneventfully, and a few hours later he sighted another TBF Avenger flying just a few hundred feet above the island. The pilot circled overhead several times and inspected the bearded, ragged sailor carefully before dropping a small package a few yards from him. Miller tore it open and found a bandage, a small bottle of iodine, and a D-ration, which he immediately consumed. It was the only complete meal he ate during his long ordeal. However, Miller said it was the iodine, along with the Japanese boots, that did the most to help save him. He applied the antiseptic to the cuts on his feet and, after putting on the socks and boots, was able to cover greater distances with much less pain. His morale soared, but still there was no rescue.

The following night, a five-man Japanese patrol began searching for Miller.

I saw them coming in the moonlight in the woods and retreated in front of them for a hundred yards to my permanent camp. They did not hear or see me at any time. When it became evident that they were going to walk right into my camp, I decided to try out one of the two hand grenades that I had. When they were thirty yards from me in the position that I wanted them in, which was in a close group, which I knew they had to be in to come between two groups of thorn bushes, I tossed this Jap hand grenade in the middle of them and killed all five.[53]

Immediately after the blast, he darted to a predetermined fall-back position a mile into the bush, not knowing for sure if there were other patrols in the vicinity. Early the next morning he returned to the site and confirmed his kill. The former baseball player's throw must have been perfect, for three of the men were "little more than mince meat." The other two, however, provided Miller with a harvest of supplies: six more grenades, clothes, raingear, tents, haversacks, bayonets, ammo, soap, and five more tins of meat. Unfortunately, all five of their rifles were ruined. He carefully buried each of the men, planting shrubs over their level graves so that there would be no trace of them. Next, he used the soap to cleanse himself of the fuel oil that had covered him since the sinking and replaced his oily underclothes. He put each item of the recovered gear to good use. During the next three days, several more Japanese bodies drifted ashore. Miller robbed them, too, increasing his supply of grenades and personal effects that naval intelligence might find useful. On his nightly visits to the beach, he observed that the Japanese had emplaced machine guns at intervals along the coast to protect against another PT boat attack on their troop barges. He memorized their routines to pass along to headquarters when he made it back. But Miller was not satisfied with simply collecting intelligence and hiding. He was armed, trained to fight, and the enemy was in his midst. There was never a question of what he should do.

Three times between 9 and 14 August, Miller risked his life by creeping a mile and a half up the coast, positioning himself to the rear of machine-gun nests, and casually lobbing grenades into them. "I know from the blood and some equipment that I found the next day that I got some each time," he said later. He did all this despite seeing almost daily search patrols. The last night he spent on Arundel, a patrol got to within thirty yards of him. Had it approached any closer, Miller later joked, they would have "gotten some more of their very good hand grenades."[54]

About mid-morning on 16 August, Miller heard the unmistakable sound of another TBF. Jumping up and waving a white Japanese towel, he managed to attract the attention of the pilot, 1st Lt. James R. Turner, who circled him once and then flew directly to Munda to report the sighting to the marine fighter headquarters there. Within an hour, Major Vernon A. Peterson and two others set out in a tiny floatplane and landed near Miller's camp. The stranded sailor started toward the plane but struggled to stand in the heaving surf. Peterson, seeing that he was too weak to make it the last forty yards to the plane, signaled to him to wait where he was until they could inflate a dinghy. Miller, always dutiful, returned to his camp to gather up anything that might be of intelligence value. When he returned to the beach, Peterson was paddling toward him. Miller insisted that he first take the materials that he had stored back to the plane. Only then, when the documents were safely aboard, did he allow himself to be pulled into the aircraft.

Bearded and forty pounds lighter, Miller arrived at Munda just in time for lunch, where he completed his first real meal in six weeks (Munda had been seized eleven days before). After spending two days recovering and writing a report of his ordeal, he was flown to Guadalcanal to complete his recuperation in the hospital. In the bunk next to Miller was his *Strong* shipmate, Willard Langley.

It did not take long before the written report of Hugh Miller's remarkable ordeal reached Admiral Halsey's headquarters. The SPA commander was so impressed with Miller's story that he recounted it in his own memoirs. Miller's courage was officially recognized when First Lady Eleanor Roosevelt presented him with the Navy Cross while visiting wounded servicemen on Guadalcanal in September. When the president's wife asked the modest naval officer how he was able to hold out for so long, he replied: "Two things saved me. I have loved hunting all my life, and I have always been able to find my way home."[55]

The Naval Battle of Kula Gulf

On the night of 6 July, coastwatchers on Vella Lavella alerted Halsey's headquarters that ten enemy destroyers were steaming toward Kolombangara's north coast. Rear Admiral Teruo Akiyama was attempting a Tokyo Express reinforcement of Kolombangara with troops selected by General Imamura. Admiral Ainsworth was anxious to avenge the loss of the *Strong*, which had been sunk less than twenty-four hours earlier. Most of Colonel Liversedge's men had by then debarked, but as the danger of the operation increased, the admiral gave the command to abort the remainder of the mission at daybreak to escape further losses. All but 2 percent of the NLG's forces had made it ashore by the time the order was issued.[56] On the return trip, however, Ainsworth was ordered to turn around and confront the enemy destroyers. There would certainly be a brawl; the gulf was not big enough for both task forces.

It was an especially dark, moonless night, with visibility less than two miles. The navy's "Black Cat" PBY night-observation planes, hampered by the inclement weather, submitted no reports. Radar was quiet as Ainsworth's task force reached the extreme northwest corner of New Georgia, whisking through the calm sea at twenty-nine knots. Suddenly, at 1:36 A.M., the cruiser *Honolulu*'s radar picked up a cluster of ships turning into the gulf off the northeast coast of Kolombangara. It was Admiral Akiyama's 6th Destroyer Flotilla, lingering off the dark shore twenty-six thousand yards away, readying an ambush. The Japanese had used this tactic with considerable success in the Solomons, placing themselves against a shadowy beach where Allied radar was distorted by the backdrop of the islands' mountains. From there they would launch their lethal torpedoes. Only then, when their presence was revealed, did they begin firing their deck guns. Making matters even worse, Akiyama's flagship was equipped with a new radar set and had detected the Americans a full ten minutes—an eternity in naval combat—before Ainsworth learned of the flotilla's presence.

Ainsworth's nine warships moved rapidly into a single column and steamed boldly toward Akiyama's warships. The cruisers *St. Louis, Honolulu,* and *Helena* opened fire at 1:57 at a range of just over 7,000 yards. The destroyers followed and together they unleashed a curtain of murderous steel—roughly twenty-five hundred rounds of five- and six-inch shells in just over five minutes. But it was too late. Instead of overwhelming the enemy ships with his superior firepower at a range of 10,000 to 15,000 yards, Ainsworth closed to the targets and allowed the enemy to use his best weapon. Akiyama's torpedoes had already been in the water for several minutes, streaking toward their targets before the Americans commenced firing. At 2:03, the 608-foot-long *Helena* was struck by a three-ton high-explosive torpedo between its forward main battery turrets at magazine number one, ripping off a large portion of the bow with the forward turret. Captain Charles P. Cecil, unaware of the seriousness of the damage to his ship, continued to move through the gulf at twenty knots, the broken vessel swallowing seawater like an open-mouthed whale. Huge waves inundated the quarterdeck, sweeping screaming sailors into the water. Ninety seconds later, two more violent explosions rocked the wounded ship, this time breaking it in two.

The impact threw E. E. Lajeunesse off his feet and into the bulkhead of the first deck repair room. Water began to rush in and shoved him around the compartment until he found himself sliding into the next compartment, gasping desperately for air and praying for divine intervention. Lajeunesse later recalled having

no idea how the hatch door to the adjoining compartment got open. I could barely see for all the oil in my eyes. I was covered from head to foot with thick, gooey stuff. I am not sure, but I think there were 14 of us in this compartment, and to my knowledge, only two of us got out.

I got to my feet and ran aft to the next hatch. The water was already waist-deep in this compartment. I opened the hatch to get out, and the men on the other side tried to close it, seeing all the water coming in. I yelled as loud as I could that the ship had broken in two, and with the help of the water pressure on my side of the hatch, I was able to push my way through.

I made my way to the center of the compartment where the ladder up to the second deck was. As I went through the hatch at the top of the ladder, I rolled over on my side to catch my breath. Another man was also lying there. I nudged the guy to tell him we better get going, but got no response. He was dead.

The dazed New Yorker finally made it outside to the aft main deck, where he witnessed a phenomenon few have ever experienced. After wiping oil from his eyes, he could see through the swirling smoke that the *Helena*'s stern and bow had risen about 30 degrees out of the water. As the ship cracked in two amidships, it began to assume the shape of an enormous, mangled V. Trained never to jump into the ocean where it is level with the deck because of the danger of being sucked inside the sinking vessel as water gushes in, he climbed up the deck and leaped into the dark abyss, thankful that the ship was not on fire. He and the rest of the crew swam away from the drowning, ninety-seven-hundred-ton, smoke-shrouded hulk. A number of the loyal crewmen saluted as they dove off the side. "It wasn't necessary," explained SN Ted Blahnik, a 40mm-gun director, "but that's what we always did when we came aboard and that's what we did when we left."[57]

Once in the water, Lajeunesse made his

> way to a raft that was about 40 yards from the ship. The raft was full, so I had to hold onto the side with the help of someone already inside. That was a good thing, because I was so sick and vomiting from swallowing so much salt water and fuel oil that I hardly had the strength to hang on without help.
>
> While looking back at the ship as it was sinking, I could see that there were some men still holding onto the guard rail on the fantail. I do not know if they could not swim or were just scared.[58]

Akiyama's flagship, the *Niizuki,* which had ventured farther into the middle of the gulf with two other destroyers, was smothered by radar-directed gunfire from the American cruisers. Several six-inch shells hit another destroyer, but the damage done was negligible. At this point, Ainsworth's radar trackers lost sight of the enemy, so he broke off the attack and began rescuing the *Helena*'s crew. By 2:50 A.M. the battle was over. The *Helena* was on its way to the bottom of the gulf, as were Admiral Akiyama—killed in his first battle— and his flagship. A second Japanese destroyer, the *Nagatsuki,* ran aground on a reef near Vila and was finished off by a flight of B-25 bombers the next afternoon. More importantly, however, only 850 of the 4,000 reinforcements landed on Kolombangara.[59]

The *Helena*'s survivors were drifting out over a one-square-mile area. Two destroyers, the *Nicholas* and *Radford,* sailed slowly into the dark waters where the *Helena*'s crew waited, some in life rafts and others bobbing in the water blowing whistles and waving flashlights. All were covered with oil from the slick carpeting on the surface. A monument marked their location: a skyward-pointing section of the ship's bow was still afloat. The rescue operation was interrupted three times when enemy ships were picked up on radar. Three times frustrated survivors climbing onto the lowered lifeboats and nets were abruptly left in the water so the two destroyers could chase after the Japanese.

At the first hint of dawn, Capt. Francis X. McInerney, who was in charge of the rescue effort, reluctantly ordered the two destroyers to move out of the area after rescuing 745 officers and men. It was simply too dangerous to be in the area dead in the water in broad daylight. Submarines, surface vessels, and aircraft all threatened the operation. Before shoving off, the destroyers left behind four whaleboats manned by volunteers to search for the remaining sailors in the water. The courageous sailors on these boats picked up another hundred survivors and ferried them to safety on New Georgia. Among them was Captain Cecil, who assembled a crude armada by lashing together rafts filled with his oil-soaked crew and had two of the motorized whaleboats tow them. They reached an isolated barrier island off New Georgia's northern shoulder before daybreak. A few hours later they were spotted by a search plane and rescued by two destroyers. Still, there were two hundred or so men left in the water.

The morning after the sinking, the *Helena*'s twisted bow, still mysteriously refusing to sink, became visible to the survivors as it towered twenty feet above the Kula Gulf. They paddled to it from hundreds of yards away and huddled around it hoping a friendly plane would spy them. One did, and dropped a few tiny rubber rafts. More planes approached at midmorning, but they proved to be Zeros. The helpless men quietly expected the worst as the enemy fighters passed low overhead. There was no place to hide. One of the pilots pulled back his canopy and gave them all a good look, but the planes held their fire. They circled and made another pass, again holding their fire. As they turned to make a terrifying third pass, the silent prayers from the helpless men in the water were almost palpable. However, the pilots fired only a few short bursts from their machine guns as they rushed by, the lead pilot waving and smiling in a rare example of Japanese chivalry.

The startled survivors, realizing they could not stay where they were, broke up into small groups and moved away from the floating bow section. The senior officer in one group, Lt. Comdr. Jack Chew, ordered his two small four-man rafts leashed together and arranged a rotation for the paddlers. Those not working in the raft would cling to it and kick. Each could expect only ten minutes of rest every two hours. He then set course for enemy-held Kolombangara.

After paddling all day, there was still nothing promising on the horizon, nothing to show for their exhausting labor. When night fell they lost one of their injured and sadly let his body float away from the rafts to join the rest of the *Helena*'s victims. Chew led them in a prayer that was as much for themselves as it was for their deceased mates.

They were hungry after eight hours in the water, but the main concern was sleeplessness, particularly for those hanging onto the rafts. A marine, Maj. Bernard Kelly, dozed off momentarily and was awakened when he swallowed some water. By then he had lost the rafts and was alone in the darkness. Instinctively he forced his unresponsive body to swim, encouraged by several large fish nibbling at his toes. Then Kelly spotted a raft. It was one of Chew's that had become separated. He swam over and clung to it, wide-eyed, the rest of the night.

At daybreak, the discouraged men decided to erect a crude sail using paddles and clothing; this resulted in some success. During the afternoon a carton of potatoes floated nearby, and the men ate for the first time since being torpedoed. However, after another long day at sea, there was no land to be seen—only the slowly quivering horizon. Another long, unendurable night passed. At dawn on day three, the dazed men on Kelly's raft realized that ten of their number had silently slipped away during the night, unable to continue the struggle. Deprived of food and sleep, burned from the relentless sun, and physically spent from the nonstop kicking and paddling, the men became unraveled.

Then someone sighted land. It was impossible to determine how far away it was, but it seemed within reach. Nearly irrational, Jack Chew and three others left the raft to swim for it, promising to stay together as much as possible, but after six hours of drifting and breaststroking, they lost contact with each other. The distant, faintly audible roar of the surf nudging a shoreline drove them on, however.

Early in the evening on 8 July, native canoes beheld the sight of tattered, dispirited men intermittently stumbling onto their beach. Some of the islanders sprinted out to drag them from the surf. Others brought coconuts to those already ashore to refresh parched throats. The survivors had drifted onto the east coast of Vella Lavella, an island northwest of Kolombangara. It was home not only to the Japanese, but also to cranky saltwater crocodiles.[60] However, that was not important at the moment. All that really mattered was that they had reached land.

Immediately, a native runner scurried across the island's interior to a village where coastwatcher Henry Josselyn had made his headquarters, told his men the news, and showed them the dog tags of one of the survivors as proof of the story. The coastwatching station had to make sure that this was not an enemy trick to expose their location, so Josselyn's men sent out in inquiry. Minutes later, a radio message leapfrogged from Guadalcanal through Donald Kennedy confirmed that the tags belonged to a crewmember of the sunken *Helena*.

Josselyn went to work. There were apparently two different groups of survivors separated by about twelve miles. Because Japanese patrols moved up and down that stretch of coastline frequently (at the time there were about 170 enemy soldiers in the immediate vicinity[61]), Josselyn made sure the native handlers led them inland before the next morning. He personally led one crew inland himself. Lieutenant Commander Chew's group was escorted over two miles into the interior and up jungle-covered hills by a native who brought them to the secluded home of a Chinese trader. There, the party—which had grown to 104 men—met Rev. A. W. Silvester, a missionary/coastwatcher who lived nearby. Silvester organized foraging parties to gather food, which was in short supply even for the natives, and provided some medicine from the mission's store.

In the friendlier home waters of Tulagi, a small island near Guadalcanal, the men of the *Helena* who had been rescued thought of nothing else but their missing shipmates. They made daily inquiries, conducted prayer services, and endured sleepless nights. Captain McInerney seemed distant, and Captain Cecil, the *Helena*'s skipper, set about the task of writing difficult letters to missing sailors' families. No one in the Solomons was more concerned, however, than the crews of *Radford* and *Nicholas*, who were never allowed to complete their search for survivors.

When Josselyn's message reporting that he had found a large number of *Helena*'s surviving crewmembers reached Halsey, the admiral vowed to pick them up immediately. A squadron of ten destroyers was quickly assembled, making it the largest naval rescue effort of the war. However, the rescuers would be cruising in waters owned by the Tokyo Express. The destroyer squadron was dispatched to Parasso Bay on Vella Lavella's northeast coast, where a clandestine pickup would be made. With enemy airstrips less than sixty miles away, and with foot and naval patrols constantly combing the area, the two bands of men, most still wearing their oil-stained dungarees, hid in the thick tree lines in the early hours after midnight on 15 July, awaiting deliverance.

It had been ten long days since they last waited for their navy to rescue them. This time it would happen; Josselyn would see to that. Leaving a protective string of scouts around the anxious seamen's perimeter, he and three islanders paddled a canoe four miles out into the gulf at midnight and waited to guide the destroyers to their rendezvous. With only three inches of freeboard, a canoe at sea is not a place for the faint of heart. Sometimes, however, there were no other options.

"To those used to this mode of travel the exercise presented no great difficulty," recalled coastwatcher Dick Horton, "but, looking back it seems to me that the grace of God was continually about us, for the times our lives were in hazard for one reason or another are more than I can remember."[62] After an hour's wait, two ships finally appeared and were carefully piloted to the collection points without incident. One hundred sixty-five elated sailors were recovered from enemy soil and given cigarettes, beef, milk, ice cream, and hot showers on board the squadron's vessels. It was a reception fashioned for heroes, but they were simply happy to be alive.[63] One hundred sixty-eight of their shipmates, most of them entombed inside the *Helena* at the bottom of Kula Gulf, never returned.

• • •

Bull Halsey pressed his lips and nodded with satisfaction when early reports of the first Rendova landing came into his office. Between long draws on a cigarette, he composed a brief message of congratulations to Admiral Turner, who commanded the operation and who had identified Rendova as the key to capturing Munda. While not entirely error free, the successful landing had cost only a few casualties. Moreover, for the first time since February, Halsey's forces were on the move—and that was the way he liked it. Another island, another step closer to Rabaul. The enemy had made a major mistake by not holding on to Rendova. Not only did it provide a perfect artillery platform, but it also was an indispensable beachhead from which to deploy troops for the move across to New Georgia. Had Rendova been suitably defended, the entire New Georgia operation would have required restructuring, for the island guarded the only eastern sea approach to Munda. Kolombangara, safely in Japanese hands, protected the western approaches. Moreover, because Munda was itself sheltered from a frontal seaborne assault by its screen of reefs and shoals, the only other option would have been an attack from the north. That would have required a Herculean march across the island's toughest terrain, its interior spine made up of rugged, unforgiving mountains. Without the capture of Rendova, the Munda operation might have been disastrous.

Zanana

It was gospel that an invasion against a fortified beachhead should, if at all possible, be avoided. That ruled out a direct assault on Munda, which was situated on a point northwest of the Rendova staging area and girdled by a coral shield of reefs and shoals. As a consequence of the spring recon patrols and coastwatcher and native islander reports, the planning staff concluded that the two-hundred-yard-wide beach at Zanana, located roughly five miles east of the airfield, would be the best place to land the main body of troops. It was relatively close to the objective, accessible to landing craft, and undefended. The only other suitable beach was at Laiana, just two miles east of Munda. However, it was ruled out because it was within range of Munda's artillery. If the Japanese had their guns registered on that beach, the landing would be a slaughter. Moreover, although not defended at the moment, General Sasaki could correct that problem quickly enough to foil even an earnest invasion there. Zanana would have to do.

Two unremarkable coral islets blocked the approach to Zanana from Rendova. Between them was a narrow but unobstructed opening to be used by the landing craft in their approach. It was therefore crucial that the islets be secured before the invasion. Two companies of soldiers from the 169th Infantry accomplished that mission without a hitch. Then, shortly before dawn on 2 July, an entire battalion from the 172nd Infantry was sent across the channel to occupy and secure Zanana. If it could do so without encountering any resistance, Zanana would continue to be the invasion point. But again there was confusion. A native escort bearing signal lamps in canoes mysteriously vanished when the silent flotilla neared landfall. Consequently, the neat formation, which was guiding on the lights, broke up just as a cruel rain began to fall on the invaders. One by one, the lead landing craft collided with a reef. Their coxswains reversed engines at full throttle and backed up into the onrushing boats behind them, shouting curses heretofore reserved for the Japanese. The furious regimental commander, Col. David Ross, curtly ordered the battalion to return in embarrassment to Rendova. At nightfall it tried again, and this time managed to secure a toehold on the beach.[64]

At this point, General Sasaki lost his best opportunity to save the airfield. If he had ordered soundings of the narrow channels leading to the beaches at Zanana or Laiana beaches, the only two possible locations for a landing on New Georgia's southern coast, he could have guessed where the American invasion would take place—especially after 30 June, when Rendova fell. He then could have moved a few infantry companies to the barrier islets guarding the approaches or positioned them to defend the beaches themselves. Once Rendova was secured, Admiral Turner was committed to invading New Georgia's south shore and would have been forced into an amphibious assault against a defended beach. Because of the peculiar geography of the target area, the invasion had to be piecemeal,

as only a few Higgins landing craft could make it through the channels at a time. Even without enemy resistance, the 172nd had to struggle to get through to Zanana. Unfortunately, there was no other way
into Munda.

For the next two days, the remainder of the 169th and 172nd Infantry Regiments was transported to New Georgia and landed at
Zanana without incident. A third regiment, the 103rd, was held in
reserve on Rendova. Although his units were untested in battle, Maj.
Gen. John Hester, commander of their parent 43rd Infantry Division,
guessed that the operation should be over within two weeks.

By the time the last squad of troops landed on Zanana, there were
roughly six thousand others already on the island, scattered northward several hundred yards into the virgin jungle from the landing
site. However, their movement had created a quagmire that matched
the muddy hell on Rendova. Vehicles, tents, ammunition and ration
crates, radio equipment, diesel fuel, communications wire, and gear
of all sorts lay in the slime while shirtless, clay-encrusted soldiers
struggled to lift, push, and pull it with tractors.

Then more rain came. It mattered little to the men lying in their
flooded foxholes whether or not they wore their ponchos. Some
commanders ordered their mess sergeants to put together hot
meals for the men as soon as they landed and dug in a perimeter
defense. But the feeding itself became another misery. Some field
kitchens managed to assemble a meal under their kitchen tents in
the dank darkness and doled out dollops of steaming mashed potatoes, corn, or beans. The wet, sleepy soldiers squatted around the
bivouac area, searching for shelter from the slanting rain while they
tried to eat. It was no use. The rainwater sluiced into their mess kits,
creating an unappetizing slurry. Hunched low under their gleaming ponchos, they looked like members of an odd, hooded cult of
mystics lying prostrate in quiet prayer. Perhaps that was just what
they were doing.

Supporting them on New Georgia's barrier islets were an impressive five battalions of 105mm guns. These were ably assisted by
two batteries of the more powerful 155mm guns from the 9th Marine Defense Battalion, and two battalions of army 155s, both firing
from Rendova. This longer-range artillery was used against perma-

nent installations like those at Munda or to interdict shipping running across the Kula Gulf. The placement of the 105 batteries was
ideal: at right angles to the axis of advance to the airfield. Because
they were so close to Munda, they would be able to unleash a hellish hurricane of steel along the entire front as the infantry advanced
on the airstrip.

This firepower hardly comforted the green troops just landed on
the mysterious, rain-swept island, one of the world's last secret
places. At their backs, clothed in a monstrous belt of vapor, was the
sea. Just a few steps to their front was a powerful phalanx of dripping, forbidding trees, pressing them back toward the water, omi-
nously guarding the island's dark interior. Cramped on the narrow
beach between these two great forces of nature, they felt helpless.
The unfamiliar scent of rotting vegetation emanated from the jungle blended with the rain and sea spray to create an ugly, repellant
musk. Each man sensed that it was a place where they were not supposed to be, severed from all they knew and trapped in a vortex of
terror. Never before had they witnessed such a manifestation of the
forces of the universe. It anesthetized them. They passed a sleepless
night bailing water from their foxholes, fearing the darkness, wondering how they would react under fire, and pondering their in-
significance.

From an observation point on Kokengolo Hill just behind the battered airfield, fifty-year-old Maj. Gen. Minoru Sasaki calmly watched
the massive buildup on Rendova with a measure of admiration. His
adversary across the channel was sustained by a lifeline that strung
out less than two hundred miles to the southeast to Guadalcanal.
Rendova became an island fortress almost overnight, while he and
his men were forced to watch helplessly. The airstrip that they
guarded had no planes with which to strike back. They were without offensive capability. Sasaki's umbilical cord stretched much too
far—385 miles to Rabaul. Ships carrying supplies and reinforcements
were becoming more vulnerable to air and surface attacks. Because
of Allied air superiority, Rabaul was forced to end its practice of using destroyers to transport its troops and begin using barges, which
were more difficult to detect but much less efficient.

In a joint army-navy conference at Rabaul on 4 July, Admiral Kusaka was only partially successful in shifting attention to the central Solomons. General Imamura, the Eighth Area Army commander, agreed to send the three thousand troops remaining in the 13th and 229th Regiments' to rear-area echelons. This would enlarge Sasaki's command to two full regiments—not enough to regain control of the imperiled island, but enough perhaps to blunt the American offensive and grant Munda a stay of execution. There were to be a few new pawns on the board for Sasaki to use in defense of his castle. Three days later, after the U.S. offensive had begun, Kusaka, at the direction of his superiors, asked General Imamura for eleven thousand more troops with which to reinforce Sasaki. The move would allow him to mount an offensive against the Americans before they were able to introduce the entire U.S. 37th Infantry Division into the conflict. The navy was worried that its installations farther up the Solomons chain in Bougainville, the Shortland Islands, and particularly at Rabaul would be menaced. With Munda in Allied hands, their ships would be in real jeopardy. But Imamura refused the request. Fifty-three-year-old Admiral Kusaka found the refusal difficult to accept. He had hoped to retire after thirty-two years of service on his birthday, 7 December 1941, but was forced to change his plans. When asked after the war whether he planned another offensive after Munda fell, the aggressive Kusaka replied: "We were always planning an offensive until [our] planes [were withdrawn] for Truk.[65] It was painfully clear to him that the army was convinced both New Georgia and Bougainville were destined to fall to the Allies.[66] Imamura thus chose to focus on New Guinea, which he believed more crucial. After the war, Rear Admiral Samejima of the 8th Fleet laid blame for Munda's loss on the army, saying that "Because the defense of this area was the responsibility of the Navy, the Army was comparatively cool toward my request [for reinforcements], and the suspicion exists that reinforcements were late in coming because of this fact."[67]

As Sasaki gazed through his binoculars at the fresh troops crowding onto Rendova's beaches, it was becoming clear that his superiors were unwilling to commit the necessary force needed to repel the imminent assault. He may have wondered if this was to be another Guadalcanal, this time with the players' roles reversed. This time the Japanese held the ball and it was the Americans who were mounting an effort to grab it. He was sure that if he did not receive some help quickly, his two poorly supplied regiments could not hold out. As U.S. troops continued to pour into Rendova on a daily basis, he anxiously awaited orders from Rabaul indicating that his superiors were contemplating a countermove. However, the orders never came. Dropping the glass from his eyes he stared pensively across the channel and muttered in jealous tribute to his opponents' landings, "absolutely miraculous."[68]

4 Dragons Peninsula

Seven gray destroyer-transports ferrying the twenty-six hundred men of Col. Harry "the Horse" Liversedge's Northern Landing Group—composed of the 1st Marine Raider Battalion and two battalions from the army's 37th Infantry Division—groped their way through the darkness at about twenty knots on the night of 4–5 July 1943. The small task force was searching for a mysterious, dreary river that widened into Rice Anchorage, the planned debarkation point on New Georgia's frayed northwestern shore. Included in the force were twelve marines, all absent without leave (AWOL) from the hospital on Guadalcanal, who had stowed away on the transports, determined not to be left behind.[1]

Surface-sweep radar located the river's mouth through the thick curtain of rain that shielded it from searching eyes. Colonel Liversedge wasted no time unloading his mixed force of Raiders and soldiers into the Higgins boats hanging like dreary ornaments from the ships' davits. The men were understandably edgy as they descended into the blackness below. Because they were in enemy waters, there was fear that the APDs, dead in the water while disembarking the men, would be inviting targets. The skipper of the *Waters,* Lt. Comdr. J. C. McWhinnie, had developed a novel means of discharging the men while the ships were still underway. The Higgins boats were lowered only to deck level so that the troops could climb over the railing and board them. Then they were lowered into the water with their engines already running. The davit cables were then dropped, followed by the bow and stem lines, freeing the coxswains to swing away from the mother ship and head for shore.[2]

To hasten the landings, rubber dinghies carrying ten men were launched and hastily leashed to each of the Higgins boats, which then towed them for the final fifteen hundred yards to the anchorage. Using this expedient, the landing craft would have to make only one roundtrip. Once clear of open water, the boats had to travel another six hundred yards farther up the river that fed the still waters of the anchorage. The tiny river became congested with dozens of nearly blind, scurrying craft, awash in the chilling downpour while their jittery occupants whispered anxious prayers. The backwash from several of the speeding Higgins boats rippled under the dinghies tethered behind them, tossing several troops into the inky sea.[3]

This was no time to linger. Enemy 140mm shore guns firing from Enogai Inlet a few miles down the coast had discovered the destroyers and began lobbing heavy shells their way. The men on board the creeping, flat-bottomed landing craft could see little except for the bursts of occasional star shells, whose illumination momentarily managed to squeeze through the clogging rain shower, offering a brief glimpse down the darkened throat of the river that listlessly spilled before them into the gulf.

Captain Charles Henne of Ohio, a company commander with the 3rd Battalion, 148th Infantry, who was as new to combat as the men he led, expressed the views of most Americans who fought in the Pacific theater: "We had never seen a live Jap, and no one feared the Jap although the Jap had been hailed as a super jungle fighter. Listening to the war stories told us on Fiji, we had developed a nose for fiction, but never having met the Elephant, we were keeping quiet. We thought the Jap runty, slant-eyed, bandy-legged, and something less than human. We accepted without comment or discussion that they were dangerous, but they would have to prove they were better than we were."[4]

As the first gray light of dawn tinged the horizon it became much too dangerous for the stationary destroyers to continue unloading their cargo of men and equipment. Colonel Liversedge announced the code word *scram* over the radio, and the APDs pushed off, still carrying about 10 percent of the NLG's equipment on board. Among the items they hauled away with them was a high-powered radio that would be sorely missed later in the operation. The radio-telephone operators, who were Navajo Indians, would certainly have protested, but they were unaware of the oversight. (These "code talkers," as they came to be known, transmitted messages in their tribal tongue, making it impossible for the bilingual Japanese soldiers eavesdropping on their conversations to understand. The system worked beautifully for the marines throughout the Pacific war.) In their haste to weigh anchor, two army officers and sixty-four enlisted men waiting on deck in full battle gear for the order to go over the side were stranded aboard their transport. As the ship slowly pulled away in the dull light of dawn, their disappointed, guilty eyes searched for someone who could tell them why. But there was no one to whom they could complain. Their unit would have to make do without them.[5]

A warm rain fell as the first wave sprinted ashore, the men clutching their weapons, whose breeches were wrapped in oil-soaked rags to protect them from the torrential downpour. With room for only four boats at a time to nose up to the river's bank, a dangerous traffic jam soon developed. A string of landing craft and dinghies extending back into the anchorage sat idling in the darkness, waiting their turn to discharge their anxious cargoes while unseen Japanese gunners continued to lob high explosives into the water around them. The wait was a severe test for even the most rational. With each thundering boom of the guns, the men gripped their rifles tighter, squeezed their eyes shut, and prayed real prayers.

One coxswain was tailgating a dinghy a bit too closely and dumped the rubber boat's men into the choppy gulf. Not five minutes after they managed to climb back in, they were again thrown overboard by the same impatient pilot. Private Ashley Large, a normally imperturbable Tennessean, did not suffer the dunkings well. When he finally steadied himself in the dinghy for a second time, he angrily loaded and locked his carbine and pointed it at the coxswain behind him. "You do that again, my friend," he hollered, "and you're a dead man." The coxswain immediately backed off.[6]

Standing on the thin, two-hundred-yard-wide clearing on the river's south bank was Capt. Clay A. Boyd, another Raider with whom Liversedge had planned to rendezvous. Boyd and an Australian coastwatcher, Lt. J. A. Corrigan, aided by several native scouts, had been preparing the way for Liversedge for the past few weeks, cutting trails, studying the terrain, and reporting what he believed would be the most expeditious landing sites and routes of advance. Still, very little was known about the area, for the natives accompanying them were from another part of the island and feared the locals around Enogai. Nor did they have oblique-angle aerial photos of the area, which would have afforded them some hint of the tangle of jungle that would greet them shortly.

Boat by boat, the rain-soaked Raiders and GIs slipped onto the river's muddy bank, which Boyd had marked at intervals with flashlights. Beyond that, visibility was zero. Some of the landing craft were unable to reach shore, forcing the men inside to plunge into the river, hoping that their feet would hit bottom. Once ashore, everyone, including the officers, was ordered to haul the wooden crates of supplies and pieces of equipment that cluttered the riverbank into the jungle. Lieutenant James F. Regan, a navy surgeon, stumbled over a crate and bent to pick it up. As he struggled to lift it to his shoulder, he heard a voice in the darkness calling for him to follow. He approached the man and discovered it was one of his patients who had gone AWOL from the hospital. Regan said he was "loaded like a mule."[7]

The site became increasingly thick with confusion and disorganization. Men were roaming around looking for their platoons in the darkness and rain. Several simply gave up the search until daybreak. The force was supposed to move inland 150 yards and set up a defensive perimeter until morning, but a steep escarpment stopped them fifty yards short. Digging in was impossible; their entrenching tools could not penetrate the packed coral. There also was the cruel rain with which to contend. Henry Poppell and his communications section opted to find some shelter. The men were so tired after a night of stevedoring that they crawled under the beefy, lichen-covered roots of a banyan tree, pulled their helmets down over their faces, and tried to keep warm under their ponchos. Fortunately, the Japanese shore batteries were unable to find their exact location. Otherwise, there would certainly have been bloody chaos. About three hundred soldiers mistakenly landed at a point several thousand yards north of Rice Anchorage and had to find their way back to the main party the next day. Hundreds of others were separated from their units in the confusion and had to locate them at dawn. Despite these blunders, however, the only casualty was George McGraw, a Raider rifleman from Company C, who was missing from his first formation and presumed drowned.[8]

Harry Liversedge seemed like a good choice to lead the hazardous operation. Taciturn and tough but approachable, his trim, muscular, six-foot-two-inch frame had changed little since his days as an Olympic shot-putter at the University of California and as the fullback on the Marine Corps football squad. It was there that his great running ability earned him the nickname "the Horse." The colonel's easygoing, unflappable disposition and his jungle experience in the Central American "Banana Wars" would serve him well in the coming weeks.

His mission was to move eight miles south to Enogai Inlet and Bairoko Harbor and block the vital Bairoko-Munda Trail, isolating the two important enemy bases that received reinforcements and supplies from Vila and dispatched them to Sasaki and his defenders. In addition, he was ordered to clear the area of enemy forces at both locations (intelligence estimated there were about five hundred Japanese at Bairoko) and secure the uninhabited two-mile-wide Dragons Peninsula separating the outposts, thus shutting the back door to Munda. There must not be any more Guadalcanals. The original plan called for the Raiders to land somewhere along New Georgia's south shore and move overland to Bairoko. However, Clay Boyd and his recon team had convinced higher headquarters in a 19 July report that even if there were no enemy resistance, that route would take them at least a month to negotiate.[9] The decision was thus made to put Liversedge ashore at Rice Anchorage, much closer to the target villages. The raiding force would then follow three parallel trails that Clay Boyd's men had hacked out days before. Although this improved the entire scheme considerably, all concerned still greatly underestimated the malignant environment they were about to enter.

The selection of a Raider battalion to spearhead the operation was an indication of the dilemma facing Allied planners. It was imperative to press forward with the planned invasion without delay, but there was a shortage of troops trained for amphibious operations. Both the 1st and 2nd Marine Divisions were licking their wounds in Australia and New Zealand after Guadalcanal. The 3rd Marine Division, which had arrived in the Pacific in April, had not yet completed its six-month training program. There were army units available, but they were earmarked for the main assault on Munda, and their beach-assault training was limited. That left only the marine Raider battalions, which were designed for quick-strike raids rather than seizing and holding territory.

Sketchy reports to Liversedge indicated that the area to be penetrated was open jungle with overgrown hillocks and small creeks. That did not seem to be too bad—until they began their trek.[10] Leaving two companies of the 3rd Battalion, 145th Infantry, in place to guard their stockpiled food and supplies, they set out, hoping that the warrior gods ruling this chunk of wet-green, primordial wilderness would be kind to them. They would travel lightly; 60mm mortars would be their only artillery. There were heavier 81mm mortars with the army battalions, but they were being held at Rice until needed. Weapons platoons would be converted into rifle platoons to lighten the load, and they would carry only three days' worth of ammo and rations—mostly K-rations. Each unit packed about three thousand calories in a six-by-two-by-two-inch box weighing less than two pounds. (Troops preferred them to the bulkier C-rations, and the combustible waxed paper used to seal them could be torn into pieces and used for fires to warm the contents: beans and franks or some other "main dish." Also included were a chocolate bar, instant coffee, sugar, crackers, and four cigarettes.) The rest of their supplies, they were told, would be shuttled to them by eighty muscular natives whom Corrigan had employed for one Australian shilling, a twist of tobacco, and some rice and tea per day.[11]

Technical Sergeants Frank J. McDevitt and Murray Harder, two combat correspondents who had been newspapermen in Philadelphia before the war, accompanied Liversedge's force and described the first day's trek:

Despite the dense vegetation rain descended in torrents, and soon the jungle floor was a veritable sea of mud. Our march began in the rain and it ended in the rain. All day Monday we sloshed through muck and mire that was knee deep. We were covered from head to foot with mud. Huge fallen trees, slippery with their coats of slimy moss and mud, and the myriad roots of giant banyans which snaked across our paths, helped slow our progress. The farther we marched, the worse the terrain became. Sharp, coral-like rocks, thick, overhanging vines and creepers, and prickly plants that pierced our jungle suits, added their hazards. Overhanging branches knocked off our helmets and sometimes the rifles we carried over our shoulders.[12]

At 3:30 the men approached a river where the trail ended and made their first bivouac. In eight hours they had managed to cover only five miles through the thick jungle. After quickly establishing a perimeter defense, the men collapsed into their freshly dug foxholes, too exhausted even to yearn for home. Then it began to rain again, beating down hard, obscuring everything within all but a few yards of them. Huddled under their ponchos in a futile struggle to protect themselves and their weapons from the downpour, they gulped down cold K-ration crackers as the water rose in their holes. The rain mercifully stopped that night, and the heavy clouds began to break above them. Cloistered under the Southern Cross, they were serenaded by the clamor of naval gunfire from the battle of Kula Gulf in the distance.

Sergeant McDevitt's writing paper had long since succumbed to the weather, so he was forced to scribble his account of the operation on captured enemy stationery, weaving his sentences around Japanese characters printed on the face of the paper: "At dark when we bivouacked we laid our ponchos on the ground and made mattresses on the broad leaves cut from the trees. We built lean-tos for overhead shelter. Pests were a constant plague. Mosquitoes, ants, crabs, and lizards crawled all about us. Huge bats flew overhead. Mysterious birds sent weird screeches echoing through the night. Sleep was fitful. What we wanted was rest. We needed all our strength for the fighting we expected momentarily. Our progress was slow, but we had managed to creep into the enemy area."[13]

At dawn the men joylessly ate their morning rations and forded the hip-deep river. At least some of the mud encrusting their uniforms washed off, but a new layer quickly replaced the old as they slithered up the opposite bank. Two hours later, Liversedge directed Lt. Col. Delbert Schultz to take his 3rd Battalion, 148th Infantry, south to the Bairoko–Munda and Bairoko–Enogai trails and establish the block as planned. Sergeant Frank Guidone, a Raider who had helped cut trails through the island's hinterland prior to the invasion, was ordered to escort Schultz to a position near the junction of the two trails. Control of the junction would isolate Enogai, frustrating any enemy plans to reinforce the village from either Munda or Bairoko. Guidone remained with the soldiers for two days, enough time to develop strong opinions about them: "This was a very green Army unit and there were many problems such as random shooting at everything that moved. I really felt sorry for LTC Schultz. He was an elderly man and a reserve officer trying to cope with inexperienced troops and officers. Now that I look back, the road block did not need a battalion. I believe that Liversedge should have sent a Marine company to do the job. We were veterans of Tulagi and Guadalcanal, and so we knew a little about the Japanese and the jungle."[14]

Meanwhile, two treacherous swamps and two more raging rivers swollen by another rainstorm that day slowed Liversedge's main body to a crawl, the gluelike muck sucking hard at their boots. Lieutenant Colonel Samuel B. Griffith, commander of the 1st Raiders, guessed that they were only a quarter of a mile from higher ground as the crow flies. One frustrated and fatigued Raider nearby overheard him and remarked, "That may be Colonel, but we ain't crows!"[15]

The entire force of about twelve hundred men was strung out in a single line through the ghostly brew, grasping telephone wires as guidelines. Each man carried a pack weighing seventy-five or eighty pounds, and it was not uncommon to see one of the mud-wrapped men sink to his waist while stepping between the roots of a tree. He would then have to be pulled out by his comrades. Al Carega remembered how the jungle exhaled a "deadly, moldy, wet smell," adding that the water tasted the same way.[16] Equipment of all types—boots, weapons, rational thought—surrendered to the moisture. Radios were reduced to pieces of junk, and telephone wires grounded and failed. All communications between companies and battalions with regimental headquarters had to be accomplished by runners. In one such message, Lieutenant Colonel Griffith updated Liversedge as they crossed the swollen, nine-foot-deep Tamakau River: "Difficult and slow process, but we are making progress. Estimate I can have the battalion across by 1700, but not before things get any better. Native scouts report no Nips, repeat, no Nips."[17]

Griffith remembered it taking six and a half hours for the entire force to cross the Tamakau one man at a time over a single log: "Of course, many fell in. We had linked individual toggle ropes together and stretched them across the river along the log to provide a hand line, and while the line generally expedited the crossing, it was responsible for many 'mass' immersions, when it suddenly snapped. During this crossing, Lieutenant Frank Kemp, Sergeant Simonich, and Sergeant Walsh distinguished themselves by pulling out of the river eleven men who had slipped from the log and who would have inevitably drowned had it not been for the quick action of this life-saving detail."[18]

Equipment that was too heavy to carry or too valuable to lose was floated across on rafts constructed from ponchos and branches, consuming even more valuable time. By the end of the day they were only eight hundred yards closer to the inlet.

"We stumble through swamps all day," McDevitt and Harder recorded as they struggled to keep up. "The communications men, with their heavy radio and telephone gear, are slowed to a crawl. It is raining again. We haven't washed or removed our clothes since we started. We just plod along quietly, dragging one foot after another, covered with mud and soaking in sweat."[19]

There was no choice except to bivouac in the cursed biosphere itself that night, the residence of the giant monitor lizards or "dragons" after which the peninsula was named. Grotesquely contorted banyan roots, sheathed with clammy mold, protruded from the inky sludge. Nothing moved and everything moved. Matter mutated. As the troops gathered in the rain under their ponchos, trapped in the crucible of swill that engulfed them, they wondered if fighting the Japanese could be any worse.

After getting practically no sleep, the soggy men readied themselves the next morning. It was 7 July, the date scheduled for the assault on Enogai—but that plan had been made days before in a dry tent and clean uniform, a universe away from Dragons Peninsula. Three hours later they still had not traversed the relentless bog.[20] Sergeant Guidone was in the command post area while troops were passing the colonel, who silently examined each man as he slogged by. According to Guidone: "Liversedge said to Griffith: 'Sam, look at these troops! We will never be able to fight when we get to the target area.' Sam said, 'Colonel, I have seen these men in worse condition, and when their point was hit on, they responded like fighting marines. And they will do it again and again.'"[21]

The filthy swamp finally expelled the mud-covered troops at about 11 A.M. As they emerged from the clammy fog, they found themselves under a gunmetal gray sky with Enogai Inlet just ahead. Still following their native guides, the procession clung to a trail that led to a tiny hamlet named Triri, less than two thousand yards from the objective. En route they surprised a small party of Japanese, killing two of them. Soon afterward, the column ran into a company of Japanese moving toward it on the same trail. Lieutenant Colonel Griffith quickly ordered two of his companies forward to establish a base of fire while he sent Captain Boyd's company up a steep ridge west of the enemy position in a flanking maneuver. Boyd's men then ran shrieking down the slope, spraying the surprised Japanese with gunfire and driving them back toward Enogai.

Ten of the enemy died, and Griffith lost three killed and four wounded. All seven Raider casualties were recovered and brought into Triri, where Liversedge established a primitive headquarters. A makeshift grass shack served as a hospital where three doctors attended to the wounded.

Regan then turned to a young marine who had been shot through the hand. The man was sobbing hysterically, and Regan chided him a bit for his antics. The Raider screamed back that he was not crying, but that he was "just so damned mad! Get me out of here!" Regan dressed the man's wound and ordered him to sit and rest, but when he turned to look again, the Raider had left to go back to his platoon.[22]

To defend their first captured village and the task force's new command post, Maj. Marvin Girardeau created a protective screen with men from the 3rd Battalion, 145th Infantry. One night, as he walked to a stream near the perimeter's edge to fill his canteen, he almost stumbled over a six-foot-long lizard feeding on hundreds of maggots that were crawling all over the rotting, bloated body of a Japanese soldier. It was a disgusting sight, but Girardeau took it in stride: "I became accustomed to the sight of these giant lizards, which gave one the eerie sensation of living in a prehistoric era. A number of nights the same lizard, or one of the same size, would pass within a couple of yards of me and climb up to his nesting place, about ten feet off the ground, in the tangle of buttress-like roots of a huge banyan tree."[23]

Liversedge decided to use Triri as his base of operations, so he ordered Girardeau and his men to stand guard while he sent the 1st Raiders ahead to assault Enogai. It marked the third time since the landing that the task force commander had split his forces. None of the four groups—at Rice Anchorage, the trail block, Triri, or the Raiders en route to Enogai—was near enough to support any of the others immediately. Even if they had been, radio communication was unreliable, no artillery support was available, and food and water supplies were dangerously low. Morale in the ranks continued to be good, however. If they could just seize Enogai quickly, its location on the coast would allow for easier resupply and reinforcement before the attack on the garrison at Bairoko.

The Capture of Enogai

A quick victory would not come easily, though, for the enemy at Enogai had been alerted to the presence of the Americans. Two more battles flared the next day during the Raiders' approach to the coastal village, one a three-hour-long ordeal that involved a furious exchange of mortar and automatic-weapons fire just beyond Triri. First Lieutenant Joseph Broderick of Monmouth, New Jersey, whose platoon had infiltrated the Japanese perimeter and jumped the shocked defenders, said his men "yelled and screamed like a bunch of banshees. We made so much noise they couldn't hear their commands. Without one to tell them what to do, the Jap is helpless."[24]

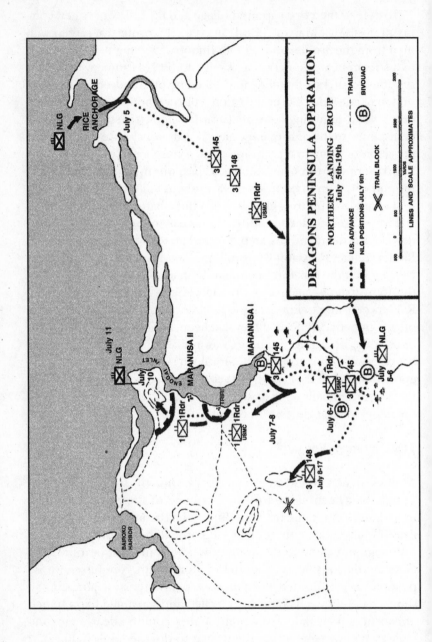

Several enemy soldiers returned the favor by shouting commands in English, but that only gave away their positions. One even stood up in his foxhole and yelled, "Come down and get me, you souvenir-hunting bastards!" He was shot dead. When they searched his body, they found a University of Washington class ring on his finger.[25] Fifty of his comrades died with him. Three marines were killed and several more were wounded. Although Liversedge still was unsure how many of the enemy faced him, the noose around Enogai's neck was tightening.

The real problem now was food. The three days' worth of rations they had packed for the mission had lasted them five days, but now they were gone. Schultz's battalion back at the trail block was in exactly the same predicament. The men were reduced to foraging in their bleak environment or scouring the bodies of dead Japanese for rice balls or anything else edible. The little that was found was distributed to the wounded. Their only source of fresh water was rainfall collected in ponchos. Poor radio communications compounded the problem. More often than not they were unable to reach higher headquarters, located just twenty miles away, with the poor equipment on hand. Liversedge had requested a parachute food drop on his headquarters and a preparatory air strike on Enogai, but there was no assurance that he had been heard. Messages were sent with the hope that a nearby station would intercept the transmission and relay it up the chain of command. It was in this debilitated, unendurable condition that the parched Raiders prepared themselves for combat the next morning.

The men of the 1st Raider Battalion arose at first light on 9 July, their bodies protesting the prospect of another day of madness. Their motivation to fight and capture Enogai was fueled by the hope that they would find food, and their steps quickened as they approached the village.

At 9 A.M. Japanese defenders scrambled frantically to their bunkers as the *whooomph, whooomph, whooomph* of Allied bombs shattered the stillness. Liversedge's request for an air strike had gotten through. The sound of the explosions worked like an elixir for the wilted troops, the sudden rush dulling the savage hunger that clawed inside them. Even in this weakened condition they were at their very best, their hyper-acute senses made raw by seven days of hell on the island.

Shortly after the air strike lifted, Sam Griffith's men reached enemy outposts scattered around Enogai and shoved them eighteen hundred yards back up a ridge despite an incessant fusillade of machine-gun and rifle fire. The advancing marines took one prisoner: a young runner carrying a message from Enogai to Bairoko. It turned out the Japanese radios worked no better than the Allied variety in the jungle, forcing the enemy to rely on physical communication, too. The prisoner resisted violently, however, and refused to cooperate, so he was dragged into the bush and stabbed to death.[26] At 5:30, with night fast approaching, Griffith halted the advance and they dug in for the night, ringing the area with riflemen, machine guns, and mortar crews. They would wait until morning to move into Enogai.

That night, one of Regan's corpsmen crept up to him shivering violently, his teeth chattering so much that he was hardly able to talk. It seemed like the man was having a bad malaria attack, but the young marine whispered: "It ain't fever, Doc. I'm—I'm scared. I'm scared as hell. Am I different from the other guys, Doc?" Regan assured him that every man there was as terrified as he was. The next day the man performed his duties well.[27]

The haggard, hungry marines attempted to sleep in the vast, forested stillness. It seemed much quieter that night than it had been. Perhaps it was their exhaustion. Perhaps the jungle creatures, sensing the morrow's fight, crept more softly out of respect for their human companions. Suddenly a loud *CRRRAAAACK* shattered the tranquility. An immense limb, partially severed from one of the massive banyan trees, fell directly on top of unsuspecting Sgt. Joseph A. Szakovics and several others who lay nearby. The limb had probably been hit by fragments from the bombs dropped that morning and, since then, had been hanging precariously high above the jungle floor. Szakovics was crushed to death by the enormous weight of the limb, and three others were injured in the mishap. The battalion's best radio was also destroyed.[28]

Sergeant Szakovics's death brought to ten the number of Raiders lost in the past twenty-four hours. The deaths were in addition to several more wounded, including Pfc. Thomas F. Powers, who was missing after his patrol ran into a squad of Japanese riflemen earlier in the day. An intense firefight erupted, and ten Japanese were killed. However, Powers lost contact with the rest of his patrol in the chaos. After his comrades unsuccessfully searched the area, they concluded that he was either dead or captured. But Powers was neither. While probing through the jungle in search of his patrol, he stumbled upon two enemy soldiers and emptied the eight-round clip in his M1, killing them both—but not before catching a .25-caliber slug in his abdomen. He spent a painful, lonely night hidden in the dank undergrowth, wondering if it was to be his fate to bleed to death undiscovered. If that was the case, he at least wanted his buddies to know that he had taken two Japanese with him. He also wanted his family to know that he died as a marine. Powers was reunited with his unit during the final drive on Enogai, still ready to die like a marine.[29] However, he never was able to lose his new nickname: "Jinx."

At 7 A.M. on 10 July, three companies of gaunt-faced marines emerged from their jungle den about eight hundred yards from the enemy village and began to surge forward abreast, raking the area with vicious mortar and small-arms fire. The Japanese were waiting and responded with a barrage of mortars and automatic weapons, hoping to turn back the assailants. After two hours, Company B penetrated the defensive line in its sector, and 1st. Lt. Thomas Pollard's reserve platoon was ordered forward to exploit the gain. A flock of mortar shells screamed into the perimeter, driving more of the defenders from their machine-gun positions. Pollard's men followed the barrage, tearing recklessly through the enemy defenses in a mad lunge down the slope, yelling and firing like Japanese conducting a banzai charge. Pollard's aggressive assault totally unhinged the enemy's defense. Recalling the episode later, the lieutenant explained his platoon's success: "That stunt is just as hair-raising to them as it first was to us. The Japs were paralyzed with fright."[30]

Swarming marines seized the abandoned weapons, barrels still smoking, and turned them on their former owners. Some of the desperate Japanese tried to escape by swimming to safety across a lagoon near Enogai Point. However, a number of unrepentant marines led by GySgt. Michael Sosnowski gunned them down, tarnishing the lagoon's pristine beauty. So cut off from their former world, so estranged from civilization were they, that they performed their gruesome chore with stony delight, firing into the backs of the fleeing, terrorized enemy soldiers as they flailed wildly in the water until there were forty-five floating corpses. Much of the damage was caused by Sergeant Sosnowski's machine gun. Frank Guidone later said Sosnowski "played the machine gun like Heifetz played the Stradavarius."[31]

Liversedge and Griffith both narrowly escaped being killed when they stumbled into the line of fire of a well-hidden machine-gun nest covered by snipers. Liversedge, always unflappable, continued to survey the battle before him while Griffith insisted that he drop to the ground. He finally complied, but not before making a quick estimate of the situation.

By midafternoon the marines were in control of the outpost and its four intact 140mm guns, which had fired at them when they first entered Rice Anchorage six days before. The guns' breechblocks had been removed and hidden, but they were soon uncovered and replaced. Once a perimeter had been established, Griffith permitted small parties to search for food. Amidst the human debris and wrecked shelters, they collected large supplies of canned fish, rice, soy sauce, and even sake. It was their first taste of food in thirty hours. Some Raiders discarded their tattered uniform blouses and replaced them with cleaner ones taken from the Japanese. An hour later there was more relief. A carrying party arrived bearing K-rations, water, and ammo that had been parachute-dropped earlier the previous evening near Triri. It was the first of twenty airdrops on Dragons Peninsula for the victorious NLG.

The Raiders' losses were high: 59 dead and 91 wounded. The enemy, however, lost anywhere from 150 to 350 men—the entire contingent of defenders. Most of them were members of the 6th Kure SNLF. There were no reports of prisoners. Liversedge's three surgeons and twenty-three corpsmen went to work administering morphine and plasma, retrieving lead, setting bones, and patching up ninety-one torn bodies. One marine's hand was blown to pieces. A Japanese grenade had flopped near where he was crouching, and he had attempted to scoop it up and throw it back. It exploded just as he released it. He sauntered into the makeshift aid station and asked politely: "Can you fix me up, Doc?" It was as though all he needed was a Band-Aid for a scratch. While Dr. Regan worked on him, he joked: "I guess I'll get me a tin can and some pencils."[32]

On a nearby stretcher lay Cpl. William Cain, one of the most popular men in the battalion. He was delirious and mortally wounded. "Just before we left our training base, he learned he was a new father," recalled Dr. Regan. "He had been excited and deeply moved. Now, in his delirium, it is the one thing on his mind. Some men die quickly, but Cain fights furiously for his life. He shouts over and over, 'I don't want to die! I want to see my baby!' Morphine had little effect. His WILL keeps him alive. Men crowd around the doorway. 'Hey, Doc! Can I help? Hey, Doc! Need some blood, huh? I got plenty.'" Although they did all they could for him, Cain died that night, "screaming defiance to his last, sobbing breath."[33]

That evening, Colonel Liversedge reestablished his headquarters at Enogai and looked forward to a much-deserved respite from combat. He radioed news of the victory and requested air evacuation for his wounded, food, and supplies. The next morning, however, an hour-long bombing raid reminded them all that the war was far from over. Three more marines were killed, bringing to fifty-four the number of deaths during the week-long campaign to seize Enogai. Patrols orbiting their new perimeter encountered only occasional resistance from a handful of Japanese survivors who had scattered and hidden in the bush. In one such brush with the enemy, a squad of GIs opened up on a small group of shrieking, suicidal enemy soldiers who charged at them with bayonets. A withering blast from a BAR cut them down; only three escaped. The Americans gave chase, later killing two and capturing the third, Tatsuo Miyantani, who they found asleep wrapped in a GI shelter half and suffering from wounds to his cheek and shoulder. Caught by surprise, he had no chance to resist and was taken back to Enogai. Miyantani, a former fisherman, had been assigned to the 13th Infantry, the "Pride of south Japan." He was typical of the type of man who filled the ranks of the Imperial Army: hungry for combat, poorly educated (he had only six years of formal schooling), and very tough. Members of his unit often settled their arguments with knives. If they found themselves low on ammunition, they were trained to fix bayonets and charge.[34] It is no wonder the Japanese inflicted so many casualties despite their manpower and materiel inferiority.

At 5:25 the next afternoon, three PBY Catalinas landed in the inlet and began loading the most serious of the eighty-nine surviving wounded, who were slowly being shuttled to the planes on rubber boats. Before the job was completed, however, the rescue mission's fighter cover ran low on fuel and flew home, leaving the PBYs like fat ducks on a pond. It did not take long for the Japanese to jump them. Within a few, short minutes, the marines heard the low drone of two approaching enemy floatplanes, so Liversedge stopped the ferrying operation and ordered everyone to man their weapons. The enemy aircraft made a strafing pass at about two hundred feet, each dropping the one bomb that it carried. One of them exploded just thirty feet from the bow of one of the PBYs, wounding the pilot and shredding its wings and fuselage with fragments.

A Raider who had been standing nude in the shallow water helping to push a PBY off of the coral reef on which it rested while the cabin was being loaded, vanished when the bomb detonated. It was not until several days later that the unit received word from Guadalcanal that he had survived. The explosion had blown him into the plane's cabin, and the stunned marine made the trip with the others, unhurt but still naked.[35]

The PBYs themselves were almost defenseless. One of their two .50-caliber waist guns had been dismounted to provide more room for the wounded. Hurriedly, the crews, with the help of some of the wounded Raiders already aboard, worked to reposition the weapons before the next run. Meanwhile, the others back on shore responded by firing a furious barrage at the lumbering, low-flying aircraft. Undaunted, the enemy pilots circled and returned to deliver another punch, albeit at a higher altitude. But the defenders' fire was beginning to find its mark. After making a third pass, the two planes finally disappeared, no longer willing to risk being shot down by small-arms fire. They left several more wounded, however, including two of the PBY pilots. The evacuation resumed anyway, and before dark the air ambulances lifted off and ferried their precious cargo to the safety of a rear-area hospital.[36]

Alongside the wounded on one of the PBYs was Liversedge's communications officer, Maj. Bill Stevenson. He was sent to personally report the mission's status to Admiral Turner. In his two-hour meeting with the amphibious force commander, Stevenson outlined to Turner the enormous supply and communications problems facing the men on Dragons Peninsula and received a promise that both areas would be immediately addressed. Most importantly, Turner acceded to Liversedge's request for the 4th Raider Battalion—which was recuperating on Guadalcanal—to bolster the NLG for its upcoming attack on Bairoko.

Enogai may have appeared to be a relatively small victory for the Raiders, but its capture was quite significant. The Japanese had intended for their four 140mm guns to help maintain control over Kula Gulf. Now, however, navy PT boats and destroyers could operate more freely in their effort to interdict the Tokyo Express's reinforcement and resupply runs from Kolombangara to New Georgia. More immediately, the village served as a staging area for Liversedge's planned attack on Bairoko, the stronger of the two Japanese garrisons on the godforsaken peninsula. There was precious little time to enjoy the victory, however.

Inside his little hooch on the edge of the hamlet, less than ten hours after his Raiders had liberated Enogai, Liversedge joined an informal huddle with his staff around his rain-stained map. The colonel allowed the crusty combatants a few minutes to relax before he spoke. He enjoyed listening. Cigarette smoke swirled lazily about as they squatted on their steel helmets in a tiny circle, chatting as marines always do about their last victory. But there was no revelry, no laughter. Just an unspoken, mutual veneration, the quiet chemistry that binds all fighting men after their noses have been bloodied in combat and they know that they performed well.

The commander sensed when it was time to refocus and redirected their attention to the map. After a few words he slowly dragged his forefinger across the paper, following a pair of broken parallel lines that led southwest toward Kula Gulf and a cluster of tiny, black squares labeled "Bairoko."

At the same moment the marines were moving on Enogai, Lieutenant Colonel Schultz and his 738 men at the trail block had their own concerns. A small Japanese patrol had discovered their presence on the morning of the eighth, and the men of the 148th Infantry, occupying dug-in positions on a tadpole-shaped ridge overlooking the narrow trail, were expecting an attack. The enemy advance, however, was hardly characterized by stealth or crafty tactics. Well before they came into view, they could be heard noisily wandering down the trail. When they finally did appear, the soldiers had their rifles slung casually over their shoulders as though the trail were secure. Schultz's machine gunners were ready. They had twisted and stretched their canvas ammo belts to ensure flexibility and checked the alignment of the bullets so there would be no feeding problems once the fight began. Mortar crews could not lay their rounds on the ground because of the moisture, so they had untaped the packing tubes and loosened the caps so the shells could quickly be removed. Riflemen and automatic riflemen had prepared their two-man slit trenches by stacking extra ammo magazines and loose grenades on the ledges of their holes for easy access. The Japanese were strolling into the teeth of an ambush.

When about a dozen enemy soldiers came into view, the riflemen manning the forward outpost opened fire. The survivors of this initial barrage rapidly scattered into the bush, leaving a handful of dead and wounded on the trail. No one attempted to rescue the wounded or recover bodies. Perhaps nothing more distinguished the Allied forces from their adversaries in combat. An American knew that he would never be abandoned, even under the most difficult situations. Decorations for bravery were awarded to Allied troops for rescuing wounded buddies under fire perhaps more often than for any other action in the war. Risking one's life for another was a huge part of the ethos of the American infantryman.

The GIs manning the outpost pulled back to the main defensive line while Pvt. William Kuckne of Company I covered their withdrawal. When Kuckne ran out of ammo and stopped firing, four screaming Japanese charged him with bayonets. He held his ground, however, flailing at them with his rifle until they savagely stabbed him to death.[37] He was the battalion's first casualty of the war.

The men on the ridge now knew for certain that a general assault would soon follow. It came forty minutes later. But again the enemy troops were surprisingly clumsy, shouting to each other in loud tirades and stumbling noisily through the heavy underbrush as they staged for the attack. Then, said Captain Henne, "The yelling and shouting stopped, and out of the quiet came the shout of a Jap, probably an officer. He had their attention. The Jap shouted a lengthy harangue that meant nothing to us. When he finished, the Japs started to advance again, but only for a few minutes and then quiet. This quiet was broken again by the same Jap. This time he shouted, *'Tetsugi Banzai!'* Then a hundred voices shouted, *'Tetsugi Banzai!'* As they yelled, they charged."[38]

A heavy pall of fear descended on the Americans. The dug-in defenders grasped their rifles and stared anxiously ahead, trying to guess where the howling enemy would appear. When they finally did, jungle creepers, groundcover, trees, and other obstacles had forced them into dangerous, clustered groups, bumping and shoving at one another as they labored to regroup in an orderly formation. Then, brandishing their bayoneted rifles, they charged the ridge. Machine guns rattled, grenades exploded, and M1s spit out round after round into the disorganized assailants.

"When the leading ranks were shot down in a heap," recalled Captain Henne, "those following faltered, slowed, and then turned and ran. When they disappeared from sight, the sound of their running was dampened by the bush, and then the jungle became very quiet. On our side it was quiet for a while, and then our men couldn't hold back. They shouted and cheered."[39]

An hour elapsed before the enemy reappeared, this time sent running by a short but effective barrage that pounded them before they were able to mount another assault. Another hour went by. Soon, thick darkness would engulf them. Once again the enemy came, in much the same insane fashion as before—and with much the same result. Seven Japanese were killed and roughly twenty wounded. Schultz lost four more men. As the sun dipped behind the treetops, shadows fell reverently across the torn corpses of the enemy, slowly covering them like death shrouds.

That night, dozens of the cursed island's immense lizards came forth from their moldy lairs to nibble on the bloating bodies.[40] The noisy creatures spooked the Americans, who instantly assumed that the rustling movement was the prelude for a night attack. There was nothing to fear from the hissing reptiles, for they frightened easily.

However, after the screaming assaults of the day, the sound of them feeding on human remains in the darkness of their jungle tomb produced macabre illusions. The enemy chose not to probe the perimeter that night, but there was one curious exchange. In the middle of the night, an English-speaking Japanese soldier called out: "Hey, Marine. Where are you? What is your company?" A machine gunner answered him with a long burst. Then someone screamed from a foxhole: "Hirohito, eat shit!"[41] The machine gunner's response was a clear violation of orders stipulating that absolutely no weapons were to be fired unless there was a general raid on the camp. This was because the muzzle flash would give away the position of the defenses. Men were told to use grenades if they sensed there was an enemy intruder approaching. Reprimands were handed out the next morning.

At noon on the tenth, the marauders attempted to storm the ridge for a fourth time—and for a fourth time they were hit hard and fell back, losing fourteen men in the process. Again they trumpeted their move with noisy yelling and again they were bunched together when they materialized from the jungle. It was a strategy that they seemed to cling to despite its lack of success. An hour later, however, their fortune turned. They came with brash inconsequence but without the loud fanfare, targeting a junction between two GI platoons. An estimated two-company force plunged ahead so aggressively that one of the platoon leaders pulled back to escape the murderous gunfire. A squad from his platoon followed him to the rear, allowing the Japanese to move ahead and occupy a finger on the ridge leading into the center of the battalion's position. The enemy dug in and beat back an ill-conceived counterattack that lacked mortar and machine-gun support. Night came with the Japanese still in control of their little salient. Fortunately they had no stomach for a deeper penetration. The enemy abandoned the position early on the eleventh and continued on to Munda.

Twenty-eight wounded Americans, some of whom had been hit five days before, were evacuated to Enogai by native carriers. Captain Ben Ferischel, the battalion surgeon, was short on supplies and relied on jungle medicine to save lives. Not too proud to realize he needed help, he enlisted the aid of native medicine men who suggested applying maggots to the wounds. The maggots, although disgusting to look at, ate infection-causing bacteria. More than a few soldiers had Captain Ferischel to thank for his open-mindedness.[42]

At this point, their own food situation was critical. Lieutenant Colonel Schultz ordered rations to be reduced to one-ninth of a D-bar—a hard chocolate bar specially designed for use in the tropics that the troops disliked but which tasted much better the hungrier they got—and one-ninth of a K-ration per man. Like Griffith's Raiders, they had left Rice Anchorage a week before with just three days' worth of rations, assured by their superiors that Enogai would be secure in two days. A fair amount of raw, still-hulled rice was lifted from the enemy bodies that lay scattered around their position, but they were not sure how to cook it. When hunger got the better of them, they built a tripod, suspended a helmet over a fire, and tried to boil it, hulls and all. The result was an inedible, glutinous paste. They tried adding salt tablets and even threw in a few D-bars. Nothing worked, so they dumped the noxious mixture.[43] The troops began harvesting palmetto hearts to supplement their meager meals, sometimes mixing them into a soup made from canned corned beef hash. The broth was then thinned until there was enough to feed ten men. Native carriers brought them a small supply of D-rations overland from Rice Anchorage during that period, but it was insufficient. The same aircraft that made the parachute drop that replenishing Triri on the tenth had trouble spotting Schultz's smoke grenades in the thick jungle canopy and badly missed the mark. Three supply bundles were recovered, but they contained primarily mortar ammunition. The remaining supplies fell into Japanese hands. Consequently, Schultz was forced to cut rations again, this time to a twelfth of a K-ration per man. The men resorted to chain-smoking to help mask their hunger. Smoking was forbidden at night, however, and it was then that it really gnawed at them. Finally, on the twelfth, three hundred pounds of rice arrived from Triri by native carriers. The half-starved men boiled it in their helmets and feasted on the simple food.[44]

Despite the heavy pressure being placed on Munda by mid-July, the battalion had not seen any sign of troop movements since its 10–11 July encounter. Colonel Liversedge, convinced that enemy reinforcements should have been heading from Bairoko to Munda by then, visited Schultz to discuss the situation. After spending a day there, he decided that the blocking position was useless and ordered the battalion back to Triri on the seventeenth for a short recovery.[45] The men surely needed it. Trapped for two weeks in their putrefied environment without a change of clothes or a bath, they were debilitated from malaria, malnutrition, and severe diarrhea. Consequently, only about half of them were combat-ready.

The weary soldiers buried thirteen of their own before leaving. The effort was hardly worth it. When the battalion first reached the trail, it was immediately clear it had not been used much. It was not the major resupply route to Munda that the intelligence officers had proclaimed it to be.[46] Records show that General Sasaki brought in thirteen hundred reinforcements from Bairoko on 13 July by simply moving them over a more obscure route.[47] The new troops were intended to bolster the force preparing to assault the 43rd Division's unprotected right flank. If the bold stroke was successful, Munda could be rescued from its stranglehold.

The Naval Battle of Kolombangara

On the afternoon of 12 July, Admiral Halsey's message center received word of a rather large squadron of enemy ships speeding southeast down the Slot from Rabaul. The light cruiser *Jintsu* and five destroyers were shepherding four destroyer-transports to Vila with more troops from the 13th Infantry Regiment. Admiral Ainsworth was immediately ordered to intercept. It was only a week after the Kula Gulf battle, and two hundred members of the *Helena's* crew were still missing. Their welfare was foremost in Ainsworth's mind when he climbed back aboard the light cruiser *Honolulu* to ready his force for what would be his fifteenth combat mission in the Slot. Ten destroyers and two other cruisers would sail with him, including the H.M.N.Z.S. *Leander*, which was replacing the *Helena* and the *St. Louis*. All were looking to avenge the loss of the *Helena* and its crew.

They departed from Tulagi at 5 P.M. as a tepid breeze, absent all day, kicked up from the west. By the time the ships approached the coast of Santa Isabel under the protection of planes from the Russells, a creamy quarter moon faded in and out between scudding clouds. Midnight found the squadron cutting across the Slot toward Kolombangara's northern coast when Ainsworth received word that a PBY Black Cat reconnaissance flight had spotted six enemy ships about twenty-six miles ahead. That report was followed thirty minutes later by a radar contact at fifteen miles. Hearts raced as Ainsworth increased his task force's speed to twenty-eight knots while slowly forming his twelve ships into a battle column.

Kolombangara's distant volcanic peak was visible in the distance when, at 1:09 A.M., Ainsworth, certain he had gotten the jump on the enemy, gave the order to fire torpedoes at a range of ten thousand yards. Unfortunately, the Japanese, using a new radar detection device, were able to trace the U.S. squadron's radar signals, allowing them to plot the bearing of his unsuspecting flotilla. *Jintsu* was ready and responded with gunfire and torpedoes while illuminating the lead American ships with its searchlights for the destroyers. Ainsworth's three cruisers responded with salvos from their own six-inch batteries as soon as they were within range. *Honolulu*'s rounds fell short, but a correction from a Black Cat spotter plane circling above remedied the error. Shellfire soon enveloped the Japanese cruiser and it exploded amidships. The three U.S. cruisers pumped out 2,630 rounds and scored ten more hits.[48] Okinawan Isamu Toyoda was at his station in the message center when he was almost thrown from his chair by an explosion on the port side.[49] A torpedo from one of the destroyers had struck the ship in its engine room. It was followed by a second torpedo just moments later. That about did it for the *Jintsu*. The ship cracked in two, the fragments burning like a pair of giant signal flares in the darkness. Other than Seaman Toyoda and a few of his mates, there were virtually no survivors from the 482-man crew. Among those lost was RAdm. Shunji Izaki, the second Japanese admiral to be lost with his flagship that week.

While Ainsworth's crews were watching the spectacle of the *Jintsu*'s destruction, a Japanese torpedo slammed into the *Leander* while it was executing a course change, killing twenty-eight crewmen and forcing the New Zealand cruiser to the sidelines.

The four Japanese transports managed to make it to Kolombangara's east coast, where they successfully discharged their troops. The enemys five destroyers turned and ran, drawing Ainsworth after them. Radar picked up two of the ships, but the admiral was unable to determine if they were ships he had sent ahead earlier or the enemy's. He held his fire until their movements convinced him that they were Japanese. That delay was crucial, for just after he gave the order to commence firing, a long-lance torpedo crashed into the *St. Louis,* just aft of the *Honolulu,* as it was turning into position to fire. The entire bow below the third deck was ripped away and seawater began to rush into the stricken ship's hull, braking its speed to eight knots. More of the deadly torpedoes flashed by the admiral's flagship, which adroitly danced its way through a swarm of four or five. The destroyer *Gwin,* steaming ahead of *Honolulu,* was not as lucky. It caught one amidships, violently exploding before Ainsworth's eyes at 2:14. Not long afterward, a third torpedo found the *Honolulu,* just nipping the tip of its bow. The *Gwin* could not be saved, despite a Herculean effort to keep it afloat.[50] The destroyer was scuttled later that morning with two officers and fifty-nine enlisted men somewhere in its twisted wreckage. Meanwhile, the three cruisers managed to limp back to Guadalcanal, arriving late in the afternoon on the thirteenth under the cover of fighters from the Russells. When they reached their anchorage at Tulagi, Ainsworth's squadron was greeted by cheering sailors. When the admiral appeared, the Marine Corps band struck up "Anchors Aweigh." The reception apparently was arranged after the base received erroneous reports that Ainsworth's ships had sunk five enemy ships rather than one.[51]

It was an expensive battle for the Allies. In addition to losing a destroyer, the two American cruisers were absent from the fleet until November, and the *Leander* was out of action for a year. Nevertheless, it was a milestone in the slugfest for control of the Slot. It was the last time the Tokyo Express operated there. The operation had become too costly for the Japanese. Piecemeal efforts to build up New Georgia's troop strength would continue between Vila and Bairoko by barge. Thereafter, however, all major reinforcement and resupply efforts would be managed by a much longer route along the west coast of Vella Lavella to Arundel's western shore, where troops still faced a protracted march across that island before reaching New Georgia. In the aftermath of the naval battle of Kolombangara, the Imperial Fleet conceded Kula Gulf to Bull Halsey and the Allied navy. Admiral Samejima, commander of the Eighth Fleet, admitted as much in 1946, blaming a lack of air support and the interception of radio transmissions for "an extremely difficult time."[52]

After Kolombangara, both navies retired to their corners. Yet neither opponent was ready to quit the fight. Even though it appeared that the two enemies were just trading punches, the Americans were getting stronger just as their adversary's knees began to wobble noticeably. Admiral Kusaka's naval forces simply could not stand toe to toe with the Americans over the long haul, even though they were fighting with skill and heroism.

With Enogai in American hands, Rice Anchorage lost its importance. On 12 July, Colonel Liversedge ordered virtually all of the men and supplies there, including the army's 81mm mortar crews, to augment his own forces before the move on Bairoko. Lieutenant Colonel George Freer, who commanded the 3rd Battalion, 145th Infantry, jumped into a Higgins boat at 4:30 P.M. and led ten others down the coast toward Enogai Inlet. Freer's boat was far ahead, circling in Kula Gulf near the coast awaiting the others when it was surprised by two Zeros. The enemy planes made a few passes and heckled the boat for a quarter of an hour, then sped off without firing a shot. However, in his attempt to elude the planes, Freer's coxswain moved farther into the gulf and became disoriented. Several miles out in open water, they made their way east toward the ragged shoreline, hoping to find the inlet. They finally spotted an opening that looked to be Enogai according to the map the navy lieutenant on board was clutching. He directed the pilot to head for it. Freer, however, was not convinced they were where they were supposed to be, so they checked out the harbor carefully as they motored into it at twilight. With his anxiety level growing by the minute, Freer suddenly ordered the coxswain to turn around and head back into the gulf. As they headed back out to sea, they came upon a large group of about twenty Japanese barges crammed with soldiers moving rapidly into the harbor. They were carrying men from the 13th Infantry sent from Kolombangara to reinforce General Sasaki at Munda. The barges were just fifty or sixty yards off their port bow. The sighting confirmed what Freer had suspected all along. They had unknowingly ventured into the enemy outpost at Bairoko, just a bit over three thousand yards down the coast from Enogai.

Freer yelled at everyone aboard to get down and ordered the coxswain to open the throttle and hug the shoreline opposite the fast-approaching barges. Seconds elapsed glacially. As they passed the barges in the narrow neck of the harbor, the trembling occupants ducked low in their tiny craft, motionless, waiting with breath suspended. The coxswain sat rigidly and stared straight ahead, ignoring the hundreds of Japanese riflemen aboard the barges. Miraculously, the Japanese ignored them and simply passed by. The lieutenant's navigational error had been so grievous that their presence aroused no suspicion among the Japanese. Less than an hour later, the shaken crew motored into the safe waters of Enogai Inlet.[53]

Even with the added strength of Freer's soldiers, it was still believed that another battalion (roughly six hundred men) would be needed to conquer Bairoko. Liversedge waited impatiently for the answer to his request for the 4th Raiders, wondering how he would take Bairoko if the answer were no. The next day, a Catalina ferrying Major Stevenson from Guadalcanal glided into the harbor. He not only brought with him Turner's approval, but also a sack of mail for the homesick men. It was just the tonic Liversedge and his men needed.

The troops read their letters over and over, put them carefully away for a while, and then read them again, repeating the routine daily. They would press letters from their sweethearts to their lips and search for traces of the scent from the perfumed hands that had brushed across those pages. Even those receiving notes from anonymous high school girls who had volunteered to write to an unknown GI overseas felt ennobled. Letters were reminders that even though they might not have been awarded medals, they were still heroes to the folks back home. For many, it was the first time someone had ever been proud of them. Whatever romance the young recruits may have had with the armed services was by now long dead, but it was still very much alive with their families and lovers. Rank was irrelevant; officers and enlisted men both carried their letters with them everywhere. This was especially true for photos mailed with the letters. In the New Georgia bush, the only sure method of keeping valuables like photos dry was to stuff them into condoms or inside the watertight cans used for issuing cigarettes to the men.[54] During off-duty hours the letters and especially the photos might be shared with a buddy who had been more than a few times briefed on the girl's beauty. Sadly, there were always those who received no mail, so they often asked their buddies to read their letters to them out loud. It was not quite as good as receiving one personally, of course, but it still helped boost their morale.

These innocent letters were also blunt reminders of how unhinged their lives had become from their previous existence. They had disappeared from themselves. Would family and friends ever understand what they had seen on this implausible island? How could anyone articulate it all? Even if the experience could be properly deciphered, would they ever want to reveal the horror of it to others? That was most unlikely. No one else, then, would ever really know the secrets of their fraternity, forever whispered only among their brothers, who themselves had been scourged by the merciless jungle. As they pulled off their helmets, wiped the grit from their foreheads, and kicked back to read their letters once more, they slowly began to realize that the world being described in them had somehow become frighteningly foreign. Even the people who penned those cherished letters had in some odd way become strangers. A connection had been irreparably broken. It became apparent that the world they now occupied was, always had been, and would always remain the only real world. They had not been banished to some unfathomable, dark corner of the universe after all, as they once had thought. Rather, it was their families and friends who existed in a semifictional netherworld. Deep within the din and death of war there was never any distortion or charade or pretense, just inexplicable clarity.

Kula Gulf was roiling early the morning of 18 July when four destroyers slowed a few hundred yards from Enogai Point and then anchored, their bows bucking in the surf, the gray sky stretching above them like a tattered tarpaulin. After a seven-hour cruise from Guadal-canal, Lt. Col. Michael Currin's 4th Raiders, veterans of Viru and Vangunu, were about to debark and join Colonel Liversedge's NLG, bringing its strength to roughly three thousand men. They were far from fresh troops, however, particularly the Raider battalions, yet it was they who were to shoulder the toughest assignment. The 1st Raiders were at only about half strength, and the 4th Raiders were at roughly two-thirds strength due to casualties and illness. Never-theless, their presence, along with the forty tons of supplies and fif-teen days' of rations that landed with them, lifted everyone's spirits.

Currin spent two days orienting himself on the situation, meet-ing with Liversedge and Griffith, studying maps with his company officers, and sending out patrols. His men, on the other hand, bus-ied themselves with more mundane chores like cleaning and oiling their weapons and performing perimeter duty. One especially odi-ous job was assigned to Anthony Walker's company the day it arrived. The men were placed in charge of disposing of the bodies of a hand-ful of Japanese soldiers who had been decomposing on a coral ridge since Enogai's seizure more than a week before. The blackened, bloated corpses were crawling with maggots and reeked of death. Nothing but death could ever smell quite so awful. Walker's men ap-proached them after first pulling their shirts over their faces to pro-vide some protection from the stench. They decided to drag the bod-ies a short distance to a deep ravine, push them in, and shovel some dirt on top of them. As they did so, a leg would sometimes tear away from a body. Skulls also had a tendency to come loose after a body had been dragged a few feet and had to be rolled to the ravine.[55] It was a most disagreeable task, but not as unpleasant as their next op-eration.

Their target was the tiny village of Bairoko. Enemy reinforcements coming across the Kula Gulf from Kolombangara continued to pass through it en route to Munda. It also possessed the only pier on the island capable of accepting significant amounts of supplies for Gen-eral Sasaki's New Georgia forces.[56] Its seizure would complete the NLG's end run and sever the flow of supplies destined for the air-field's defenders. It would no doubt be a tougher nut to crack than Enogai. There was still no hard intelligence on the number of enemy troops at Bairoko. The original estimate had placed the number of defenders at both Enogai and Bairoko at five hundred. Japanese casualties during the operation had been heavy, so the best guess was that only about two companies remained in the garrison. It was wrong.

What the planners overlooked was the unchecked flow of reinforcements from Kolombangara into Bairoko Harbor during the week following the fall of Enogai. Actually, Liversedge would be going up against a force of about fourteen hundred determined combat veterans. Aerial photos showing the location of gun emplacements, stores, and strong points would also have been helpful, but Liversedge had received practically none.[57] Moreover, the element of surprise that had helped the Americans at Enogai was gone. The Bairoko garrison commander, Comdr. Saburo Okumura, whose force included the 6th Kure SNLF and the 2nd Battalion, 13th Infantry, knew Liversedge's strength and exact location. Furthermore, he had had ten days in which to prepare his defenses. This time the Japanese would be ready.

Surrounded by coconut palms, Father Paul J. Redmond, the 4th Raiders's beloved Catholic chaplain, prepared to say mass the evening before the assault. He tied a small American flag to a tree and stacked several wooden ammo crates in front of it, forming a crude altar. He then draped his white vestment, embroidered with a large crimson cross, neatly over the crates so that the cross was upright. When he finished, Redmond sat down and prayed silently while the men finished eating. Soon, small groups of them began walking toward the lush grove curving along the edge of the peaceful inlet. They sat on steel ammo boxes and ponchos and helmets, forming a semicircle around Father Redmond. Their battalion commander, Lieutenant Colonel Currin, was among them. Nobody talked. Faces were grave.

"*Dominus vobiscum*," the priest began. Only a few of the men responded in Latin. Most of the others were deep within themselves. They watched him face the makeshift altar, standing erect, hands and arms outspread as he murmured the prayers, his head cocked downward toward the missal that lay before him. Occasionally he would turn to face them, his voice growing louder, soliciting more responses in Latin. At the consecration of the bread and wine, the congregation knelt on the damp earth, heads bowed reverently at the sight of the simple chalice held high above them, and begged for redemption. They were Protestants, Catholics, and even Jews. Some had never been to a religious service, but each was in touch with his personal god. Each seemed to sense that the next day's battle would be brutal, that many of them would die. Father Redmond could sense it, too. When he turned to give the final blessing, he looked out over them wondering who would survive what some later called the toughest battle the Raiders faced in the Pacific war.

Assault on Bairoko

Five days behind schedule, the NLG commander completed his plan. The two Raider battalions, the 1st followed by the 4th, would move parallel to the coast along a trail that ran about a mile through a narrow grove of coconut palms from Enogai toward Bairoko and strike from the northeast. Meanwhile, Lieutenant Colonel Schultz's 3rd Battalion, 148th Infantry, would attack from the south, using the Munda Trail to make its approach. Lieutenant Colonel Freer's 3rd Battalion, 145th Infantry, would defend the rear-area base camps at Enogai, Triri, and Rice Anchorage. Colonel Liversedge knew well that his real weakness was the absence of artillery, so he was counting heavily on the aviators at Henderson Field to soften up the harbor's defenses. On the evening of 19 July he radioed a request for a mission in support of the next morning's attack. The request was received but it was never acted upon because of an administrative oversight.[58]

Assaulting a fortified position without artillery, air, or naval support would imperil the mission and the lives of the men. To complicate matters, there was the poor intelligence estimate of enemy strength. The Raiders would have only a two-to-one advantage, far lower than the three-to-one or higher ratio prescribed for an assault of this nature. Liversedge should probably have pulled back until he could send another request for an air strike or obtain naval gunfire support. But that was not to be.

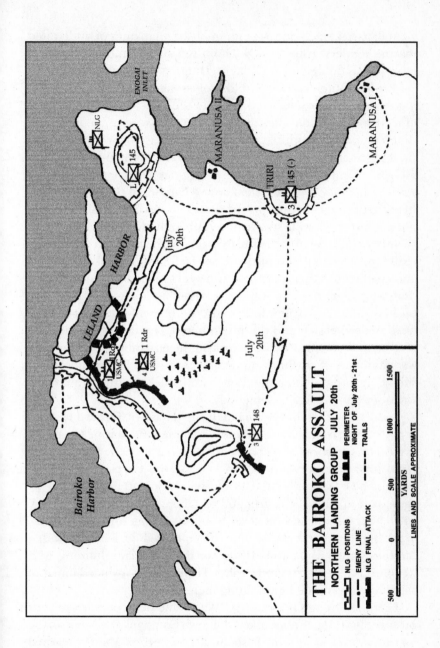

THE BAIROKO ASSAULT JULY 20th

NORTHERN LANDING GROUP JULY 20th

NLG POSITIONS
EMENY LINE
NLG FINAL ATTACK
PERIMETER
NIGHT OF July 20th - 21st
TRAILS

YARDS
LINES AND SCALE APPROXIMATE

At 8:30 A.M. on 20 July, a column of six companies of undaunted marine Raiders, roughly eight hundred strong, moved out once more. It was the seventeenth day on Dragons Peninsula for Griffith's 1st Raiders—their seventeenth day of eating out of a can and fighting diarrhea, their seventeenth day in the same clothing, their seventeenth day without decent sleep. But they rose uncomplaining, their combat packs stuffed with extra ammo, grenades, and mortar shells. Virtually anything a man could not eat, shoot, throw, or drink was left behind. Military-issue canvas leggings had been ditched long ago because they became inflexible and hard when coated with mud. Instead, the men cut the blue nylon parachutes used to airdrop supplies into six-inch-wide strips and wrapped them around the tops of their boots and up over their calves to keep the mud out. The nylon really appealed to the troops, who used it for ground sheets, scarves, and headbands. After more than two weeks in their brown and olive-drab world, the colorful trappings helped to lift spirits. Looking a bit like latter-day rogue pirates with the blue adornments spilling from under helmets and down weathered, bearded faces, the men reveled in their vulgarity. To complete the ensemble, they slung extra bandoliers of machine-gun ammo around their tired necks and shoulders, ornamenting themselves for battle. Now they were ready to do serious damage to somebody.

Perhaps the most interesting of the men was S1c. Richard H. Maurer, a Seabee from Seattle. Maurer had joined the Marine Corps Reserve a month short of his sixteenth birthday in 1937. When he applied for active duty after Pearl Harbor, the Corps rejected him because he was color-blind. Undeterred, he joined the navy and became part of a naval construction battalion. But Maurer was dissatisfied with his job, and he never lost his yearning for infantry duty. While stationed on Guadalcanal, he cultivated a friendship with a marine Raider who briefed him on their specialty training with weapons, rubber boats, and stealth. The marine convinced him that the Raiders were the best fighting men on earth.

That was enough for Maurer. "What's the best company in your outfit?" the young Seabee asked. His own Company C, of course, the marine answered without hesitation. Later, when Maurer learned that the Raiders were about to embark on a mission to New Georgia, he decided that he would go with them.

Sure enough, when the Raiders finally readied themselves to board the destroyers for transport to Enogai, Seaman Maurer was there, too, part of a working party that was going out to the ship. When the time came for the Raiders to board, he simply jumped into the line and strolled up the gangplank with the others. No matter that he was weaponless, bareheaded, and carrying only a canteen dangling from a belt loop. No one seemed to notice. Once on board he found his way to the ship's fantail and hid inconspicuously between cargo crates and equipment. When they arrived, he debarked with the others, lowering himself into a rubber boat for the trip to shore. Still no one questioned him. When he was sure that every transport had left, he set off to locate Company C, figuring they would have no choice but to let him stay.[59]

For two and a half hours, the Raiders humped over jagged hills of volcanic matter peppered with dense undergrowth and "wait-a-minute" vines draped from huge trees with erupting root systems. Griffith's marines thought the terrain even more unforgiving than what they had experienced on their move to Enogai two weeks before. They broke through a four-man enemy outpost eight hundred yards from Bairoko with little trouble, but as they advanced, a barrage of gunfire greeted them across their entire front as the pitch of battle rose to a new crescendo. First Lieutenant Jim Lucas was in the thick of it, trying to avoid the Japanese .25-caliber rifle fire:

I dived back of a banyan log. The firing continued, then ceased abruptly. We edged forward, darting from bush to bush, tree to tree, and falling flat on our bellies. I reached Captain Morrow. He pointed into a ravine. A dead Jap, his head split by a single burst of a Browning automatic rifle, lay sprawled across the jungle floor. He went to inspect the body while we spread out. . . . I was on the left when a Jap broke out from the bush and attempted to get back into the jungle, fired instinctively, and he fell. Later, when one of our men found a picture on his body—of a young Jap and his mother—I felt sick all over. She was a sweet-faced old woman, and I never thought of Japs as human beings with sweet-faced mothers. It was my first kill, and I didn't get over it for days.[60]

Two more hours of heavy fighting followed, with marines subduing foxholes one at a time. Then the enemy dropped back to their main line of defense. The scheme utilized a series of four parallel coral ridges, blocking Liversedge's axis of advance just a few hundred yards from his objective. Designed by Commander Okumura, it was a superb shield indeed. The ridges housed a labyrinth of mutually supporting, interlocking coconut-log-and-coral bunkers protected by Japanese snipers in nearby trees and cleverly concealed machine-gun fire lanes. The well-camouflaged positions, many hidden carefully under banyan tree roots, were resistant to all but a direct hit from a mortar round. Underground tunnels connected many of the bunkers so that they could be abandoned or reinforced as necessary. It soon became obvious that the ten days since Enogai had fallen had been busy ones for the vigilant defenders, who had been reinforced with troops from the 13th Infantry on Kolombangara, elements of the 45th Regiment, and an artillery battery from Bougainville.

Captain Royal F. Munger, who had been the finance editor of the *Chicago Daily News* before rejoining the marines, wrote this report about the defenses:

> It's a good deal like Indian fighting in American frontier days. Each soldier has to be his own tactician, his own general, his own advance guard. Somewhere ahead is a Jap, perhaps in a thick tangle, perhaps in a tree, but most likely in a little "grave" in the ground, covered over with solid coconut logs and earth of coral, the whole camouflaged with palm branches. Down in his hole, looking out through a small firing port, the Jap is safe from almost anything. He is hard to see. You can come within thirty feet of such a camouflaged position before you notice it. Yet you cannot afford to let the Jap see you first, for at that range not even a Jap could miss.[61]

That was often exactly what happened. The Raiders leading the way "on point" suffered the highest losses, for enemy riflemen firing from their concealed pillboxes would simply wait until the last moment to gun them down. They never had a chance. An estimated half of all small-arms casualties in the Pacific were hit within twenty-five yards of a Japanese position.[62] While advancing through this type of terrain, the enemy would almost certainly be located only when a few of the men were blasted by gunfire. That is why point men were rotated often.

Once the enemy weapons opened up, everyone dropped and the hard work began. It required a squad of about ten men to defeat a bunker. Half of them would keep the occupants of the bunker occupied while the others tried to outflank it so they could lob in a grenade or a satchel charge or kill the defenders by crossfire. But any attempt to maneuver around one position carried the attackers into the line of fire from another. The only way to break through was to silence each bunker, but doing so meant sacrificing many of those in the maneuver element. Without artillery, there was simply no other way.

Not long after the attack began, the Raiders heard a sound that they hoped not to hear: mortar rounds launched from ahead of them. They were of the 90mm variety, and the Raiders had nothing for counterbattery fire except their own 60mm tubes. It was hardly a contest. Seconds later, a hailstorm of lethal shells began exploding among them, catching the Raiders with no place to hide except behind the trunks of palm trees or niches in the coral escarpment paralleling the trail. The Japanese had registered their mortars days before, and the deadly barrages sent fragments of sizzling-hot steel—some tiny and some the size of a man's fist—hurtling through the boiling air, tearing indiscriminately into the marines' flesh. Men began to fall everywhere. Unlike bullets, which are more likely to leave a clean wound, jagged shell fragments recklessly carve into human tissue with gruesome savagery. One nineteen-year-old marine's abdomen lay open, his gleaming intestines hanging from his stomach cavity. A young corporal's face was a bloody mess after an explosion took his jaw and cheek away. Arms were left hanging to elbows by shreds of skin. The heavy odor of blood and burning powder crept over the living. Terrible screams of pain split the air, punctuated by random death. Somehow, Henry Poppell managed to scribble a few lines in his diary: "We keep moving forward against very heavy machine gun fire for a few minutes and then mortars begin to bark. We are low but the Nips have found the range and they are pounding us mercilessly. Each shell seems to get five or six men. The struggle has become a seesaw battle. If we only had air support or a little artillery. We can't even bring our mortars into action due to the heavy bush."[63]

Captain Tony Walker of the 4th Raiders said he "never saw a dead Jap that afternoon. Only dead Marines."[64] Father Redmond scurried around in a crouch, helping a corpsman attend to a wounded Raider, sharing a cigarette or a canteen with another during a long lull. Later, behind a dripping mahogany tree, amid rocking explosions and the disarray of the assault, he was seen hovering calmly over dying Raiders, his grimy white vestment draped loosely around his neck, reverently intoning the Latin liturgy for the repose of their souls: "*Per istam sanctam unctionem indulgeat libi Dominus quidquid delequisti.*" He then took a small glass bottle filled with holy oil from his chaplain's pouch, dribbled a bit of it onto his right thumb, and anointed their sweaty, blood-stained foreheads with tiny crosses while continuing to pray. When a Raider expired, Redmond, head bowed low, would brush his fingers gently across the lifeless face and whisper his own benediction for the man and his family. Each grieving family that lost a Raider received a personal letter from him.

Seaman Maurer, who had managed to get the proper equipment and a rifle issued to him, found his way to Company C, now firmly in the grip of combat. The impetuous twenty-two-year-old asked someone where the skipper was and he was led to Captain Walker's foxhole. He identified himself, explained briefly how he had gotten there, and told Walker he wanted to be a Raider. Walker remained totally composed. Without hesitation he assigned Maurer to a machine-gun crew that was shorthanded and hastily sent him off with a curt order: "You'd better do a good job."[65] Maurer's new boss, a corporal, handed him an ammo carrier's bag filled with boxes of .30-caliber ammunition for their Browning machine gun. The corporal told Maurer his job was to cover the other five men in the crew with rifle fire as they rushed forward. When they stopped, he was to drop down between the gunner's legs and "keep them snipers off our ass."

Before Maurer had a chance to get settled, Walker yelled out: "They're right in front of us. Let's go get 'em! Gung Ho!" The entire company leaped up, screaming wildly and shouting as small-arms fire began to crackle from both sides of the jungle. Maurer's crew would drop and lay fire on a position, then jump up, rush forward, and repeat the process. Tiny geysers of coral dust mushroomed around them as enemy gunfire reached closer. A mortar round exploded just a few yards away, upending the machine gun and wounding several members of the crew—including the gunner, who ordered Maurer to take over the gun. He fired until it malfunctioned, then scampered ahead in a low crouch until he reestablished contact with another machine gunner. Maurer cleared his weapon and both began firing at the tree line ahead until things quieted down somewhat.[66]

Milton Robert, a Company C BAR man, ran out of ammo four times. He scavenged cartridges from the dead and wounded Raiders lying all around. When his supply dwindled again, he crawled over to where another downed leatherneck lay to replenish his supply. When he turned the man over, he saw the face of his buddy, Watson, who had begged Robert to arrange for him to carry a BAR, too. It never happened. Robert drew his K-bar knife and cut Watson's belt to see how serious the wound was. It was too late; he was already gone. The angry Raider then moved forward and, with some satisfaction, took out an enemy machine-gun nest with the ammo he had retrieved from Watson's body.[67]

Ivan D. Shurts was running in a low crouch through the middle of the shellfire when a Japanese soldier jumped up and shot a man who fell to the ground screaming in pain. The bullet had ripped open the man's stomach and his organs were oozing out on the ground. Seconds later, the enemy rifleman was riddled by bullets himself. Shurts relieved him of his rifle and shoved some ammunition into a pocket before moving on. Later he noticed that the points of the Japanese bullets he had pocketed had been crisscrossed with a file so that they would fragment upon impact.[68]

By 11:30 A.M. the Japanese had stopped the Raiders' forward movement altogether, and casualties really began to mount. Corpsmen scampered around attending to the wailing wounded, cutting off blouses and pants, shoving morphine Syrettes into them, sprinkling sulfa over wounds before binding them, and then quickly moving off to the next man. Liversedge grabbed his communications sergeant and instructed him to try to reach Shultz and his 81mm mortars, but the line was dead. His radios failed as well, victims of the wet New Georgia jungle. Cursing the aviators for failing to show up that morning, he decided to commit the 4th Raiders on his left in hopes they would find a weakness in the enemy line. Companies B and C, along with a reserve company from the 1st Battalion, pushed forward but were stopped cold in front of a thirty-yard-wide clearing that was covered by an enemy platoon with a half-dozen Nambus machine guns and several knee mortars. What weakness in the enemy line? There did not seem to be one. Then the men in Company D got the word that they were to charge across that open field into the maelstrom. Somebody thought it was the right thing to do.

What happened next was one of the most unusual, if not comical, events of the Pacific war. Company D's three platoon leaders were to signal the charge by throwing white phosphorous grenades into the clearing. Besides synchronizing the attack, the grenades would also provide a smoke screen for the Raiders as they galloped across the field into the Japanese buzz saw. Just seconds before the lieutenants threw their grenades, however, they heard the eerie sound of screams and wails from the enemy position. It sounded as though the Japanese were preparing to mount their own banzai charge. John McCormick, a Company D tommy gunner, said they

were more than half way across the narrow clearing before we realized that not a shot had been fired our way. It was incredible. We had expected to be greeted by machine guns or blasted by mortars, yet no man in our charging line had gone down. Right then a line of Japs rose at the end of the jungle immediately to our front and banzaied. It all happened so fast that they were right on top of us in a few seconds.

It was a thing that was not supposed to happen: both sides charging each other simultaneously. So unexpected was it that both Marines and Japs forgot to yell, forgot to fire. Going at top speed in opposite directions, they ran right past each other. A Jap rifleman with his long bayonet fixed ran by a yard to my right. I could see that he was struggling to angle toward me, but momentum and the fixation of the banzai took him past me. Meantime, I was struggling to overcome my own momentum, my own fixations on the charge, but as he rushed by I could not bring my tommy gun to bear.[69]

The marines made it untouched to the opposite side of the clearing, where they finished off a couple of dazed machine gunners by lobbing grenades into their gun pits. Behind them they heard the clatter of gunfire, which quickly surged to a roar. The Japanese had run into Company B's position.

Meanwhile, the Raiders in Company D kept plunging ahead, hoping their good fortune would continue. They fought their way slowly forward through heavy and continuous fire and managed to seize a small ridge on the enemy's right flank. A small victory like this needed to be exploited quickly. But that required the assistance of the army's 81mm mortars. Since he was unable to reach Schultz by phone or radio, Liversedge sent a five-man party to find him and deliver the urgent order for help.

Slowly, the Raiders battled their way through two of the four ridges to their front and finally managed to claim a piece of precious high ground. From that spot their combat-stained eyes could see the harbor just three hundred yards away. They were killing the enemy efficiently and making progress, but with each tiny gain they encountered a new line of samurai just a few yards ahead. Frank Korowitz, a communications specialist who was feeding a busy machine gun, admitted later that he was almost petrified with fear. "I remember feeling," he said later, "that I wanted to get up and run. I also felt that I would rather be killed than have anyone know I was scared."[70] More 90mm shells greeted the Raiders, who crept down the back hump of the ridge where they were confounded by reverse slope machine-gun bunkers that abruptly halted them and turned them back. A mortar round exploded near Pfc. Francis Hepburn, a runner attached to Liversedge's command group. His face scored by jagged coral, he ran bleeding in a crouch with a message for Captain Walker. On the way he saw a buddy jamming his bayonet through the throat of a Japanese soldier who lay on his back, his legs flailing and thumping. The Raider, seeing that Hepburn was watching him, yelled that "the son-of-a-bitch" had been pretending to be dead.[71]

Corporal John Hestand, who survived the war to become a detective with the Los Angeles Police Department, felt like he had been "kicked in the stomach by a mule" when he caught an enemy bullet. A three-by-three-inch M1 ammo clip on his web belt had taken the blow and saved him from a serious wound. Minutes later, however, he felt a thud and then a burn on his right thigh. "There were mortars bursting in the tree tops and on the ground all around us and all kinds of other stuff was flying around, coming from all directions, twinging, whirring, and thunking," he recalled later. "A lot of our guys were getting hit and needed corpsmen. After a while I found the aid station and there must have been a hundred guys, bleeding, hurting, being bandaged, etc."[72]

By 3 P.M., Liversedge's fatigued and bloodied men had assembled in a line of roughly seven hundred poised to advance into Bairoko. A few Japanese could be seen retreating, perhaps an indication that their line was finally crumbling. Griffith penciled a quick message to Liversedge and had it hand-carried to him: "Line advancing. . . . On left O Co., center Dog, right B (less one platoon), P protecting left rear on high ground . . . casualties appear heavy, but no count yet. I had two officers killed. I urgently recommend two fresh battalions (from the 145th and the 148th) sent here quickly. There are plenty of Nips here yet, but think we've got them on the run."[73]

This was the classic moment where the commander was supposed to commit his reserve. But Liversedge had none to commit. Besides, the defenders still occupied two more ridges ahead of them, and their mortar fire continued to score hits all along the Raider line. Casualties were unforgivably high. Should the methodical assault continue without heavier fire support? Even though the Japanese seemed to be cracking, they were clawing back with the savagery of a cornered panther. Moreover, a scout who had succeeded in tunneling his way through the Japanese defenses to Bairoko reported that five barges of enemy infantry had just landed.[74]

While the Raiders had their hands full, Shurts battalion was stalled a thousand yards south of the harbor. After an arduous six-hour hike through the peninsula, the GIs had encountered more of Okumura's defenses, a strong outpost of one or two machine-gun bunkers on a hill overlooking the tired troops. Squeezed between a lagoon and an impassable swamp, the gun emplacements made maneuver difficult, but they had received neither small arms nor mortar fire. Clearly, Shurts had not reached the main line of enemy resistance, but rather a lone (or possibly a pair) of Nambu machine guns. An entire battalion of seven hundred men packing BARs, M1s, machine guns, and grenades was stymied by one or two small-caliber machine guns. Marine radioman Henry Poppell was unable to conceal his frustration: "Hours pass and no word from Dutch Schultz and his Army troops. . . . This is the first time we have ever operated in conjunction with the Army and too this is the first time in over twenty engagements that we have faced the Nips that we failed to take our objective. We know not the reason for Shurt's failure to close the gap and hope tomorrow will bring us word that he is intact."[75]

Meanwhile, the team of messengers sent by Liversedge arrived at Shurts command post at around four, after having repaired the telephone lines. Shurts rang the NLG commander and explained that his unit could not reach him until after dark. That was no good. Liversedge needed the relief immediately.

The marine in Liversedge told him that they should complete the job. The harbor was in sight and they had already slugged their way through half the 6th Kure SNLF's zealous defenses. To withdraw now meant that the heavy losses his men had suffered—forty-eight killed and 191 wounded, more than 25 percent of his force—would have been in vain. But he was commanding a Raider unit, a commando-style outfit that was designed for speed and quick, hard-hitting raids. They were clearly miscast for the capture of Bairoko, facing a dug-in and tenacious force that required heavier weapons such as tanks, heavy mortars, and artillery, or perhaps naval gunfire or combat air support. Short of that, he would need the 3rd Battalion, 148th Infantry. None of those things were forthcoming, however. A light infantry assault from their position into the Japanese compound would mean a bloodbath, and he did not want to sacrifice any more of these fine men in a mission for which they were not suited. They were short on ammo, their water was almost gone, and they had now been in fierce combat for six hours. Besides, if the scout's report was correct, there was a good chance that more reinforcements from Vila were on hand to blunt an advance. Before Liversedge made his decision, however, he wanted a consensus from his officers on the line. He sent a runner to Griffith with a message instructing him to consult with Currin, size up the situation, and report back to him pronto with their recommendations on whether or not to continue. The two battalion commanders moved along the line and conferred with their company commanders.[76] Shortly afterward, Griffith reported to the command post and confirmed what Liversedge already knew. He issued orders at 5:15 for the NLG to retire immediately. What was arguably the toughest day of fighting since the beginning of the Pacific war. Griffith, who survived the war to receive a doctorate from Oxford and become a noted historian and translator of the works of Mao Tse-tung, later summed up the decision to withdraw:

> By this time (5:00) the Raiders—1st and 4th—had nearly 250 casualties. We had another 150 men tied up getting them to aid stations and to Enogai. There was nothing to do but pull back and reorganize, re-equip, get some rest, try to get something to cope with the Jap 90-mm, and get the wounded out. The final determining factor was the Japanese capability to reinforce from Vila-Stanmore during the night by barge. We were already up against a stone wall, low on ammunition and out of water and had a responsibility to 200 wounded men. In any case, reorganization was a paramount requirement. Colonel Liversedge had a mission and was understandably loath to abandon it. [But] I felt the decision to withdraw was entirely sound and the only sensible one.[77]

Liversedge's actions amplified his reputation for sound leadership. He showed good judgment in consulting with his battalion commanders (and they in parlaying with their company officers) before he broke off the attack. He consulted often with Griffith, in particular, during the campaign, picking his brain to help remedy problems. The decision to halt the attack took more courage than if he had simply continued onward. He felt a greater responsibility to his men than he did to Admiral Turner and the mission, which had developed into something very different from what was envisioned when the plan to invade the Dragons Peninsula was being drafted. He would pull back, resupply, and beg for more resources before he made another attempt. He was not going to abandon the mission. They would return soon enough.

Meanwhile, the navy surgeons and their assistants were inundated with casualties. The wounded came in so fast that it was impossible to evacuate them back to Enogai. James Regan found a level place in the jungle protected by a low coral wall and established his aid station there. By nightfall, scores of casualties were crammed into the tiny clearing, fully a fourth of them litter cases. It smelled like a hot summer afternoon in a Chicago slaughterhouse. By the end of the battle, the Raiders had taken almost 30 percent casualties, including 47 killed and 199 wounded. One of the dead and 3 of the wounded were corpsmen who were shot as they attempted to administer medical help. Nine corpsmen were awarded the Silver Star for their courageous actions during the battle.[78]

Back in Bairoko, Commander Okumura was elated. They had beaten back the American attack despite their numerical inferiority, thus becoming the only Japanese unit during the New Georgia campaign to do so. They had fought tenaciously and courageously, as they usually did, and they had outwitted the Americans with their uniquely and cleverly arranged bunker system, which had capitalized on terrain features, cover and concealment, and well-planned fields of fire. Moreover, their casualties were relatively light. The contrast with their poorly executed and piecemeal assaults against Shurts at the trail block on 8 July was remarkable. The Japanese were demonstrating that when their intelligence information was good (which was not often) and they had some time to prepare for an attack, they could be an extremely formidable defensive force. Small pockets of them could likely force much larger units to falter, particularly if the terrain was rugged. On the other hand, their assaults were sloppy and governed more by foolish valor than well-reasoned tactics.

When Lieutenant Colonel Shurts received the order to pull back, he was in the process of preparing to attack the unyielding positions to his front. The plan was dropped, however, and the GIs began withdrawing back to Triri, thus allowing the frustrated battalion commander to save face. Schultz had managed to lay down a blanket of 81mm counterbattery mortar fire on Bairoko's defenses, but it was too little, too late.

Farther north, the Raiders began to pull off the line two companies at a time, leapfrogging back to less tenuous positions with the full retirement to Enogai scheduled for six the next morning. After the ninety or so litter cases began the move (with the help of seventy native carriers using ponchos and tree limbs for stretchers), the remaining Raiders moved out behind them with the weapons of their dead and wounded comrades slung over their tired shoulders. There were so many casualties to carry that nearly every capable marine was assigned to that detail, four to six per stretcher. Sometimes the blood from wounds pooled in the ponchos and leaked to the jungle floor through the head slot, leaving a grisly trail for the others to follow. A few men perished in their makeshift stretchers and were left on the trailside to make room for other wounded marines. With no one to spare, the dead would have to be recovered later.

Richard Maurer was part of the rearguard covering the retreat. As he backpedaled toward Enogai, he passed near the torn, crumpled body of a marine lying alone in the bush on his back. Even though he was losing contact with his squad, Maurer dropped to one knee for a moment—not only to study the corpse, but also out of respect for his comrade. The Raider's bandages, now stained black after several hours in the sun, were partially unwrapped. That indicated to Maurer that the man had died while receiving medical attention. He wondered how long the man had been forced to suffer before he died—or if he ever knew he was going to die. How would that feel, knowing that you were not going to make it? Did he have time to make peace with the Lord? Did he have a family?

Maurer rose to leave. But then he looked solemnly down over the uncovered body and wondered hard if his bold prank would have been worth it if the day had ended in his own death. Until that moment, it had never occurred to him that he might have died. Twenty-two-year-old Richard Maurer, who had stowed away on a ship to be in that terrible battle, suddenly realized it could just as easily have been him lying there instead.

Just two years out of high school, Olin Gray of the 4th Battalion was probably the last Raider to pull back. One minute he was scrambling toward the Japanese defenses with his machine gun, the next he was a teenager all alone just yards from the enemy. "I found myself at the tail end of the evacuating line—the last to leave," he recalled. "I have always been the last one to get the word." A half-century later, the Distinguished Service Cross recipient vividly recounted the details:

I recall a lot of shooting up ahead when our squad was called up. A young lieutenant and his runner . . . started to lead our squad around the base of a hill to set up our gun position. Then all hell broke loose. Just beyond the hill we were sprayed with Japanese machine gun fire coming from at least two directions. The lieutenant and the runner were killed, and R. A. Taylor (his partner) had part of his hand shot away. William Regan, who was in front of me, was killed, and before I could catch my breath, Dale Massen, who was behind me, hollered out, "I'm hit!" From where I lay on the ground, I looked back and saw him rolling and staggering away.

I found myself alone with the machine gun and no tripod (which Taylor carried). To this day I don't know how, but I returned fire that afternoon until almost dark. It couldn't have been more than two hours from the time the fire fight started, but it seemed like forever. Before it got dark, I counted less than a hundred rounds left for my gun. I had 2,000 starting in.

In the dark I felt the still-warm barrel of my machine gun and knew it had to be leaded up inside real bad. I don't know how it came to be there, but our extra barrel was in its case next to me. All our training really paid off then. I replaced the barrel and laid down waiting for daylight which I thought would never come. We were very close to shore because I could hear the Jap boats running over to Kolombangara Island and other noises at Bairoko. I thought they were bringing in more reinforcements, but they were carrying away their wounded.[79]

As soon as they made it to high ground, the main body began to dig into the hard coral for the night. Those who were not wounded took positions around the perimeter. Soon, a relief party from the 3rd Battalion, 145th Infantry, reached the Raiders with enough water, food, and medical supplies to hold them for one more day.

The enemy made only a half-hearted pursuit, a night patrol that probed the 1st Raiders' perimeter at 2 A.M. Nine more of Griffith's men were wounded in the ensuing firefight. An eighteen-year-old corporal went forward to drag one of them out of danger and was hit by a burst of fire. Corpsmen tried to reach him, but they were pinned down by heavy rifle fire when they received the order to pull back. The badly wounded marine yelled at them from a distance, begging them to shoot him, but they had no intention of going back without him. Four Raiders moved up and began firing to draw the enemy's attention away from their stranded comrade while two corpsmen scurried up and rolled him onto a litter. Meanwhile, the rest of the unit had retired, so the small band of men curled back down the trail alone, hauling their buddy and dodging sniper fire the entire distance. The young corporal did not make it. They buried him along the trail after nightfall.[80]

James Regan recorded these details of the night attack in his diary entry for 21 July:

We were pinned down under heavy fire at nightfall. At midnight the Japanese staged one of their celebrated suicide bayonet charges, screaming like madmen. A false rumor started that we were going to withdraw and leave the wounded. My Pharmacist's Mate Brownie (Jay A. Brown), a stubby, easygoing chap crept over to me. "If we are ordered back, Doc," he said quietly, "I'll stay here with the wounded." I said, "Do you realize what might happen to you?" He said soberly, "Yeah, I know all right. But if the boys can take it, I can take it."

Of course, we were not ordered back. The wounded had neither food nor water during the night. We started them back to
sick bay at Enogai at daybreak today. Having no litters, we im-
provised them by rolling ponchos on limbs of trees. They were
unsatisfactory; the ponchos would slip and let the wounded fall.
Their stoicism is incredible; even half-conscious, they are thinking of their fellows. I knelt beside one man who had fallen. He
thought I was his stretcher-bearer, and muttered through
clenched teeth, "That's okay, Mac. You couldn't help it."[81]

Just before daylight on 21 July, the NLG commander radioed a
request to Guadalcanal for an air strike on Bairoko at 9 A.M., making it clear that it was needed to cover their retreat. This time Air-
Sols answered with gusto. Beginning at 10 A.M., all available aircraft
hit the harbor hard all day long. Bombers of all types dropped 133
tons of explosives, and scores of fighters swept through the area blowing up fuel dumps and damaging equipment. The aviators flew more
than 250 sorties, making it the heaviest air strike thus far in the campaign.[82] By the end of the day, the entire NLG had successfully completed the withdrawal.

At Enogai, the 3rd Battalion, 148th Infantry, was already manning
a perimeter defense when the first of the eighty or so walking
wounded appeared on the trail. They stumbled in, gazing blankly
ahead with bloodless lips pressed tight. The battalion's medics rushed
forward with stretchers to administer to their wounds—wrapping
them with bandages and giving them morphine. Shell fragments,
probably from the enemy's 90mm mortars, had caused most of their
wounds. Surviving gunshot victims usually ended up litter cases.
Those unfortunates moved in next, borne by their comrades and native carriers. Frank Guidone remembered that the islanders' feet were
bleeding under the burden of their heavy loads. Some were even
weeping.[83] Their morale still noticeably high, the wounded were surprisingly composed and spoke rationally about their ordeal. Even in
defeat they understood that they had displayed extraordinary courage
in face of a zealous, unbending enemy force. An hour later, the rest
of the Raiders began to dribble through the perimeter a platoon at

a time. It was obvious to the GIs manning the line that they were a beaten bunch. There was none of the usual sardonic joking that accompanies a combat unit as it returns from the field. Quietly they wormed into the encampment, faces drawn with disappointment and fatigue. After taking off his helmet and lighting a cigarette, a Raider captain talked about what happened:

> We moved out in good fashion, and there was no sign of Japs until we were close to Bairoko. We never had patrols go that far, and I was beginning to wonder if the Japs were still there. We continued our advance until we could see pill boxes. Then all hell broke loose. The Japs were obviously waiting for us. The whole front opened up at the same time with rifles, machine guns, and mortars. It was the damned mortars that hurt us the worst. It was very bad. Men dropped all around me. We tried flanking, but the mortars followed us wherever we went. Nothing we tried worked, and the men continued to drop. Finally, the order came to pull back.[84]

Yet they would all be ready to fight again. "All we needed," crowed Sergeant Guidone, "was decent chow, clean clothes, maybe movies and a little beer, and our morale would zoom back to Quantico level."[85] The next morning, volunteers set out to recover the dead. All the missing men were accounted for, properly identified, and given dignified burials.

Guadalcanal had received few radio reports from Liversedge thanks to the unreliable equipment with which the Raiders were burdened. Efforts to reach the NLG had repeatedly failed, so the decision was made to send a small patrol out to determine the task force's status. Martin Clemens, a coastwatcher on Guadalcanal, volunteered to go. He selected just two partners for the mission: an experienced Solomons bushman who knew a good trail to Enogai and a sharp-eyed American Indian U.S. Army scout. Clemens and his companions happened upon several Japanese patrols on the trail, so they shifted to a parallel route that was considerably more difficult, but safer. Late in the afternoon on their second day out, they stumbled onto the fresh boot prints of an American. Minutes later, as they made a turn around a hillock, they could hear movement. Clemens and his men readied their weapons and sprang out of the bush. There in the trail were Colonel Liversedge, his pistol still lodged inside his holster, and Lieutenant Colonel Griffith.

His face worn from the strain of combat, the NLG commander reported that they were short of food, ammunition, and medical supplies, and that his radios were no longer working. Clemens recalled that Griffith, using a piece of tracing paper,

> sketched what they knew of the Jap positions, their weapons, fields of fire, casualties, and the considerable number of wounded for whom they had few facilities to care. No means of evacuation other than a couple of landing craft at Rice Anchorage. He reported the list of spares required for the signalers' radio sets and what else was required if they were to make another attack. This interesting document was folded and refolded, and put it in my matchbox. Very early the next morning I and my two offsiders hightailed it back for Munda, most of the time straight down the trail. We got back in and reported. A couple of Catalinas were laid on, and I briefed them, and off they went. All wounded were then evacuated.[86]

For the next thirteen days, the dead-faced, depleted men of Liversedge's task force garrisoned Enogai, Triri, and Rice Anchorage, enduring daily air strikes and performing routine reconnaissance patrols. On one such operation, a squad of Raiders in the bush heard a noise and froze. Someone challenged with "Who is it?" An unseen voice not twenty-five yards away cried out "Rites!" With hardly a hesitation, the men opened fire. It turned out to be a small ambush. When the firing stopped, the Raiders searched the enemy position and found a dog tag on one of the dead Japanese. It belonged to Pfc. Norton D. Retzsch, who was listed as missing in action on 9 July. Retzsch had always firmly insisted that his name be pronounced "Reetz" rather than "Rites." That error cost the Japanese their lives.[87]

A particular nuisance the men of the NLG were forced to endure was a Japanese floatplane that flew slowly at low altitude over Bairoko every night and dropped small bombs. The men called their antagonist "Washing Machine Charlie" (or "Piss Call Charlie") because of the rhythmical humming of the plane's noisy engines. Like his American counterparts, the PBY Black Cats, Charlie was never very accurate. He caused few casualties, and damage from his nightly attacks was slight. He did little more than disturb their sleep. Still, his regular runs became increasingly bothersome as he flew back and forth overhead in search of a target. Once the pilot located one, he would dive, cut his engines until he leveled out to drop his payload, and then gun his engines for a quick exit. Each time he made a pass the men on the ground were forced to grab their rifles and move to a more secure position. They would wait for him to cut his engines, then sit anxiously in the eerie silence wondering where his bombs would land. One attack like that was not so bad, but he came back night after night, multiplying the nuisance factor exponentially. In August, the garrison finally received 40mm antiaircraft guns with which to answer his nightly visits. There was never a happier moment in the encampment. The night after the guns were set up, the men waited in gleeful anticipation for Charlie's arrival, hoping the gunners would finally get a piece of him. When the pilot cut his engines and began to glide overhead, the 40mm guns opened up. "You could almost hear his sphincter snap shut as he clawed for altitude," recalled Capt. Jack Goulding. Charlie sped away and never returned. "In a perverse way, we missed him," mused Sergeant Guidone.[88]

Waiting for their next mission was tedious and boring, the common complaint of warriors for centuries. One of the few things for them to do during the time they were not on patrol was to clean their weapons and write letters home. The latter was a problem because of a shortage of paper. The men would tear apart K-ration boxes and scribble a few lines on the unwaxed side of the cardboard. There were, of course, no envelopes, but the post office still delivered their field expedient missives. There also was time for religious services. Their chapel was a clearing under the branches of a huge banyan tree. For communion, the Raiders's Father Redmond used K-ration biscuits and wine served from an aluminum canteen cup. The men who attended, regardless of their religious background, reported that these primitive devotionals were the most moving and prayerful of their lives. Douglas MacArthur perhaps said it best: "There are no atheists in the foxholes of Bataan." Their only real entertainment was trading souvenirs pilfered from enemy corpses. There were wallets, family photos, caps, flags, pistols, and even a few swords in their stash. Navy and Air Corps people would pay well for these when they got back to Guadalcanal.

One day, however, the routine was broken. A returning Raider patrol brought back a seriously wounded Japanese soldier. The man kept repeating, "Me die. Me die." A member of the patrol decided to oblige him. The marine dragged the man into the bush and lopped off his head with a machete, upsetting at least one soldier, who was startled by the slaying.[89]

On 3 August the NLG was ordered to occupy key positions between Munda and Bairoko to prevent the enemy from withdrawing from Munda. The airfield was expected to be in American hands within forty-eight hours, and surviving Japanese troops would most likely attempt to escape to Bairoko from their fallen citadel. For six days the GIs and Raiders scouted the area around them for Sasaki's defeated troops. On 9 August, lead elements of the 27th Infantry Regiment—part of the army's 25th Infantry Division, which had been called in during the closing days of the main assault on Munda—made contact with the NLG.

The next day, Liversedge's command was placed under the operational control of Maj. Gen. J. Lawton Collins, the 25th Division commander, and ordered to conduct another assault on Bairoko. Fresh soldiers from Collins's division, joined by the 3rd Battalion, 145th Infantry, would take the Raiders' place in the attack. The marines, weakened by dysentery, malnutrition, malaria, and combat fatigue brought on by their long jungle ordeal, were in no condition to mount another offensive. Of the 521 men remaining in the 1st Raiders, only 245 were combat-ready. In Currin's 4th Raiders, medical officers deemed only 154 of 412 men healthy enough for action.[90]

The newly organized NLG moved forward on 24 August, easily overwhelming the last outposts feebly guarding the harbor. Most of the main body of defenders had been evacuated to Kolombangara when, in the late afternoon, a company from the 3rd Battalion, 145th Infantry, moving up the same trail used in the aborted 20 July attack, entered Bairoko unopposed. There amid the scattered wreckage they found the remains of Pfc. Paul D. Lehey, a runner from the 148th Infantry who had been captured during the original assault. He had been tied to a post and bayoneted and hacked to death, probably just before the Americans arrived. His body was so badly mutilated that he could be identified only by his dog tags.[91]

There was no celebration. Colonel Liversedge radioed word of the mission's success to General Collins's headquarters and, in a flat monotone, asked for a prompt APD pickup. The next morning, Harry "the Horse" Liversedge and what remained of his two weary Raider battalions boarded a fast transport headed for Guadalcanal.[92]

Was the NLG's sacrifice worth the effort? Certainly it prevented General Sasaki from benefiting from the thousand or so men left to defend Bairoko Harbor. Most of those men would have enhanced Munda's defense and helped postpone its capture. However, the task force's primary mission was to stem the flow of men and supplies to Munda during the main assault, a strategy born of the experience on Guadalcanal, where the Tokyo Express landed two full divisions in spite of significant Allied efforts to disrupt the landings. Admiral Turner and his staff did not want New Georgia to become another Guadalcanal. Yet Bairoko hardly mattered at all. Although it had the best facility for accepting supplies from Kolombangara, the Japanese quickly found alternate routes for resupply—across the island of Arundel, for example—that Admiral Turner discounted. If cutting Munda's lifeline was the goal, the way to do it was for the navy to control barge traffic in the Kula Gulf so as to prevent more troops from reaching New Georgia.

The real blame for the troubled campaign belongs to the planners who misjudged New Georgia's forbidding terrain. This oversight created the most crucial gap in Admiral Turner's plan, in particular, the failure to provide adequate fire support by artillery, naval gunfire, and air strikes. After Enogai was secured, for example, a battery of 105mm howitzers could have been landed there to support Liversedge's bloody assault. Failing that, naval gunfire support from the Kula Gulf on the morning of the assault would probably have made the difference. However, with the main attack on Munda bogged down and in trouble, no one was willing to spare anything for the sideshow on Dragons Peninsula. Finally, Turner's intelligence staff should have provided the NLG a better estimate of Bairoko's strength. It turned out that Commander Okumura had a supporting artillery battery from the 6th Field Artillery, as well as a battalion from the 45th Infantry Regiment to augment his own 6th Kure SNLF and troops from the 13th Infantry Regiment. It proved to be much too formidable a force for two light infantry battalions to attack under those severe conditions.

Even the Joint Chiefs of Staff (JCS) in far away Washington recognized Liversedge's predicament. On 22 July, without mentioning his name, the JCS admonished Turner for his shortsightedness. "The Marine Raiders," the JCS report stated, "are equipped for surprise operations. Such lightly armed troops cannot be expected to attack fixed positions defended by heavy automatic weapons, mortars, and heavy artillery." In surprisingly frank language, the report went on to imply that the NLG was abandoned by Turner, comparing the failure to reinforce it with his earlier "abandonment" of the 1st Marine Division when it first landed on Guadalcanal.[93] Captain Tony Walker endorsed the disturbing report years later: "If we had been provided the gunfire of one destroyer, we may well have won. Generals and admirals are supposed to think of this."[94]

Unfortunately, the New Georgia jungle continued to occupy center stage during the assault on Munda airfield. It served the Japanese well, for they shrewdly made it their most important ally. For the army's 43rd Infantry Division, which had landed at Zanana beach On 5 July, it became a nemesis equal to General Sasaki's defenses.

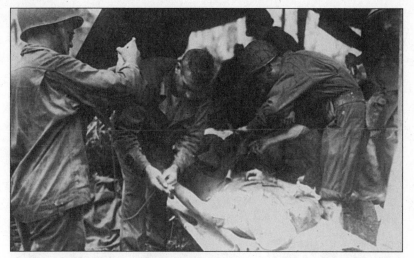

On Rendova, a Marine helps a buddy as two men administer plasma at a front line dressing station. Two others work on a leg wound, cutting away clothing. (This after the initial Japanese air attack.) Casualties probably from the Marine Defense Battalion. (Marine Corps Historical Center)

PLANTATION BUILDINGS ON HILL

CLEARING

From coconut field to airfield to rubble. Munda Field is shown. Enemy development of the airfield was followed closely by Navy photo reconnaissance. (Marine Corps Historical Center)

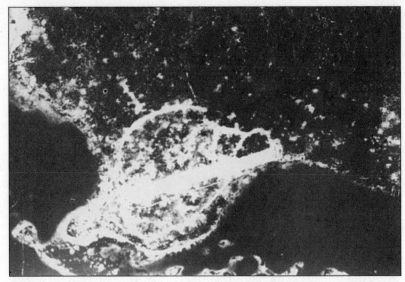

Heavy shellfire and aerial bombings blasted the Munda airfield into shambles. Photo taken from a Navy plane. (Marine Corps Historical Center)

Getting ready to load and fire 155mm howitzer on Rendova behind a revetment of sandbags and coconut logs. (Marine Corps Historical Center)

Munda airfield. Essential support of the move up the "ladder." This is what it looked like after the Americans took over. (Marine Corps Historical Center)

SBD Dauntless dive bomber based at Guadalcanal and the Russells. (Marine Corps Historical Center)

A corduroy road—117th Engineers, 37th Infantry Division, 11 August 1943.

A flame-thrower from the 43d Infantry Division, near Munda.

A camouflaged radio truck, 37th Division Command Post area on New Georgia, 5 August 1943.

Troops of the 37th Infantry Division from the 145th Regiment moving forward, 5 August 1943.

Soldiers of the 117th Engineers laying a corduroy road, 11 August 1943.

Engineers carrying projectiles to an artillery battery.

Engineers bathe in a jungle creek. Purified water was reserved for eating and drinking. Photo was taken from road above.

Technician 5th class Melvin Cummings of Michigan operates a switchboard of an army field artillery exchange in an oversized fox-hole. Operators were on duty twenty-four hours a day.

Perfect camouflage. A prefab tank for storage of 100 octane aviation fuel.

Fiji scouts at rest probably talking about the enemy. Called South Pacific scouts or Fiji commandos, the pipe is their favorite pastime. A New Zealander in command crouches behind them, 26 July 1943.

Japanese money found on an enemy body. Shown are troops from H Company, 161st Infantry, and E Company, 148th Infantry.

Casualties on litters waiting for LST at Munda.

After being brought out of jungle, wounded were put on a Higgins boat for evacuation, 7 July 1943.

U.S. Cemetery at Munda.

Lonely, untended grave near water point at Laiana, made hastily during combat. It was later moved to a permanent site. Photo taken 16 September 1943.

Opening valve on a flame-thrower ahead of a pillbox near Munda. The target is just ahead of the operator and partner, well camouflaged.

A rare hot meal, as soldiers of I Company, 148th Infantry use their helmets as plates.

Carrying hot food through jungle and swamps, 17 August 1943.

Men of the 3d Battalion, 148th Infantry hold a raffle for good, dry socks.

Photo from bulldozer shows a guard on lookout for snipes. Escorts were assigned after bulldozer operators were shot. There were nine guards for this machine.

Troops of the 65th Engineers are shown cutting road parallel to a trail through the jungle.

Soldiers of Battery B, 169th Field Artillery are firing on the enemy from 5500 yards, 10 August 1943.

Native scouts waiting for orders to move out.

Soldiers struggle to move a 155mm howitzer at Zieta after five miles through mud. Tractors were used to get them there, manpower was used to emplace.

High steps were necessary to make one's way through the thick vegetation. In the background is a soldier looking upward for snipers.

Marine Raiders ford one of the numerous rivers that sliced through New Georgia. The third marine from rear carries a "boys" 37mm rifle over his soldier. (U.S. Marine Raider Asscociation)

A BAR man in the bow of a rubber boat provides covering fire as a ten-man crew of marines reaches an undefended beach in the Russels. Boats like these carried Raiders in both the Viru Harbor and Rice Anchorage operations. (Marine Corps Historical Center)

Marine Raider Col. Harry Liversedge, commander. of the Northern Landing Group, cuts a cake in honor of the Marine Corps birthday, 10 November 1943. (Marine Corps Historical Center)

Navy lieutenant Hugh B. Miller being congratulated by First Lady
Eleanor Roosevelt and Admiral Halsey in September 1943 after being awarded the Purple Heart and Navy Cross. After his ship was sunk
in action, Miller survived an incredible ordeal on an enemy-held island before his rescue. (Marine Corps Historical Center)

Natives stand watch
near a peaceful surf
on Morovo Lagoon,
near Segi. (Marine
Corps Historical
Center)

5 Terra Incognita

A heavy curtain of forest pressed against the gray-faced soldiers of Maj. Gen. John Hester's 43rd infantry Division as they felt their way into the murky, swollen darkness of southern New Georgia. It was shortly before dawn on 6 July when they began their attempt to align themselves for the assault on Munda airfield five miles away. Waist deep in vegetation, their creeping movement from Zanana beach disturbed the opaque stillness, each unsteady step releasing an odor of organic decay that choked the young soldiers. They blundered through a thick tangle of brambles, thickets, rocky hills, and banyan roots, which pierced and bruised them as they prepared for their first brush with fear. Visibility during the day was no greater than a few yards, and a man could walk miles without once stepping into sunlight. Everything around them shimmered with movement, for the jungle's huge population of tiny creatures was constantly occupied with the business of hunting. There were so many oversized frogs, centipedes, lizards, and caterpillars stirring about that the earth itself seemed to crawl. Sleek green snakes inched their way up tree trunks, unhurried by the clumsy movement of humans through their habitat. Then suddenly there would be an explosion of color as hundreds of strange birds swept through the quilt of branches and erupted above the tree line, leaving the jungle throbbing with their screams. It was a place they did not belong.

Colonel Liversedge and his Northern Landing Group were inching toward Enogai when the 43rd's 169th Infantry, a Connecticut National Guard regiment, occupied a position about three miles north of Zanana, followed closely by another Guard regiment, the 172nd Infantry. Once in place, they would turn west and move toward

Munda abreast of each other until they reached the Barike River, using it as a line of departure for the assault on the airfield. A battalion from the division's other regiment, the 103rd Infantry, along with tanks from the 9th Marine Defense Battalion, would prepare the way for the final attack by landing near the airfield itself two days after the initial assault. The rest of the regiment remained in reserve on Rendova.

By afternoon, all three battalions of Col. David Ross's 172nd Infantry had reached the whiskey-hued Barike, encountering only a few small enemy patrols that quickly vaporized in the jungle growth that crowded around them. The novice GIs were feeling their way through their first experience of combat, each wondering how he would react once the fighting began. The men of Company F had an early epiphany. Moving west along the coast toward the Barike, they came under fire from Japanese 57mm knee mortars. The men flung themselves to the ground. First Lieutenant Ben Sportsman, the acting company commander, saw one of his platoon sergeants drop his weapon, turn, and sprint to the rear. It appeared likely that the others in the platoon would soon follow, so the young officer coolly stood up and, waving his rifle, screamed as loud as he could that he would shoot the next man to flee. That stopped the hysteria. The mortar fire soon ended and they continued on their way.[1]

There was worse trouble elsewhere. The 3rd Battalion, 169th Infantry, moving in a column of companies through the thick trees and underbrush, was ordered to destroy a platoon from the Japanese 229th Infantry on a small rise blocking the Munda Trail, a primitive path on which native guides were leading the regiment toward the river. Native Nekale and Fasala trees rose limbless from the damp jungle floor, abruptly extending their leafy arms to fashion an almost impenetrable tent about 150 feet above the men, blotting out the furnace-bright sun and subjecting the GIs to steamy, rigid air. Sinister vines coiled around their warty trunks, penetrating them here, bulging out again there as they slithered upward toward the sky. A glutinous sludge sucked at the soldiers' boots, belching jungle gas that reeked of decay.

Japanese machine guns were zeroed in on them near the trail's end, and the thick jungle concealed others along the trail's flanks. The battalion, after taking its first casualties in the green quagmire, did not challenge the enemy stronghold. Instead, the order was passed to dig in for the night three hundred yards east of the trail block. A few machine guns had stalled an entire battalion. Larry Buckland, a rifleman in the 169th, tried to make some sense of it: "You go through this training and it's what you're going to do to the enemy and the objectives you're going to do. But no one tells you that maybe you're going to get your face blown off or an arm shot off. Once you get in there and see this misery and suffering, now it's a different ball game."[2]

Instead of configuring a tight perimeter, the inexperienced, jittery GIs dug their foxholes more than six feet apart and did not bother to string tripwires so as to provide early warning of enemy infiltration attempts. Nor were orders given to maintain fire discipline inside the foxholes. This was crucial because the Japanese made it a practice to attempt to draw fire from the perimeter positions because the muzzle flash from weapons gave away their exact locations. The operation proved to be on-the-job training for the division's officers and men. No one seemed to know what to do, and indecision spread quickly. Everyone knew they were supposed to hit the deck when they encountered hostile fire, declared rifleman Alfred Cassella. But what next? "You wait for someone to tell you what to do. Those commands were not forthcoming."[3]

The Allies may have controlled the daylight hours in the Pacific on land and at sea, but the Japanese owned the nights. The U.S. Navy learned the hard way to respect the enemy's deadly skills with their superior optical equipment, torpedoes, and flash-suppressing devices. The Imperial Army took advantage of the jungle at night to neutralize the huge American advantages in firepower that they were forced to endure during daylight hours. Americans avoided movement unless they could be assured of artillery cover, so at night, when artillery adjustment was impossible, troops stayed put, dug in, and tried to get some steep.

The nightmare for Col. John Eason's 169th Infantry began around midnight. The darkness melted into mysterious sounds as voices, invisible in the inky-black wetness that entombed the GIs, began to call out, mocking them. Creeping to within a few yards of the perimeter, the Japanese yelled in English the code names of the battalion's companies, made references to the unit's training in Louisiana, and

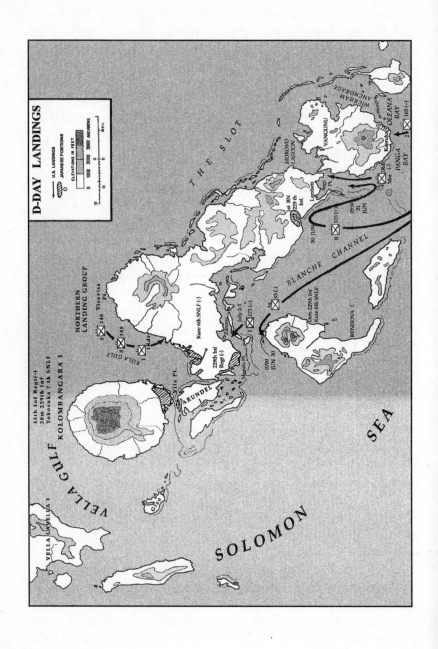

taunted the Americans to come out of their holes and fight.[4] One voice even challenged 1st Lt. Aubern Marr by name.[5] They called for cigarettes, for help, and for water. To the green troops huddled in their muddy holes, the blackness seemed to be collapsing onto them, smothering them in a claustrophobic grip of fear. Their minds began to play tricks on them—the phosphorescence of rotten tree limbs and the screams of flying foxes and fruit bats became enemy signals. Squirming land crabs, attracted to the food particles remaining in empty C-ration cans, became infiltrating Japanese. It was surprising how much noise those shelled creatures could make in the pitch-black night. Larry Buckland was sure that the crabs drew more than a few grenades.[6] A GI in Company F, mistaking the sounds made by land crabs for enemy movement, panicked in his foxhole, swung his machete, and killed his partner.[7] From inside a foxhole, said Sgt. Norvil Wilson, those "crabs sounded like a human crawling on his belly. Made a lot of noise. They were about the size of your fist. In the day they'd hide in banyan tree roots. Only come out at night. They were brownish-red. You'd kill one and it would stink like hell."[8]

Fantastic stories circulated throughout the division about ape-men from Borneo who would swing down at night from the treetop dwellings and slay the unsuspecting in their holes.[9] Marine veterans of Guadalcanal, having a little fun at the army's expense once that island had been secured, generated rumors of how the enemy raiders would sneak into the perimeter wearing long, black robes and drag men away with ropes and hooks.[10] It was comical at the time, but the images conjured up by the rumors, coupled with the wailing of the nocturnal marauders, were enough to keep the GIs sleepless and on edge all night. Misinformation about the enemy was so widespread that it prompted an article in the *Infantry Journal* that attempted to humanize them. Entitled "Battle Facts for Your Outfit," the December 1943 piece was written by two New Georgia veterans who debunked, among other things, the myths that all Japanese spoke fluent English, hosed poison gas into foxholes, and were high on drugs during combat.[11]

However, the loss of sleep was only a negligible consequence of the soldiers' jungle ordeal. More dangerous was their habit of throwing grenades blindly into the darkness. Often, the errant grenades hit trees, bounced back, and exploded among their own positions.[12] Men also would fire their rifles at anonymous sounds. The gunshots in turn tended to create an infectious panic of blind shooting that exposed their positions to the enemy, caused friendly casualties, and created chaos inside the perimeter. One enterprising battalion commander checked this problem in his outfit by offering a twenty-four-hour respite in a rear area to anyone who could silently kill a Japanese infiltrator. Offering this bounty turned his men into predators and had a calming effect during the long, dark nights.[13]

During that terrifying night on the Munda Trail, a report circulated among the men that the enemy had infiltrated their position. By morning, soldiers along the perimeter were swearing that they had seen Japanese jump into foxholes and bayonet the occupants. According to Bill Kean, "It was a nightmare that you couldn't imagine. Guys were getting hurt. Guys were fighting against themselves. There was just too much confusion."[14] When it was finally light enough to see, the men searched the area and found no enemy bodies anywhere. There were, however, dozens of stabbed and lacerated GIs.[15] Medical teams later determined that about half of the machete and knife wounds were actually inflicted by the wounded men's terrorized buddies.[16]

There was no need for an event to trigger an outburst. Sometimes all it took was for someone's imagination to run amok. Such a situation occurred in the 169th. Technical Sergeant Sal LaMagna of Company F was sharing a foxhole with his buddy, Joe Lapinski, who had begun to show signs of cracking under the strain. Lapinski's once-animated face, now void of all but fear, betrayed this affliction. When he kept muttering that he heard enemy soldiers sneaking around, LaMagna assured him that it was only land crabs, but his answer fell on deaf ears. An hour later, LaMagna, feeling the weight of something on his shoulder,

> reached up and felt a grenade. The pin was still in. I felt Joe . . . lay another grenade on my shoulder. I grabbed his hand and asked him what the hell he was doing! He was getting ready for that $&*@ Jap and wanted the grenades where he could get them fast. . . . About an hour later he stood up in our hole and yelled

for the Japs to come on. I yanked him down, but he kept on rav-
ing. . . . I rapped him across the mouth with my .45 pistol and
told him that if he didn't stay put, I'd shoot him. That did it. He
slumped down in our hole and slept.

The next night, Lapinski was moved to a three-man hole about
twenty feet away so someone would always be alert to watch him. During the night, LaMagna heard shouts and gunshots from Lapinski's
hole. When morning came, LaMagna discovered what had happened. Sometime during the night, Lapinski had gone berserk,
grabbed his .45-caliber pistol, and begun shooting, wounding one
of his comrades in the chest and leg. The other man quickly grabbed
his rifle and shot Lapinski. The survivors rolled Lipinski's limp body
out of their hole, leaving him face-up in the moist mud, his face a
frozen mask of fright.[17]

Such psychiatric casualties were the result of "war neurosis" or
"shell shock," as it was known in World War I. Marines on Guadalcanal called the condition "jitterbugging." The symptoms included
stupor, tremors, amnesia, or the inability to move, speak, or hear.
Some men would curl up in a fetal position. Others suffered from
paranoid schizophrenia. Hallucinations were also common. Ray
Winialski of Company H, 169th Infantry, had a buddy who swore that
a Japanese soldier had approached his hole during the night and
asked him about his mother and father.[18] Sergeant Norvil Wilson of
the 37th Infantry Division, who saw his first action on New Georgia,
clearly remembered other symptoms: "I had a man in my company—
a mortar shell landed just a few feet from him. After that he didn't
even know his name. Went into shakes. Couldn't hold a cigarette.
Couldn't eat. It took him two weeks to come out of it. Didn't remember anything. And I seriously think that if I had been in combat another month, I would have cracked. The strain that you're under all the time. For ten years after the war I'd have nightmares. My
wife would wake me up. I'd almost be screaming."[19]

Another sergeant said his unit

took care of shell shock cases in our foxholes. Some of these
were very bad and were unable to walk alone. They could not
talk to make themselves understood. Water would be "wa wa wa

wa" and cigarette was "sss sss sss sss," both of which they took in great gulps. If one can imagine a big strong man using both hands to hold a cigarette, he can get some idea of his condition. It was too late at night to take them back out of the area, but the medical men gave them a shot of morphine that kept them more or less quiet, and eventually they fell into a kind of sleep.[20]

Captain Joseph Risman, a medical officer in the 169th, treated a number of neurosis cases, including one while his unit was moving down a trail:

> I saw soldiers struggling. A big husky lad had suddenly lost his head and began to strike out about him with his trench knife. The rest of the detail dragged him down, and three men held him while a fourth twisted a knife out of his hands. The soldier was completely mad, his eyes rolled, he struggled and grunted while his buddies tried to calm him and bring him to his senses. I gave him a gram of morphine, tied his wrists together behind his back, and two of his companions led him struggling back down the trail. It was pathetic watching them, the old friends vainly pleading and entreating the struggling soldier to recognize them. They recalled events of the past, but still he struggled. The prolonged hardship, strain, lack of sleep, lack of food, and physical exhaustion, combined with the stench of the unburied dead and the groans of the wounded requires a strong mind.

He recalled numerous other cases as well, most of which occurred during night bivouacs after Japanese troops had heckled the men for hours. As is evident from his description, however, not all displayed the same symptoms:

> It was dawn. I checked up on casualties. One minor shrapnel wound and three neurosis cases. The chopping and screaming were evidently merely harassing tactics. Effective too. The characteristic [neurotic] just lays on the ground, hangs on to the branch of a bush, and trembles. He pays no attention to any-

one. Just hangs on to the branch and shakes. With each rifle shot or other noise the trembling becomes more marked. Routine treatment—morphine, cut down with a machete the bush that he held to, and evacuate by litter. It was impossible to remove the branch from their hands.[21]

After a psychiatric casualty was evacuated to a rear-area medical facility, the prescribed treatment was rest, quiet, and, for those who showed no improvement, sodium Pentothal.

There were less humane ways of subduing the poor victims. Recognizing that the condition was dangerously contagious, Capt. Arthur Davis revealed that the standard practice in his unit was for the nearest sane man to club the victim unconscious with a rifle butt. Later he saw shiploads of psychiatric casualties returning to Guadalcanal in LSTs "shaken, disoriented, and with distorted faces. A ghastly scene."[22]

Colonel Frank T. Hallam, the chief surgeon of XIV Corps, the 43rd Division's parent organization, outlined the condition in a letter to his superiors:

At least 50% of these individuals requiring medical attention on entering medical installations were the picture of utter exhaustion, face expressionless, knees sagging, body bent forward, arms slightly flexed and hanging loosely, hands with palms slightly cupped, marked course tremor of fingers . . . , feet dragging, and an over-all appearance of apathy and physical exhaustion. About 20% of the total group were highly excited, crying, wringing their hands, mumbling incoherently, an expression of utter fright or fear, trembling all over, startled at the least sound or unusual commotion, having the appearance of trying to escape impending disaster. Another 15% showed manifestations of true psychoneurotic complexes. The remaining 15% included the anxiety cases.[23]

Even after the campaign was over, when there should have been a sense of great relief and triumph, there were those who fell prey to the neurosis. Joe O'Hara of the 135th Field Artillery was heading back to Guadalcanal with his battery on an LST when tragedy struck:

"About three bunks from me, one of the guys puts his toe to the trigger and puts the muzzle in his mouth and shot himself. He was kind of getting a little mental. You'd talk to him and he wouldn't answer you. Real moody. The shot didn't kill him, but he was in the hospital for eight or nine years. He was lying in his bunk. When someone shoots a rifle in a confined area, it's a big explosion. I thought we were being hit with artillery! I saw blood and thought a shell had come in and hit him."[24]

Approximately 1,500 soldiers (including a battalion commander) from the 43rd Division's three line regiments were diagnosed as war neurosis victims during the month of July 1943 in the New Georgia area of operations. That number amounted to almost 16 percent of Hester's infantry strength and was over three times the average number of medical admissions for psychoneurosis armywide during the war.[25] Roughly 700 came from the 169th, 450 from the 172nd, and 350 from the 103rd.[26] These three regiments contributed only 40 percent of the troops in the New Georgia campaign but suffered a startling 80 percent of all psychiatric casualties there.[27] The other two participating divisions, the 37th and 25th, were introduced into combat later in the campaign and, suffered fewer such casualties. By mid-June, one medical unit reported that the number of war neurosis cases it treated equaled the number of men wounded by enemy fire.[28] Another medical report said 125 casualties were processed daily at an aid station at Laiana (on New Georgia) from 22–29 July, and most of those were identified as war neurosis or "battle fatigue" cases.[29]

Immediately after the campaign was over, General Hester's successor ordered medical personnel to identify anyone who might not be able to perform satisfactorily in combat. Colonel Hallam screened one thousand war neurosis cases from all three regiments in the combat zone and surveyed officers and enlisted men of all grades from units both with and without high numbers of neurosis cases. As a result, many men were reassigned to service units or transferred to base commands. The study also generated a report attempting to catalog the causative factors of war neurosis. From the data collected, Hallam concluded that poor leadership was the primary reason for the large number of psychiatric casualties in the 43rd Division. Some company-grade officers, he stated, "were not able to instill confidence in their men nor [able] to control the wave of 'infectious' hysteria which seemed to permeate a unit when one or more men showed signs of breaking." Also, whenever a platoon leader, platoon sergeant, or squad leader was evacuated for the disorder, the number of cases in his unit increased dramatically.[30]

Captain Robert Schwolsky, a company commander in the 2nd Battalion, 169th Infantry, verified that finding when he described what happened after his battalion commander broke:

> I'd have to go around in the morning and check on the men for war neurosis. I'd have a tree branch and would put it into their hands to hold on to so I could pull them up from their holes. Shaking. One of them was one of my platoon leaders. They couldn't take it after a couple of nights. Officer and enlisted. I had a battalion commander who took off. My communications sergeant said, "What's good enough for the colonel is good enough for me. And I never saw the sergeant again. He took off too. I didn't do anything. I was too busy to be affected by it. After New Georgia, the rest of the fighting for the rest of the war was easy.[31]

The conclusion was drawn that some commissioned and non-commisioned officers (NCOs) had "failed to gain the confidence of men under them, or had failed to knit together a smoothly organized unit capable of operating as such." Colonel Liversedge attested to this when he complained that army junior officers in his command lacked proficiency in map reading, scouting, and patrolling. Platoon leaders were not only unable to report the enemy's location, but often their own as well.[32]

One mistake like that would immediately erode whatever trust an officer's men might have had in him. According to James Salafia:

> The captains had maps, but in the jungle, none of them knew where their units were. One got so lost he called the artillery in to drop a smoke shell to verify his position. We ran like hell to get away from that officer. I heard a briefing. The colonel asks, "Where is B Company?" Someone answers, "I don't know."

The colonel asks, "Where's C Company?" And hears, "I don't know." He went through all the companies like that.[33]

Colonel Hallam suggested that many of the noncoms and officers in the National Guard units were selected because of their affability rather than their leadership skills. This was undoubtedly true in some cases. One soldier remembered that one of his line officers returned to a secure area in the rear after losing his glasses. He later "found" them, but the officer never returned to the unit.[34] Staff Sergeant Arthur O'Connell of the 118th Engineers claimed that some of his officers "appeared to avoid combat, feigning illness or stress."[35] Corporal Maurice LaPlant saw two noncoms get it. "It was probably stress," he admitted, "but we thought it was cowardice."[36]

Another cause of war neurosis, according to Hallam, was the failure to inform men what they should expect from day to day. "Information," said army historian S. L. A. Marshall, "is the soul of a soldier's morale." Major General Oscar Griswold, the XIV Corps commander, agreed, complaining that he saw far too many of these dangerous, troubling cases. "A man who is beside himself with fear is pathetic and dreadful to see, and the thing is like an infectious disease." His solution was to adequately prepare the soldiers for what they would expect to experience rather than "waiting to let them learn it in battle—the hard way."[37]

Louis Burton of Company H, 169th Infantry, said that much of the information about the terrain and the enemy, all bad, came from marines wounded on Guadalcanal who were returned to New Caledonia. Their stories, filled with hyperbole, half-truths, and falsehoods, resulted in a spurious portrait of the enemy as half-human, half-animal marauders who could see in the dark, climb trees like monkeys, grab a fly between their fingers without crushing it, and crawl for hours without making a sound.[38]

Sailor James Fahey watched curiously one day as an LST, just back from New Georgia, pulled alongside his ship anchored in Purvis Bay at Guadalcanal. Three hundred casualties were on board, most of them war neurosis victims. Fahey stared at the procession of stretchers and caught glimpses of the horror frozen on the faces of some of the men. Many had to be strapped down and given sedatives. Curious, he questioned some of the crewmen aboard the LST about the casualties and recorded their remarks:

> They said our troops go for days with very little sleep. They live in foxholes and when they get wounded or hurt, cut their clothes off to bind their wounds. The wounded troops who they brought back had hardly any clothes on so sailors gave them theirs. Fighting the Jap is like fighting a wild animal. The troops said that the Japs are as tough and fierce as they come; the Jap is not afraid to die, it is an honor to die for the Emperor, he is their God.
>
> A lot of fierce fighting is done at night and you can smell the Japs 25 yards away. The jungle is very hot and humid and drains the strength quickly. The jungle is also very thick; you could be right next to a Jap and yet you could not see him. . . . The Japs watch from coconut trees in the daytime and then when it becomes dark they sneak into your foxhole and cut your throat or throw a hand grenade. A 200 pound soldier was pulled from his foxhole and killed in a short time. You hear all sorts of noises made by the animals and you think it is the Japs. This is too much for some men and they crack up.[39]

How did others feel about the psychiatric casualties? Most men were sympathetic, perhaps amazed that they themselves had not broken down—and not a little proud of the fact. Their buddies' unfortunate condition was something that could easily happen to them as well, and they felt compassion and empathy for them. "Those guys were sincere," according to Carl Grotton of the 103rd Infantry, whose views were representative of the majority. "When a body breaks, it breaks. You don't condemn them."[40] Louis Burton's friend Marty was stricken by war neurosis. "Bullets everywhere. Close. He started to shake. Couldn't talk. His brain was okay, but he was unable to do anything." After a brief respite from the combat zone, he returned to his company. (Three-fourths of the victims rejoined their units anywhere from a few days to a few weeks later.[41]) When he reappeared and his buddies asked how he was doing, he recoiled, obviously sensitive about what had happened to him. No one mentioned the matter again.[42]

Although there is no data available, there were probably a significant number of men who experienced a recurrence after returning to their units. Sergeant Franklin Phelps of the 169th Infantry was sitting beside a trail in the jungle with his rifle company awaiting the signal to move out. There was some erratic sniper fire and an occasional enemy mortar round passed overhead, but nothing more. Phelps noticed a rifleman in a foxhole "acting queerly" before he began to shake all over, so much so that he was unable to hold onto his weapon. He was on his knees furiously trying to burrow deeper. Phelps went over to the man and tried to help him up. When the man failed to respond, he was sent to the rear.[43]

Of course, there were a few healthy men who pretended to be victims of war neurosis in order to get evacuated. Most such men were eventually exposed and disgraced. Soldiers have always found ways to punish those who violate the ironclad code of their unique society. Besides, most GIs were thankful when the gutless malingerers took themselves out of the fight, even if only temporarily, for they were considered liabilities and even threats to the entire unit. Colonel Hallam's analysis of the causes of war neurosis was certainly valid, but what he overlooked was the impact of the jungle itself. The tribulation of combat in that fetid environment magnified each factor he identified. To this must be added the insidious jungle skin diseases that bred in armpits and crotches, dengue or "breakbone" fever—which earned its nickname because of its impact on the body—and malaria. Author John Hersey, writing about the campaign for *Life* magazine, said that there was a psychological quirk about fighting in the jungle. Soldiers there felt trapped by the war, unlike those who fought in more open terrain like North Africa or Italy. The "stifling vegetation," he remarked, "seems to hold time back."[44]

General Collins, whose 25th Division participated in the Guadalcanal campaign, called movement on New Georgia "the worst physical ordeal I had during the whole period of the war."[45] Few of the men on that island jungle knew it, but each of them was free-falling down the dark tunnel into madness. For some, the descent was faster, the tunnel shorter. But *all*, to some degree at least, fell victim to the repellent horror of jungle combat.

In his autobiography, Admiral Halsey, like most high-ranking officers, did not take kindly to the high number (360) of psychiatric casualties in the 169th Infantry. Halsey's deputy, Maj. Gen. Millard Harmon, met with the evacuees personally and promptly returned three hundred of them to their units.[46] General Collins was more sympathetic. At first he did not believe there was such a condition as war neurosis—at least not if a unit had good leadership. He angrily ordered medical personnel to refrain from even using the term, thinking that giving it a name would only validate it. However, his attitude changed when he noticed that one of his men who had been awarded the Distinguished Service Cross on Guadalcanal collapsed on New Georgia, unable to function. "This man," he admitted, "was a brave man."[47] War neurosis was unquestionably real, and a majority of those developing symptoms needed to be either hospitalized or given a brief respite from combat before they could be returned to their units. All but 550 of the 43rd's twenty-five hundred psychiatric casualties were evacuated to Guadalcanal and beyond. Seventy-five to 80 percent completely recovered after three or four days' rest, showers, and hot food.[48]

Perhaps half of the men diagnosed as war neurosis casualties actually suffered from "combat fatigue." These soldiers exhibited some of the same symptoms of the more serious disorder, but their condition improved rapidly with proper rest.[49] Finally, there were the malingerers who took advantage of the avalanche of medical cases leaving the island (8,394 patients of all types were shipped out of New Georgia during the months of July through September). Using every subterfuge, they simply tagged themselves and lined up with the others on LCTs for evacuation in the absence of any type of screening.[50] One regimental commander pointed out that a few of these people jumped ship and scattered all over the Pacific. According to reports he received, a couple of men were discovered as far away as San Francisco.[51] Because of the initial difficulty identifying true psychiatric casualties, it is understandable that field-grade officers often had little sympathy for the lot of them. Three weeks into the campaign, authorities ordered medical officers to screen straggler lines for slackers.[52]

In 1941, 58 percent of all Veterans Administration hospital patients were World War I shell-shock victims. That figure alone should have alerted the Medical Corps to anticipate another flood of such cases. The psychiatric discharge rate for World War II combatants was 250 times that of the earlier conflict.[53] Nevertheless, it was not until November 1943, after the New Georgia operation ended, that the War Department authorized the assignment of a certified psychiatrist to each infantry division. That same year, the School of Military Neuropsychiatry opened in Atlanta at Lawson General Hospital. Both those moves were meant to address the unacceptably high number of psychiatric casualties coming from not only the jungles of the South Pacific, but also from North Africa and Italy. After almost two years of war, a more professional approach to the diagnosis and treatment of war neurosis was finally established.

It is interesting to note that after the New Georgia campaign, the 43rd Infantry Division, minus the men reassigned to noncombat duty, spent four months recuperating before its next assignment. With sleep, better food and water, and recreation away from the battlefield environment, the division waged a bitter five-week campaign in 1944 on New Guinea, where the conditions were similar to New Georgia. Yet during that time, only 199 psychiatric casualties were recorded, and many of those were quickly returned to duty. One difference was that the men were kept informed of current missions down to squad level, thus giving them at least a simple picture of their daily role in the operation. Later, in the Philippines, further steps were taken by the division to minimize psychiatric casualties. Most successful was the establishment of rest camps providing clean clothes, hot food, and relaxation for anyone displaying the telltale symptoms of war neurosis or battle fatigue. Each man sent to these camps was returned to his unit in five days or less, and of the more than five thousand casualties of all types suffered by the 43rd Division during the tough six-month campaign there, only ninety-two were neurosis cases—less than 2 percent.[54] Compared to New Georgia, where the figure was 40 percent, it becomes obvious that the division effectively eliminated the embarrassment and debilitating effects of war neurosis and became a competent fighting force. The about-face was slow, however. For the time being, the New Englanders would first have to make do without any of the enlightened changes that were made later and endure their baptism of fire on the detestable island.

• • •

Shortly after dawn on 7 July, the unnerved men of the 3rd Battalion, 169th Infantry, assisted by a company from their sister regiment, the 172nd, began converging on the trail block. When they encountered machine-gun fire, Maj. William Stebbins ordered his companies to deploy. Company I mounted a series of frontal assaults against the stronghold, but each time was beaten back with heavy losses, including three of its platoon leaders. The Japanese occupied well-camouflaged, mutually supporting coconut-log machine-gun bunkers protected by riflemen. The enemy was almost invisible, and the GIs caught no more than shadowy glimpses of their adversaries as the Japanese moved stealthily through the jungle haze. It was difficult to determine the exact locations of the bunkers because the Japanese weapons produced little muzzle flash and smoke. A few GIs crept forward, guiding on the clatter of the enemy's small arms, hoping to use grenades against the bunkers, but they were thrown back by enemy fire. Finally, the battalion's 81mm mortars were brought forward and the men began cutting overhead branches. This was necessary because mortar rounds striking even a small twig after leaving the tube would detonate, subjecting the men below to a lethal hail of shell fragments. Forward observers took up positions only thirty yards from the suspected enemy bunkers in order to adjust the fire. The order was given to commence firing, and the mortar crews pulverized the enemy position for thirty minutes, shredding the forest.

But even this did not reduce the stubbornly held "Bloody Hill," as it came to be known. After five hours of combat and a loss of six dead and thirty wounded, the 3rd Battalion was forced to retire two hundred yards back down the trail to a windless bivouac at midafternoon while the 172nd waited on the Barike. If close air support for the infantry had been available at this stage of the war, the hill might have been taken. But it was not. Air strikes against Japanese shore defenses were usually effective, as at Enogai and Munda. When enemy jungle emplacements were encountered, however, the airmen could not be counted on for help. Efforts to mark targets with smoke were ineffective because the Japanese would employ their own smoke shells and grenades to confuse the aviators. The marines began attaching air-liaison parties to infantry units so as to place them in direct communication with the pilots, but the first such makeshift teams were poorly trained and equipped with unsatisfactory radios.[55]

The battalion was thus forced to endure another frightful night deep in the womb of the groaning jungle. Again the men reported Japanese infiltrators jumping into foxholes after dark, swinging machetes and knives, and jeering at them in English. The terror was paralyzing, but there was no escape. Privates Thomas O'Brien and Harold Rothstein quickly learned to manage their fear by recognizing and accepting it. Fear was constantly with them on the front line, according to the two riflemen, but it was sustained, not hysterical. It became part of their daily routine in the bush. "The fear and suspense and danger are never over in the jungle," they reported. "They just go on and on. And you go on and on."[56]

In the morning the battalion dispatched patrols to investigate the trail block. The GIs found only the scattered remains of some of the defenders, their bodies perforated by mortar blasts. The rest had abandoned the position. However, that platoon of about forty Japanese had managed to delay the six-thousand-man attack on Munda—scheduled to begin on 8 July—a full day. A frustrated General Hester requested and received a one-day extension for launching the assault. His increasing appreciation for the enemy's defensive skills led him to cancel plans for using the 103rd Infantry and the 9th Marine Defense Battalion in an amphibious attack on the airfield. The operation clearly was not going to be as simple as everyone had thought.

On the ninth, the two regiments were strung out from south to north along the Barike in preparation for the assault on Munda, the 172nd's left flank along the coast, and its right flank tied in with the 169th's left to the north. Their orders were to advance westward from the river, seize the high ground overlooking Munda, and take the airfield. General Sasaki had established his main defenses in the rugged, thickly covered ridges southwest of the Barike, running about three thousand yards inland from the coast. If the positions there in any way resembled the pattern of interlocking bunkers on the ridges outside of Bairoko, the 43rd would be in for a very tough trial indeed—even though it was less than four miles from the objective. Concern was mounting in Bull Halsey's headquarters in New Caledonia. The admiral was well aware of the difficulty Lieutenant Colonel Currin was having reaching Viru Harbor. His Raiders were highly trained elite troops, and yet even they labored to traverse the island. Moreover, if a single platoon of Japanese troops could delay an entire regiment for twenty-four hours, what would happen when Hester's untested National Guardsmen went up against three thousand Japanese defenders dug securely into New Georgia's Jurassic landscape?

General Sasaki was awakened at 5 A.M. on the ninth by the thunderous, deafening roar of American artillery. For the GIs groveling in their mud holes, it was sweet music that had been composed especially for them. But for the Japanese commander, it was a screaming terror like nothing he had ever experienced. He could feel the ground tremble as he put on his boots and scrambled to his protected command post on Kokengolo Hill near the battered airfield. For nine hours, every available gun of Brig. Gen. Harold Barker's Force Artillery Group pumped out deadly ordnance, blanketing the high ground between the 43rd's sleepless troops and the airfield. During that time, two batteries of 155mm guns, two 105mm howitzer battalions, and two 155mm howitzer battalions fired fifty-eight hundred rounds. The fire initially was concentrated behind enemy lines for half an hour, then shifted to a thousand yards in front on the Barike River and slowly "walked" west toward Munda.[57] Twelve minutes after the army's guns opened fire, four destroyers that had slipped into Blanche Channel before dawn began unloading 2,335 five-inch shells, firing continuously for an hour into suspected enemy defenses near the airfield. The navy had offered to soften up the bunker system west of the Barike for the 43rd's troops, but General Hester declined, fearing that rounds fired from the ships' guns might accidentally fall short on his men.[58] Then, as if that were not enough punishment, eighty-eight navy and marine dive-bombers pummeled the jungle-covered hills just ahead of the Barike with high-explosive and fragmentation bombs.

Terrified Japanese troops recoiled in their bunkers, the smoking wilderness around them quaking and churning. Huge, hundred-year-old banyan trees were ripped effortlessly from the ground or simply disintegrated in the explosions, transforming great chunks of the rolling jungle into a steaming sea of mangled matchsticks, shredded and splintered at their tops. Powder-burned air, heavy with swirling coral dust, descended from the jungle ceiling, smothering the defenders. Violent detonations rocked the earth beneath them again and again, creating a huge dust cloud that polluted the disturbed island's dawn. Several tormented souls were crushed when their bunkers cracked and yielded to the relentless pounding. One poor wretch, his mind shattered by the bedlam, fled sobbing from his shelter-tomb and sought relief somewhere above ground. Those who were able to endure the madness prayed to their emperor to give them the courage to withstand the hellish barrage.

The Americans were displaying the one decided advantage they had in the New Georgia campaign. Although General Sasaki had an antiaircraft detachment and a mountain artillery regiment under his command, many of the heavier guns were needed at Enogai, Bairoko, and Vila. The remaining artillery pieces were either destroyed by repeated Allied air attacks or were without ammunition much of the time.[59] In fact, U.S. artillery batteries emplaced on the barrier islands off New Georgia's southern coast reported no counterbattery fire from Munda after the ninth, even though they were well within range of the enemy guns. Aside from automatic weapons and woefully few converted antiaircraft and shore guns, all the Japanese had to stem the assault from the east were mortars.

Despite the awesome display of American firepower, however, the Japanese suffered surprisingly few casualties from the bombardment on 9 July and subsequent fire missions. Their skillfully built log-and-coral bunkers protected them from all but a direct hit. One prisoner admitted after the campaign, however, that many of his comrades preferred to remain outside of the bunkers for fear of being buried alive, something that happened to five or six men in his unit.[60] The shellings proved to be of immeasurable value to the operation's success. They removed so much foliage that visibility was vastly improved for the advancing troops. At night, the guns provided protective fire around a battalion or regiment's perimeter. Tree snipers were all but eliminated, and night attacks were discouraged. Finally, the constant artillery fire significantly boosted the GIs' morale and greatly demoralized the enemy. Prisoner reports made it clear that the Japanese also suffered from war neurosis, and artillery fire was the leading cause. At the very least it produced sleeplessness. One enemy soldier confessed that artillery was the one thing that was universally feared by the Munda defenders. Another claimed that the airfield's defenders would have held out longer had it not been for the big guns.[61] By the conclusion of the New Georgia campaign, the American 155mm and 105mm guns and howitzers had fired 30,052 and 82,894 high-explosive rounds respectively, smothering the enemy's positions and hastening the victory.[62]

Compounding the problem for the Japanese was the blistering assault from the skies, most of which went unanswered. On 10 July, for example, 106 Grumman TBF Avengers and Douglas SBD Dauntlesses struck Munda with impunity. The following day, 86 more planes pounded the airfield. Again there was no sign of Japanese interceptors. On the twelfth, after plastering Munda with fifty-two tons of bombs, a force of 69 more TBFs and SBDs was menaced by enemy Zeros, but the Rendova fighter patrol burned 7 of them before they could jump the busy bombers. Two more strikes by 85 and 46 aircraft respectively hit positions in and around Munda on the thirteenth. All pilots returned without encountering a single enemy fighter. The same was true on the fourteenth, when 46 bombers hit Munda, encountering only light and ineffective antiaircraft fire.[63] That pattern continued throughout the remainder of the campaign. The sole relief General Sasaki's men got from the steady aerial punishment was when the weather turned sour and AirSols shut down operations for a while. That he and his men persevered throughout this onslaught is testimony to the courage of the Japanese infantryman.

Meanwhile, on the Barike River line, the Americans anxiously awaited the order to attack. Most of the men had gone without sleep for more than two days, and all of them cursed the jungle's clogging humidity. Medical officer Joseph Risman observed the void faces of the men as they moved farther into the jungle and remarked:

For the first time I noted the battle expression characteristic of the first part of the campaign. These men who had not changed clothes or had two continuous hours of sleep had the same expression. Their hair was matted and muddy, their beards were ½-inch in length, their eyes were sunk in, dark, and had a strained expression. Gait was plodding and methodical, no spring or bounce. When they stopped walking they fell in their tracks until it was time to proceed again. It was all I could do to go forward with no load. How those men carried up to 80 pounds, I shall never be able to understand. As we approached the Barike River, the terrain became mud. Men tripped on roots under the mud, fell flat on their faces, picked themselves up, adjusted their loads, and proceeded. No breath was wasted on cursing or talking. Strength was not unnecessarily expended.[64]

Compounding their misery was the army's new jungle gear, which was universally damned by the men. The canvas-and-rubber jungle boots issued to them made it impossible to keep their feet dry in New Georgia's swampy environment, resulting in hundreds of cases of infection from sores or jungle rot, a terrible fungus that destroyed layer after layer of skin. If not arrested soon, the disease could lead to amputation. Their newly issued jungle uniform was another torment. The uniforms were painted with irregular patterns of green, brown, and black camouflage, but the paint trapped body heat and humidity inside their clothing and it was not long before they began slitting air holes in the fabric. Many men cut their camouflage suits in two at the waist, tying the two halves together in an effort to overcome the dreadful garment's greatest design flaw: the lack of a seat flap. Unless one performed such radical surgery on the cursed suit, disrobing was required when nature called. Packs, cartridge belts—everything had to come off except helmet and boots. According to Captain Henne, that could be more than just an inconvenience on New Georgia:

It was easy to imagine that a Jap might be out there taking a bead on you while you were sitting on your ankles, jungle suit pulled in a bunch around your knees, trying to hit a cat hole. What a hellava way to go—killed while taking a crap. Once I moved out into the bush, dug my cat hole, and sat on my an-

kles to do my business. I had no more than settled when out of
the leaves and mud rose a huge monitor lizard. He angled toward me hissing, declaring that I had invaded his turf. I didn't
want to use my trusty .45 caliber pistol cradled in my hands, but
vowed that if the sucker moved much closer, I would blast him.
I must have stared him down. He stopped, looked me over,
hissed a couple of times, and then turned and ambled away. For
a few moments I thought that my first target on New Georgia
would be a lizard, not a Jap.[65]

The extreme annoyance caused by their uniforms should not be
underestimated. It served to reinforce the prevalent belief among
frontline soldiers that their leaders were incompetent fools. Why
had they ever allowed such miserable uniforms to be issued? Why
had they not trained for jungle warfare back in the states or somewhere else in the Pacific before they were sent to this godforsaken
island? All their tactical training was based on the concept of "open
warfare," a doctrine better suited for the open terrain in the European theater.

Sergeant Frank Phelps forgetting his discomfort for the moment,
rejoiced at the sound of friendly artillery fire. Earlier that night, the
Japanese had continued their harassment of his position, throwing
grenades, yelling, and even exploding firecrackers to confound the
New Englanders. Now it was their turn, he thought, to listen to some
noises:

I thought that under the cover of all this noise our friends . . .
might try to sneak in. Waiting with trench knife in one hand
and a heavy machete in the other, my eyes tried in vain to pierce
the darkness. It seemed as if dawn would never come.

We could hear the far away reports of the heavy guns as they
discharged their missiles of destruction. Next was the sound of
rushing air akin to the noise of a Twentieth Century Limited
as it passed a railway station. We could visualize trees falling,
dirt and debris flying into the air, and the enemy crouched in
their foxholes. I hoped the little yellow dogs that were plagu-
ing us would appreciate the show we were putting on for
them.[66]

At breakfast, everyone had a tale to tell about the night. Several men reported that Japanese soldiers had passed right by their holes into the perimeter. Two men in Headquarters Company were injured—either by knives or grenade fragments—seeming to validate their stories.[67] But danger lurked not only at night. Even the morning could be a dangerous time. A common practice was for the Japanese to silently position a sniper near a bivouac site. The man would remain until daybreak or midmorning, sometimes in a tree, looking for an open shot at an opportune target. It was a suicide mission, for the sniper would inevitably be killed. However, before he was, he would often bring down a few unsuspecting GIs, particularly if he were toting a light machine gun.

H-hour for the attack was set for 6:30 A.M. on 9 July. The torpid, waist-deep water, covered with a greenish scum, meandered through the amphitheater of crowded trees all the way to the sea, forming an easily identified line of departure. When the order to move came down, the attackers, clutching their rifles above their heads, forded the river in the gray half-light of dawn, pushing through the network of spider webs that dangled before them like jeweled necklaces in the morning dew. Wait-a-minute vines, some as thick as a man's leg, dropped down to entangle them. They tripped on hidden banyan roots and spilled into the water, swallowing the foul liquid.

But there was more trouble. For one thing, the operations order called for the regiments to move with battalions abreast in two-hundred-yard bounds, after which they would pause briefly to reestablish contact. The order, however, did not allow for the almost impenetrable bulwark of growth that cascaded to the airfield. It soon became clear that it would be impossible for even squads of ten men to advance abreast through the menacing tangle, where visibility was twenty feet or less in all directions. The attack's planners should have known better. The area had been scouted beforehand by local guides and Fijian commandos brought to the island by the Australians. Unfortunately, either their reports were too optimistic, or they were simply ignored. Commanders began to call back their leading elements, resulting in enormous confusion.

The order came down to change the attack formation to a column of files, a configuration more suitable for penetrating the dense undergrowth but inappropriate for an assault—and much more vulnerable to ambush. Units were forced to advance along a single native path on which small bands of Japanese lay in wait. When the lead elements were engaged by a few invisible Nambu machine guns, the entire assault ground to a halt. Three hours after the order to begin the attack was issued, Brig. Gen. Leonard Wing, the 43rd Division's assistant commander, received word at his command post that not one battalion had advanced forward of the river—and the main enemy defense line was still 2,500 yards away.

Darkness came early in the jungle, so the order to dig in for the night was given at 4:30 P.M. By that time, the 172nd was only about 200 yards west of the river, although the lead elements reported they had covered 1,100 yards. The reports were not intentionally falsified. The regiment legitimately perceived itself to have traveled farther because of the necessity of zigzagging through the thick brush, and therefore greatly exaggerated its true forward progress.[68] The hills and ridges twisted and bent in all directions, forcing units to move as much laterally as forward. The initial line of attack was 1,300 yards south to north along the river. It was now half that distance, with the two regiments threatening to blend together.

To the north, only one battalion from the 169th had managed to cross the river. Perhaps the regiment was suffering from lingering psychological effects from its night encounters with the enemy. Maps were still scarce and inaccurate, and junior officers were not properly briefed on what they were likely to face. This created an infectious doubt and a loss of self-confidence that almost certainly was conveyed to the men in their commands. Then, too, supply and wire communications had been completely severed by the Japanese. Compounding the problem, the 169th encountered more enemy activity than did the 172nd, particularly at night, and it had considerably rougher terrain to traverse. Whatever the cause, however, there was consternation in division headquarters. Heads undoubtedly would roll if things did not improve rapidly.

Before they tried to grab a few hours of sleep, Maj. Joseph Zimmer, commander of the 169th's 1st Battalion, met with his staff over a dinner of cold C-rations. Using a fallen log as their dining table, they discussed the day's progress and their plans for the next day.

When supper was over, they discarded their trash and set off in search of a suitable place to spend the night. The next morning, a security patrol discovered that a Japanese infiltrator had been hiding under the very log that Zimmer and his staff had used the previous evening.[69]

It was a relatively quiet night in the 3rd Battalion, 169th Infantry, camp—until a single shot from an M1 shattered the stillness, followed by more gunfire as the agitated troops fired into the surrounding jungle. Then a strange thing happened: The entire battalion held its fire when a thunderous, Tarzan like yell erupted from one of the foxholes. Sergeant Ernie Squatarito stood up in his hole, thumped his chest, and bellowed out another yell. Several other GIs followed suit and laughter soon rippled up and down the line. That bit of humor brought an end to the panicky shooting, and normality was restored for the rest of the night.[70]

The solemn, churchlike hush that enveloped the jungle on the morning of the tenth was broken by the movement of hundreds of men preparing to resume their push through the forest, which gleamed after the night's drizzle. The 169th finally forded the Barike, and down the line matters seemed more in hand. But forward progress was still painstaking.

The 172nd Infantry continued to make good progress, encountering little resistance, but then the 169th encountered another stubborn trail block in the early afternoon after advancing about fifteen hundred yards. A single company from the Japanese 229th Infantry, occupying a camouflaged position on a low rise near a trail junction, jumped the regiment's 3rd Battalion, which was in the lead. Colonel Eason ordered the men to fall back and called in mortar and artillery fire, which scorched and pounded the enemy position with high-explosive rounds that rearranged the landscape, shattering trees and replacing underbrush with freshly dug craters. As the smoke from the bombardment lifted up through the brambles and branches that still remained, Eason ordered an attack. Dozens of unseen heroic acts punctuated the fighting as the green troops struggled to advance. But the Japanese stiffened and held, compelling the regiment to bivouac in an odious mud swamp below the trail block. Once again, a much smaller force had stymied hundreds of men.

Things were not going nearly as smoothly as General Hester and his superiors in New Caledonia had hoped they would. The largest concern was logistics. The division's supply line now extended over two miles to Zanana, and there was nothing on the 43rd's northern right flank to protect the rear area from attack. Since there were no roads to Zanana, casualties had to be carried back in litters, and food, supplies, and ammo had to be hand-carried to the front—which further sapped the division's strength. The 118th Engineer Battalion worked tenaciously to carve roads, but the going was exceedingly slow. Heavy graders were unavailable, so the roads could not be crowned for drainage. The decision thus was made to corduroy in the lowest areas because of the heavy rains and mud. That meant that scores of trees had to be felled and positioned securely across the roadbed, a labor-intensive and time-consuming task that nobody wanted. Every foot of road also had to be surfaced with six to twelve inches of sand or crushed coral trucked in from coral pits near Zanana. Bulldozer operators were prime targets for Japanese snipers, and casualties became such a problem that metal shields (crafted from a beached Japanese landing barge) were welded to the vehicles' chassis to afford them some protection. Later in the campaign, three riflemen were assigned to walk with each of the hard-working machines, so important was it for them to complete their job.[71] Despite these extraordinary conditions, the engineers were able to construct an average of two hundred yards of roadbed a day.[72]

Nevertheless, General Hester was worried. Although the engineers were making good progress with their road to the Barike, once they reached its eastern bank, swampy mud required them to make a wide northern detour upriver without flank security and away from the troops the road was meant to support. They laid road for more than two miles before they found ground suitable to sholder two trestle bridges to cross the river, causing a forty-eight-hour delay. Each day, the 43rd became further estranged from Zanana's resources. It appeared to Hester that the engineer road would never catch up to the front lines in time for it to be of much use. In spite of assault units' slow forward progress, they were outdistancing their supply line.

Laiana Beach

The offensive had reached a critical stage. Sasaki's main defenses were about to be reached, and the fighting was sure to escalate in the face of both 7.7mm and 13mm machine guns, supported capably by 90mm mortars and the 57mm and 90mm mountain guns that were sure to unload on the beleaguered New Englanders. The rugged terrain was ideal for interlocking bunkers and mutually supporting positions for the riflemen and machine gunners. Both regiments would need a road over which to evacuate casualties, bring reinforcements and supplies forward quickly, and keep communications open with the division headquarters. The problem was created weeks before when the decision was made to land at Zanana, five long jungle miles from the objective. Setting the men down on a spot that far from Munda in such a heinous environment was, according to historian Samuel Eliot Morison, "the worst blunder in the most unintelligently-waged land campaign of the Pacific War."[73] Even the heroic efforts of the 118th Engineers were insufficient to keep a lifeline open to troops on the front. Hester's men were not much better off than Liversedge's Northern Landing Group—neither could count on logistical support. Only now did the planners' mistakes become obvious. Captain Jack Wilcox of Headquarters Company, 2nd Battalion, 169th Infantry, concurred with Morison's assessment: "When we landed, people were just thrown onto the beach. No place to go. The jungle started right from the waterfront. We could have gone up the coast to land on a clearing [Laiana]. We saw the consequences of this in a week's time. We didn't know what the hell was going on—who we were firing at, where the enemy was, and it's not surprising that we had some neurosis cases. To try and move a regimental combat team with all its gear and equipment up a native path in a thick jungle was very poor judgment."[74]

There was only one thing to do: Hester ordered the 169th to continue moving southwest toward Munda while the 172nd swung south to secure the beach at Laiana, just two miles from Munda. If a new supply base could be established there, it would supplant Zanana and shorten the logistical lifeline to the men by some five thousand yards. There was, however, one major problem with this course of action.

The main Japanese defenses were only five hundred yards west of Laiana beach, and it was likely that it, too, would be defended. Nevertheless, taking Laiana from the north would be infinitely easier than an assault from the sea.

At 10 A.M. on 11 July, roughly the same time that the NLG was storming Enogai and Allied troops in Europe were landing on Sicily, the 172nd began its detour to Laiana. Almost immediately the regiment was forced to churn through a hundred-yard trough of liquid mud while enduring a hailstorm of mortar fire. The ordeal was so exhausting that the GIs managed to cover only 450 more yards during the remainder of the day. By late afternoon on the twelfth, the aching troops, drunk with fatigue, ran into machine-gun and more mortar fire from well-prepared pillboxes connected by trenches about five hundred yards from the beach. Colonel Ross decided to halt his hungry and thirsty regiment there on the edge of a mangrove swamp and sketch an assault for the following morning. Meanwhile, the men suffered through mortar registration fire and occasional rifle shots that kept the bedraggled unit awake all night in that awful slough. They were not the only sleepless troops on New Georgia, however. Ships offshore heaved their shells on Munda again that night. Four cruisers and ten destroyers fired 8,600 five- and six-inch shells for sixty sustained minutes. It was the largest bombardment group to assemble during the entire Solomons campaign, and it dished out a blistering cannonade.

The shelling left behind a great deal of chewed up jungle, but there was little else to show for all the trouble. The Japanese suffered only an inconvenience. As soon as the huge guns began to fire their salvos, the airfield's defenders moved fast toward the American lines and inside the mile-wide safety zone along the 43rd's front into which naval guns were forbidden to fire. General Hester, unaccustomed to working with naval fire support and still concerned that the ships' rounds might fall short on his men, identified targets so far forward of his front line that the bombardment was of little direct use to him. General Sasaki in turn had his own heavy mortars dump rounds into the 43rd's positions moments after a U.S. artillery barrage so the GIs would think they were being hit by friendly fire, encouraging in them a lack of confidence in their own artillery. It

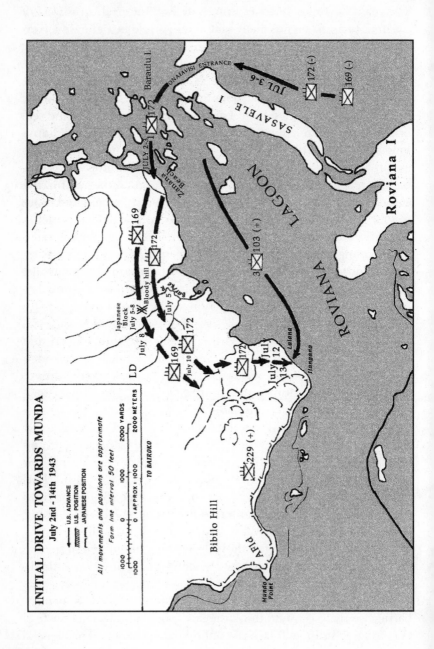

INITIAL DRIVE TOWARDS MUNDA
July 2nd - 14th 1943

sometimes worked. Soldiers throughout the campaign complained about inaccurate and dangerous friendly fire, both from the navy and from the division's batteries.

That same afternoon, a formation of Japanese bombers escorted by fighters from Kahili on Bougainville, the enemy's key Solomons airbase, showed up to drop supplies to Munda's defenders. They were greeted by navy Chance-Vought F4U Corsairs which, along with the highly regarded army P-38 Lightning and navy F6F Hellcat fighters, were fast replacing the older navy F4F Wildcats and army P-39 Airacobras in the Solomons during the summer of 1943. Forty-five Japanese planes were shot down by the rugged, fast-climbing, gull-winged fighters, which had a top speed of more than four hundred miles per hour. Their major adversary, the Japanese Zero, could attain only 331 miles per hour. Dubbed "Whistling Death" by the Japanese because of the scream from its air intakes, the Corsair could slice a plane in half with a single burst from its six .50-caliber machine guns. Place a well-trained pilot with a bit of experience in its cockpit, and it became almost invincible. It was one of those instruments of war that helped tip the scales in favor of the Allies. In dogfight after dogfight, it was fast becoming the same story for the outclassed Japanese pilots and their increasingly inferior aircraft. Henceforth, Japanese air combat losses would always be many times those suffered by the Allies.

Another air battle erupted on the fifteenth, with roughly the same results: 45 downed enemy aircraft out of 70, as opposed to only 3 Air-Sols planes. Thereafter, the Japanese wisely began conducting bombing missions only at night and at high altitude, significantly reducing their chances for success.[75] It was almost as though Rabaul had conceded New Georgia to the Americans. One artillery officer even expressed a rare bit of sympathy for the frustrated enemy:

> The poor Jap Air Force has a hell of a time of it. Our Air Force has established complete superiority of the air from dawn to dusk and when the Jap does attempt to fight back, he gets blasted right out of the sky. He is no match for our pilots no matter what he tries. At night unopposed he sneaks in a plane now and then for nuisance bombing or reconnaissance, but he

is seldom dangerous, and it usually ends in nothing more than the loss of a little sleep for those of us who are on the ground. The nightly Jap bombings and reconnaissance are becoming so commonplace and ineffective, it hardly seems worthwhile to report them anymore.[76]

During the week the men of the 43rd had spent in the jungle, they developed somewhat of a routine for the hellish nights. First they dug two-man foxholes a few feet apart to form an exterior perimeter around a company position. One-man holes were discouraged because there was a better chance that a lone rifleman would become hysterical under the stress and vacate his position. Then they sent out pickets who stretched communications wire festooned with noisemakers made of ammo clips or C-ration cans filled with pebbles outside the perimeter to provide early warning of enemy infiltration attempts. Sometimes the men added booby-trapped grenades rigged with trip wires. At twilight, the pickets would leave the wire screen in place and recede back into the interior of the perimeter, where they dug three- or four-man positions. They lined the floors of these muddy cavities with their ponchos and partially covered them with shelter halves to afford some protection from the rain. However, the slit trenches still filled up quickly, and it was impossible to stay dry. The men usually slept with their helmets on to keep their ears out of the water and grime.

A strict rule had evolved since those first terrorizing nights on the line: No one was to fire after dark unless the perimeter came under all-out attack. This order was so strictly enforced that a lone Japanese soldier could stand in front of a rifle squad and no one dared fire. Inside their holes, the men held knives or machetes for protection against enemy infiltrators. Anything that moved above ground was presumed to be Japanese and was liable to be stabbed. A soldier who had to defecate did so in his hole; helmets became urinals.

According to Collinsville, Connecticut, native Lester Goldstein: "We were curled up in our foxholes with a machete in one hand and a bayonet in the other. The first night they killed three of our men. The second night we lost three or four men and on the third night we lost nine."[77] However, on that same third night, GIs manning some of the 169th's outposts dragged enemy soldiers who got too close into their holes and quietly dispatched them.

Inside the perimeter, two of the men in a four-man hole would try to sleep while their partners stood watch. Talking or smoking was taboo, of course, and the GIs in neighboring holes would pelt men who violated this restriction with rocks. A simple code was developed for communicating. If a man thought he heard or saw something unusual he would tap his partner with his index finger. A one-tap reply meant the buddy had seen or heard it, too. Two taps meant there was nothing to worry about.[78] Frank Giliberto of Hartford, Connecticut, remembered that men often would not move at all for fear that a knee or elbow would crack, and when morning came they had to work on each other's "frozen" limbs to get the circulation going again.[79] Once, a mortar shell hit a three-man foxhole on an especially dark night. At dawn, the surviving occupants discovered to their horror that their buddy's arm had been torn off at the elbow and he had bled to death in silence.[80]

New replacements trickling in from Guadalcanal were no different from the others during their first nights on the line. They had been fed the same nonsense stories about what the enemy-infested jungle was like after dark. Often their fear got the better of them. Leonard Hall told about an incident in Company G, 72nd Infantry, which received a few replacements after reaching Laiana. During their first night in the humid darkness, two of the new men began shooting at what they believed was an enemy infiltrator. They climbed out of their hole and moved toward another replacement's hole thinking that he was the intruder. The soldier in the foxhole knew them both and called out their names and identified himself, but it did no good. They kept shooting at him, forcing him to return fire. He killed them both. There was no formal investigation of the unfortunate tragedy, and both men were listed as killed in action.[81]

After dawn, before emerging bleary-eyed from their mud holes, the men saturated the surrounding treetops with BAR fire to ensure that no snipers were waiting there. One soldier likened the practice to spraying for mosquitoes. That done, some of the men continued to stand watch while the remainder opened cans of C-rations and ate breakfast. Next, they lined up for their Atabrine pill, a medication used to combat malaria but which the men did not like to take because it was rumored that it caused impotence. Unit officers thus were required to dispense the pills individually. Many still spit the little pills out anyway, so the order came down for officers and NCOs to watch each soldier swallow it. Once that onerous task had been accomplished and canteens refilled with rain or swamp water spiked with purification tablets, the dreary band was ready to go.

As the 172nd Infantry snaked through the muddy swamp that sheltered Laiana five hundred yards away, the men could hear the beach being pounded by dive-bombers and 105mm and 155mm rounds tossed at them from Rendova and the barrier islands. Yet despite its ferocity, the bombardment had little effect on the enemy. The moist, gluey earth absorbed much of the bombs' blasts, and even a slight delay in the artillery fuse settings caused the rounds to burrow deep into the ground, forcing the explosions up rather than out peripherally. Once, a five-hundred-pound bomb detonated twenty yards from a regimental commander. He was shaken by the experience, but escaped with no more than a ringing in his ears.[82]

The dark wedge of attacking troops slogged slowly forward, transporting a mounting number of their own litter cases. This in itself was a great drain on Ross's unit, for each stretcher required between four and eight bearers, amounting to three and one-half companies.[83] However, the weary soldiers were aware that this was the last push. Once they made it to the beach, they were promised resupply and maybe even a swim. The thought of that indulgence quickened their pace somewhat, for a week in the bush had seemed to fix them in a condition of irreversible decay. Enemy fire hounded them the entire way as they clumsily but resolutely lunged forward in the sticky cauldron of muck, and by early afternoon they gained their prize by default as General Sasaki's soldiers pulled back to their main defenses to await the knockout punch.

That night, a dozen vessels carrying food and water and hoping to evacuate the wounded crossed over from Rendova searching for the beachhead. However, the 172nd, probably out of fear of a Japanese night assault, failed to light signals for the craft, which were forced to return when they could not find it. The next morning, General Hester ordered the 3rd Battalion, 103rd Infantry (part of the division reserve), a tank platoon from the 9th Marine Defense Battalion, and teams of flamethrowers, demolition experts, and engineers to land at Laiana. With fighters from the Russells providing top cover, more than twenty Higgins boats approached the beach as Japanese artillery sprayed the landing craft. General Barker's guns fired five hundred white phosphorous and high-explosive rounds to blind the enemy's forward observers, and the entire reinforced battalion disembarked safely. Once the reinforcements and supplies were ashore, the 172nd was fed, its wounded transferred to the field hospital on Rendova, and the engineers began to build a jeep trail inland.

A Japanese report discovered several weeks later claimed that two thousand Americans attempted to land on the beach that morning, but that at least half of them had been killed. The report made no mention of Japanese casualties.[84] General Sasaki himself greatly exaggerated the size of the landing and lied about its results to his superiors in Rabaul. He claimed the entire operation was aborted after his men sank fifteen large troop carriers out of the approximately seventy boats participating in the invasion.[85]

Meanwhile, the beleaguered and poorly supplied 169th Infantry's ranks were rapidly thinning from malaria, war neurosis, and wounds. Sadly, more than a few were self-inflicted. During a quiet breakfast one morning, for example, a pistol shot rang out. Soon a soldier appeared, blood pouring from a bullet hole in his hand. Another reported to a medic with a gunshot wound in his toe. He claimed that he had seen something in the bottom of his foxhole and had fired his rifle at it. Things were so bad that an antitank platoon in the 1st Battalion was forced to discard and bury its .50-caliber machine guns, a flamethrower, and other equipment because there were too few people to operate them.[86]

Despite these difficulties, the 169th pressed ahead. However, without any prominent terrain features on which to guide, navigation in the dense jungle was nearly impossible. Every hill and stream looked alike, so maps were of little help, and high-angle photos showed only layers of monochromatic jungle. Units began requesting artillery barrages to their front, then moved toward the billowing smoke. Flamethrowers were also used for this purpose. By having a neighboring unit fire a flamethrower straight up, the requesting unit could shoot a compass bearing toward the black smoke and then orient in that direction.[87] Even reconnaissance patrols were of little help in the jungle. A patrol could, for example, claw its way to a location like a hilltop and report back that it was undefended. But by the time the main body arrived there, the GIs might find it swarming with ruthless Japanese soldiers who could shift from one position to another within the wide defensive arc curling like a convex shield around the airfield. Even worse, General Sasaki was beginning to send hundreds of his men into the gap that had opened up between Hester's two regiments when the 172nd detoured to Laiana.

On 10 July, Colonel Eason's lead battalion slammed into a dogged enemy company occupying the high ground above a trail junction. Machine guns, heavy mortars, and artillery chewed away at it while nagging infiltrators and snipers menaced the battalion's flanks. When it became clear that the battalion would be unable to pierce the blocking position, Eason was forced to order a withdrawal to a bivouac site in an unpleasant swampy area. Worse, the regiment had advanced a mere fifteen hundred yards. The next morning, Eason struck hard at the ridge and by nightfall the GIs had managed to fight their way to the top and dig in. It was the 169th's most important success thus far in the short campaign. Ironically, it proved to be Eason's swan song.

Colonel Holland Takes Over

Major General Millard Harmon, Halsey's deputy commander, impatiently watched the cautious pace of the assault and let it be known that something had to be done. If Sasaki's defenses were to be cracked, the 169th Infantry would need an infusion of fresh leadership. General Hester, sensing his own career was on the line, needed no further prodding. On 11 July he relieved Eason of his command and axed the regiment's executive, intelligence, and operations officers despite the regiment's fine showing during the previous twenty-four hours.

Colonel Temple Holland, commander of the 37th Division's 145th Infantry Regiment, was chosen to succeed Eason. Selecting someone from outside the 43rd was evidence that Harmon and General Griswold, the XIV corps commander, were losing confidence in the 43rd. Holland's was only a temporary appointment, intended to restore the regiment's fighting spirit while a permanent replacement was being sought. Holland, believing a clean sweep was needed in the 169th's headquarters, asked for and received permission to bring his entire staff with him. Perhaps the men of the 169th would respond well to officers untainted by the blunders of the past week. The whip had begun to crack.

Holland, a Regular Army officer like Eason, was a strict disciplinarian who was disturbed by the reports he had received. Later on, he witnessed certain things himself. Officers and NCOs were frequently killed because they were forced to move ahead themselves before their men would follow. Commands often were issued in the form of suggestions, and the most odious were ignored. During firefights, soldiers would advance while burdened with water and rations, or worse, captured souvenirs at the expense of ammunition or commo wire. This last practice particularly incensed Holland, who reported seeing "men and officers carrying as many as four Jap rifles—mortars, etc., in addition to their own, using all the time and care in the world to keep the souvenir equipment cleaned and oiled, while their own weapons were in such shape as to be practically unserviceable."[88]

Fraternization between the National Guard officers and enlisted men apparently was the cause. They may have been classmates in school or they might have worked for the same business. Sometimes junior officers had civilian bosses who were enlisted men in their Guard units. The situation was too awkward for many to handle well, so the entire unit suffered for it.

The day after he took command, Holland received his first attack order. Ahead of the regiment, the Munda Trail led through a draw flanked on both sides by two heavily wooded ridges. Beyond the draw was a junction with another trail heading south to Lambeti, an abandoned coconut plantation along the coast a thousand yards east of

Munda. The enemy held both the draw and the ridges on each side of the trail guarding the trail junction that was the regiment's objective. Holding one battalion in reserve, Holland mounted an attack at 8:30 A.M.

As they advanced, a sniper fired on Sgt. Franklin Phelps and his men from the 1st Battalion. Phelps stopped beside the trail and began searching the treetops for the source of the enemy fire. "In one tree I saw a sudden movement," he recalled. "Another fellow saw it too. Cleverly hidden in the leaves was the dim outline of a little green man. We both took careful aim and fired. That was all. Without a sound a rifle dropped out of the tree and out of a large branch hung one dead Jap. He was tied to the limb and swung gently back and forth. One or both of us had done a bit for our side."[89]

Despite tough opposition, the 1st Battalion pushed ahead three hundred yards to the ridge. By afternoon they had reached the crest, but they were forced to withdraw. Blindsided by machine-gun and mortar fire from both flanks, they had no choice.

Sweeping fire from the ridge north of the trail pinned down the 2nd Battalion. Heavy overhanging branches from huge banyan trees prevented the use of the regiment's 81mm mortars, so Holland called for and received artillery support. The big guns fired a rolling barrage that began fifty yards forward of the regiment's frontline trace and walked forward at a rate of roughly ten yards a minute. Holland hoped that his battalions would be able to advance to the trail junction behind this steel shield, but the men were unable to keep pace. Many of the bunkers were built on two levels, with a deep hole dug beneath a floor made of coconut logs. The Japanese would descend into the holes during artillery barrages and bombing attacks, then return to their weapons when the danger had passed. If a gunner died, another from an adjacent bunker would replace him, moving through the tunnels that connected each position.

What they needed, according to Holland, was a light recoilless rifle that could penetrate the bunkers. The 37th Division had been issued bazookas on Guadalcanal, but when it came time to embark there still was no ammunition for the weapons, so they were left behind.[90] They would have made a significant impact had they been available to the men of the 169th.

Late in the day, Holland called off the attack and reported to Hester that the regiment was badly disorganized. The only consolation for the men of the 169th after the day's debacle was that they were able to occupy the same holes they had been in the night before. They were totally fatigued, but there would be little rest for them that night—the Japanese saw to that.

By the time dawn broke, Colonel Holland had a much better appreciation for his new regiment: "Words beg description of those night raids by the Japs. They used their entire bag of tricks: dual purpose guns, mortars, commando tactics, yelling, screeching, hand grenades, knives. . . . May it forever be said to the credit of those men of that New England regiment—they stood their ground and kept their heads, killed what they could, and took their losses in stride."[91]

Bob Casko, a Connecticut Guardsman in Company H, 169th Infantry, described that hellish night with haunting brevity in his journal entry for 12 July: "Lost several men during last night and early this morning. Hogan and Cerina were killed. Roger Hedman, Jacobs, Bennett, Roberson, Ella, Rabalais, and Hebert got war neurosis. Jordan was wounded. Crockett also got neurosis."[92]

The next day, the regiment again set out to seize and hold the ridge over the trail junction. The steep, rocky eastern slope—which just days before had been thickly carpeted with trees and shrubbery—now had devolved into a bizarre, pockmarked landscape of huge bomb craters surrounded by shredded and splintered tree trunks and fallen limbs. Sergeant Phelps recalled reaching

the crest of the ridge without much trouble, but going down the other side was something else. The trees and shrubbery were very thick, and in the top of every other large tree was a Jap sniper. . . . Then heavy Jap resistance was encountered. . . . Up in front, another one of our machine gunners was hit, and many of the men in the rifle companies were put out of action. Men were screaming and groaning all around, and I hated to walk about and see just how bad it was. It seemed as if it took the heart out of every company. . . .

Contact was made with the enemy who were heavily entrenched with machine guns cross-firing in front of every position. . . . Every advance was costly. The brave and able commander of B Company knew it would be tough and well neigh impossible to carry out the orders [that] he had to give [to] his command. Seconds later he stepped into the path of a Jap machine gun and was riddled with bullets. The fire was simply murderous. Most of our men never saw the source of the fire which mowed him down.[93]

With only about half the regiment's original strength of twenty-eight hundred men available for combat, Holland committed his reserve 3rd Battalion to the battle, ordering it to join the other two in a new drive up the Munda Trail on the thirteenth. It was against conventional practice, but the colonel needed all the help he could to break through. Despite the critical shortage of troops, however, he ordered a full company from the 3rd Battalion to remain in the rear to guard his command post during the day's assault. This was an unnecessarily large number of men considering the circumstances and, despite his competence as a commander, exposed him to the charge that he was a "rat holer." This accusation was believed by some in the regiment, especially after word spread that Holland's standing orders were to cut the commo wires leading to his headquarters at dusk so that Japanese infiltrators could not trace their way to the command post.[94]

Following a twelve-plane dive-bombing attack on the south ridge and another artillery preparation ordered for the purpose of "cutting grass"—clearing the hill of the tangle of growth that shielded the defenders—the regiment wobbled forward. The 2nd Battalion targeted the draw while the other two battalions assaulted the ridges skirting each side of the trail.

Four hours later, Lt. Col. Fred Reincke's 3rd Battalion, short-handed by one-third with the loss of one of his companies to protect the regimental command post, reached the base of a two-hundred-foot hill near the trail junction after an arduous journey through the charred, smoky woods. The battalion's two remaining companies sliced their way upward through the unbroken din of gunfire and exploding Japanese mortars, searching for the unseen enemy. About halfway to the summit, the point men came under heavy fire and could move no farther. Casualties were heavy, with men falling everywhere. However, they finally triumphed, reaching the summit before sunset. Reincke, knowing his enemy all too well, hastily established a perimeter defense. The battalion had achieved the regiment's most notable success so far, and in their elation the men named the rise Reincke Ridge. From that vantage point, the emaciated Connecticut soldiers squinted into the setting sun and saw Munda airfield, littered with the twisted shells of about two dozen enemy aircraft, outlined by the blue water of Blanche Channel as it curled around Munda Point.[95]

Meanwhile, things were not going as well for the 2nd Battalion in the draw itself. Heavy machine-gun fire halted the battalion's forward progress, and when artillery was called in, the men claimed that some of the rounds had fallen short, causing several casualties. The dispirited battalion began to splinter, and panic-stricken men began falling back down the trail in disarray. It looked like a route might be developing that the enemy could exploit to split the regiment in half. Then a strange thing happened: The fleeing soldiers collided with Capt. Jim Rankin of the 3rd Battalion, who was moving in the opposite direction on the trail toward the front. Rankin faced the GIs and angrily screamed at them to halt, which they quickly did. He then deployed more than a hundred riflemen from his own company across the trail to block not only any approaching Japanese, but also to ensure that the 2nd Battalion personnel did not take another step farther. Rankin's prompt reaction brought an end to the panic and the 2nd Battalion men returned to their companies.[96]

On the northern ridge, broken trees and bomb craters provided even more protection for the stubborn Japanese defenders, who repulsed each thrust with savage bursts of gunfire. Artillery might have remedied the problem, but the 1st Battalion was too close to the Japanese positions for that. In desperation, one company commander ordered his men to fix bayonets and advance into the teeth of the withering enemy fusillade. It was a foolish command and his men obeyed without objection. However, he quickly called them back after the first men up the hill were killed.[97]

Holland, after deciding it was time to cut his losses, ordered the 1st and 2nd Battalions to pull back and open a supply line to the isolated 3rd Battalion on Reincke Ridge. The battalion's position formed a salient protruding five hundred hard-fought yards into Japanese territory and overlooked the trail junction. It was also the only significant high ground the regiment possessed. Holding it would be a huge step in reducing the enemy's hilltop positions opposite the draw and securing the trail junction. The 3rd Battalion was almost entirely surrounded, however, so ammunition, rations, fresh water, and medical supplies had to be carried up on a trail that was menaced by snipers. Regardless, Reincke's men needed help, and every spare soldier and native in the regimental rear was utilized. Medical personnel packed mortar shells along with their first-aid pouches as they ground their way up the trail to the threatened troops. At night, the supply parties continued their shuttle to the top of the ridge, using commo wire that led from the hill back to the regimental command post to help guide them. Once, a native guide leading a crew of green replacement medics and a few native supply carriers decided that he did not need to follow the wire and took a short cut. Captain Joe Risman, who was following the man, recalled:

After we had covered about a mile, the guide, with an incredulous expression on his face, said he was lost! We turned about and retraced our steps. The natives didn't approve of this and began to get restive. I didn't feel so good myself. A sniper opened up and the natives dropped the mortar shells and took off, followed by the new medics. We hit the ground, crawled away from the sniper fire, reassembled, and cursed and yelled until the natives and medics returned. Again we picked up the shells, went back to the wire, and then went forward to the 3rd Battalion. On arrival discovered one medic missing. I later found out that he kept going through the jungle. He encountered a Jap on the Barike River, struggled with him, and finally drowned the Jap in the river. Then this medic made his way back to his outfit.[98]

By late afternoon the GIs could see columns of Japanese moving in from all directions, preparing to regain control of the ridge. At 4 P.M. they began their assault. For the next thirty-six hours, Reincke's men were bludgeoned with mortar and artillery fire, enduring probe after probe by light infantry until the early morning of the fifteenth. The artillery units supporting the regiment from the barrier islands had registered their guns immediately after the summit was seized and thus were able to lay a protective curtain of fire around the ridge a mere three hundred yards from the battalion's positions. The margin for error was thin, however, and the rumor quickly spread that the GIs again were being shelled by their own guns. Whenever someone radioed in a complaint, the guns would have to stop firing so that the allegation could be checked. That was exactly what the Japanese wanted. In response, General Barker, the 43rd Division artillery commander, made a personal visit to the ridge, where he exhumed a shell fragment bearing Japanese markings from a crater. That dispelled the rumor once and for all.[99]

The 105s offshore fired twice each hour at irregular intervals with concentrations on call, and mortars firing from the ridge supplemented the artillery by covering likely enemy approaches. The result was that the Japanese were being pulverized. One artillery forward observer requested a twenty-five yard correction even though the effective radius of a 105mm round was thirty yards. When the fire direction center questioned his odd command, the observer replied: "I missed one of the little bastards."[100] The next day, the victors counted ninety-nine enemy corpses on the faces of the ridge.

This was the first time that a 43rd Division unit was forced to fight a defensive battle during the operation. Although the battalion acquitted itself well, the men were short of food and medical supplies, and they had been forced to fill their canteens from rain puddles for the past several days. The engineer trail from Zanana was still five hundred yards from the regiment, and hand-carrying supplies up the trail to the ridge under the watchful eyes of the enemy was increasingly inadequate and dangerous. Provisions were finally dropped by parachute. Unfortunately, the Japanese retrieved some of the supplies, and others were hung up in towering tree branches. The battalion was able to grab a few crates, however—barely enough to keep the men from starving and running out of ammunition. At the end of the day's fighting the Connecticut soldiers clung determinedly to the top of the vital hill after losing 16 dead and 85 wounded. Company L had suffered the worst: Only 51 enlisted men remained, and all of the company officers were dead.

For the dead, their persecution was at least over. The others had to endure. Among the tormented defenders was Captain Risman, who for some time was the regiment's only physician. Two of the regimental medical officers had been wounded, one was evacuated with war neurosis, yet another had malaria, a fifth suffered from exhaustion, and the regimental surgeon and dental officer were sent back to Rendova. As Risman attended to the wounded, he

> ordered my men to find holes and crawled into a hole already occupied by two infantrymen. One had neurosis and moaned and groaned all night. I fished out a morphine syrette from my pocket and gave him an injection. In a short time he quieted down. In about an hour a voice from the next hole called me. A soldier with both legs shot off was moaning softly in agony. I adjusted his dressing, gave him morphine, and left an extra syrette to his buddy to administer if necessary. I then gave him a lecture on the proper method of administering morphine, a silly thing to do in the middle of the night with Jap mortar shells dropping in our midst.[101]

While the 3rd Battalion was being clubbed on Reincke Hill, Lt. Col. John B. Fowler's 2nd Battalion was feeling Japanese counterblows as well. Casualties began pouring into the regimental aid station after 90mm mortars pounded Fowler's positions. Most of the men suffered from shrapnel wounds, but there were a number of war neurosis victims as well. Reportedly, some of the medics were tagging each other and heading for the rear, but the majority of cases were legitimate psychiatric casualties. One soldier with crazed eyes had surrendered completely to the jungle, lunging and biting anyone who came near him. The men were forced to tie him up like a wild animal until he could be evacuated.[102] Two Japanese mortar shells had detonated simultaneously on each side of one of the battalion's junior officers during the night. The man was miraculously left unhurt by the blasts, but his mind collapsed and he had to be evacuated. After two weeks of rest on Rendova, he was released at his own insistence and returned to his battalion. Colonel Holland spoke to the officer for a few minutes upon his return, and he seemed pleased to be back. However, when a mortar barrage fell on the officer's unit not long after his return he went to pieces again and had to be sent home.[103]

With so many casualties, one can only imagine the workload faced by the regiment's medical personnel. Reincke's battered unit was without a doctor as Risman was off tending to the 1st Battalion's casualties. The only medical help forthcoming was given by Sgt. Louis Guilitti and his heroic team of medics, who scrambled all over the hill during the shellings, attending to the wounded as they groaned and writhed on the smoking hillside. Unfortunately, because of the acute lack of supplies—particularly morphine, plasma, and sulfa powder, which was used to prevent infection—they were limited in what they could do. The 43rd Division's operations plan required that all field units initially carry a thirty-day supply of medical supplies, which would be doubled in a later delivery. However, because of the disorganization during the muddled landing at Rendova, crates of medical supplies were haphazardly mixed with ammo, rations, and quartermaster stores and never sorted in time for the assault on New Georgia. Consequently, the units carried only about a ten-day supply, and within three days of the landings, the shortages became apparent.[104]

Hundreds of yards back in the regiment's rear, staff officer George Mayo received word of the medical supply shortage. Without orders and at great personal risk, Mayo gathered a few volunteers and set off for the ridge up the supply trail. When they reached the base of the ridge, it was pitch-black, so Mayo climbed toward the summit screaming out his name. When the pickets were convinced of his identity, Mayo returned to the carrying party and led the men up to a grateful Sergeant Guilitti.[105]

The valor and élan displayed by men like Guilitti and Mayo, just two of the hundreds of examples of noncombatants who performed courageously during the chaos of the battle, is testimony to the character of the soldiers in Hester's embattled division. Twenty-one Purple Hearts, a Legion of Merit, three Silver Stars, and a Medal of Honor—to Pfc. Frank J. Petrarca—were awarded to the 43rd army medics during the operation.

Even more disturbing than the medical supply shortage were the woefully inadequate evacuation and hospitalization services. For the first four weeks of the operation, there was only a single 125-bed clearing station on Rendova to care for the wounded and the hundreds of patients suffering from diseases like malaria, which incapacitated twenty-nine hundred throughout the campaign. Dengue fever and dysentery added to the caseload, as did the men who suffered from war neurosis. There were only enough beds for 1 percent of the patients, and it was not until 28 July, after 90 percent of the casualties had already occurred, that the 250-bed 17th Army Field Hospital arrived and set up shop on Kokurana Island near Rendova. A soldier on New Georgia in need of medical attention before that hospital became operational would be given immediate first aid by medics on the spot and, if necessary, be moved to a rear-area aid station. If a man required more attention, he would be shipped to Rendova. Those in need of advanced care had to be transported by LST to Guadalcanal, a voyage that took nearly an entire day. Sixty-seven hundred or 87 percent of New Georgia's casualties, including the noncombat injured and sick, were ferried to Guadalcanal 100 to 200 at a time by LST, attended by only one medical officer. When available, PBY floatplanes would fly the most serious casualties to the hospital. It thus was as much as seventy-two to eighty-four hours from the time a man was hit until he reached a surgeon's table on Guadalcanal. This deplorable situation was at least partially a consequence of the 30–35 percent shortage of medical personnel in the division. Roughly 90 percent of the replacement medical officers assigned to the South Pacific had little field training and no combat experience. The Medical Corps was stretched beyond its limits throughout the entire Pacific theater. Nonetheless, it is difficult to understand how a major assault by a division-size force could have been so neglected.[106]

The 169th Infantry was gradually turning into an excellent combat force, and the men knew it. Morale improved and the number of war neurosis casualties began to subside. They had seized from the Japanese a prized piece of property that they wanted badly, and when the enemy tried desperately to recover it, the 169th had held them off. Some of the credit should go to Colonel Holland, but the

lion's share belongs to the men of the 169th—who had learned the
hard way how to fight in the jungle. They knew their enemy and
themselves better, and they knew what to anticipate. Now that their
on-the-job training was completed, they were ready to exploit the 3rd
Battalion's hold on Reincke Ridge.

Kelley Hill

During the battle, the 2nd Battalion captured the hill on the north
side of the draw, the Japanese having withdrawn sometime during
the night of the fifteenth. That gave Holland control of the draw for
good and allowed him to use his two new positions as pivot points
on which to swing southwest toward the airfield to secure another
hill. He assigned this task to Maj. Joseph Zimmer's 1st Battalion. After an artillery preparation that included support from the 60mm
and 81mm mortars on Reincke Ridge, the battalion moved out at
8:30 A.M. on 16 July. A weapons platoon climbed up the hill's eastern slope without meeting the enemy and set up its .30-caliber machine guns on the summit to cover the rest of the unit's ascent from
the south, which also was unopposed. Japanese gun emplacements,
bunkers, and foxholes were everywhere, but there were no defenders occupying them. Munda's commander was probably attempting
to husband his outnumbered forces for a last determined offensive,
for he surely must have understood that Munda would fall. The
Americans simply packed too much firepower and possessed too
many resources for him to defend what was once an airfield. By mid-
June it had become nothing more than a barely discernable path of
cratered and buckled coral. Nevertheless, the conflict continued. If
he could not hold on to Munda, Sasaki planned to fight a war of attrition, a tactic that was fast becoming Tokyo's strategic plan for the
entire Pacific theater. Sasaki, however, envisioned an active defense.
In short, the Japanese were on the run, but their retreat would be
brutally slow, punctuated by assaults on the American positions. The
43rd Division would continue to pay dearly for its inexorable march
to Munda.

Zimmer's men spent the rest of the day improving the hill's defenses. They worked in an area about 150 yards by 75 yards, clear-

ing fields of fire, digging foxholes, and positioning mortars and automatic weapons. Artillery was registered by firing out at a safe distance and then walking the rounds back toward the hill. After about the third volley, artillery forward observers could see well enough to lay the rounds on identifiable targets within 300 yards of their defenses. It was hard work in the sweltering heat and humidity, but the men were buoyed by their conquest. Shortly after noon, they were rewarded with a big sack of mail, fresh water, and rations brought up by native carriers.

The outer perimeter, made up of two-man foxholes, began more than halfway down the slope. Before they withdrew to the summit for the night, however, they set booby-trapped grenades along the wire stretched around them for early warning. In some cases they placed older .03 Springfield rifles in the ground, loaded and ready to fire, pointing at a likely avenue of approach. Long strings were tied to the rifles' triggers and the other ends of the strings were brought back into their night positions. When the enemy began firing their mortars, the men would pull the strings, causing the rifles to fire. Strangely, this seemed to stop the barrages.[107]

At 4:30 P.M., a Japanese patrol surprised the battalion's forward outposts. The lead man carried a light machine gun and hit two GIs sharing the same hole squarely in the head, killing both men instantly. One of the .30-caliber machine-gun crews on the crest cut loose in response, and within moments six or seven of the enemy were down. One man was almost minus his head and another was nearly cut in two at the waist. The whole engagement did not last longer than a minute.

Like hungry predators, a few of the soldiers stumbled down the hill to scavenge the still-warm corpses. They found some crackers, rice, and canned meat (one enemy soldier had hidden four dill pickles in his hat) as darkness quickly descended upon them.[108] However, before they could return to the safety of their positions, the baleful *whoomph, whoomph, whoomph* of Japanese artillery and mortar fire sounded in the distance. Within seconds the deadly shells engulfed the hill in a convulsion of violence. The stench of burned powder swirled with screams from the wounded. Jagged metal fragments sliced through the air as men pressed themselves hard against the erupting earth to escape the conflagration. The unit's Catholic chaplain and a doctor were killed when they jumped from their fox-holes to attend to the dozen or so men who were hit in the first vol-ley. After that, Colonel Holland gave strict orders that patients should, if possible, be brought to a doctor's foxhole during a mor-tar or artillery barrage.[109] A total of fourteen men died in the bloody carnage, including 2nd Lt. John R. Kelley, a beloved officer in whose honor the hill was named. Major Zimmer and twenty-nine others were wounded.

Captain Risman, who floated from battalion to battalion in the regiment, now found himself on the hill, imperiled along with the 1st Battalion. He was a reluctant witness to the madness:

> A Jap mortar shell had landed squarely in a hole killing one, blowing the legs off the second [Lieutenant Kelley], and a hole in the back of a third. For the first time Butch Messina was not with me to mix the plasma, so I sat down, read the directions on the can, and mixed the plasma myself. Meanwhile, Sexton and Tucker had dressed the wounds and given morphine. They held the plasma bottles while I went to report to Major Ramsey. Snipers opened up, and Sexton continued to stand un-til the plasma had been completely administered. Voices could be heard yelling for him to take cover, but he continued to stand. "I got to give this plasma," he answered.
>
> Looking about, I realized why we had so much trouble tak-ing this particular hill. All about it was a series of communi-cating trenches joining together deeply-dug pill boxes covered with coconut logs and dirt.
>
> When the mortar shells began to drop around me, I jumped into a trench and crawled along until I got to a pill box. In it was one man with shrapnel wounds in his right foot and right arm with a tourniquet above the arm wound. By this time it was dark. Since the floor was watery mud, instead of a dressing I put several pairs of stockings on his foot and loosened the tourniquet. By this time my medical pouch was empty, so I took the dressing from my belt and redressed the wound.
>
> Right behind me came an infantry soldier and a lieutenant from our supporting artillery on forward observation. Unfor-tunately, the lieutenant had dysentery, and since the mortar

shells were dropping, he could not leave the hole. He relieved himself in the corner and then fell asleep. He was really sick.

The wounded man had accumulated our canteens and began to drink, a symptom of acute hemorrhage. Then he began to vomit. That hole was a mess. The mortar shells fell all night, and from all directions the moans and groans sounded. I thought that was our last day on earth. The tears rolled down my face. Two mortar shells landed within ten feet of the hole. One piece of shrapnel whizzed past my ear and embedded itself in the wall of the hole. We flattened out in the mud. At dawn the mortar fire ceased. Not a sound could be heard. We felt that the rest of the battalion was wiped out and waited for the Japs to come. We prayed.

After a while the fire started up again, and from all sides came the call for medics. One man got out of his hole, and a sniper got him through the stomach. Another boy got up, the sniper fired, and back to his hole he went. Again it was silent. Then again the moaning and groaning began until I could stand it no longer. I did not want to die, but I had a specific job to do, so I crawled out and began to check up on the holes. Approximately nine dead and thirty-two wounded. Since we were by this time all out of medical supplies, there was not much to be done. I readjusted some of the dressings and used up the remainder of the morphine. There was no way of evacuating patients because we were completely surrounded. The Japs must have miscalculated our strength, because we were so low on ammunition, they could have walked up and massacred us. During the day the sniper hit eight more men. [He must have had a scope on his rifle, for every one of his victims was hit in the stomach, according to Frank Phelps.] Each time a man was hit, I dashed for his hole. Each time I moved, the sniper fired. I still don't know why he missed me. He had eight round trips in which to get me.[110]

Major Zimmer sent out a patrol to find the sniper. The men came back a few hours later with a pair of Nambu machine guns and ammunition and reported they had killed two snipers. This was the first good luck the battalion had had since taking the tree-mangled hill. The machine guns were hastily emplaced along the perimeter and probably helped save their lives, for that night the Japanese massed in the draw between Kelley Hill and Reincke Ridge and rushed the forlorn battalion. It was the unit's first encounter with a nocturnal banzai charge. Mortar bursts seared the dense atmosphere, sending the GIs even deeper into their cramped holes. When that lifted, they could hear the enemy moving toward them from below, guiding on someone who was snapping two sticks together like castanets. Then, screaming like tortured animals, they stormed the hill. It was a sight Frank Phelps would never forget it:

> It was 9:00 and all was still when from the hills to our front came the most blood-chilling yells and cries that I have ever heard. It seemed to come from thousands of Jap throats, and to our already tired nerves, it was a fearful shock. The blood-thirsty screams rose to a tremendous volume of sounds and then died away only to occur again with the same intensity. I must admit that I had a real case of the nerves. . . . In my mind's eye, I could see thousands of dusky Jap warriors, swarming down the hills in a tide that would destroy us all. Tired and disorganized, our thin lines and shaken crews could never hold against such an attack as I had visualized. I made ready as best as I could, inspected my rifle, had ammunition in readiness, laid out my hand grenades, and affixed my bayonet. I'm afraid that I thought that this was the end, but I resolved to sell my life dearly.[111]

When the Japanese began firing, they revealed their position to the 3rd Battalion's mortars less than a thousand yards away on Reincke Ridge. The mortar crews zeroed in, but the enemy continued to swarm over the face of the hill. When the gunners manning the captured Nambus spotted the Japanese muzzle flashes, they laid down a withering barrage of fire. The attackers may have been confused by the clatter of their own weapons in the dark, for they seemed to walk into the face of the furious fusillade. Then the assault broke off, at least for the moment. Just before daylight, however, the Japanese tried again, this time coming from the battalion's right rear with even more fervor, but again they were repelled. The attackers even tried creeping up to the battalion's holes, but well-placed grenades tore them apart. They flung themselves at the Americans in bold, suicidal rushes, but brutal automatic weapons fire stopped them cold. Three times the enemy lunged at Zimmer's men, and three times they were rudely thrown back. The ravaged enemy finally withdrew into the jungle at 8 A.M. after one of the most heroic and hard-fought battles of the campaign.

When they emerged from their holes, the Americans counted 107 enemy bodies strewn in scattered, contorted clumps about the hillside. A dozen were discovered twisted together in a huge bomb crater. They had probably been seeking cover there when a mortar round fell in their midst. The frail battalion on the hill had endured, but the Japanese remained in the jungle waiting to try again. Colonel Holland directed the 2nd Battalion to stab through the draw between Kelley Hill and Reincke's Ridge to ease the pressure on the other two battalions, but the GIs were forced back. When a party carrying twenty of Zimmer's litter cases was ambushed east of Kelley Hill and forced to return, all on the hill knew that they were virtually surrounded on their steaming outpost.

Sadly, among the American casualties after the battle was a soldier with a self-inflicted gunshot wound through the hand and another who had nearly severed his arm with his own machete. Sergeant Phelps noted in his memoir that two Headquarters Company officers also decided that they had had enough and reported to the medics for evacuation.[112] One, he said, had a shrapnel scratch on his leg and the other had arthritis. It is difficult to believe that the medical officer on the hill would have allowed their evacuation considering the battalion's precarious condition. Either Phelps had diminished the seriousness of their wounds in his own mind, or he simply was not aware of the extent of their medical problems and was simply speculating that they were capable of abandoning their unit in a pinch. Whichever the case, his perception of what happened is revealing because it demonstrates the low opinion many of the men in the regiment had for their officers. It is perhaps worth noting that Phelps held officers who performed well in high regard, lending credibility to his serious charge against the two unnamed officers. Risman's description of the hellish conditions on Kelley Hill serves to underscore the heroism of the men of the 1st Battalion who had the courage to continue:

No shade, no clouds, and a hot sun. No water. By noon our distress was acute. Many of the wounded died. I chewed on a D-ration chocolate bar, but it merely made my thirst more acute. We got two canteens from a puddle in a shell hole. It must have been recently occupied by a long-dead Jap. We each drank and vomited. We then added some lemon powder from the C-ration, and this partially took the curse off, and the boys with strong stomachs could hold it down.

About 3 P.M. Chaplain Dudley Burr arrived with a large patrol carrying litters, food, water, and ammunition, and orders to hold the hill at all costs. There were not enough litters to hold all of the litter patients, so I told the litter bearers to dump off a boy shot through the stomach and take on a boy with both hands shot off. This boy was holding his guts in his hands with despair in his eyes. At least the hand injuries had a chance to live. The buddy of the stomach casualty cursed me like I've never been cursed before. I bent my head and walked away. There was nothing I could do.[113]

Phelps remembered Chaplain Burr as an "angel of mercy" who made two trips between Kelley Hill and Reincke Ridge helping to evacuate the wounded.[114]

That night it rained buckets, but the filthy little army on the hilltop welcomed it. The men chanced taking off their helmets to catch the rain and fill their canteens with fresh water for drinking and then for washing their mud-encrusted faces and beards. However, their holes soon filled and the sludge was back. So were the Japanese.

At fifteen minutes past midnight, the same time the enemy had mounted their attack the night before, the gunfire commenced. Again the battle extended long into the night. This time the Japanese supported their assault with plenty of automatic weapons fire from a ridge across the draw. Tracers exposed their location and soon the 169th's mortars were barking back. The terrified soldiers manning the perimeter remained steadfast in the face of a rain of mortars and grenades, and allowed no Japanese soldiers to penetrate the position.

At daylight on 18 July, the GIs collected weapons and ammunition from the 102 enemy corpses that lay around the hill. In addition to inventorying the dead and stripping the bodies of documents for the division's G2 staff, the men searched for food and souvenirs, which were always in great demand. As they searched the still-steaming hillside, Frank Phelps and a companion noticed a live Japanese soldier, unarmed and yelling, near a shell crater. Weapons at the ready, the pair approached him. They shouted for the man to surrender and he replied, but they could not understand him. They waited for a while and then threw a grenade his way. When he started to run, Phelps fired a short burst from his tommy gun, dropping him immediately. But the man was only slightly wounded. The poor wretch was shaking with fear and begged them to kill him. Instead they brought him back to battalion headquarters for evacuation to an interrogation center on Guadalcanal. He was the only POW the 1st Battalion took during the entire campaign.[115]

Four C-47 transport planes loaded with crates of rations and supplies loomed into view, heading over the battalion's position to execute a badly needed airdrop. The famished men watched anxiously as dozens of parachutes mushroomed beneath the planes and began descending to the ground. However, as with other airdrops over the island, many of the supplies were lost to the enemy or became irretrievably tangled in the surrounding trees. The C-47s flew eighteen of these missions during the course of the campaign, delivering 118 tons of supplies to the isolated infantrymen on line, but only about half of the rations dropped were ever recovered.[116]

That same day, Lieutenant Colonel Fowler's 2nd Battalion pushed its way up to the ridge and joined Major Zimmer's beleaguered unit in defense of the hard-won real estate. Besides food and extra ammunition, the men of the 2nd Battalion brought with them rumors that they were about to be relieved. Unlike the majority of rumors heard in combat, this one turned out to be true. Three days later, fresh troops from the 145th Infantry Regiment trudged up Kelley Hill under the cover of a smoke screen with orders to relieve both battalions. A few days of rest on Rendova was in store for the men of the 169th before the regiment returned to New Georgia to take part in the final drive on Munda. As the 145th moved into the line, Colonel Holland relinquished command of the 169th and took over his old unit. It was a pleasant surprise for the New Englanders, who had no idea that the brass had decided a week before to throw three more infantry regiments into the mix. The dangerous daylight relief operation was accomplished with a minimum of casualties despite being conducted only two hundred yards from enemy lines.

The hill had been a hellish, miserable residence, and the men were happy to leave it. Nevertheless, it was an important turning point, not only in the operation, but also for the men themselves. As the men of the 1st Battalion staggered down that bloody ridge, they knew in their hearts what they had accomplished. It did not really matter to them if anyone else ever knew.

On to Munda

On 14 July, after securing Laiana, Colonel Ross and his 172nd Infantry had begun plodding methodically toward Munda airfield. Almost immediately to the west of the landing area, a battalion from the Japanese 229th Infantry Regiment occupied a semicircle of well-constructed bunkers anchored by a steep, sparsely wooded hill that provided an open field of fire for the defenders and barricaded the American advance.

The defenses appeared impregnable. Each bunker, measuring about twelve feet square and ten feet deep, was painstakingly constructed of coconut logs, mud, and coral. The walls were strengthened with the logs or sand-filled oil cans, and crossbeams layered with even more logs formed an almost impenetrable, protective roof covered with earth from which grew native plants and weeds for camouflage. Because of the prolific jungle growth, the structures rapidly became part of the landscape. The occupants of these impressive emplacements would stand on steps to fire their weapons out of narrow slits in the walls or descend to the floor for almost complete protection. Every bunker was surrounded a few yards away by four to six riflemen in foxholes. The gunners themselves wore bulletproof vests of a sort, canvas garments of six pockets each with a small steel plate inside. Their job was simple and direct. They were expected to die at their positions. Soldiers more often than not would walk directly into their fields of fire never sensing their presence.

Negotiating their way through this web of rugged defenses would only be the beginning, for Sasaki had fashioned a defense-in-depth all the way to Munda field similar to the impervious design of mutually supporting bunkers and pillboxes that guarded Bairoko. If his men were bent back, they would be able to withdraw to an equally steadfast position in a new bunker and fight it out again with the frustrated Americans. Although he never received the requested infantry division, Sasaki could always count on a steady, albeit limited, supply of soldiers to man his elaborate defenses. Men ferried over on barges from nearby Kolombangara (via Bougainville) continued to stream into Bairoko despite the Northern Landing Group's efforts.

On 15 July a new weapon was introduced in the war against the treacherous bunkers: M5 Stuart light tanks. Tanks had been used on a limited basis at Gifu Point on Guadalcanal and by the Australians at Buna in Papua New Guinea. They had also been tested when the New Georgia Occupation Force (NGOF) first landed at Zanana. However, there was no solid footing for their grinding treads on the drive to the Barike, so they were withdrawn. The ground near the beach was firmer, though, and they were reintroduced into the fighting after Laiana was seized. Anticipation was high. Perhaps they would be the key to cracking the difficult defensive system that extended sixty-five hundred yards east to Munda and three thousand yards inland from the coast, effectively shielding the airstrip. Emboldened with a fresh battalion from the 103rd Regiment and a platoon of eight of the usually reliable fifteen-ton tanks (two had broken down immediately and were never used) from the 9th Marine Defense Battalion, the assault resumed.

The going was difficult for Capt. Robert Blake's armored vehicles. Even though the jungle was not nearly as dense along the coast as it was near the interior, there were still fallen trees and soft riverbeds to negotiate. Sometimes an unseen log would turn a tank belly up. They were constantly forced to reverse their course because a stump or thicket of mature trees blocked their path. Six riflemen and a native scout were assigned to each of the awkward vehicles, which were placed in the vanguard about seventy-five yards forward of the advancing regiment. They furnished security and vision for the four-man crew buttoned up inside, protecting the creeping iron creatures from flank assaults and firing tracer rounds that pinpointed targets.

Blake had an easy go of it on his first penetration west of Laiana, encountering no fortified bunkers. His own and two other tanks formed a wedge and began slowly carving their way through foliage torn by shellfire. As the lead tank commander, he had his head and shoulders out of the turret hatch, barking directions to his driver through the tank's intercom. They saw nothing but abandoned pillboxes scattered about.

A quarter hour went by and there was still no sign of the enemy. Frustrated, Blake pulled out his Thompson submachine gun and began firing it from his perch atop the tank into the recesses of the jungle. Still no response. Then, just as he descended to replace the gun in its holster, a Japanese machine gun opened fire, its bullets spanking the tank's armor. Inside, Blake and his gunner felt the sting of hot metal splinters. Slugs from the Japanese machine gun were hitting the open turret hatch and ricocheting inside. The smell of scorched metal and smoke began to swirl inside the tiny, hot compartment.

Suddenly, there was a lull in the firing. Blake pulled down the hatch and vigorously traversed the turret in an effort to locate his tormentor. Steel continued to rain down on them until the clanging threatened to drive them mad. At any moment, they thought, an antitank round could slam into them and they would all broil to death. Buttoned up inside, he peered through his periscope carefully and finally spotted tiny red bursts through the bush not fifty feet away. Blake called for a canister round, which was like a huge shotgun shell filled with hundreds of pellets designed to tear and maim dozens of men with a single blast. This time, however, it would be fired at one man at close range. With the M5's motor grumbling loudly beneath him, he aligned the 37mm gun on his adversary just as the man finished reloading a new belt of ammo. Blake watched as he yanked back the gun's charging handle and waited for him to begin firing again. The tank recoiled and a split second later dirt and smoke billowed up from where a man had been. Blake's crew cheered.

Several more Japanese were vaporized by the tank's main gun. Each event was a scarcely disguised suicide mission, for without more appropriate weapons, the defenders could not hope to slow an armored advance. Yet strangely, rather than seep back into the safety of the jungle, they continued to fire at the advancing tanks. Once, Blake's tank ground to a halt as it approached a steep embankment. Just as it did, another machine gun opened up, blanketing the vehicle with meaningless rounds that did nothing more than call attention to it and irritate the tank's crew. The weapon was in the center of a trail without camouflage of any sort for the gunner, who crouched low over the gun. Blake again called for canister. The blast hurled the soldier's torn body several yards back against the trunk of a tree, leaving little more than a bloody heap of tissue.

The whole affair turned into an ugly blood sport for the tankers. Their fighting spirit was fueled more by sheer hatred of the Japanese than by any sense of duty. Earlier in the day they had seen the rotting bodies of two American medics, their bloated, disfigured remains astride a bullet-riddled stretcher. Nearby were the bodies of a half dozen or so GIs who had likely died of wounds. It was obvious that the two medics had gone forward to evacuate the most seriously hurt and had been gunned down themselves. Blake and his crew never forgot the image of Americans bleeding to death and the heroic medics who died trying to save them. The tankers bristled at the thought of it as they searched for more targets.

Farther ahead they spotted another enemy machine gunner lying prone, hammering away futilely. There he was, face-to-face with a tank, standing his ground, knowing full well that in seconds he would be obliterated by the vehicle's main gun. This time, Blake called for a high-explosive round, the kind designed to rip apart a ten-man squad. The macabre overtone to his narrative is unmistakable:

The Jap . . . lifts his head to have a cautious look. . . . Slowly his hand goes up for the trigger. The upper part of his body lifts from the ground. I level the cannon at the soft of his stomach. I watch as he swings the barrel toward us. . . . *BAMM.* The projectile socks into the ground in front of the Jap and glances up into his exposed stomach. There is a sharp explosion and the top half of the enemy's body spins into the air—like a rag doll in a wild dance—then crumples over the breech of the machine gun.

A howl of triumph goes through the tank. "Best shot of the day!" "You blew him in half!" "Aw, hell," says Amurri, "a driver doesn't have any fun. Let me run over just one little old Jap."[117]

Continuing along at a pace of only a few miles an hour, the three tanks located their first occupied bunker, deployed back into wedge formation, and began heaving 37mm high-explosive rounds at the target. This time, however, their fire seemed to have little effect. Enemy soldiers killed by the bursts were rapidly replaced by others from nearby bunkers or foxholes. More bunkers were uncovered by the blasts of the tank guns, and Japanese infantry could be seen crawling from their sanctuaries and disappearing into the jungle. Blake decided to try something else. He ordered armor-piercing rounds fired at the coral-and-log enclaves, creating holes in the structures large enough for high-explosive rounds to go through. This tactic did the trick, flushing the stunned enemy gun crews out into the open where they made easy targets for the infantry's waiting rifles and BARs and the tanks' machine guns. They exposed other emplacements by firing canister rounds into thickets from which they were receiving fire. The canister stripped trees of their leaves and roughly tore away underbrush that camouflaged the enemy positions. Then the tank crews served up armor-piercing and high-explosive rounds that penetrated the burrows. After several hours of these exchanges, the easternmost terminus of the Japanese line of defense was reduced. It was the first real gain the regiment had made against the Japanese in that sector since Laiana fell.

Meanwhile, three more M5s closed on the center of the Japanese bunker line, where a steep hill blunted the 172nd's advance. Five well-disguised bunkers on its forward slope made the hill a formidable position for foot soldiers alone to defeat, but the light tanks made the going easier. They lumbered toward the hill and raked it with .30-caliber machine-gun fire while using their 37mm guns to uncover the enemy dugouts and gun ports masked by the jungle's natural architecture. At times they were so close to their targets that the gunners were unable to depress the muzzles of their main guns far enough to engage the enemy, relying instead on their machine guns. The outgunned defenders tried to sling mortar rounds at the metal monsters, but they were impervious to anything the Japanese possessed. Soon, the enemy abandoned their sturdy bunkers. The following day the tank-infantry team continued to press on, destroying five more bunkers with only light casualties and no damage to the tanks. Munda was less than two thousand yards away.

Meanwhile, the 3rd Battalion, 172nd Infantry, was having a hard time keeping pace. The M5s wrecked five more bunkers and several more dugouts hidden in the palms and underbrush along the coast, allowing their infantry escorts to move onto an important coastal hillock. As the advance continued, however, mortar fire escalated and the riflemen scattered and fell behind. Nowhere to be found, they left the three tanks unprotected from enemy magnetic mine attacks. This device was an explosive charge with four magnets on its base and a grenade fuse. An enemy soldier would run up to a tank, pull the safety pin, and hit the striker to arm it, much like he would with a grenade. Then he would slap (or throw) the mine onto the vehicle's back deck and run. There was just a six-second delay.

Realizing their vulnerable position, Captain Blake reluctantly gave the order to pull back to their original line of departure after seizing two hundred tough yards of real estate. Slowly they reversed their progress, traversing their turrets left and right and furiously firing canister rounds into the jungle to keep the Japanese attackers away from them. Backing out was no easy matter without the benefit of their infantry guides. Broken trees tightened around the gawky machines, sometimes snarling them in the tangled jungle growth while enemy troops rushed at their blind flanks. Entombed inside their steamy, suffocating crypts and staggered by the brutal mine explosions, the men struggled to break free of the enemy's grasp. Finally they shook loose and limped to safety with a minimum of damage.

Armored vehicles are most effective when they operate with infantry in a team. But the arrangement could sometimes be dangerous for the soldier-chaperons, for the tanks drew more than their share of enemy small-arms and mortar fire. Nor was New Georgia the ideal venue for armored operations. Because of the problem of parallax, a projectile fired from the main gun might hit a tree not seen through the tank commander's sight, making dangerous premature explosions a common occurrence. This is the most likely reason why the GIs, untrained in cooperative assault tactics, were so reluctant to advance alongside their iron partners. In any event, the battalion commander assured Blake that the tankers could count on close support for their next strike.

Satisfied by this assurance, the M5s plowed forward again and traveled about fifty to a hundred yards past their previous position when heavy machine-gun and mortar fire halted their thrust and wounded several soldiers. The rest went scurrying for cover away from the tanks, now idling in a cosmos of crowded trees and jungle growth so thick that visibility was less than twenty feet. The tangled environment concealed the Japanese and encouraged them to come forward with their deadly mines. Each of the tanks was hit, but again none was seriously damaged. Once again the armored trio retired to the staging area.

Blake, a marine officer, blamed the soldiers for abandoning them, leaving them unprotected in the face of the enemy. The GIs, meanwhile, claimed that it was the tanks that were too quick to back down. Robert Gilman of the 103rd Infantry shared that opinion. When things got hot, he said, they would "pull up and get the hell out of there."[118] Jealousies and mistrust were keen between the different branches of the military, and this fact partially explains the dispute. Finger-pointing commonly occurs in the aftermath of frustration. In this case, however, neither side was correct and neither was wrong. The real reason for the blunders was that trained personnel were needed to execute the coordinated attacks. Neither the marines nor the soldiers involved had been given any instruction on how to communicate with each other during the attack—a key element of the tank-infantry team's success.

The nights were especially harrowing for the weary tankers. Images of Japanese suicide attacks wove in and out of their fitful sleep, and the jungle itself intensified their insomnia. Captain Blake wrote after the war about one particularly memorable night:

We lie down on a blanket or a strip of canvas, pistol in hand or rifle or Tommy gun close against our ribs, fingering the trigger guard. Darkness, utter blackness. Silence among the resting men, but the jungle rustling with movement. There is a whistle in the night, repeated. The call is answered from the opposite direction. There is a call far away, then one very close. Now whistling is everywhere. *Clack! Clack! Clack!* Sticks being pounded together. A branch cracks from a tree and falls thrashing through the foliage. You listen, breathless. There comes screeching in the trees and the heavy flap, flap of wings. Birds. You breathe again.

But something is crawling through the brush not six feet away. Slowly, you lift your head, straining your eyes into the darkness. You play with the idea that you may be blind; you move your spread fingers back and forth in front of your eyes, so close they brush your eyebrows. Nothing to be seen; probably a land crab crawling through the brush. You relax, laying your head down slowly, so as not to make the slightest sound.

Voices and the sound of a motor far up ahead. The noise grows louder. What can be moving at this hour? Near at hand among the men, you hear quiet clicks as hammers are drawn back on pistols and the bolts of rifles slide a round into the chamber. Maybe the Nips have one of our jeeps and are trying to get through our lines by talking loudly and making a great racket. Down the trail they come. You can make out English words, "A little this way. . . . Watch out for that tree." But the Nips often use English. The camp is still and black. We will let the strangers go right through, keeping our guns on them in case they discover us. Into our circle they come, into the crossing and crisscrossing lines of fire. No sound. They are passing through—a jeep and several men. There is the Jap odor of fish and smoke. "Hey, medics! Where are the medics! We have a wounded Jap! Someone tell us where the medics are!" They kept talking and calling out, but no one answered and they went on, never knowing they had passed through a camp.

We hear the jeep bouncing, tools and chains clanking as the incessant talking and exhortations fade out down the trail. There is no shooting at the wire. Evidently, the strangers knew the password and really did have a Jap bound for the hospital. But theirs had been a dangerous journey. Had one shot been fired as they passed the camp, they would have been torn to ribbons, no one believing what they said. But jungle-wise troops do not fire at night. They lie still and kill with a knife.

A long time later, some movement again roused me with a start. I felt the muscles of my heart contract, shooting a cold fluid through my veins. Something was creeping along a little trail toward me. I peered through the night. The moon had risen, and the bright white light, filtering through the jungle canopy, was mottling everything with brilliant patches. Where I lay was bathed in a stream of light. I felt that my face was glistening in the moonlight. Something invisible moved nearby. Slowly, I raised my head, watching steadily. With a jab of freezing terror, I saw movement in a patch of moonlight. This is it, I thought. I will never see morning.

With the light bright above me, I was afraid to raise my pistol, afraid to move. I strained to hold my head up and keep my eyes on the shadow. I was in no position to shoot. My pistol was in my hand by my side. I would have to bring it up to my head to fire. It was a long move. I would wait until the figure was in the middle of the moonlight, and then, with one move, throw out my pistol against him and fire. If only the figure did not see me, did not fire first.

Just then one of the men nearby sighed in his sleep and turned over. At the sound, the figure on the trail grunted and went bouncing away. It had been some animal—a wild boar, a rat, a lizard, or a coconut bear.

I relaxed and laughed to myself. But I was wide awake by then. I damned the long, long night and wondered if the darkness would ever end. I dug my wrist watch out of my pocket where I had put it to conceal the glare of its luminous dial. I stared at the tiny hands until my eyes could focus. It was only half past one.[119]

After a night like that, Blake welcomed the new mission that was given to his tanks on 17 July. This time, however, there was a change. The 3rd Battalion, 103rd Infantry, which had not yet seen action on the island, relieved the 172nd's weary 2nd Battalion. Although the new battalion commander assigned thirty troops to cover each of Blake's tanks, the commander warned the battalion's officers that he would withdraw his M5s if the promised escort abandoned them. He would not again place his tankers in jeopardy. Not long after they began their advance through a knot of snarled vines and bushes. Grinding through the brambles, Blake broke through the enemy positions and ordered his crews to fire canister rounds at the fleeing enemy troops. Just then a grisly explosion, caused by a mine that had been deftly inserted in the crevice between the turret and hull, shook one of the tanks, wounding two of its crew. The enemy also employed a flamethrower for the first time on the island, showering another tank with fuel. It did not ignite, and the Japanese soldier who was responsible was quickly killed, but the mere knowledge that such weapons were present was enough to frighten even veteran tankers.[120] Japanese troops carrying mines made bold, suicidal lunges at the remaining tanks, perhaps heartened by the sight of the burning tank. Although no more tanks were lost, the order came down to fall back. The disabled tank was pulled out by one of the other M5s using tow cables.

The tanks had demonstrated their usefulness in their first encounter with the enemy on New Georgia. Despite some weaknesses, they proved effective against the Japanese bunkers, certainly saved lives, and hastened the advance to the airfield by clearing a four-hundred-yard wedge in Sasaki's defenses along the division's left flank. Soon, another tank platoon from the Russells was ordered into action.

While the 43rd Division continued to inch its way toward Munda, Sasaki was being reinforced. On 19 July, 1,300 men from Col. Satoshi Tomonari's 13th Infantry Regiment arrived from Kolombangara via Bairoko. Another 1,200 arrived the following night. Those 1,200 were joined by a like number transported by a convoy of destroyers that collided with Admiral Ainsworth's Task Force 18 in the sea battle of Kolombangara. The reinforcements were the ones that had been promised five days before by Eighth Area Army headquarters in Rabaul to invigorate the effort on New Georgia at the expense of the New Guinea campaign. Help came as a result of an urgent message sent by the frustrated Sasaki outlining his precarious situation and explaining that he would have to evacuate to Kolombangara if relief was not immediately forthcoming. He also suggested a bold offensive plan for the reinforcements when they arrived. The scheme pleased his reluctant superiors, who promptly radioed back: "The very best possible plan. Highest confidence and expectations in the attack."[121] Operations against MacArthur would continue, but for the moment at least, New Georgia was to receive priority.

The crafty Sasaki had been waiting for this help since the Americans first lined up along the Barike. With two full regiments of veteran infantry at his disposal, he could put his plan into action. He would use the fresh troops to strike at the 43rd Division's exposed right flank and drive through to the practically undefended division command post at Zanana. If coordinated well enough the entire American invasion force would be threatened with envelopment. On 7 July, Tomonari's column reached the upper reaches of the Barike and awaited orders to attack while Hester's men looked westward. The success of this ambitious ploy would determine the outcome of the struggle for Munda.

6 A Dark Corner of Hell

By mid-July, after almost two weeks of stumbling toward Munda, General Hester's two exhausted regiments had stalled in front of the heart of General Sasaki's stubborn defenses. Moreover, they were a week behind schedule. Hester's decision to order the 72nd south to secure Laiana was sound, but the maneuver had opened a dangerous gap between the 172nd and the 169th on the high ground at the trail junction. It was one of combat's cardinal sins. General Sasaki seized on the opportunity and promptly plugged the gap with his veteran infantry, threatening to drive a wedge that would crack the attacking division in two. Colonel Liversedge had seized Enogai, but the Northern Landing Group was inactive for the moment, awaiting reinforcement by the 4th Raiders before the assault on Bairoko, which would not kick off for another week. Meanwhile, fresh Japanese troops continued to funnel through Bairoko with intelligence reporting a new batch of enemy reinforcements en route from Kolombangara. There was real concern in higher headquarters that the entire operation was in danger of collapsing.

Prior to D day, plans had been made to place Maj. Gen. Oscar Griswold, the XIV Corps commander, in charge of the New Georgia Occupation Force—which included all army and marine units fighting on the island, navy Seabees, and other supporting elements scattered around the New Georgia group. This would occur after Munda fell. Griswold visited Rendova on 11 July for a routine look-see and to get a general feel for things, but he quickly discerned that there was trouble. He landed just as Hester was diverting the 172nd to Laiana.

Studying the situation map and attending daily intelligence brief-ings, he began to get an uneasy feeling about the mission. Two days later, Griswold advised General Harmon at SPA headquarters that things were "going badly," and asked that Maj. Gen. Robert S. Beightler's 37th Infantry Division (made up of Ohio National Guardsmen) and a regiment from the 25th Infantry Division be em-ployed immediately to relieve Hester's dispirited men. Simply stated, Griswold was asking for double the number of men sent to seize Munda two weeks earlier. The 43rd was "about to fold up," and he felt strongly that the struggling division would never take the airfield. This was so, he very incorrectly surmised, despite the fact that "en-emy resistance to date [was] not great."[1]

This extraordinary message sent a shock wave through Halsey's headquarters. Things were not going well. Despite accurate and al-most continuous artillery support from three 155mm and three 105mm howitzer battalions, naval bombardments, and incessant air attacks flown from Guadalcanal, there was no discernable break-through. The psychological impact of the constant bombardments on Munda's defenders had to be enormous, yet their morale ap-peared to remain high, as evidenced by their determined and ag-gressive assaults along the front lines. If one accepts the number of noncombat casualties as an indicator, then Japanese morale was ar-guably higher than the Americans'. There certainly had been no en-emy desertions, and, most dissatisfying of all, there was little pene-tration of the Japanese defenses. Something had to change quickly.

Halsey, never one to hesitate, met with his deputy General Har-mon, placed him in control of all ground operations on New Geor-gia, sent him to Guadalcanal so he would be closer to the action, and ordered him to "take whatever steps deemed necessary to capture Munda."[2] Harmon in turn notified Griswold that the two requested divisions would be made available to him soon, and ordered Gris-wold to prepare to assume command of the remodeled NGOF im-mediately. Formal orders were cut, and at midnight on 14 July Op-eration Toenails officially became a XIV Corps campaign. For morale purposes, Halsey described the move as a "reorganizational relief," rather than a "yank-out."[3] For the time being, General Hester re-mained in command of the 43rd.[4]

The 37th Division already had an artillery battalion, the 145th Infantry, and the 148th Infantry's 3rd Battalion committed. Once the remainder of the 148th Infantry, which was stationed in the Russells, arrived on the embattled island, two full regiments from the 37th would be in the contest. Priority was given to relieving the battle-worn 169th, which had been clinging tenuously to the high ground overlooking the Lambeti plantation. After Harmon flew to Guadalcanal, he ordered General Collins, whose division was responsible for Guadalcanal's defense, to ready his 161st Infantry Regiment for movement to New Georgia, where it would be attached to Beightler's division. What had begun two weeks before as a task for a single reinforced division of four regiments had burgeoned into a much more sizable operation requiring the application of seven regiments from three different army and one marine division. Roughly thirty-two thousand soldiers, all of Halsey's available forces, would be on or around New Georgia for round two. Griswold hoped that this force would punch through the outer Japanese defenses, link up with the NLG, and finally break what he called the "Munda nut." He was under enormous pressure to make it work.

Meanwhile, General Sasaki was itching to launch his ambitious but complicated countermove, the success of which would turn the American effort on its head. Defending the airfield, he believed, meant more than constructing and manning imaginative defenses-in-depth. It also meant taking offensive action. Although he recently had been reinforced, it is improbable that Eighth Area Army headquarters in Rabaul maintained any illusion that Sasaki could defeat the Americans. However, he was certainly capable of inflicting severe punishment on the 43rd Division, slowing the American offensive, and perhaps buying time for a grand defense of Japan's bases farther up the Solomons when, presumably, more resources would be available. Already this strategy was paying dividends.

Hester's forces had failed to penetrate Munda's primary defense corridor for reasons already addressed. The Japanese commander offered this explanation for the 43rd's fumbling: "They awaited the results of several days' bombardment before a squad advanced. Positions were constructed and then strength increased. When we counterattacked at close quarters, they immediately retreated. . . .

The infantry did not attack in strength, but gradually forced a gap and then infiltrated. Despite the cover provided by tank firepower, the infantry would not come to grips with us and charge."[5]

In plain language, he was saying that the Americans were faint-hearted warriors, if not outright cowards. It was a view widely held by most Japanese during the war. The Americans, they believed, avoided hand-to-hand combat, would not attack without artillery, were cautious in the attack, and were able to succeed only when they had fire superiority.[6] From the Allied viewpoint, the Japanese were murderous, subhuman criminals, heedless of life itself. Both appraisals reveal misunderstandings, not an uncommon occurrence when two nations are slashing away at each other in desperate combat. According to historian Eric Hammel, each side was simply using the resources that it had in abundance. For the United States it was the modern hardware of warfare; for Japan it was a willing population. Charles Henne, a retired colonel who served as a platoon leader and company commander in the 148th Infantry, said the Japanese army was obsolete and overrated, not much more advanced than a World War I outfit. "They never improved it," he added. "We could have fought their kind of war—one-on-one in the bush. That would have been stupid. We used our outstanding artillery and our all-capable bulldozer to remove the jungle. Doing so made the Japs hold up and wait for us to kill them."[7]

There is no need to defend the performance of the American fighting man during the war. Sasaki misinterpreted the American reliance on technology as timidity. What he failed to understand was that emphasis was placed on airpower, artillery, tanks, and more lethal weapons because they were simply more effective and helped achieve Allied objectives more quickly without unnecessary loss of life. His mistake was in equating prudence with cowardice. On the other hand, it was Japan's cultural enigmas that caused the Allied misunderstanding. Critics inside and out of Japan have claimed that its people's extraordinary devotion to the emperor and the Bushido code had become so corrupted that the emperor himself was aghast at the orgy of death. Still, these zealous beliefs that truly defined Japan were alien to Westerners, who attempted to interpret Tokyo's suicidal military forces in terms familiar to them. Sadly, these misunderstandings continue into the twenty-first century.

• • •

Like a master chessman, General Sasaki began maneuvering his forces into position for the assault. A battalion of the newly arrived 13th Infantry Regiment had already wedged itself between the over-burdened 169th Infantry and its companion 172nd Infantry, which, in its haste to make for Laiana, had failed to maintain contact between them. This error invited enemy exploitation, and it was not long before the Connecticut GIs were cut off, particularly the 169th's 3rd Battalion on Reincke Ridge. Secondly, Sasaki planned to press forward against the 172nd, threatening Munda from Laiana. He would do this with the main body of the 13th Infantry, along with the 229th Infantry, which was still poised in its dugouts along the southern coast. This move, Sasaki hoped, would distract Hester from the next and most important component of his plan: an attack on the 43rd Division's command post (CP). A three-hundred-man raiding party from the 13th Infantry would swing around the 169th Infantry's unprotected right flank, block the Munda Trail from Zanana to cut the regiment's supply lines, and penetrate deep into the American sector as far as Hester's CP, located a mile and a half north of Zanana. The possibility of such an attack was what had prompted Hester to give the order to relocate farther west to Laiana, where the CP and logistical and medical centers could be tucked behind the two frontline regiments. However, because of the inevitable logistical delays, all relating directly to the jungle's snare, the repositioning was postponed. To ensure the attack's success, the Imperial Navy agreed to send a squadron of destroyers into Kula Gulf to shell the 43rd's headquarters. Finally, RAdm. Minoru Ota's Combined Special Naval Landing Force would conduct a series of landings west of Laiana, move east to destroy supply and communication centers there, and cut off both of Hester's regiments from their sustenance.

As the time to launch the counterblow approached, Sasaki sent an urgent request to Rabaul for more reinforcements and massive air and naval support to ensure victory. Without this help, he pleaded, Munda was in jeopardy and the Japanese would likely suffer their second defeat in the Solomons.[8] For some reason, however, his message was never acknowledged.

Like most operations planned on situation maps rolled out over a table someplace, things appeared to be much simpler than they turned out to be when men were forced to traverse New Georgia's sharp ridges, trees, swamps, and dense undergrowth. On 14 July, Colonel Tomonari began a three-day ordeal in the jungle, moving his men north to swing down and pounce on the unsuspecting Americans. He was ready by the 17th, but by then other elements of Sasaki's plan were unraveling.

Back at Munda, the coordinated advance against the 172nd halted when a huge, sustained artillery preparation followed by air strikes shook the 229th to its bone. That was followed by the two-battalion attack led by the M5 Stuart light tanks, which temporarily pushed the defenders off balance and disrupted the attack plan. The advent of the tanks cast a pall over Sasaki's headquarters and caused the Japanese to doubt their ability to win. The heavy air and artillery bombardments also upset the plan to land Admiral Ota's force behind American lines, for they disorganized the pool of armored troop-carrying barges and lighter landing craft allocated for the mission. The only part of the plan carried off without a hitch was the isolation of the 169th Infantry. But even that success was only temporary, as the bold aggressors were unable to capitalize on the maneuver and were gradually squeezed back out of the gap between the frontline regiments.

Colonel Tomonari, who was uninformed about these events, was about to commence a most hazardous raid, one that would net huge rewards if it succeeded. At dusk on 7 July, he and his reinforced company swung around the 43rd's dangling right flank undetected and silently hunkered down in a mangrove swamp on the Barike. From there they would move to flatten the division's supply dumps and CP. They would have to do so, however, without the assistance of the promised destroyer force. At the last moment, Rabaul canceled that mission without explanation.[9] Regardless, just as a thunderstorm began to lash down upon them, the intruders broke out of the veil of vegetation and crept stealthily through the matted jungle deadfall toward the beach.

Facing the advancing column was a weak, platoon-size security force made up of elements of the division's Reconnaissance Troop and a handful of Fijian commandos. They spied the infiltrators and attempted to stage an ambush, but their effort was woefully inadequate and the determined Japanese ripped right through them. Once this mobile screening force was smashed, Tomonari was looking at an open avenue to Zanana. Then he made a crucial move: Apparently acting on Sasaki's orders, he divided his force into small, lightly armed groups that would operate semi-independently. The operation thus was converted into a mere guerrilla raid, an uncoordinated hit-and-run rampage designed more to disrupt than to seize and hold the division CP and its support facilities. Here was still more evidence of the diminished ambitions of the Japanese command in the face of the spiraling American military might. What had begun as an imaginative, bold offensive had dwindled rapidly into no more than a one-dimensional counterpunch. The off-balance and reeling GIs were precariously close to a major reversal. A concerted, determined attack might have badly hurt the brawny American force. Sasaki, however, lost both audacity and opportunity.

These questionable orders seemed to have no appreciable effect on the individual infantrymen in Tomonari's party, however. They maintained their magnificent élan and courage throughout the attack. It still proved to be a difficult brawl. With the exception of a few legitimate combat types, like those from the 9th Marine Defense Battalion, all the remaining troops assigned to the division's rear area were support personnel: assorted motor pool, mess, medical, and commo crews, clerk typists, and engineers. Although they carried their own weapons, most had only fired them for qualification in basic training, and the men were uncomfortable with the thought that they would have to use them.

Their moment came that night as they listened to the terrible sounds of hunters stalking them in the angry darkness. Closer, louder, then the rattle of gunfire mingled with screams. The horror-struck defenders were irregularly dispersed north and west from the hub of the command post. Since the enemy was also divided into small combat teams, the onslaught became a collection of brief but furious firefights. The marauders overlooked several of the outposts, while others were located by following commo wire straight into the encampment. Some were quickly overrun, their hapless guardians firing at everything and nothing. Prostrate and sweating in the mud-swill of their holes, the courageous Americans continued shadow boxing with the Japanese until the final blow. Here anonymous lines held. There they broke. A few abandoned their positions and fled, searching for sanctuary deeper in the jungle gloom. Most of the men, resigned to their fate, traded death with their unseen opponents, firing aimlessly into the leafy void and receiving fire from improbable sites above and all around them. Radios crackled with curses and urgent pleas for help while the wounded chanted their own haunting choruses.

Meanwhile, on Rendova, General Hester, who had been tending to his chronic stomach ulcer, began receiving reports of the attack just before 9 P.M. By then, roughly a hundred of the invaders had converged on a trail running along the shore that connected Zanana to the command post, their objective. They turned east and headed up the trail, where they were spotted by a marine patrol that quickly made it back to report the hostile force's presence to a fifty-two-man platoon from the Special Weapons Group. These units, designed to beat off air strikes or amphibious assaults, had quite an arsenal of weapons, including 40mm and 20mm cannon intended for enemy planes, ships, or barges. That night the gunners used them as antipersonnel weapons. The platoon leader, 1st Lt. John Wismer, left half-crews on the guns and then ordered the remainder of his men back from the beach and into the tree line about 150 yards from shore. There he had the men redeploy on a hillock overlooking the trail beneath them.

It was a perfect position for an ambush. Hidden in the jungle night, they could fire down on a surprised enemy that would be trapped between the marines, the platoon's heavy guns, and the sea. On Wismer's right was the 172nd's antitank platoon; his left was covered by a handful of medical, mess, communications, admin, and artillery personnel who had become riflemen for the night. To augment their firepower, the marine platoon searched for and found damaged .30-caliber machine guns that had been discarded in the salvage dump. By cannibalizing other weapons for parts, they were able to assemble two complete weapons and put them in working order. Wismer then cleverly set the trap, placing the two machine guns forward of the rest in position to fire down the trail. The bal-

ance of his platoon dug in on the little rise under a low roof of cluttered branches and waited for the enemy to come. At about 9 P.M.
the intruders moved quietly up the trail and began setting up mortars. Wismer, wanting the surprise to be complete, gave strict orders
that no one should fire until they heard his command. Anxious
marines and soldiers could hear the unsuspecting Japanese creeping along the trail before them, their shadowy forms occasionally sil-
houetted against the dull glow of the New Georgia sky. It was truly a
rare opportunity. Close encounters with the Japanese for them normally meant duels with enemy planes on a low strafing run. Now they
would feel what it was like to be infantry. When the lieutenant was
sure that most of the enemy troops were strung out on the trail, he
raised his head and yelled, "Open fire!"

A sheet of flame illuminated the wood line where the Americans
lay in waiting, heralding an explosion of gunfire that stunned the
Japanese. Scores of dead and wounded fell on the trail—perhaps a
quarter of the entire party, maybe more. The others tried lamely to
return fire more or less in the direction of the ambush, but to no
avail. Within minutes, the survivors were limping back up the trail
as their enraged officers screamed. Round one had gone to the
Americans. However, Wismer knew the night was not over, and the
men along the line braced themselves for the anticipated counterattack, silently reloading magazines and fixing more grenades to
their pack straps. Sure enough, the Japanese began noisily re-
grouping in a dark corner of the trail, their officers harshly barking
out orders. Surely both the soldiers and marines recognized the pattern. The Guadalcanal vets had shared enough stories of the crazed,
inhuman attacks with them. This was their first real encounter with
fear and the dull nausea that inevitably accompanies it for most of
the GIs. They stared silently into the darkness before them and
prayed. Some made peace with the Lord, but most just begged
humbly for the strength to do what needed to be done.

Their meditations were interrupted by the growing noise of men
tramping through the heavy forest undergrowth. Then they heard
the loud banter of their phantom rivals. Clearly, the Japanese wanted
them to know that they were coming. "Kill me!" they seemed to be
crying. To them, death was a glorious victory. Such behavior bewil-

dered the waiting Americans, who had constantly had the need for cover, concealment, and stealth stressed to them. It was also terrifying. The enigmatic Japanese not only defied death, they welcomed, embraced, and even worshiped it. After what seemed an eternity, the broken Japanese columns sprang from the curtain of coconut trees and surged toward their adversaries. Once again a fusillade of fire greeted them, but this time the enemy kept coming, overran some of the forward pickets, and forced the others to pull back to where the 20mm and 40mm guns waited with barrels depressed and pointed down the trail in the direction of the attackers. This would be their last line of defense. However, a second banzai charge never materialized.

The credit for breaking the back of the Japanese attack goes to Cpl. Maier J. Rothschild and Pvt. John J. Wantuck, the marines manning the two cannibalized Browning machine guns that guarded the trail. The pair had bravely held their positions and covered their comrades' withdrawal during the furious assault, expending belt after belt of ammunition, creating a lethal crossfire that tore into the rampaging, screaming hoard of Japanese. Several approached to within a few feet of the busy gunners. Once, an officer charged at Rothschild, advancing until he was right on top of the smoking gun and twisted its ammunition belt with his boot, jamming it. Unable to fire, the alert corporal coolly drew his pistol and shot the man dead at point-blank range.

The next morning, the men counted more than a hundred enemy corpses strewn indecently about the forward slope of their perimeter. The two heroic marines were responsible for at least eighteen of them. Among the enemy dead was the body of Private Wantuck. There were no cartridges left in his machine gun, and his ammo box was empty. Eight enemy bodies were piled nearby, victims of his last grenades and trench knife—which his sullen buddies found resting on the ground inches from his body. They found Corporal Rothschild under some brush, wounded but alive. He was encircled by the contorted bodies of ten Japanese troops who had stormed their little salient. The two marines, who along with timely artillery fire may have saved the division rear and beachhead area, had repulsed four enemy assaults. Both were awarded the Navy Cross.[10]

• • •

A single long chow line began to form around 5 P.M. at the 43rd Infantry Division CP, which was nothing more than a clearing measuring about thirty by fifty yards alongside the winding, muddy road the engineers had been building to the Barike. Olive-drab tents serving as offices, a kitchen, and a hospital mushroomed haphazardly between pyramids of wooden supply crates and metal containers of all shapes and sizes. The cartons made suitable dining tables for the seventy or so men assigned to the CP, who sat there in the sticky evening devouring their meal of fish, canned meat, and cocoa.

Before they finished their meal, a GI ran into their midst and breathlessly demanded to see Gen. Leonard Wing, Hester's deputy who was in command during the CO's absence. Colonel Ernest Gibson, a former U.S. senator from Vermont serving on the division staff, confronted him and inquired what was wrong. The panicky soldier explained that a large Japanese force, perhaps two hundred strong, was coming down the road in their direction. The enemy had saturated their old CP location with mortar fire and machine-gunned two unsuspecting water carriers. The soldier fled when they turned to attack the handful of remaining engineers and medical people. General Wing emerged from his tent and had the man repeat his story, questioning him about numbers and weapons, figuring that the enemy would press ahead along the road looking for them. He guessed they had no more than half an hour.

Each of the approximately seventy officers and men present jumped to action to improve the CP's feeble defenses, which amounted to a handful of light machine guns spaced twenty yards apart in an arc along the compound's northern rim. The fifteen or so soldiers manning these forward positions, the first that the intruders would likely face, were fortified with BARs, Thompsons, and an extra helping of grenades. The rest of the men were strung out in a thin line on opposite sides of the road, the probable Japanese line of advance. Cooks dropped their serving spoons, picked up their M1s, and joined the medical and staff officers on the right flank. Signal Corps and engineer folks shouldered a line that curled west and south to the road's left. Someone remembered that there were two tripod-mounted .30-caliber machine guns somewhere in the weapons tent. The two guns were quickly emplaced on the CP's fragile western and southern flanks about seventy yards apart, making mutually supporting fire, the crux of a solid defense, impossible. If the attack came from either of those directions, the Americans would easily be overrun.

The irregular cadence of entrenching tools tearing feverishly at the ground drowned out the sound of men scampering here and there, lugging ammo to their holes, opening crates of grenades, and laying barbed wire. Intelligence personnel collected the war correspondents' notebooks and burned them along with everyone's personal mail. Official documents and maps were placed in a pouch and readied for quick destruction. A new password was issued. Without it, no call for help would be answered. Any movement outside the perimeter was to be interpreted as enemy, but no one was to fire unless ordered to do so. Each man was ordered to take a knife with him into his hole.

Storm clouds blanketed the islands as night fell, escorted by a western wind that quickly dropped temperatures into the high seventies. As the men climbed into their undersized mud trenches, a hard rain began to fall, flogging them as they lay shivering in the slop.

At exactly 7 P.M. the impassive jungle came alive with a roar of explosions and gunfire, causing the men in the holes to momentarily forget their misery. They stretched their necks to peek out into the endless darkness and strained their eyes as they looked for flashes of movement, firing at the occasional shadowy figures scurrying through the damp, crowded thickets to their front. Enemy machine guns began to sweep the area, violently shearing the umbrella of trees above them. Branches cracked everywhere, sprinkling the GIs with fluttering leaves. Several men unbolted a pair of .30-calibers from their jeep mounts and placed the machine guns on the trail leading to the CP while soldiers scrambled to dig more holes before the attackers reached them. In less time than it takes to tell, they were surrounded. The porous perimeter security was breached by a trickle of wildly screaming interlopers who ran through the area firing their weapons and throwing grenades. The air swelled with invisible animation. Supply dumps exploded and burned, casting lurid, dancing shadows on the jungle floor. It was bedlam. Fortunately, most of the division's logistical support had been moved to Laiana. The division staff and its radios were still at Zanana, however, and the beach there remained XIV Corps's primary landing point. They had to hold on.

In one of the holes on the southern edge of the perimeter was a weaponless war correspondent named Jack Mahon, one of four reporters who had been caught in the attack. Sharing the terror in his three-foot-deep hole was another noncombatant, Father John Culliton, a Catholic chaplain from Connecticut who had arrived just a few hours before. Mahon survived the ordeal and wrote the following about the experience:

> For almost thirty minutes there was a continuous roar of fire. The earth trembled. Suddenly, there was a series of familiar, short explosions right on the rim of our hole. Dirt rained down on us, and a moment later something struck me on my back. I thought I had been hit, but, rolling over, found that the concussion had toppled a good-sized rock on the small of my back. Those tremors had been too familiar, and we knew in a flash the answer: the devils were throwing grenades.
>
> There was no way of telling where the fire came from. You couldn't look out of your hole; that would be suicide. All you could do was lie there and wait. Lie there, wait, and sweat. Lie huddled on your belly, your mouth pressed into the red earth, not knowing where or when the Jap would strike next; not knowing whether that was friend or foe moving out there in the bush not thirty yards away. But knowing very well what you heard of Japs leaping into holes, their knives lashing out in hate.[11]

Then the demonic shrieking began. It was like nothing they had ever heard before, a low, guttural moan that quickly grew into a wavering, tortured soprano wail. Shrieks were punctuated with loud, angry chatter in the enemy's native tongue, an unnerving sound by itself in the midst of the pounding rain and withering gunfire. Was their fiendish opponent mounting a banzai charge? Were they about to die half-submerged in the sludge at the bottom of their holes? Through this relentless tumult, however, a single, clear voice man-

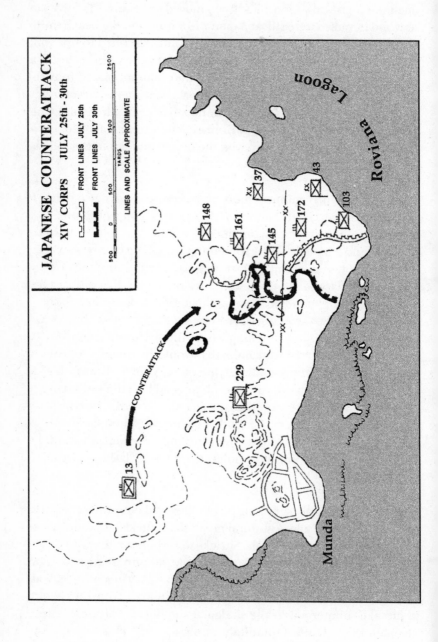

aged to reach the defensive sector where Mahon and the chaplain lay. "Help me, help me! Get me water, get me water! I'm wounded. Help! Help!" There was no question that the man was nearby and in trouble. His petition was all too real. However, his accent was clearly not American. For two or maybe three long hours, the man moaned piteously for help. It was impossible to ignore, and yet they must, although his pleas tested their Judeo-Christian instincts. They had to remain hidden. They fully understood that it was the darkness and rain that kept them alive. Then, as suddenly as it began, the moaning stopped. Each man who lay there that gruesome night would be haunted by his cries for years after the war. The next morning, they confirmed what they already knew: The wounded man was a Japanese soldier who lay not fifteen yards from their holes, half his stomach blown away by a grenade.

Four hours into the battle the two tortured noncombatants were still in their hole, silently cursing their misery and praying for the sun to bring an end to the carnage. As the night dragged on, recalled Mahon, they would "steal a peak at a wrist watch. Ten o'clock. We'd been lying there since six and there was no relief in sight. Hours and hours stretched ahead of us, long, dark, and foreboding. We couldn't get out of the hole for even a minute, and the thought of being crammed in it for eight or ten hours was torture."

Then another voice cried out from ahead of the perimeter: "This is Sergeant Bowers. Please don't shoot. I must get ammunition." Mahon wondered again if it were a trap. This time, though, the voice sounded American. The soldiers in the holes around the reporter kept their rifles at the ready, remained very still, and expected the worst. But the voice persisted: "I must see the general! Please let me come in! Please don't shoot! Answer me. Answer me!" All eyes peered in the direction of the voice, hoping to see some evidence of his identity. But the tangle of jungle debris around their holes was too thick for them to see much more than six feet ahead.

"For God's sake, let me come in! I'm no Jap! I swear it! This is Sergeant Bowers of the 103rd. I must get ammunition for my machine gun. My men are running low and the woods out there are full of Japs. You're supposed to be officers. For God's sake, answer me— answer me!"

They did not. Even though they were fairly sure he was legitimate, they were not about to grant entry without first hearing the password. The enemy had too many American-educated troops in the Pacific, and no one was foolish enough to take that kind of risk and expose their position. There was a rustling sound as the man moved closer. Again he pleaded with them to accept him, promising to take off his helmet and stick out his head so they could see that he was an American. "Please don't shoot. You can see me now, can't you? Please don't shoot."

Mahon caught a glimpse of a shadow moving just ahead of a pile of dirt on the rim of his hole and lifted his head to steal a took. There, crouching low, was a dirty-faced, sweating American youngster. It was Sgt. Leroy Bowers of the division's Headquarters Company Defense Platoon. Mahon and Father Culliton grabbed him by his blouse and dragged him into their mud pit.

As soon as he caught his breath and chided them for not answering, he explained his urgent situation. His machine gun was almost out of ammo, and an estimated fifty Japanese were threatening to overrun them. Bowers had volunteered to return to the ammo dump. The priest blessed him as he crawled out of the hole to continue his search. Before he left, however, they advised him to continue to repeat his name as he approached other defenders and promised him that they would not challenge him when he returned if he used the password. He agreed. Slipping quietly out of their hole, he shuffled on all fours through their tent, which lay directly behind their trenches, and was gone.

Life in their hole had become almost unendurable now that the rain had intensified, testing the patience of even the clergyman. Father Culliton suggested that they slither back to the tent to get some shelter from the chilling showers. The gunfire in their sector had diminished somewhat, he reasoned, so they could chance leaving their hole. Mahon agreed. For the moment they preferred to take their chances with the enemy's machine guns. They felt fortunate to have the option. The hapless riflemen, who were solely responsible for their sector's defense, had to remain in their hellholes. Less than an hour later they heard the sound of movement outside the tent, followed by the whispered password. It was Bowers. Gasping for breath, he squirmed inside juggling four wooden ammo boxes. They were small but heavy, difficult for a single person to carry. Nevertheless, the determined sergeant intended to deliver them to his comrades. The war correspondent and the priest begged him to reconsider, but the impetuous, young machine gunner refused to listen. He kept muttering that he had to get back to his men. He assured them that he would be all right, that his men knew his voice after being with him daily for the past year.

When the rain abated, Bowers was ready to go. Again they pleaded with him, grabbing him roughly by the arm for emphasis. It was suicidal, they insisted. Besides, there had not been much firing in their sector in the past hour. Did they really need the ammo now? It was not worth it. He thanked them for their concern, but he was single-minded and would have none of it. Mahon described the scene at his departure:

> We shook hands with him, the padre patting him reverently on the shoulder, and he crawled past the cot, down the hole, up the other side. He crouched there, the speckled jungle suit shining in the moonlight. He dropped one of the boxes and had a hard time wrestling it back into the crook of his arm. Then, bent almost double, he started creeping. We raised our heads and watched his tortuous journey for maybe thirty seconds. Suddenly the jungle swallowed him up and we could see him no more. We thought of the magnificent courage of this kid we had never seen before; of the guts it had taken to make that journey even one way; of his devotion to his men.[12]

Less than a minute later, a Japanese Nambu machine gun stuttered briefly in the darkness. Mahon and Culliton strained to listen in the ensuing silence, which was shattered by the flat crack of a single rifle shot. Inside the tent, neither man spoke or moved for a long time. In the morning they found the young noncom's bullet-riddled body less than thirty yards from their foxhole, lying in the mud next to four unopened ammunition boxes. It was sacrifices like his and those made by hundreds of others on New Georgia that elevated the simple tasks of soldiering to the level of the epic. Sergeant Leroy Bowers was awarded the Silver Star.

• • •

Help in the form of men and artillery was only a few miles away on Oniavisi Island, just off New Georgia's southern shore. However, the Japanese found the telephone lines leading across the channel to the batteries, cut them, and then smashed the switchboard, making it all but impossible for General Hester to maintain contact with General Wing, who remained at the CP in the midst of the chaos. Somehow, though, the Japanese managed to overlook the underwater cable linking the headquarters with the 136th Field Artillery Battalion on Rendova. Getting support from the gunners was not as simple as picking up the telephone and asking for it, however. The unit's guns, which were trained on Munda, had to be repositioned. Moreover, huge trees blocking their new fire lanes had to be cleared before they could respond to calls for fire.

Two of the 155s came on line just as a large number of enemy troops were preparing to assault the CP. Because of the enemy's proximity to the headquarters, the forward observers were forced to practically call artillery on themselves. This required a high degree of expertise from the men in the fire direction center who determined the solutions for the missions, the gun crews who fired the shells, and the forward observers who relayed target coordinates and adjusted fire on the enemy. General Harold Barker, the division artillery commander, was at the CP with General Wing. Rather than allow someone with less experience to adjust fire, he picked up the phone himself and helped Capt. James Ruhlin, the division artillery liaison officer, and an enlisted man bring in the rounds as close as possible in a box bombardment. They managed to have most of the rounds impact between one hundred and five hundred yards from the edge of the bivouac in order to discourage further enemy penetration. Steady and composed throughout the ordeal, the trio shifted fire from one point to another while the gunners maintained a furious pace, sliding the projectiles into the scorching breeches of their guns as fast as they were handed to them.

The artillerymen were using a method of fire adjustment called "sound and fragment." The guns would fire a volley a considerable distance ahead of the forward positions, and then the observers walked them back slowly by listening for the rounds' impact and then ordering the gunners to fire the next volley a little bit closer. They continued to adjust the strike of the shells until fragments began falling in the vicinity of the troops dug in around the CP. It was far from a scientific method, and extremely dangerous. There was always the threat of a shell falling short and landing on friendly troops. But desperate times called for desperate measures.

The shelling was harrowing for the men defending the CP. For a while, the men thought they were being hit from the rear by Japanese naval gunfire, and throughout the bivouac area men pressed deeper into their holes as the shells whined overhead and exploded nearby, sending fragments singing through the trees. They soon discovered that the 43rd's own offshore artillery was responsible for the devastating barrage. However, any relief that information brought was tempered considerably by their fear that a round might fall short. Still, they surrendered to episodes of fitful sleep during the brief interludes in the bombardment, only to be nudged awake when the earth again quivered beneath them.

As more trees were cleared from around the batteries and guns were retrained on target, the battalion's remaining 155s joined in one at a time until all twelve were slinging high-explosive rounds at the enemy troops gathered around the CP. The ground lurched as they plastered all potential staging areas for an assault. This went on for nine hours, with Barker ordering fire missions at irregular intervals, then adjusting by the sound of the barrages since it was impossible to see. Only one round fell short the entire night, and that was an early registration round. It was a magnificent display of finesse in an environment where finesse was a stranger. The bombardment kept the enemy off balance and tentative and unquestionably helped save the CP from utter destruction. Marines, who rarely had words of praise for their army counterparts, added their voices to the chorus of accolades for General Barker and his men. It was truly one of the most impressive feats of the campaign.

Later that night, General Griswold directed a battery of artillery and a battalion of infantry to Zanana from Rendova to help protect the CP, but by then the enemy had retired back up the Barike. General Barker was so grateful for the expert artillery support that he grabbed a spot on a supply shuttle to Rendova the next day and visited the 136th, where he personally thanked the gunners for saving their lives.[13]

The next morning crept in hot and still. From six to seven, only a few scattered gunshots were heard. Mud-encrusted men slowly began to emerge from the stifling slop in their rifle pits. There were surprisingly few casualties: five dead and about twice that number wounded. A few unnerved GIs were ordered to locate and count the enemy dead. They found the eviscerated corpses of about twenty-five enemy infiltrators near the trail and scattered throughout the CP. Ashen-faced and silent, they kicked their way through lumps of shredded flesh. Their metamorphosis had been rapid. Only a short time ago, their behavior was barely adolescent. Silly jokes, laughter, girl-talk, music, and pranks betrayed their youth. Two weeks in the loathsome jungle war, however, had reduced them to the level of barbarians, insensitive to the unspeakable horror. They had been embraced by evil and had not struggled to break free. They accepted it and even befriended it. They grew contemptible of everything and anything except their comrades, sullen and degenerate, their souls darkened. They had forever lost themselves somewhere in the madness of the deviant island.

Massacre at Butcher's Bridge

Five lone jeeps from the 118th Medical Battalion carrying seriously wounded soldiers in a litter convoy back from the front lumbered down the freshly constructed engineer road east across the bridge straddling the Barike. The casualties were from Major Zimmer's crippled 1st Battalion, 169th Infantry, on Kelley Hill, and their destination was the aid station at Zanana. Those who were still conscious grunted every time the vehicles hit a hole. The quarter-ton trucks were utility vehicles without much of a suspension system to soften the ride. But at least there was the prospect of a respite from the bloodshed, however brief, along with a Purple Heart to forever validate their courage. As the little convoy made its way to the rear, they sometimes were able to make out the staccato bark of gunfire from a distant contest. Imagining that their unit was still engaged with the enemy back on the hill, their minds were beset with guilt. They had known the guys in their outfit for years, and even though there were more than a few who were unworthy of much praise back home, things were different here. Leaving any of them in a lurch was traitorous, even if there was a piece of lead in your chest.

Darkness began to fall, bending the arching panoply of jungle growth down on the open jeep as it slowed to negotiate a sharp right turn. Just as the driver downshifted, they were greeted with a storm of rifle and machine-gun fire. It was an enemy trail block, just a few miles southeast of Zanana and a good four miles behind American lines—although the term *lines* had by then lost its meaning.

The drivers and medics attending to the wounded jumped from the jeeps and began hosing the gnarled forest with gunfire. The firefight's tempo increased while the forsaken wounded lay in excruciating fear on their pallets. The Americans located the enemy machine gun but failed to silence it. Unable to punch through the block, they had no choice but to do an about-face. They shrank rearward into the deadfall flanking the trail until full darkness allowed them to pull their jeeps back to the bridge over the Barike, where there was a small clearing that served as an aid station and water point. The scowling jungle was alive with Japanese who had isolated them from the beach evacuation point. Until the enemy could be cleared, they would be trapped there.

At the bridge, twenty-six-year-old 2nd Lt. Nicholas T. Kliebert, pulled temporarily from the 172nd, commanded a platoon of thirty-six men from Company E, 169th Infantry, who had been attached to the engineers in order to secure the bridge and casualty collection point. The simple wooden structure straddled the Barike where it pushed down between two overgrown hillocks, narrowing as it bisected the dense terrain, then disappearing into the island's green realm until it reached the sea. He and his men had been there for three uneventful days. Now, on 17 July, their mission suddenly became more complicated. Casualties were piling up at the tiny clearing while hundreds of nocturnal Japanese killers stalked them within their own lines.

In the twilight, Kliebert, a former shipping clerk and first sergeant in the Michigan National Guard, had the most serious casualties lowered carefully into the positions they had prepared for the BAR men in his perimeter defense. The others would have to make do on their stretchers until more holes could be burrowed. With enemy troops nearby, the men guarding the bridge were especially alert. They would vigorously defend the wounded men now entrusted to them, but they kept their distance emotionally.

The jungle was alive that night with the savage rattle of gunfire, rupturing the intermittent stillness. No one slept. Embedded in their shallow trenches, the wounded wondered if their dark, coral enclosures would become their tombs. But the night passed without incident.

The next morning, fourteen of the strongest walking wounded and an equal number of litter casualties again tried to reach Zanana. This time they were successful, circumventing the trail block and reaching the medical tents before dusk. Kliebert, meanwhile, sent for help. A platoon from the newly arrived 145th Infantry answered his call, but the newcomers, like those before them, discovered that without a trail, finding the bridge was considerably tougher than expected. When they failed to reach Kliebert's position by 4 P.M., they turned around and retraced their steps before the sun set. Later it was calculated that the platoon was only a hundred yards from Kliebert's perimeter when the platoon leader decided to pull back. That unfortunate bit of bad luck would prove costly.

Late in the afternoon on the eighteenth, more casualties moved into the tiny clearing from the front. Kliebert soon had about forty wounded in his care, sixteen of whom were confined to stretchers. There was little the medics could do for the casualties beyond changing their dressings, administering morphine, and giving them cigarettes. The smell of the muddy earth beneath them blended oppressively with the musk of decomposing leguminous matter. Without a breeze, the sickening odor settled over the clearing where the litters were scattered. Lying on their backs, sucking on cigarettes, the wounded stared through an open dome of leaves and branches at the sheet metal–gray sky and pondered their fate.

With no reinforcements forthcoming, and out of radio contact with the regiment, Kliebert did what he could with what he had. He positioned the jeeps and drivers on the trail east and west of the bridge and along the outer edge of the perimeter. More holes were dug to accommodate the most serious of the new casualties comfortably within the defensive ring, which itself was nothing more than a series of four-man slit trenches. The medics remained near the wounded and were given strict orders not to fire. The outer defense, they were assured, would handle any attack. If a large force approached, they were to withdraw into the surrounding woods. Kliebert placed his six BARs, the only automatic weapons available, at strategic points along the perimeter. The platoon leader himself would be on the west side of the river with most of the litter patients and half of his men. His platoon sergeant, John Finn, was with the remainder of the men on the eastern bank. The scheme was solid, probably good enough to stop a platoon-size force. However, no one knew how many of the enemy were out there, so another dreaded night of suspense lay ahead.

About a hundred Japanese troops left the trail block and began moving surreptitiously in column formation toward the Barike bridge with orders to create as much turmoil, destruction, and disorder as possible before they withdrew. They were divided into four subunits, each larger than the entire force defending the bridge. Their scouts came within sight of the bridge and clearing sometime around 8:30 P.M. Less than an hour later, as the moon was beginning its ascent into the clearing sky, they crept into Kliebert's perimeter. Sergeant Ken Dietlin of Winsted, Connecticut, was asleep in his hole when his buddy awakened him and pointed out eight enemy soldiers standing carelessly on the trail near the bridge. When they opened fire on the tantalizing targets, all hell broke loose.[14]

There was no organized assault. Small groups of the enemy rambled through the perimeter, firing here and there, scavenging the bivouac for food and equipment in between bursts of sporadic gunfire. They seemed leaderless, each group independent of the others, undisciplined and unfocused. But they heavily outnumbered the Company E defenders. Fire from a Nambu emplaced on the rise east of the bridge showered down on the scared GIs, prompting the BAR men to fire back until its muzzle flashes were permanently extinguished. The abrupt crack of enemy rifle fire, more frightening now that night had descended on the woods, would rise in intensity to a rattle, then ebb for long minutes. The battle continued for four and one-half hours as groups of from four to six infiltrators attempted to rush across the bridge to the river's west bank. Some nearly always got through the hail of gunfire and shrapnel, firing at anything they saw inside the loose circle of Americans. There were terrifying face-to-face encounters everywhere, the two adversaries now little more than a bayonet's thrust away from each other. Some men were reluctant to fire blindly through their perimeter for fear of hitting their own. Sergeant Finn's men stood up or knelt in their holes, throwing grenades and unloading magazine after magazine of ammo. Several of the BARS, which were supposed to be fired in short bursts, overheated and jammed as their gunners hammered away at the scores of targets around them. They accounted for "quite a lot of them," according to Sgt. Harold Ashton of Company E, who expended all but thirty rounds of his ammo before his own weapon seized in the middle of a long burst. The battle burned for hours with several lulls, said 1st Lt. Albert Wells, a litter patient who clung tightly to his pistol while praying that he would remain unnoticed in his trench.[15]

Lieutenant Kliebert had just dozed off when the babble of BAR fire broke up his half-sleep. Before he could reach for his M1, several screaming Japanese were upon him. There was no time to think:

I had my machete in my hand and swung it in front of me, missing a Jap by about 3 inches. The Jap got up and ran towards the bridge. I grabbed my rifle and ran in the opposite direction about 10 yards and laid down with a group of other men. As I laid there, some man ran towards me from the direction from where I come from, and I grabbed him by the arm [he offered no resistance]. I pulled him down beside me and told him those were Japs who were attacking us. As I grabbed him, the man beside me said, "That is not an American, It's a Jap!" Not being able to use my rifle because he was right beside me, I held on to the Jap, still had a hold on his arm, and with my left hand pulled out my trench knife and drove it into his stomach. He grabbed my knife and got up and ran about 15 yards and fell. I heard no more sounds from him. Then everything was quiet for a while.[16]

Fifteen more Japanese attempted to steal quickly across the bridge, four abreast, running in step through the maddening din of combat. About a third of them made it across. One of the enemy discovered the hole where a captain, seriously wounded in the ambush the day before at the trail block, was still hiding. Apparently an officer himself, he blew a high-pitched whistle and directed fire into the hole. Kliebert finished the man off with a single shot. Then twenty more made a rush to cross over. Half were cut down by the withering cross fire from positions on both banks of the river. But now the invaders were swarming deep inside the perimeter. Kliebert later reported:

> To my left there was a BAR and I realized if he opened fire toward the enemy, it would endanger the lives of the wounded lying nearby. I shouted at the Japs at this point. As I shouted, one of my men shouted, "Watch out!" I saw . . . three of the enemy coming toward me. I got up and ran about five or six feet and one of the Japs grabbed me by the seat of my pants. I jerked quite hard and twisted and got loose and ran approximately 10 feet in the direction of the BAR position and then turned around and fired my M-1 from the hip. I believe I got the leading Jap, but I don't know if I got the other two, although all three hit the ground.[17]

Meanwhile, Sergeants Dietlin and Finn and sixteen other members of the platoon south of the trail on the east bank continued to slug it out with small groups of Japanese as they continued to cross the bridge. Firing from under a thatched cover designed to provide some concealment for the troops within the trenches, Dietlin was rushed by two enemy soldiers who had crossed back over the bridge. They ran directly toward him and his partner. As they did, two BARs opened up and sent the two men scurrying. Some of the Japanese tried to drag their wounded comrades away into the undergrowth; they, too, were driven away. Dietlin later said the enemy

> threw grenades at us and they might have used knee mortars. It was pretty loud, some of the explosions across the road from where I was. There were three bursts of BAR fire from our holes. They were long bursts, but after three it ceased. They

rushed us again; the BARs beat them back. This went on for some time until finally . . . they blew the top of our hole down on us. In order to get ready for another rush, we had to push right up through the top and throw the leaves right off to one side. That left us exposed in the moonlight and after a few minutes exposed, I decided that we should move—to the jungle.[18]

Meanwhile, his rifle cradled in his arms, Lieutenant Kliebert, who was opposite Dietlin on the west side of the river, low-crawled to a slit trench about twenty feet from the trail, where four of his men were huddled. It probably took him less than a minute to cover the distance but it seemed much longer. As he inched forward in the brightening moonlight, dragging his chin through the jagged coral and sod, he prayed that the enemy would not spot him. Later he confided that he had always wondered how he would respond in combat. He could be comforted by the fact that he had performed well thus far, remaining calm and unafraid in front of his men. But his nightmare had only begun.

Sometime before midnight, the Japanese had taken control of the clearing on both sides of the bridge, and most of the defenders had consequently wormed their way from their darkened holes into the web of forest growth that encircled them. Some were able to drag away a couple of the wounded. They were the lucky ones. Inside the clearing, fourteen litter patients were still helplessly trapped inside their holes. One by one they were uncovered, and the awful savagery began.

The Japanese slid from hole to hole, pulled off their blankets, and lined up to take turns stabbing, bayoneting, and slashing with machetes at the defenseless innocents inside. The victims cried out with wrenching howls, begging for the help they knew would not be forthcoming. A few of the bandits flipped grenades inside the holes or mercilessly gunned down the hapless wounded as they stared up in terror at the killers standing above them. The first to be slain were at least spared the anguish of the wait. The others were left alone with their thoughts, wondering how they would be butchered as the morbid sounds of pain and death moved inexorably closer. One poor GI was slashed from the top of his head to his feet while the Japanese laughed deliriously. One of them finally shot him in the skull.

Most were executed in their dirty trenches, but one unfortunate soul was pulled from his hole, stood up against a tree, and held in place while an enemy soldier bayoneted him in the stomach. Another suffered a particularly slow, agonizing death. His gruesome murder evoked a visceral racism in Sgt. Franklin Phelps, which he shared with many Allied servicemen who served in the Pacific: "They dragged him a long ways over the ground and broke both his legs. On his body were over two hundred small gashes. How he must have suffered before he passed out. Strange creatures these fanatic little yellow men. Sometimes they will stab a dead man as much as fifty times, mutilating him beyond all recognition. It isn't hard to acquire an undying hatred for such a race."[19]

Amid the heinous brutality there was magnificent heroism. Private First Class John Patrizzo of the 169th Infantry's Service Company saved the lives of his three partners when he jumped atop and smothered a Japanese grenade. He survived the blast and was awarded the Distinguished Service Cross for his uncommon deed.[20]

When the bloody bacchanal was over, some of the killers sat down and ate the medics' rations or refreshed themselves with their water, talking and joking with each other as though they were enjoying a family picnic. Others packed away as much blood plasma as they could carry. They tossed aside the bodies in the holes and used the bloodstained stretchers for their own wounded. The victors were relaxed; one NCO even ordered a bit of close order drill while taunting an American prisoner who was forced to march with them inside their ranks. When the man stumbled and fell, they kicked him and prodded him with their bayonets. Lieutenant Wells, one of the wounded who survived the attack, claimed that he heard a few of the Japanese speaking English.[21]

As the screams of the men being slaughtered reached the trench where Lieutenant Kliebert and four other occupants hid, each man fought to control the panic welling up inside them. They no longer heard any friendly fire, which meant only one thing to Pfc. Earl Angelle: The Japanese had overrun their perimeter and they were the only ones left alive. "We knew the Japs were taking over," said SSgt. Adrian J. Demers of Manchester, New Hampshire, who heard the enemy chatting and concluded that the situation was hopeless. He made one attempt to reach Sergeant Finn across the river, but as he crawled slowly over the rim of his trench, shots hit above and around him, driving him back.

Kliebert, too, pondered the fate of Finn and the rest of his men. However, without radios, and with enemy soldiers streaming all about, communication with his platoon sergeant was nearly impossible. "I would have had to go across open ground that was well lit up by the moon in order to do so," said the frustrated officer. "The Japs had put a machine gun into a tree and fired every time anyone made any sort of an attempt to move in the hole I was in, and the hole was very much exposed. . . . Myself and the men tried dozens of times to get up to fire or observe, and this machine gun would open fire and was hitting the parapet of our hole every time."[22]

At first, Kliebert whispered that they should try and take out as many of the enemy as possible. He later recalled thinking he had eight rounds left in his rifle and that he would "get seven Japs with seven rounds and use the last one for myself." He eventually relented: "Having heard noises to the rear of the attack . . . , hearing the wounded groan, hearing the Japs attacking the pill boxes in the area, hearing no fire of our own, and only one or two shots from the Japs . . . , and hearing them jabbering and yelling for all they were worth . . . , I came to the conclusion that everyone in the area except ourselves had been killed or had left the area."[23]

The lieutenant was the first to slither out of their trench since he was closest to the shadowy sanctuary of the nearby jungle. Each of the others alligator-crawled behind him, taking care not to make a sound. It was several minutes past midnight.

After roughly an hour of simply lying still, Kliebert and two of the others moved silently northward through the woods for fifty yards, waded across the Barike above the bridge, and traveled until 4 A.M., hoping to reach division headquarters for help. They rested in the mute jungle until dawn and then resumed their trek. At noon, the grizzled threesome met three more members of their platoon and continued on to the east, forced to navigate by the sun after Kliebert's compass malfunctioned. Occasional sniper fire slowed them still more. After a second night in the bush, they finally reached headquarters at noon on the twentieth. After the hungry and exhausted men were refreshed with food and drink, they reported the details of the bloody event near what became known as "Butcher's Bridge."

By 7:30 on the morning of 19 July, a musty vapor murmured above the torn bodies as about fifty survivors trickled from the smoky gray of their hiding places and into the clearing to behold the aftermath of the battle. Many had retreated into the cover of the jungle, but a few, like Lieutenant Wells, had remained undiscovered in their holes throughout the entire wanton ordeal. The stench of fear clung to them. Some of the corpses had been obscenely dismembered, the men's eyes frozen wide in horror. Many of the bodies were altogether unrecognizable. Gaping holes now blackened by blood gave stark evidence that they were bayoneted or shot at point-blank range. A captain left on a stretcher to fend for himself had been so badly mutilated that he could only be identified by the bandages wrapped around his wounds. The men's dog tags were so heavily caked with blood that they had to be washed in the river before the Graves Registration personnel arrived. The wrecked shells of a dozen jeeps were scattered among the dead. Several more victims were found stretched out on their stomachs, their fingers dug into the mud as though they had tried to drag themselves under the vehicles. One of the jeeps sported a note that had been placed on its windshield by one of the English-speaking enemy, a morbid calling card announcing their terrible crime. There were conflicting reports of the number of bodies recovered, the best estimate being around twenty. Only one of Company E defenders was killed; the rest of the dead were litter patients.

Lieutenant Kliebert was nowhere to be found, so Wells took charge from his stretcher. He sent a patrol to Zanana beach with orders to obtain help and told the men remaining with him that if help did not arrive by noon, they would attempt to reach the beach themselves. They really had no other choice. The remaining wounded, including fifteen litter cases and an equal number of walking wounded, had been deprived of all but the most rudimentary medical attention for more than two days, and they were out of food. When help did not arrive, they began the four and one-half mile trek through the jungle, stopping every hundred yards to allow the litter bearers to rest, some of whom were walking wounded. They made the trip without incident except for occasional sniper fire, reaching the 118th Engineer Battalion's bivouac area near Zanana before dark.

When enough information about the atrocity had been collected, an investigation was conducted. Blame for the tragedy was fixed on Lieutenant Kliebert, who was court-martialed on 31 October on two specifications of violating Article of War 75. The charges read: "In that 2nd Lieutenant Nicholas T. Kliebert . . . then of Company E, 169th Infantry Regiment . . . did, on or about 18 July 1943, shamefully abandon the said platoon and seek safety in the rear, and did fail to rejoin it until on or about 21 July 1943. . . ." He was also accused of "shamefully abandoning a litter train of patients, which it was his duty to defend." The proceedings began on 29 November, almost four months after the New Georgia campaign ended. Kliebert was assigned two officers as defense counsel and a panel of ten officers was appointed to hear the case. Seventeen witnesses testified during the week-long trial, eight of them for the defense.

The trial established that Kliebert acted courageously throughout the attack. At no time did he lose his composure. His abandonment of the platoon may have been negligent, but it was prompted by poor judgment rather than cowardice. Nevertheless, he had failed to determine the status of his platoon and the condition of the wounded he was obliged to protect, and he left no orders for anyone to assume command before he left, basing his actions solely on presumptions. The court exonerated Kliebert of "shamefully" abandoning his men and "shamefully" abandoning the patients, but found him guilty of failing to determine whether his unit could continue to resist the Japanese and withdrawing before exhausting all "reasonable efforts to rescue the litter train." He was dismissed from the military.

The judge advocate officer who reviewed the case thought the sentence was too light. "Mere dismissal of an officer convicted of an offense of this type," he complained, "is not adequate punishment."[24] Perhaps hoping to send a message to similar tribunals in the future, he approved the findings but suggested that Kliebert should have been imprisoned. General Harmon endorsed the reviewing officer's remarks, stating that Kliebert's punishment was not commensurate with his actions.[25]

All things considered, Kliebert's sentence was probably just. He was correct in attempting to reach headquarters for assistance, but he should have sent someone else. The fact that it took him a day and a half to reach division headquarters, whereas Lieutenant Wells and his entire litter train made it to Zanana in an afternoon, did not help his case. Although he was under no obligation to stay in the foxhole, it was his duty to remain near the clearing, even if hidden in the jungle like the others, until the Japanese left. His unit suffered only one dead and two wounded, and most of their weapons were fully functional and had an ample supply of ammunition. It is reasonable to believe that he could possibly have rallied his men in the surrounding jungle and led a counterattack. Or he could have at least tried to reach his platoon sergeant across the river, despite the abundant gunfire. None of these issues would have been raised, of course, if Kliebert had had radio or telephone communication with Sergeant Finn and division headquarters.

Nicholas Kliebert was a brave man, but his bravery was not enough to save him under the strict standards of conduct dictated by war. His four-year army career was over, marred by disappointment. He was shipped out of the Solomons to San Francisco, and in April 1944 he became a civilian again. From there he went home to Detroit, where he began a career in automobile and then appliance sales.

When the terrible story of the atrocity at Butcher's Bridge reached America in February 1944, it inspired a series of government propaganda posters depicting Japanese soldiers stabbing a bandaged, kneeling American with bayonets. Displayed in manufacturing plants throughout the country, it urged workers to "Make 'em pay . . . KEEP PRODUCING." Later, the incident was dramatized in a radio program sponsored by Bell Telephone. Kliebert himself never avoided discussion of his crucial role in the atrocity. He related the story in detail to an Associated Press correspondent and even agreed to be the principal speaker at General Motors blood drives all over Michigan.[26] After marrying, he became a successful stockbroker. He died in California in 1998.[27]

Other isolated groups of Japanese stormed rear-area supply dumps, medical collection stations, support unit bivouacs, and en-

gineer water points on the night of 17 July. General Griswold betrayed real concern at the time in his diary: "Entire line of communications heavily attacked by enemy during the night from Zanana
beachhead. . . . Losses heavy. Morale low in the 43rd . . . line of communication cut. It looks bad. Front line battalions of the 169th cut
off."[28]

Most of the attacks were repelled. Although there is no official
record of casualties during the rampage, American losses were probably light despite Griswold's comment. By dawn on the eighteenth,
the serious fighting in the brief but violent counteroffensive was over,
although encounters with receding enemy patrols were reported
throughout the day.

General Sasaki had to be disappointed with his offensive, particularly the raid on the 43rd Division CP. He had made it clear in his
original orders to Colonel Tomonari that he expected the attack on
the coast to "annihilate" the Americans.[29] Had it been coordinated
with a well-orchestrated attack into the gap between the 172nd and
169th Infantry Regiment's, Tomonari's foray would have offered the
best opportunity for the Japanese to interrupt the entire Allied operation.

In 1946, Admiral Samejima, commander of the Eighth Fleet, concluded that the failure of Sasaki's counterattack was due to "fatigue
acquired during the movement, lack of heavy supporting weapons,
and the terrific American supporting fire and bombings." He also
admitted that splitting Tomonari's forces was a mistake, but he
blamed the decision on the island's "rough terrain."[30] The failed
counterstroke did nothing more than bolster Griswold's argument
that the rest of the 37th Division was needed immediately on the island to relieve the 43rd's two combat-weary regiments. Munda's dis-
advantaged defenders were about to witness what their comrades
across the Pacific would continue to see until the war's conclusion:
the unceasing swell of Allied men and materiel. "Bull" Halsey was
determined that New Georgia was going to fall. It was simply a matter of when.

7 The Final Torment

The anvil was about to drop on the Japanese. By the final week in July, General Griswold had almost twenty-seven thousand troops in New Georgia proper. Roughly ten thousand of them—five regiments (minus three battalions)—moved into the line to replace the two 43rd Division regiments that initiated the assault three weeks before. One of the biggest flaws in the campaign was thus corrected. At last General Griswold had sufficient forces on hand to meet the doctrinal requirement for success. The worn Munda defenders were about to face a force roughly four times their own size.

The fresh troops also benefited from the newly completed supply roads snaking from Laiana through the jungle to their immediate rear. There was no longer a need to hand-carry or parachute food, medical supplies, and ammunition to the frontline troops, thus eliminating one of the principal difficulties facing General Hester. The roads would also allow wounded soldiers to be evacuated more quickly and efficiently. Moreover, a fully staffed hospital had been established on Rendova to receive them. Rest camps offering hot baths, food, and cots were also established on the nearby barrier islands to attend to combat-fatigue victims. Doctors there screened incoming patients in an effort to identify and separate those who suffered from more serious war neuroses. After two frustrating weeks, movement behind the American line was finally easing a bit.

Marine pilots escalated their almost daily bombing raids against targets in and around Munda. Two days after Griswold assumed command of the operation, for example, seventy-four bombers bludgeoned the Japanese positions at the Lambeti plantation with eighty-eight 500-pound, thirty-six 1,000-pound, and eighteen 2,000-pound bombs. These earthshaking attacks transformed the landscape into a mess of steaming craters and fractured, uprooted trees. The defenders were so well dug in, however, that it is unlikely they suffered many casualties from the raids. A number of the well-designed bunkers were damaged, but they were easily repaired. In fact, the felled trees tended to enhance their defensive alignment. Thus, although the air attacks on the airfield's defenses were intensified, the men charged with rooting out the defenders still faced a costly battle.[1]

Phase two of the reinvigorated offensive was set for 25 July, and units began moving into line in preparation for H-hour. The 43rd Division's 103rd Infantry, which had been in corps reserve since D day, took over the southern sector of the line along the coast. Next came the refreshed 3rd Battalion, 169th Infantry, just back from a three-day rest on Rendova. The battalion would be in contact with the 172nd Infantry, which occupied the center of the corps line. The 169th's 1st Battalion would join in on 29 July. The 37th Division's 145th Infantry was next in line on the right, tied in with the 25th Division's 161st Infantry, which was under General Beightler's operational control. The 37th's 148th Infantry moved into position on the extreme right flank in the north, completing a line that was a little over two miles long. Orders were given for the 37th Division's three regiments to move west and seize Bibilo Hill, the high ground overlooking the airfield's northern rim. They then were to link up with Colonel Liversedge's Northern Landing Group and envelop the airfield's defenders. The 43rd Division was assigned the task of seizing the airfield itself. General Griswold's operations order emphasized the need for speed and directed that difficult strongholds should be contained and bypassed. He had no intention of getting bogged down the way the 43rd Division did when it crossed the Barike.

Between the attackers and the airfield was a two and one-half mile strip of choking vegetation, coral escarpments, and winding rivers guarded by the remnants of the Japanese 229th and 13th Infantry Regiments, and a battalion from the 230th Infantry. Corps intelligence estimated that Sasaki had lost nearly half his original force in the three weeks of fighting since 30 June.[2] However, the remaining troops were determined to fight to the last for their emperor. Despite intolerable hardships, they prepared themselves for the worst. Before they perished, though, the Americans would have to claw their way through an intricate system of defensive works bolstered by an assortment of mountain artillery, antitank weapons, and heavy machine guns brought forward from Munda. Although the Japanese knew they could not stop the powerful American advance, their spirits were high as they steeled themselves for the assault. Their final perimeter began at Ilangana Point, almost two miles down the coast from the airfield, and extended northwest along a ridge in front of the American line. The defenders waited resolutely in their dugouts, ready to kill and be killed.

Moving the neophyte Ohio Guardsmen into the proper alignment was no easy chore, particularly for the 148th Infantry, which had the farthest to move. The regiment's sector was north of the enemy's perimeter, where, functioning as a flank protection force, it would encounter little opposition in the drive west. The problem was getting there. The unit had yet to establish contact with friendly units presently on the battle line. Even the engineer jeep trails were not secure. Consequently, enemy units ranging in size from squads to companies continued to roam unmolested throughout the sector.

A small advance party from regimental headquarters was ambushed on the engineer trail leading to Reincke Ridge on 18 July. Two men were killed, four were wounded, and their truck was destroyed. The event delayed one battalion's move by a full day. Twenty-four hours later they tried again, but the lead company ran into a roadblock consisting of several machine guns. Several squads of riflemen moved into the thick jungle to suppress the gunfire, but by then darkness had settled in. Once again, a few well-placed Japanese machine guns had disrupted an entire battalion's timetable. General Griswold was beginning to understand the frustration that General Hester had experienced earlier in the month.

The next day, the 148th's commander, Col. Stuart Baxter, impatient with the 1st Battalion's unsteady first steps, ordered his 2nd Battalion to move forward from Zanana. Using an alternate route, the battalion's vanguard nearly reached its goal that afternoon. Meanwhile, the frustrated 1st Battalion flushed out the Japanese at the roadblock and began cautiously creeping forward through the dense jungle. The green GIs staggered on, unsure of themselves, feeling their way step by step, like blind men alone in an unfamiliar house. They spent another night bivouacked short of their objective.

The implacable jungle was already beginning to wear on the inexperienced Ohioans. The nocturnal clamor unnerved them, and the putrid odor it exuded sickened them. They felt like hostages in a dank, dark cell. Many of the men began to believe the inflated stories they had heard about how a single Japanese would slither up to a perimeter and mark men's helmets with phosphorescent paint to identify their positions for his comrades; or how the enemy sprinkled sleeping powder in the jungle to ensure the Americans would be unprepared to stop night attacks.[3] Unprovoked and unanswered shots rang out from the perimeter, then a few more, until dozens of the novice soldiers were firing blindly into the void. Order was finally restored, but the battalion was already succumbing to its interment in the island asylum of New Georgia.

On 21 July two battalions from the 145th Infantry replaced the bedraggled 169th GIs on Reincke Ridge and Kelley Hill. With the assistance of a smoke screen provided by division artillery, the tricky and potentially dangerous relief was accomplished during daylight hours. Sniper fire popped all around, but they were spared a mortar attack. The two regiments suffered only five wounded while making the switch.[4]

A unit's first casualties are always the most shocking. However, weeks of combat and death can easily make one indifferent to even the most unspeakable horrors. Norvil Wilson's first assignment with the 145th was to drive a jeep filled with ammo to the front. On his return trip to headquarters, he was ordered to load up two bodies for evacuation to the rear:

> They'd been dead so long that the maggots were working out. Going back we weren't in a stretcher jeep. It was a regular jeep. The trail was holed and bumpy. The bodies would fall off the jeep. We'd have to get out and pick them up and put them back on the jeep. When we got back the graves were already dug in

the cemetery. And they had about 6 inches of water in them. We put the bodies in the water, the chaplain said the last rites, and they covered them up. That was my introduction into combat. It was hard. But it didn't take too long to become immune to what you see. Later, I took a photo of a GI sitting on a dead Jap's swollen stomach eating C-rations![5]

Following the new jeep trail to Laiana, the 169th was met by fresh troops moving toward the front. They offered the grim-faced veterans cigarettes, canned peaches, and best of all, a bit of human warmth. When the battle-weary GIs reached the beach, they saw a flurry of activity: engineer outfits at work with their earthmovers, quartermaster units establishing their compound, and field kitchens preparing the next meal. Cooks gave them coffee as they slogged by. A few men came forward and carried some of the tired troops' packs. There were no cheers, but the reception they received was heartening nonetheless. The men in the rear made them feel like they were part of something good again.

Most of the 169th was shuttled to Rendova that afternoon. The others spent the night at Laiana, having their fill of C-rations (some men ate as many as five meals at one sitting) and fielding dozens of questions about the fighting. After they were asleep, an air raid siren sounded and a few bombs fell, but the veterans of Kelley Hill and Reincke Ridge hardly noticed. After a hearty breakfast, the remainder of the regiment was taken to Rendova and out of the battle zone for a while. When they landed, the gaunt troops trudged ashore feeling a bit like celebrities. Rear-area types gaped at them and peppered them with questions about the fighting. However, most of the veterans withdrew from the verbal onslaught. As soon as they reached their bivouac area, the men tore off the tattered jungle uniforms that had tormented them for the past three weeks, then indulged themselves with showers, hot food, and clear drinking water. That night they slept in clean clothing above ground under shelter halves or in cots—a luxury after three weeks in muddy slit trenches.[6]

The next day, many of them hacked off their three-week-old beards, although there were more than a few who were reluctant to part with their distinctive stigmata. They had proven to themselves that they could confront death and still function as good soldiers. Captain Robert Howard was one of those who felt that he had passed the test. "I cannot be called brave," he wrote in his diary, "yet I feel a certain satisfaction down deep, that although frightened, I never was yellow and managed to control emotion through many a trying night or day."[7]

By 24 July, all five regiments were almost in position, ready to commence the second offensive, scheduled for dawn the next day. The exception was the 161st Infantry, which occupied a five-hundred-yard sector in the middle of the corps' front. It had trouble moving up to its line of departure, which lay directly over a rather nasty, gnarled rise called Horseshoe Hill. Reconnaissance patrols had reported the presence of enemy pillboxes on the face of the hill, so two combat patrols were sent out to reduce the positions. Four were eliminated, but there were dozens more, and the four that had been silenced were quickly reoccupied.[8] Unknown to them, the men of the 161st Infantry were about to advance on one of the fulcrums of Sasaki's defense.

A hold-your-breath uneasiness permeated the XIV Corps CP on the eve of the assault. Members of the staff spoke with confidence in their plan, but the cockiness they had exhibited at the outset of the operation was missing. There was quiet seriousness throughout the compound, perhaps even apprehension or fear. A sentry on duty outside General Griswold's tent was shot and seriously wounded during the night by an officer from Admiral Halsey's headquarters who mistook the man for an enemy prowler. The corps commander tried not to allow the incident to distract him from his task, but it clearly distressed him. Late that night he sat alone on his cot and penciled these anxious words in his diary: "Moving up for D-Day tomorrow. I face tomorrow—my first test in battle leadership. I bow my head in humility and pray that I may have what it takes to properly lead my troops. God with us, we will win the victory."[9]

The attack commenced at exactly 6:09 A.M. on 25 July. For the next thirty-five minutes, seven destroyers in Roviana Channel showered the Lambeti plantation with 4,000 five-inch rounds. Each hundred-yard square was pounded by an average of 70 shells—a number that sounds awesome until one takes into consideration that a 200-shell density was required for proper target saturation.[10] Before the navy was finished, fifty-six B-24 and ten B-17 heavy bombers punished enemy emplacements along a five-hundred-yard strip of shoreline west of Lambeti with more than 250 tons of bombs. Finally, ninety-two artillery pieces lobbed several thousand 105mm and 155mm shells into the enemy positions along the front. At seven, the infantry began lumbering toward the carnage as an unearthly yellow-gray haze slowly curled above the charred jungle ahead, obscuring the morning sun.

General Sasaki, for his part, was likely untroubled by all the bluster. He and his men had suffered such indignities before and had seen the results fall short of American expectations. One is reminded of the story told by Herodotus about how a Spartan general was informed before a battle with the Persians that there were so many enemy archers the sun would be darkened when they released their arrows. The seasoned officer was unmoved. The battle would simply be fought in the shade, he replied flatly. Munda's commander was wise enough to understand the strengths and weaknesses of his own army and his adversary. He had done everything within his means. There was nothing to do now except watch his short candle burn until it slowly was extinguished.

The two 43rd Division regiments surged ahead with more poise this time. They started to engage enemy positions by 10 A.M., but machine-gun fire from well-concealed, mutually supporting pillboxes and accurate mortar barrages brought the entire advance to a halt. The air was filled with steel. Attempts to maneuver around one enemy position would draw fire from another while rifle fire popped from anywhere and everywhere. The preparatory bombardment seemed to have done little good. Some Japanese had moved closer to the American line when the hail of explosives began to fall, then moved back to their damaged positions in time to meet the ground assault. Someone in 1st Lt. James Chase's platoon came up with the idea of using concussion grenades on the bunkers, but that did not work. Another expedient did the trick, however. The men filled mortar casings with plastic explosive and attached white phosphorous grenades to them to serve as fuses. When thrown into a bunker's aperture, "It really blew the hell out of everything."[11] The problem, of course, was getting close enough to the position to flip one of the devices inside.

The 103rd Infantry's Company E managed to punch through an unprotected gap in the enemy's defenses, and by midday had created a salient. General Hester ordered a reserve battalion to exploit the company's success, but the Japanese quickly discovered their mistake and began to close in from both flanks, bottling up the attackers and cutting off the company's rear. By late afternoon, Company E was forced to surrender its gains and retreat east through the enemy lines to the regiment's position.

Farther north, Hester tried something else. Five marine tanks were brought up to help the 172nd Infantry push the Japanese from a crucial hill, but they contributed only marginally to the attack. Two 47mm armor-piercing antitank rounds slammed into the leading M5, the second penetrating its reinforced frontal armor and continuing through until it came to rest inside the rear engine compartment. No one was killed, but the tank burst into flame and had to be abandoned. The gunner froze, and Sgt. Robert Botts, the tank commander, grabbed him by the collar and dragged him out. When the enemy saw them escaping the burning vehicle, they mounted a hasty charge that was beaten back by a BAR man. One sprinting Japanese, cradling a mine under his arm like a breakaway tailback, made it to within six feet of the tank before he was cut down by the alert automatic rifleman.

After fleeing from his burning tank, Botts spotted what he believed was the antitank gun's muzzle flash. He climbed back inside and fired three rounds from the main gun, then jumped out just as the vehicle exploded. He then led two untouched tanks rearward, where they would be out of danger. Meanwhile, the antitank gun scored two hits on another of the M5s, and it, too, had to be abandoned. Small squads of Japanese infantry surged around the disabled tanks and eventually captured them despite furious fire from the retreating GIs.[12] The other three tanks broke down under the strain of steep slopes and heavy growth and had to be withdrawn. Nothing seemed to work in the fiendish jungle—not tanks, not fire and maneuver, not even the heavy air and naval bombardments.

Captain Robert Blake slumbered fitfully as midnight approached. He and his tankers knew that the three remaining M5s would be sent out to face the Japanese antitank gun in the morning, and he was more than a bit concerned about it: "I woke with a sense of dread. I had the feeling that today was a day that had come too soon, that something had to be done that I would rather not do. I got up and drank a lot of coffee. I was not hungry for anything else."[13] Despite the universal anxiety, the battle went well the next day. The 47mm gun was either destroyed by the morning's mortar barrage, or the Japanese had pulled back to another position.

There were similar problems in the 37th Division sector, where strong Japanese positions were discovered on a large hill mass west of the 161st Infantry's sector called Bartley Ridge. General Beightler, following Griswold's instructions to bypass strong points, had ordered elements of the 161st to contain the enemy on the ridge the day before the corps offensive began while the remainder of the regiment enveloped it north and south. He hoped that this maneuver would keep his three regiments on line and ready to jump off on the twenty-fifth. The 161st, commanded by thirty-four-year-old Col. James Dalton, sent a company to probe the enemy positions on the ridge after an artillery barrage. As 105mm shells smashed into the hill, Sgt. Orville Cummins of Spokane, Washington, stared at the spectacle before him. He said one Japanese soldier "went forty feet in the air, over the tops of trees, just floated up lazy-like, turned over one time and came back down. Then there was another that went up like a pinwheel, all arms and legs twisting in the air. He was an officer, I think, because I saw a saber go one way and a pistol the other."[14]

A few bunkers were reduced with the help of homemade Molotov cocktails—plasma bottles filled with gasoline donated by jeep drivers. Unfortunately, Beightler had badly miscalculated the extent of the Japanese defenses on the ridge. Heavy mortar and machine-gun fire soon stalled the envelopment, and it quickly became clear that it would require more than one company and more than one day to not just contain the position, but to seize it. The hill turned out to be an extensive fortress honeycombed with reinforced pillboxes and bunkers teeming with automatic weapons positioned so deftly that the entire regiment (and therefore the division) would be unable to move westward in force until it had been neutralized.

There appeared to be no bright spots anywhere along the 37th Division's line at the end of the day. The only exception was the easy time the 148th Infantry had on the right flank. It turned out that the regiment was north of the enemy's east-west perimeter and could have continued westward. Colonel Baxter even asked for permission to move onto what appeared to be an undefended Bibilo Hill, the division's objective. "Hell, my wedding anniversary is in three days," he complained, "and I want to get to a spot where I can send my wife a cable."[15] But General Beightler ordered him to maintain contact with the 161st. He did not want a gap developing in his line that the Japanese might try to exploit.

The first day of the corps offensive resulted in less than an impressive debut for General Griswold. The five assault regiments stumbled into the miasma looking for an invisible enemy who announced his presence with withering blasts of Nambu fire. Then the bloody duels began—dozens of nameless bouts between blazing machine guns and scared soldiers crawling forward on their bellies, armed only with grenades and M1s or BARs. Seemingly little had changed from three weeks before, when the 43rd Division began its advance from the Barike.

During the Spanish Civil War, the government issued a communiqué that attempted to put a positive spin on the grim report of a failed offensive. "The advance continued all day without the loss of any ground," it said. General Griswold was not tempted to sugarcoat the day's events. The new commander wrote honestly in his diary that he was "very much disappointed" by the corps' gains. "We have lost heavily all along the line today."[16] Perhaps he was developing a greater appreciation for what the 169th had gone through. Perhaps he was rethinking his 13 July message to General Harmon, in which he had remarked that Japanese resistance had "not been great." Perhaps he would have reserved judgment had he been aware that General MacArthur was experiencing the same problems in heavily overgrown New Guinea. Allied respect for the Japanese infantrymen had grown immensely since Guadalcanal, but some observers continued to trivialize the problems of jungle operations.

Day two was more successful on the left flank. Leading elements of the 43rd Division's 103rd Infantry pulled back a hundred yards so that artillery could go to work on a line of machine-gun nests that shielded Lambeti. After the howitzers fired for twenty-five minutes, the regiment crept forward supported by tanks and flamethrowers handled by six volunteers from an engineer unit.

Flamethrowers consisted of two metal tanks with a web harness worn on the operator's back. One tank was filled with highly volatile fuel, and the other contained a jelly-like substance that ignited and adhered to enemy emplacements. Each tank had a hose that came together in metal tubes attached to a nozzle that spewed a six-foot-wide stream of the mixture on targets up to about thirty-five feet away. The difficulty was that the operator not only had to get close enough to the target, he also had to use both hands to aim and fire. Another soldier was needed to turn the valves on the tops of the tanks to release the fluids. The contraption weighed sixty-five pounds, was cumbersome and hot (its flames often singed the operator's eyelashes and eyebrows), and had a tendency to malfunction at the most inopportune times. Even worse, flamethrowers attracted lots of enemy fire, so it was not easy finding men willing to carry them. When they did work properly, the five-gallon tanks emptied in eight to ten seconds. This required a ready supply of heavy fuel tanks that had to be brought forward by already overburdened support troops. However, if used with supporting infantry and tanks as they were in this instance, they could be most effective—especially in burning away the thick growth that so completely hid the Japanese bunkers. Flamethrowers were used a total of fifty-three times against enemy positions during the assault on Munda, and were credited with destroying twenty-three pillboxes or bunkers in the 37th Division sector alone.[17]

With tank and infantry teams engaging the enemy, a flamethrower crew and its attendant riflemen crawled to within several yards of three enemy positions. Flames quickly engulfed them, and within a minute all three were silenced. This early success was an indication of things to come. By dusk, the 103rd was eight hundred yards closer to Munda, but casualties in the regiment were becoming alarmingly high.[18]

On the twenty-seventh, the Japanese defenses squeezed tighter. The advance that had gone so well the day before collapsed in the face of intense 90mm mortar and machine-gun fire. One company in the 103rd's 3rd Battalion was unable to reach its line of departure. Another managed a mere fifteen-yard advance. In nine days, the battalion lost two staff officers, four company commanders, and eleven platoon leaders, leaving some platoons without officers or even NCOS. Enlisted casualties had reached 50 percent, reducing the size of each company to only sixty men.[19] Despite these losses, the 103rd crept closer to Lambeti behind four of Captain Blake's M5 light tanks moving in a double column about fifty feet apart. The terrain along the beach was less dense and rugged than it was farther inland. Nevertheless, the lumbering machines struggled to negotiate the broken stumps and trunks that were in their path.

Less than a half-hour after the attack began, four high-velocity antitank rounds slammed into one of the lead vehicles, filling the crew compartment with scalding metal and acrid smoke. Despite being seriously injured, the driver shifted into reverse and gunned the engine, smashed hard into the tank behind him, and executed a U-turn that took them out of range. The enemy gun then zeroed in on another tank and walloped it with a scorching round. Before it suffered another hit, the tank commander ordered the driver to back up at full throttle.

The attack was renewed at about noon. This time the armored vehicles outflanked the antitank gun, coming at it from the north supported by two rifle companies and spraying the jungle with .30-caliber machine-gun fire. One of the M5s spotted a grass shack and headed directly for it. At the last second, two Japanese soldiers leaped out and fastened magnetic mines to the vehicle's engine compartment. The explosions lifted the tank a few inches from the ground and forced it to hobble back. The 47mm gun then launched a round at the other tank, jarring the machine but causing no serious damage. The gunner, however, located the gun and sent a few well-placed rounds its way, quieting it at last.

The Japanese pulled out of their positions and regrouped that night, allowing the 103rd's tank-infantry teams to nudge farther ahead the next day. No tanks were lost and better coordination with the escorting riflemen paid off as the regiment advanced five hundred yards on the twenty-eighth.[20] After the regiment gained another three hundred precious yards on the twenty-ninth, the battle for Munda again came to resemble a handful of methodical, bloody fistfights, as the advancing tanks and infantry encountered a fresh line of enemy strong points manned by determined defenders. Patrols made up of a handful of men would probe ahead of the main body, searching for the well-camouflaged positions. Lieutenant Chase claimed to have developed a sixth sense that kept him out of harm's way: "Animal instincts would come back to you. And something would say, 'Get down.' About that time a burst of gunfire would come over the top of your head. And that happened several times to me. It goes back to the days when a man was an animal and could feel these things."[21]

Meanwhile, the 172nd Infantry inched forward over more difficult terrain, grinding its way over the last big ridge guarding the approach to Munda airfield without the help of tanks. As far as the men in the regiment were concerned, nothing had changed much since General Griswold assumed command of operations on New Georgia. The going continued to be tough. Success continued to be measured in yards. Casualties continued to mount. After twenty-two days of continuous combat, the men had had no change of clothes, they had bathed only once, and they had eaten only two hot meals. Many of the men began to wonder why their sister outfit, the 169th, had been removed for a few days rest on Rendova while they were forced to remain in the line. They felt they were being penalized because they had not suffered as many war neurosis casualties as the 169th. For the first time, their morale plummeted.[22]

The men of the 1st Battalion were told bluntly that they would have to take the key position without the aid of tanks or even the routine preparatory artillery barrage that the infantrymen had come to expect. Bludgeoning the defenders with those heavy weapons had failed, so this time they would attempt to force the enemy out using stealth and surprise. First Lieutenant Robert S. Scott's Company C was chosen to lead the way.

The company, moving out with platoons abreast, began its quiet advance up the hill's torn slope on 25 July, each man laden with two bandoleers of ammo and as many grenades as he could carry. As they neared the foot of the hill, Scott halted his platoon and went ahead alone to investigate. As he crept up the slope, he unknowingly passed directly over a large, well-concealed pillbox. Luckily, he noticed two bayonets sticking out of its gun port. He froze and then heard a faint conversation in Japanese coming from underneath him. As Scott positioned himself to fire into the rear entrance, a rifle shot from somewhere struck his carbine and cut through a piece of his finger. He dropped the weapon and sprinted away in a low crouch, slid behind a nearby tree, and began flinging grenades at the position. The first two were poorly aimed, but the next two found the mark and fell into the enemy dugout. Unfortunately, the occupants had time to throw them both out before they exploded. Scott pulled the pin on a fifth grenade, released the arming spoon, and held the grenade for a couple of seconds before letting it fly. He watched as it exploded in the face of an enemy soldier emerging from the bunker. He threw two more grenades that exploded inside, then scurried back and instructed his men to cover the pillbox while he returned to the line of departure to secure a new carbine and grab a few more grenades.

Upon returning, Scott crawled past his men and up to the crest of the hill to where a blasted tree trunk lay. As he slithered around the trunk, he saw two Japanese soldiers not twenty feet away firing knee mortars. Scott shot blindly at them until his magazine was empty, then scrambled for cover behind a huge tree. The enemy tossed several grenades at him from the other side of the hill. Estimating where the enemy were, Scott hurled a few of his own grenades at them. The Japanese then launched a wild counterattack. Scott, who had suffered a second wound during the grenade exchange, was able to beat the attackers off with carbine fire for half an hour, aided only by grenades thrown up to him by his men farther down the slope.

When the Japanese withdrew, Scott ordered his platoon to move up and deploy around the hilltop, making sure to drop grenades into each pillbox along the way. When that task was finished, the men dug in and prepared to defend their new turf. They watched as a demolition team, supported by a flamethrower crew, made sure the dugouts were clear. By the time they reached the pillbox that Scott had stepped on earlier, the engineers were out of TNT. So, instead of blowing the bunker, the flamethrower crew torched it. Twenty minutes later, four choking, gasping Japanese who had remained hidden inside rushed out into the middle of the American position. The surprised GIs gunned them down, bring the total number of enemy KIAs on the hill to twenty-eight. Lieutenant Scott was subsequently awarded the Medal of Honor.[23]

Back at the foot of Bartley Ridge, the 161st Infantry's 1st Battalion was ready for another go at its northern face, this time behind a vanguard of six M5 tanks supported by two flamethrower crews. The tanks, perhaps more so than anything else the Americans threw at them, terrified the Japanese.[24] The vehicles made good progress at first, despite a steady barrage of fire from Japanese 70mm guns and mortars. They pulverized a dozen or so pillboxes with jarring canister bursts, and GIs immediately manned the positions to keep the enemy from reoccupying them. The pace slowed when both flamethrower operators were killed and several tanks became snarled in the tangled growth or trapped in holes. Four soldiers seeking shelter behind one of the tanks were crushed when the driver abruptly shifted into reverse. One tank succumbed to mechanical problems. A foolishly brave Japanese soldier scaled up the hull of another with a magnetic mine and put it out of action before he was riddled with gunfire. Still another tank lost contact and got lost, so two crewmen dismounted to reorient themselves. While they were gone, the enemy crept up to the machine, blew off one of its tracks, and killed or wounded its other two occupants.[25] With the iron-skinned monsters struggling, the five-hour assault faltered, then stalled completely as the sun sank behind the trees. The two badly disabled tanks were abandoned.

Meanwhile, on the opposite (southern) side of the ridge, the 2nd Battalion managed to advance two hundred yards before encountering such a heavy curtain of small-arms and mortar fire from above and from nearby Horseshoe Hill that the GIs were forced to withdraw to their initial positions. The ridge was pockmarked with a nearly invincible chain of bunkers. According to Pfc. Elson Matson: "You got a few yards in front of them before you even saw them. You could throw mortars at them all day, but there would still be Japs there, burrowed under the logs and roots. Even if you grenaded them out of one dugout—others would come back to the same holes. They would never give up until they were dead."[26] The attack accomplished nothing more than adding the names of nine dead and twenty-five wounded to the casualty list.

General Hester's fate had been in doubt for some time. When the operation faltered in the opening weeks and Griswold was placed in command, the implication was that the 43rd Division had failed and needed bailing out. That suggestion, of course, is grossly unfair and mitigated for the most part by circumstances already explained here. Still, Hester's actions remain curious. Despite the eye-opening number of war neurosis cases, the relief of Colonel Eason and his key regimental staff officers, the embarrassment of having an outsider take Eason's place, and the relocation of the division CP and logistics center from one beach to another, Hester remained ensconced on Rendova. This was so even though his regimental frontages had been spread too thin, his units had lost contact with each other, and an enemy force had wedged itself dangerously between them. Faced with similar circumstances, a prudent commander would have made his presence felt by personally visiting the front in an effort to bolster morale. This is not to suggest that Hester was either imprudent or lacked personal courage. There is no evidence of that whatsoever. Perhaps the answer lies in a letter Admiral Halsey sent to Admiral Nimitz at the conclusion of the campaign. In it, Halsey admitted that Hester had "lost immediate, intimate touch" with his division, and said that he also "looked very bad." It turned out that Hester was suffering from painful stomach ulcers, an ailment that was not discovered until later. "He was traveling on his nerve," Halsey told Nimitz.[27]

General Griswold was much less indulgent. He had been disturbed by everything he observed after assuming command of the New Georgia operation. In the privacy of his diary, he revealed a much more uncomplimentary picture of the 43rd Division's fifty-seven-year-old commander. Hester's men, he wrote, seemed "bewildered" and had "the look of horror on their faces." They also appeared to be poorly trained, not mentally prepared for combat, and not doing their jobs. Hester's staff suffered criticism as well: "Was not impressed with them. Lots of loose ends." Griswold was clearly worried. "In my opinion," he stated flatly, "disaster in this operation is a possibility unless something is done."[28] Nor did Griswold keep his discontent a secret from Halsey. On 13 July he reported to the SPA commander that the operation was "going badly" and that Hester's division was "about to fold up."[29] He also held Hester personally responsible for not having his men ready for the night attacks that led to the division's grave war neurosis problem. That situation alone, he bluntly asserted, "almost wrecked one regiment."[30]

Within two weeks of assuming command, Griswold had lost all confidence in Hester, blaming him for the listlessness of the corps offensive: "We had some initial advances, but due to poor leadership, or lack of aggressiveness of Hester, the enemy reacted and drove us back to our starting line. . . . I am afraid Hester is too nice for a battle soldier. He is sick. Tonight I am requesting his relief from the Division."[31]

The corps commander dispatched his request to General Harmon, who in turn consulted with Halsey before relieving Hester on 29 July. Hester left New Georgia and was hospitalized in New Zealand before returning to the states, where he held several posts until the war's end. His temporary replacement was Maj. Gen. John R. Hodge, commander of the Americal Division, which had seen action in Guadalcanal. Hodge's experience in jungle combat and his reputation as a hard-nosed soldier made him an excellent choice for the job.

Horseshoe Hill

Meanwhile, the men of the 37th Division prepared to resume their attack on Bartley Ridge, an area that, along with neighboring Horseshoe Hill, turned out to be the linchpin of the Japanese defenses. General Beightler ordered the 145th Infantry's 2nd Battalion to seize Horseshoe Hill's northern slope. Occupying this high ground would make the enemy's defenses on Bartley Ridge untenable and open the way for the stalled 161st Infantry. On 27 July, two companies from the 145th Infantry slugged their way three hundred yards up the hillside and, after bitter fighting, managed to seize a small knob (which was nicknamed Wing Hill) protruding from a spur on the hill's skirt. Their success was short-lived, for the position was exposed to heavy mortar and machine-gun fire from two nearby position. Both companies were pinned down and had to pull back. The slightest move brought more fire, however, so it took over an hour of tedious crawling for the entrapped men to slip away.[32] To their credit, they brought back all forty of their dead and wounded. Captain Robert Howard was among them. Suffering from a slight but painful shrapnel wound on his hand, he refused evacuation because he felt safer on the line with his unit than on the trail back to the medical collection point.[33]

The next morning, the 2nd Battalion was ordered to try again. However, before the GIs could mount their assault, the dull, metallic *thwung, thwung, thwung* of Japanese 90mm mortars again erupted from Horseshoe Hill. One company commander recalled hearing an explosion

about half way between the Japs and where we were standing. Then another explosion about half way between where the first landed and where we were. There was no doubt about it now. The next shot would be close to us. I hit the dirt, just at the feet of Lt. Melvin G. Johnson and an orderly of H Company. I hadn't been sprawled out on the ground more than a few seconds when the next Jap shell hit. I remember being thrown over and over and being showered with dirt and rocks. My helmet was blown off, landing up the hill. I stumbled dazedly after it for about twenty feet, then looked around. Both Lt. Johnson and the orderly had completely disappeared. That 90-mm mortar shell had apparently hit between them and blown both to pieces. I know it was a miracle that I was not killed, also. I believe that I was too dazed from this time on to even feel any fear.[34]

Others never succeeded in conquering their fear. Colonel Holland recalled watching as a GI knelt in prayer, head bowed, at the bottom of his foxhole. Through the din of the detonations, he could hear the man nervously wail the "Our Father."[35]

The war chorus ceased at 8 A.M. and the thinning line of the 2nd Battalion's three companies again advanced on Wing Hill. With their own mortars supporting the attack, the dazed troops confronted the same pillboxes, now reoccupied, that they had fought so hard to reduce less than twenty-four hours earlier. It seemed like madness.[36] Within an hour they were back atop the knob, but again they came under small-arms and mortar fire from nearby positions farther up the hill. This time, however, instead of creeping back to their start line, the GIs clung to the small defile in the saddle connecting the two hills and, by methodically destroying pillboxes one at a time with grenades and rifles, the two lead companies reached Horseshoe's summit by midafternoon. Unwilling to concede the high ground, the enemy poured in heavy fire from both flanks and from the opposite slope of the hill. Unable to hold on in the face of the violent barrage, the gallant battalion, less thirty-six more casualties, crawled down from the crest and dug in for the night thirty-five yards from the Japanese positions.

While the 145th was scuffling with the enemy on Horseshoe Hill, a ten-man patrol from the 161st probed the face of Bartley Ridge on 28 July, encountering only sporadic resistance from a few outposts. The men had fought on that slope for so many hours that they knew which tree stump would shield them from the line of pillboxes along the crest. Offering more protection were the many craters that blemished the helmet-hard coral ridge after days of repeated heavy shelling. They alligator-crawled from one crater to another, inching closer and closer to the enemy positions. One of the men got to within a few feet of the gun port of a bunker and saw movement inside. Before the gunner could raise his Nambu to fire, Sgt. Leroy Norton, a tough lumberjack from Bend, Oregon, shoved a grenade into the slit. Norton slithered around the smoking bunker and approached a machine-gun nest manned by three groggy Japanese. He dispatched one of them with a well-placed round from his M1, then caught a glimpse of another Japanese scampering up the slope. Norton turned and sent a bullet through the man's chest before swinging back to finish off the remaining two crewmen. Meanwhile, Pfc. Joe Shupe and Sgt. Charley Dick nailed a sniper just as he awoke. The men tossed grenades at bunkers, taking them out one by one. Private First Class Cliff Gibson sidestepped and then curled around a machine-gun nest that opened up on him. He crawled up to it, leaned over its top, rammed his BAR into the gun slit from above, and unleashed an entire magazine of ammo into the dark space. An enemy rifleman in another dugout raised up to fire but was killed by Sgt. David Stewart before he got off a shot. The dead man's arm lay outside the position, his wristwatch exposed. Stewart crawled over and tried to pull him out by his arm, but the more he pulled, the heavier the man seemed to get. The sergeant peered over the lip of the dugout and saw a Japanese soldier tugging at his buddy's legs to keep him inside. Stewart fired again, pulled the watch from the dead man's arm, and kept moving.

By the time they reached the crest of the hill, twenty-one Japanese lay dead and fourteen positions were neutralized without a single friendly casualty—all in less time than it takes to smoke a cigarette. It was quite a performance and, like all skilled professionals, they made it look easy. Without interlocking fire from connecting bunkers, the enemy's defense broke down. Isolated pillboxes were extremely vulnerable to fire and maneuver. However, the real reason for their quick success was that the tenacious enemy had begun to abandon Bartley Ridge after five days of combat, some of them equal in ferocity to the bloodbath at Bairoko.

Although the crest of the ridge was in American hands, the Japanese withdrawal would be incremental, with an undetermined number of them still clinging tightly to the reverse slopes. More than a dozen of the enemy attempted to infiltrate the American perimeter that night. A Japanese grenade rolled into one foxhole and into a helmet that was lodged between one of the defender's legs. When it exploded, it blew away his calf and tore into the other two men, but none made a sound until daylight, understanding well that even a whisper might bring death to each of them. A mortar shell in another foxhole ripped off a soldier's arm below the elbow. His buddies did what they could to staunch the flow of blood, but at dawn he was gone, having bled to death without breaking the strict code of silence.

Darkness fell on 31 July as the main body of battle-weary GIs swept over the ridge's bloodstained face. They counted what had stopped two infantry battalions during those seven bloody days: forty-six re-inforced log bunkers and thirty-two pillboxes, which had sustained no more than four hundred defenders.[37]

While the 37th Division's other two regiments were struggling to move forward through the thick jungle, Col. Stuart Baxter's 148th Infantry was toiling to move backward. Simply put, the regiment had advanced too far westward—about fifteen hundred yards beyond the division line (to a point north of Munda)—and had lost contact with the 161st Infantry to its left (south). Although Baxter claimed that he remained linked to the 161st by patrols, he clearly had violated the spirit of Beightler's orders by allowing a gap to widen between the two regiments as his men advanced in pursuit of pockets of en-emy resistance to their front. Meanwhile, a force of two hundred Japanese soldiers had wiggled through the gap between the two reg-iments and played havoc in their rear. They were most likely troops from the 13th Infantry, which occupied positions north of Baxter's right flank. Breaking up into small squads built around their auto-matic weapons, they had the potential to further disrupt the corps timetable.

Baxter began his about-face on the twenty-ninth, but his two lead battalions were fragmented and vulnerable, out of contact not only with his supply line, but also with each other. Along the way, platoons and companies were stopped by Nambu fire coming from some unidentifiable place in the green gloom. The hidden enemy am-bushed a truck convoy, a survey party of engineers, and a bulldozer crew; cut off and ran over a mortar section; and attacked a ration dump. Then the bitter jungle darkness forced both battalions to bivouac in complete isolation from each other and the division, taunted by nocturnal jackals in the thick growth around them.

Another day passed without reaching the 161st. The fighting grew increasingly bitter, and heavy rains added to the delay. General

Beightler lost all patience and ordered Baxter to continue moving even if it meant doing so at night. Still, by the end of the next day, only a third of the regiment was on line with the 161st. Finally, three days and 190 casualties later, the 148th was back on line with the rest of the division—but not before Baxter felt the fury of his commander.

The 145th Infantry's 1st Battalion experienced comparatively routine days during the week after it occupied Kelley Hill and Reincke Ridge. On 22 July, water-carrying parties were ambushed in the morning and ration parties received small-arms fire on a new supply train in the afternoon. At 6:15 A.M., a distant enemy shore gun plastered Kelley Hill, killing nine and wounding eight. One of those killed was a surgeon who was administering plasma to a seriously wounded soldier. The next day was more of the same. Four times the Japanese pounded the hill with mortars and artillery. Four more men died. This routine continued for seven more days as the 161st Infantry struggled to clear the nearby high ground. There was nothing to do but patrol, curse the rain, try to sleep between shellings, hug the mud during them, and wait for the order to attack.

The order finally came on 28 July when a reinforced company from the battalion was ordered to join the attack on Horseshoe Hill. The GIs made it only a hundred yards up the slope before rifle fire sliced into them from their right and right front. One platoon maneuvered to outflank the enemy and managed to destroy six pillboxes before being subjected to devastating fire from enemy positions on higher ground. The men scampered for cover and pressed hard against the earth as bullets whined through the air around them. Sergeant Ben Kielliject fired three rifle grenades directly into the aperture of one of the pillboxes, but all three failed to detonate. A flamethrower was brought up and, under covering fire from rifles and BARs, its operator worked his way to within fifteen yards of the enemy positions and sprayed them with jellied gasoline, turning the holes into funeral pyres. The defenders never had a chance. However, after refilling his tanks, the flamethrower operator was severely wounded during his encounter with the next Nambu nest.

At 3 P.M. another company was ordered into the fray. An hour later it was on line and both companies began creeping forward behind a shield of 60mm mortar fire. Casualties were heavy and some platoons were reduced to fifteen men. Still, the two broken companies managed to push forward to within about fifteen yards of the crest. They would, however, get no closer. Darkness fell upon them even faster, or so it seemed, than it usually came in the Solomons. The order was given to dig in for the night right where they were.

Mortars and grenades serenaded them continuously until dawn, when the GIs lunged ahead once more. The Japanese had been reinforced during the night, however, and threw an even heavier volume of fire at them. The battalion's 81mm heavy mortars were directed in on the hilltop just above them and effectively reduced a number of stubborn pillboxes, but it was no use. More men were needed to surge over the crest, and at 10 A.M. they heeded the order to withdraw. As the Ohioans fell back, a horde of screaming Japanese counterattacked, but the regiment's mortars, some so heated up from overuse that they turned orange, caught them in the open and wrought havoc on the attackers.

Unlike in the triple-canopy jungle cloaking the island's interior, the mortar was the queen of battle in the struggle for these hills, whose surfaces were relatively clear of the clutter of jungle growth as a result of multiple artillery and air strikes. Consequently, the weapon not only could be fired without fear of an overhanging branch catching a shell on the way up and exploding it, it also could be adjusted by sight instead of sound. The mortar observers could actually see where the rounds impacted.

A few hundred yards behind the combat line, mortar crews worked feverishly in response to calls for fire. In between these furious assignments, shirtless, bearded men labored in the stifling air to unload crates of ammunition from bulldozers, jeeps, or anything motorized that happened to be coming up the trails. Piles of cardboard ammunition tubes mounded around the mortar positions as the crews stripped from them the rounds, which they stacked neatly near each tube, ready for the next mission. Unfortunately, the Japanese used their own mortars with equal effectiveness, bringing an end to hopes that the hill could be captured without another attack. The failed two-day engagement on Horseshoe Hill cost the 1st Battalion ninety casualties, including the deaths of twenty-five officers and men.[38]

Fierce fighting continued on the twenty-ninth, with the 2nd Battalion, 145th Infantry, pushing farther over the mangled hilltop, devoid now of any standing growth. Enemy mortar fire intensified, however, and at 5:15 P.M. the battalion was ordered to return to its previous night's positions below the charred, broken crest of the hill. There were many acts of heroism, none more memorable than that of Cleveland native Pfc. Frank Petrarca, a medic with Company F. Petrarca scooted from one fallen GI to another, cleaning and binding wounds and injecting morphine. Through the clouds of coral bits that still hung in the air, he saw a crumpled-up man writhing in pain in an open area in front of the Japanese bunkers. Petrarca belly-crawled over to where the man lay with the intent of dragging him to safety. The man was too seriously wounded to be moved, however, so Petrarca administered first aid, using his own body to shield the dying man until he finally succumbed to his wounds.

The next morning, the battalion beat off a counterattack without suffering any casualties, then waited all day in a fierce rainstorm for a follow-up assault, but none came. They then spent another macabre night in the squalor of their holes—this time among the bloating, shredded carcasses of the men they had killed in the morning's action.

Early on 31 July the men of the 2nd Battalion were ordered to punch forward again. This time they surprised several Japanese officers at breakfast. Moving closer, they watched in astonishment as three of the officers continued to sit calmly, eating from their bowls of steamed rice as the battle raged not 150 yards away.[39] The fighting, which lasted most of the day, proved to be the bitterest of the week.

Farther south, the 3rd Battalion, 169th Infantry, refreshed from its respite on Rendova, moved across the faces of the unoccupied hills left of the 145th on 25 July, sealing the gap between the 172nd and 103rd Infantry Regiments. Two hours later, soldiers from the 161st Infantry crawled over the north face of Horseshoe Hill, a move that finally brought the three regiments in the center of the corps front in direct contact with each other, as it always should have been. With Munda in sight, Griswold and his two division commanders could breathe easier knowing that Sasaki was unlikely to attempt another rear-area penetration. Most important of all, the corps was aligned and ready for the final push. However, it had taken eight days and cost hundreds of casualties, a performance strikingly similar to that of the sharply criticized 43rd Division's earlier in the operation.

General Hodge was especially interested in the 169th Infantry's performance. The regiment still bore the stigma of the large number of war neurosis casualties it had suffered in the first two weeks of the New Georgia campaign, and the new division commander was watching it carefully. The 3rd Battalion was already in contact with the enemy when Hodge arrived on the island, and all the reports were good. By 24 July, the 1st Battalion had returned to the island as part of the division reserve with many of its psychiatric casualties restored to their squads. However, on the day he took command, Hodge purposely assigned it to the front line so that its confidence could be restored as soon as possible.

The tactic worked. The battalion demonstrated a desire to fight and, along with the other two battalions, gave an excellent account of itself during the remainder of the campaign, although Hodge later relieved its commander for unfitness.[40] Moreover, Hodge revealed in a letter to the 43rd Division chief of staff written after the campaign that he still harbored doubts about the 169th, especially its officers: "We were able to bolster them up temporarily and get some fight out of them while I was there, but they lacked the long, hard training that is essential to make a top outfit, even though I think the enlisted men are as good as the other two regiments."[41]

At 5:15 P.M. on the thirty-first, with about a third of Horseshoe Hill firmly in American hands, the Japanese fired another blistering mortar concentration that sent dozens of GIs twisting to the ground in pain. One of the wounded lay just over a small crest, exposed to the murderous Japanese fire. Again Private Petrarca rushed to help— for the last time. His partner begged him not to crawl over the crest, but he pushed ahead anyway, almost reaching the injured GI before being torn by a mortar blast himself. Enraged by his own painful wounds, he struggled to his feet and inched ahead, then staggered and dropped to his knees, screaming curses at the Japanese before he finally fell dead on the smoking hillside.

• • •

The men of Company F, 145th Infantry, took inventory after digging in for the night. None of its platoons had more than eighteen men left. Casualties had gutted the officer ranks, and one of the acting platoon leaders was only a corporal.[42] The situation was much the same in the other companies. Although they needed replacements and rest badly, they were instructed to resume the attack in the morning. This time, though, it would be coordinated with a battalion from the 161st. As the men emerged from their holes, they encountered no resistance. This confirmed the assessment of an officer who had told Generals Hodge and Wing during their visit to the 145th Infantry's CP the night before that he was certain the enemy had abandoned their positions and withdrawn toward the airstrip.

By 6 P.M. the two battalions were in complete control of Horseshoe Hill. In a week of heavy, protracted fighting there, the Japanese had absorbed three thousand 81mm mortar rounds, beaten off six tanks, and quelled the fury of two determined infantry battalions. Although they had finally released their grip on the gnarled ridges, they had done so in good order after successfully delaying the American advance.

A wild heat rose from the ground coral of the hill's strangely silent summit, magnifying the stench of excrement and the sickly sweet odor of decaying flesh. Sullen-faced, the GIs drifted through the demolished remains of the enemy's defenses, decorated with human detritus, abandoned gear, and broken weapons—a visual testament to the past week's horror. But there would be more. From the hill's peak they caught a glimpse of the tough surviving defenders of Horseshoe Hill withdrawing westward to regroup for their final stand before the airfield.

"Keep 'em Dying"

Optimism permeated the American ranks. Along the coast, the 43rd Division now occupied the last lattice of hills protecting the airfield, and the 37th Division was in control of Bartley Ridge and Horseshoe Hill. In addition, the 25th Division's 27th Infantry had

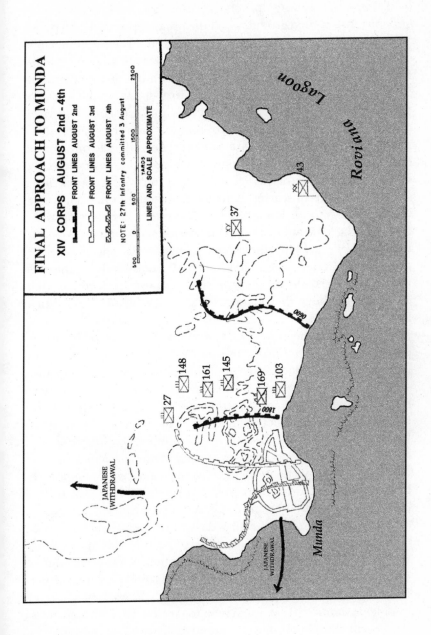

FINAL APPROACH TO MUNDA

XIV CORPS   AUGUST 2nd - 4th

▄▄▄▄▄   FRONT LINES AUGUST 2nd

▭▭▭▭▭   FRONT LINES AUGUST 3rd

▰▰▰▰▰   FRONT LINES AUGUST 4th

NOTE: 27th Infantry committed 3 August

YARDS   LINES AND SCALE APPROXIMATE

500   0   500   1500   2500

Roviana Lagoon

43

37

148

27

161

145

169

103

0090

1800

Munda

JAPANESE WITHDRAWAL

JAPANESE WITHDRAWAL

landed and was moving up to bolster the right flank. On 1 August both divisions gained ground with little or no opposition, and by the end of the day the 103rd Infantry had filtered through the remains of the Lambeti plantation, reaching the easternmost lip of the airfield's taxiways, where it tied in with the 169th Infantry on the right. They had Air New Georgia to thank. Thirty-six SBDs and TBFs hit Japanese gun positions on the plantation's northeast corner and tore open the stronghold. It was one of the rare occasions when Allied planes provided effective close air support. According to one marine correspondent, Lambeti was "one of the most ghastly and unusual sights I have seen either at Guadalcanal or on New Georgia. Not a single tree stands unscarred. Literally hundreds of once tall, swinging palms lay strewn along the beach. Crater after crater pits the earth's surface. Japanese equipment is scattered along the road and the stench of dead Japs still in their pillboxes fouls the air."[43]

Even with General Griswold's impatient troops nudging the edge of the runway, General Harmon was unwilling to forecast when Munda would be in their hands. Such was the respect he now held for his adversaries.[44]

Noisy M5 tanks accompanied the 103rd all the way to Munda, experiencing few of the problems that had beset them in the much more hilly and forested interior. The regiment also received a few air missions since the terrain was now more open and it was easier for the pilots to see. However, these were suspended after a dive-bomber came in parallel to the lead companies and dropped its lethal ordnance on the crest of a hill occupied by U.S. troops. No one died, but twenty men were treated for shrapnel wounds and concussions.[45] To the north, the 37th Division kept pace, advancing seven hundred yards against almost no resistance. For the first time in eleven days, the 161st Infantry suffered no casualties.

It was easily the most effortless day of the operation. Perhaps the cumulative effect of American artillery and bombing missions was finally taking a toll. The Japanese 229th Infantry was reduced to an effective force of 1,245 troops, and some of its rifle companies were left with only twenty men. To compensate for these losses, its commander brazenly ordered each man to take ten GIs with him before he was killed.[46] The wounded were without medical attention, and food was scarce. Colonel Liversedge and his men had forced the Japanese garrison at Bairoko to remain there in order to keep Sasaki's tentative supply line open. However, it was constantly harassed by Allied planes, destroyers, and PT boats—the latter now operating from two bases in the area—slowing the flow of supplies to barely a trickle. The Japanese were virtually trapped—a situation General Griswold knew made his tenacious enemy even more dangerous.

The real reason for the GIs' surprisingly easy day was that General Sasaki had pulled almost entirely out of his Munda defenses. Two days before, an Eighth Fleet staff officer had come to Munda to evaluate the gloomy situation. It was readily apparent that Munda itself could no longer be defended, so he ordered Sasaki to abandon his positions and withdraw northward to high ground about two miles inland. What he feared most was the wedge that Griswold's men were driving between Munda and Bairoko, threatening to sever all contact between the two strongholds.[47]

Sasaki immediately set about making the best of the situation. A powerful delaying force supported by six 75mm antiaircraft guns and a number of twin-barreled 25mm guns was emplaced on a 250-foot-high, triple-ridged knoll called Bibilo Hill, which overlooked the runway to the northeast. At least fifty land mines were scattered along its uneven slopes, and rolls of barbed wire completed the design. Closer to but still north of the runway was Kokengolo Hill. It, too, was solidly defended. Although they were conceding Munda airfield to the Americans, the staff officer assured Sasaki that General Imamura was not abandoning the operation. Substantial reinforcements were en route to New Georgia via Kolombangara, he promised.[48]

The airfield could hardly be identified as such any longer. Over a period of five weeks, Allied aviators had dropped 950 tons of explosives on the tiny coral point, turning it into a grotesque moonscape. The runway itself was hardly discernable under the litter of scorched and twisted aircraft, weeds, and rainwater that had puddled onto its cratered surface. Here and there were scattered an array of ammo crates, demolished construction equipment, and collapsed bunkers occupied by rotting corpses.

Sergeant James Salafia of the 169th Infantry had seen his platoon reduced from more than forty men to just seven during the month-long campaign. As they neared the edge of the airfield they had fought so long and hard to reach, he and the others expressed disappointment: "This is what all the work was for? What a shitty airfield! . . . There was nothing there except shell holes."[49]

On 2 August, elements of the 169th, 172nd, 145th, and 161st Regiments began encountering small suicide squads occupying positions on the coastal plain and dug into the high ground around the airfield. These rear guards had been left to slow the American advance while the rest of Sasaki's men made their escape. When they reached the foot of Bibilo Hill that afternoon, the Americans were stopped by thunderous fire from the 75mm guns sited there. It was the first time they had encountered these frightening weapons on the island. The men called them "whiz-bangs" because, as Pfc. Elson Matson of the 161st Infantry explained, they "fired with a swish and then an ear-splitting crash as the shells exploded." The Japanese aimed them just over the heads of the attackers. Their muzzle blasts were so powerful that they knocked people to the ground, "deafened and dazed."[50] Sergeant Norvil Wilson remembered the guns shattering treetops and causing near panic among the men. One soldier was so unnerved by the bursts that he frantically tried to dig a hasty foxhole under a fallen log with his mess kit.[51]

Medical officer Joe Risman was sitting at the bottom of a large bomb crater seeking protection from the 75mm guns when someone called to him that one of the platoon leaders had been hit with shrapnel about a hundred yards away. The surgeon and his aide grabbed some plasma, dressings, sulfonamide, and morphine, waited for a lull in the shelling, and scooted out of the crater. Three shells exploded just seconds after they emerged from their shelter, one just fifty feet to their front. They fell to the earth and tried to dig into the coral with their hands as shell fragments whistled overhead. They advanced another few feet during the next lull and jumped into a crater that was still warm from the blast that had sent them diving for cover minutes before. Risman finally reached the writhing lieutenant, who lay in the open with his guts in his hands. A jagged shell fragment had ripped across the anterior wall of his stomach. After checking the officer's pulse, he administered morphine, hoping that it would cause him to stop straining and prevent more of the man's gut from being pushed out. Next,

> We dusted the wound with sulfonamide powder, covered it with a large dressing, and held the entire bulging mass in place by buttoning up his shorts over the dressing. All this we did while lying flat on the ground with shells bursting and shrapnel flying overhead.
>
> The lieutenant was clear and conscious and he watched the entire proceeding. "This is it, isn't it, doc?", and his voice was flat and dull and hopeless. I lied and said a little operation would fix him up.[52]

Ten minutes later, litter bearers from the collecting company had him on his way to the rear. Risman subsequently learned that the officer had indeed recovered.[53]

Heavy mortar and artillery fire hammered Bibilo throughout the rest of that day and the next. Enemy soldiers not killed by the blasts were chased from their pillboxes and cut down by machine-gun fire. The intensity of the barrage made it dangerous that planes were unable to fly support missions. A mortar round hit the wing of a navy Corsair strafing the hill, tearing it off and sending the plane into a death spin. The pilot bailed out and was rescued.[54]

At about midnight on the third, an ammo dump was hit, causing a huge explosion. The GIs watched from their foxholes as the pyrotechnics lit up the dreary night sky. By morning, the hillside was nothing more than a groaning wasteland of broken trees, disabled dual-purpose guns, and shell craters, some so deep that engineers would later drill just a few feet more and find wells of fresh drinking water.[55] Scattered groups of Japanese defenders were eliminated, and the 75mm guns were finally silenced. The end of their long assault was at last in sight.

Meanwhile, the 25th Division's men continued northwest in an effort to make contact with Colonel Liversedge's NLG, which General Griswold had ordered to reestablish the roadblock on the Bairoko–Munda Trail and intercept the fleeing enemy. The pincer had finally closed tight.

Farther south, the 43rd Division occupied the southern shore of Munda Point. Facing it was the enemy's last redoubt, Ķokengolo Hill. Now the American troops were fighting in open country, permitting them to use their tanks and mortars effectively. They were followed closely by trucks carrying food and ammunition. The fanatical defenders in their pillboxes and bunkers held them back for one day, but with the assistance of eleven marine tanks spearheading the final assault, the attackers subdued the enemy pillbox by pillbox. For the first time many of the GIs were able to see their detested enemy, now so hopelessly outclassed even the 169th's Sergeant Phelps betrayed a stroke of compassion for them:

> It was almost pitiful to see those little devils. Some of them running about without rifle or helmet appeared half-stunned. They staggered about not knowing where to go. I saw one blown out of his hole running for cover somewhere else. The next shell picked him up and carried him 20 or 30 feet through the air. He lit and seemed to start running again. Then a shell burst right on him and he disappeared. Another one running for cover was cut down by machine gun fire. Taking a grenade, he struck it and held it against his chest till it exploded. . . .
>
> All our guns delivered fire on that hill. It was a thrilling sight. . . . There were so many light and heavy mortars firing in the same general area, it was a problem to tell which burst was which. . . . It must have been tough on those Japs. Sometimes I could hear them screaming, and often logs and debris from pillboxes would fly into the air high over the tops of the trees.[56]

On the afternoon of 5 August, the last of the Kokengolo's defenders were killed or driven from their bunkers and tunnels. Japanese-American interpreters tried to talk the Japanese hiding inside the tunnels to surrender, but without success, so TNT charges were detonated, entombing them beneath tons of earth.[57]

That same afternoon, Bibilo Hill fell into American hands. A battalion from the 145th Infantry skirted north of the hill and cut the main enemy escape route, the trail to Bairoko, hastening the Japanese' decision to abandon their last stronghold. The troops dug in on the face of the denuded battered hill, preparing to defend against an attack that never came. Most were able to get some sleep anyway, as exhausted as they were.

"You get so tired, you hope you get shot," recalled Norvil Wilson. "I will never forget—Bibilo Hill—making our last drive. A Jap sniper was popping at me—shooting 'daisy cutters'—just a few inches off the ground. I said, well, if he hits me in the leg, I'm going home. So I just kept moving. You get to the point where you're so tired, so numb, you don't give a damn if you get hit. As long as it wasn't going to be fatal."[58]

From his two-hundred-foot perch on the hill, a triumphant General Wing gazed down at the smoldering airfield and telephoned General Hodge: "Munda is yours at 1410 today."[59] General Griswold in turn notified Admiral Halsey, presenting the island to him as its "sole owner." Halsey's response was a verbal "custody receipt for Munda, and for a gratifying number of enemy dead. Such teamwork and unrelenting offensive spirit assures the success of future drives and the implacable extermination of the enemy." He followed that comment with a characteristic closing: "Keep 'em dying."[60] Two days short of the anniversary of the initial landings on Guadalcanal, all organized Japanese resistance at Munda ceased.

About a hundred of the last defenders, cut off from Bairoko to the north, left their positions and waded into the surf. As the water deepened, they discarded their weapons and began to swim toward the nearest island, several miles away. It made little difference to the infantrymen, artillerymen, and support troops lining the beach firing at the helpless fugitives. Some swam beyond rifle range, so 60mm mortar shells were lobbed at them. When division headquarters heard about this, they sent Japanese-Americans with loudspeakers to the beach to persuade them to return. Positioning themselves in the middle of the firing GIs, the Nisei troopers promised the enemy soldiers good treatment and pleaded with them to give up. It did no good.[61] Others emerged from hidden spider holes around the airstrip, held grenades against their bodies, and blew themselves up. To the Imperial soldier, surrender was apostasy; only death brought purification after defeat.

When GIs snooped through the rubble, they found plenty to satisfy their unbending curiosity about the enemy. There were the remains of thirty planes, some so badly battered by artillery and bombs that they hardly resembled aircraft any longer.[62] Several still squatted on the runway while others lay shattered in their collapsed revetments. Stamped on their bent and broken engines were the familiar markings of Pratt and Whitney, the engine manufacturer located in East Hartford where Hugh Finkle of the 169th Infantry worked before he joined the Connecticut National Guard. He remembered that the Japanese were "buying the engines as fast as we could make them in late 1939 to early 1940."[63] Three wrecked trucks used by Japanese construction crews to haul coral received considerable attention—they were all right-hand-drive models made by Ford, Dodge, and Chevrolet. Most enemy buildings were torn apart by bombs and artillery, but under the piles of debris the men came upon large quantities of rice, tinned meat and fish, tea, candy, and cigarettes. They eschewed the Japanese tobacco, but the food offered them a much welcomed break from the monotony of C-ration stew and hash. The repair garage, with tools intact, still stood amid the carnage. It was the only building left relatively unscathed. Personal gear like watches and binoculars were strewn everywhere.[64] A bloody Japanese flag taken from the body of a dead defender made one souvenir hunter happy. Several half-starved Chinese forced laborers also were discovered during the sweep of the airstrip.[65] A GI found something on another Japanese body that he would never forget. As he opened the dead man's pack searching for something to catch his eye, he found the soap dish he lost two weeks before on the Barike River.[66] A Japanese captain captured alive was stripped of his saber, cap, and tiny flag by the hunters. Surprised by the enthusiastic attention paid to this mindless enterprise, he said sarcastically in rather good English, "We fight for Tojo. You fight for souvenirs."[67]

The Japanese inexplicably left a great deal of material with significant intelligence value for the victors. The most useful document was a list of enemy code designators for various geographic locations throughout the Pacific. Another important find was the Southeast Area Fleet directive outlining the enemy's current strategic plan. They also discovered the minutes of a Southeast Area Fleet conference held in mid-June at Rabaul.[68]

While some men hunted for mementos, most headed for the beach to bathe in the clean surf. Without orders, they simply dropped their rifles and equipment on the shoreline and waded into the cool ocean, clothes and all. A few men took turns riding a pair of bicycles discovered inside a shed, acting more like eleven-year-olds than combat-hardened veterans.[69] Someone unveiled a stash of sake and Chinese beer, which the liberators dutifully opened, passed around, and drank to celebrate their victory.[70] The revelry continued even after a sniper opened fire on a marine tank a hundred yards or so away. His bullets pinged off the tank, which returned fire with its 37mm gun. The GIs started booing the tank when it fired back, and cheered whenever the sniper fired.[71]

Seabees began work on the airstrip's repair almost immediately. On 9 August an LST slid up to the beach and disgorged engineer equipment. Within hours the men of the 73rd Construction Battalion were filling craters and clearing debris from the runway even as patrols continued to clear the area of Japanese stragglers. Disregarding the threat of enemy air attack, the Seabees strung up bright lights so they could work around the clock. Interestingly, on the day work on the field began, an air raid warning sounded and everyone immediately scattered for shelter. Minutes later, three enemy dive-bombers flew in low over the pockmarked runway with their wheels down as if trying to land. They evidently had not yet gotten the bad news. Machine guns peppered them with fire and they rapidly leveled off and flew away without dropping a single bomb.[72]

On the afternoon of 13 August, five days after the Seabees began work and four days ahead of schedule, four P-40 fighters landed at Munda for refueling. Now, every enemy base in the Solomons was within the range of Allied land-dased airpower. The following day,

Brig. Gen. Francis Mulcahy, the Air New Georgia commander, inspected his newest base.

The pace increased when the 24th Construction Battalion arrived from Rendova to lend a hand. In no time Munda became a major base. Taxiways were overhauled, more roads were built, and the extensive tunnel system dug by the Japanese was cleared of bodies. A cavity inside Kokengolo Hill became the headquarters of AirSols.[73] By early October 1943, the runway had been almost doubled in length to two thousand yards, with an eighteen-inch-thick coral base capable of handling bombers. It soon replaced Henderson Field as the busiest strip in the Solomons. Average daily departures and arrivals in October, for example, reached about four hundred.[74] Suffering from the constant hammering from the skies, and recognizing that the situation would only get worse, Rabaul began transferring air and naval forces from its Bougainville bases in August.[75]

While the airstrip was being repaired and readied for Allied use, the enemy launched only two serious air attacks against it, despite having almost five hundred aircraft in the sector. Both were intercepted and turned back before they could reach Munda.[76] The airstrip was visited almost every night by lightly armed floatplanes, and sometimes a few light and medium bombers, but they caused little damage.[77] Japanese failure to respond aggressively to the fall of Munda illustrated the rapid shift that had occured in the balance of power in the South Pacific since their disastrous pullout from Guadalcanal in February.

Incident in Blackett Strait

While Munda was slipping away from Sasaki's control, the focus shifted to preventing the enemy's escape from New Georgia and the reinforcement of its sister islands, especially Kolombangara. From the beginning of the campaign, the thirty-eight-ton Elco Motor Patrol Boat (PT boat) had been used to intercept Japanese barge and destroyer runs to and from Bairoko, Vila, and other enemy ports. Four PT squadrons with a total of more than fifty boats operated out of two bases, one on Rendova and a second at Lever Harbor on New Georgia's north coast. The Rendova squadrons sought to interdict the Tokyo Express runs from the southern coast of Vella Lavella to southern Kolombangara through Blackett Strait and then up to Vila, while the Lever base intercepted barges coming down to Vila from Kolombangara's northern coast. Although their record may seem modest at first glance (ten barges sunk out of ninety-nine engaged from 21 July through the end of August), their mere presence hampered the enemy reinforcement effort.[78] In response, the Japanese began placing shore batteries along the barge routes and mounting 40mm guns on their barges.

The PT boats, which could carry up to four torpedoes, were also sent to intercept destroyers. They enjoyed no success whatsoever in the struggle for New Georgia against these vessels, however. Still, the effort against them continued. On 1 August an urgent communication from Guadalcanal came into the PT base at Rendova indicating that Vila was to be reinforced that night, so a plan was made to cover both sea approaches. A task force consisting of destroyers and PTs would cover Kolombangara's northeastern coast. Farther south, fifteen PTs were assigned to cover the western end of Blackett Strait. One of them, PT-109, was commanded by Lt. John F. Kennedy.

Allied intelligence was correct. Nine hundred Japanese soldiers and 120 tons of supplies were en route to Vila on three destroyers with another serving as escort. PT-159's radar located the ships at about midnight and, along with PT-157, began closing on them. PT-159 fired its 20mm cannon at the destroyers and launched three errant torpedoes. Minutes later, two more PTs joined the fray, each discharging its entire supply of four torpedoes. All eight missed their mark. The four ships managed to evade twelve more torpedoes fired from three more boats and made it to Vila, where they unloaded their cargo in three-quarters of an hour. The anxious crews wasted no time shoving off, and the destroyers were soon racing back toward Blackett Strait, hoping to evade the ambushers they knew awaited them there.

At around 2:30 A.M. a lookout on Lieutenant Kennedy's PT-109 spotted the *Amagiri* bearing down on his small vessel. "Ship at two o'clock!" he screamed frantically.[79] The skipper yanked hard on the wheel, but it was too late. Seconds later, the speeding destroyer's sharp bow sliced into the starboard side of the eighty-foot plywood boat, split it in half, and continued on its way. Kennedy was thrown flat on his back and lay there stunned as he watched the black vessel wedge through what remained of his boat. Half of his crew was tossed into the water. One of the men was badly injured and two were killed. The stern quickly sank, so the jittery survivors clung to the bow. Kennedy and his officers, Ens. Leonard Thom and Ens. George Ross, swam out and recovered five of the men, including two of the injured, who were scattered up to a hundred yards from the boat. It took Kennedy an hour in the strong current to rescue Patrick McMahon, who was suffering from serious burns on his face and extremities, and drag him to safety. The skipper then retrieved two others who had drifted away. Three hours later, the eleven survivors were together.

Reg Evans, a coastwatcher on a small island west of Kolombangara, spotted a small gasoline fire burning near the wreckage. The next morning he received a message from his counterpart on Rendova that a boat had been lost in Blackett Strait. Evans later spotted an object floating in the waves and sent out word for his native scouts to be on the lookout for survivors. By then Kennedy and his men had decided that it was best to try to swim to a nearby island with the two injured crewmen in tow.

On the night of 2 August, Kennedy swam out into Fergusson Passage, the southern entrance into Blackett Strait, armed with a .38 pistol and the boat's lantern tied to a life jacket in hopes of flagging down help. He came upon a reef, rested, and then headed out into open water, where the current swirled in a huge circular path and carried him back into Fergusson Passage. Despite his extreme exhaustion, he knew that it was now or never, so he made for a tiny islet and collapsed on its beach. Kennedy swam the final half-mile back to the island the next morning, arriving hungry and completely spent. The next night, Ensign Ross volunteered to swim out to the passage. His foray ended with the same result.

Their supply of coconuts was nearly depleted, so they swam to another island with Kennedy pulling McMahon as he piloted his men through the choppy sea to their next home. The three-hour swim brought them to tiny Olasana Island, where they found enough coconuts to sustain them for a few more days. But they were becoming desperate.

Well aware that their strength was rapidly ebbing from a lack of food, Kennedy decided the next morning to try to swim to Nauru Island on the eastern fringe of Fergusson Passage while he still was physically able. Earlier they had seen an Australian P-40 strafe the island, a signal to them that it was enemy-held. But where there were troops, there would also be food. He knew they would be killed if the Japanese found them, but he had to take the chance. As soon as they awoke, Kennedy and Ross discussed with the others what they should do if the two failed to return.

At 3:30 in the afternoon on 5 August, about the same time Munda fell, the two officers reached Nauru Island and sought safety in the tangled jungle along the shoreline. After resting quietly for some time, they moved cautiously across the narrow island's interior until they reached its eastern shore. There they spotted a small box stuffed with Japanese crackers and candy. After devouring some of it, they continued on and were delighted to find a barrel of fresh water and a one-man canoe. While inspecting their discovery, they saw two natives paddling by offshore, but were unable to get their attention. The others needed the food desperately, so Kennedy loaded it into the canoe and set out to deliver it to his hungry crewmen. Ross spent a sleepless night alone on the island and began the swim back in the morning.

It was nearly midnight when Kennedy reached Olasana. To his astonishment, the two natives he and Ross had seen in the canoe off Nauru were with his men. Ensign Thom had managed to convince the wary natives they were Americans. At daybreak on the sixth, Kennedy and the two natives paddled back to Nauru, where the natives had hidden a two-man canoe. Before they arrived, however, they spotted Ross in the water and pulled him out of the choppy sea. The natives guided the sailors to a canoe seaworthy enough to negotiate Fergusson Passage. Before debarking, however, the officers used a knife to scribble a message for each of the natives to deliver to Rendova: "Native knows posit. Can pilot. 11 alive. Need small boat. Kennedy."[80]

That night, Kennedy and Ross slipped out into Fergusson Passage, optimistic that they would be able to signal any rescuers who might still be looking for them. The wind picked up, however, and a driving rain stung them as they dug their paddles into the growing waves. A few hundred yards from the island the canoe capsized, plunging them into the turbulent water, where they were rudely swept against a reef protecting the island's southern shore. Ross was injured slightly, but they managed to make it to the beach. They went to sleep that night knowing their fate was in the hands of the two natives.

On 7 August, after a breakfast of coconuts, they noticed a large canoe bearing four natives headed their way. One of them was carrying a message from one of Reg Evans's assistants instructing the senior officer to go with his scouts to Evans's island hideout, where the coastwatcher would arrange for their rescue. Kennedy insisted on first delivering the food that the natives had packed in their war canoe to the rest of his crew. After that they made the journey to Evans's base camp, arriving at 4 P.M. Evans greeted Kennedy warmly, served tea, gave him a change of clothes, and arranged a rendezvous with a squadron of PT boats in Fergusson Passage that night.

At 10:30 Kennedy stepped into the native canoe for the last time. PT-157 spotted them forty-five minutes later and picked up the gaunt PT-109 skipper. The natives then guided the boat to the rest of the marooned crew. As soon as the men were aboard, they sped off to their base.[81] Thus ended the valorous exploits of the man who later became one of America's most beloved presidents.

The Battle of Vella Gulf

While General Sasaki was retreating north with most of his beaten forces hoping to escape across the Kula Gulf to Kolombangara, four overburdened Japanese destroyers crammed with more than sixteen hundred men and fifty tons of supplies left the Shortland Islands after dark on 6 August. Their mission was to reinforce and resupply him there. With its airfield at Vila, the Japanese assumed that the island would be the next Allied target. The shortage of troop-carrying barges was so acute, however, that Rabaul was forced to use destroyers for the mission even though they were much more likely to be spotted by radar or aircraft.

Two weeks before, RAdm. Theodore S. Wilkinson had replaced Admiral Turner as commander of the South Pacific Amphibious

Command. Determined to stop enemy reinforcements from landing at Kolombangara, he ordered six destroyers under the command of Comdr. Frederick Moosbrugger to sweep Vella Gulf. At 2:30 P.M. on the sixth, a search plane spotted the Japanese task force sailing southeast toward the northern tip of Vella Lavella and reported the discovery to Moosbrugger, who correctly estimated that the enemy would arrive in Vella Gulf near midnight and made plans to greet them.

A half-hour before midnight, the four Japanese ships turned the corner around Vella Lavella and sped into the gulf heading south at 550-yard intervals. Moosbrugger's radar picked up their formation at 19,700 yards. At 6,300 yards, he ordered his three lead ships each to launch a spread of eight torpedoes at the enemy ships, which were still unaware of the U.S. destroyers' presence.

The Japanese vessels continued on course at twenty-five knots, while soldiers on board were spread about their decks trying to sleep. A lookout on one of the destroyers identified the U.S. ships, but it was too late. At 11:46, five minutes after they plunged into the water from their tubes, the torpedoes began to strike three of the enemy destroyers. One was hit amidships, ripping apart its fire rooms. An ammunition magazine below the bridge exploded on another, ripping the bow from the rest of the ship. The third caught fire after a torpedo impacted, then was stunned by another that caused a huge explosion. The *Shigure,* an older, slower vessel a half-mile behind the others, was struck by a dud that went completely through its rudder. It was able to fire eight torpedoes before turning and running, but all missed their targets. Moosbrugger's other three ships lined up to fire more torpedoes and five-inch shells. Their gunners had little trouble pinpointing their targets, which by then were burning fiercely. Dozens of rounds scored hits all over the three steel infernos. PT boat crewmen twenty-eight miles away in Kula Gulf saw the glow brighten the sky and thought Kolombangara's volcano was erupting.[82] A few minutes before midnight, the *Kawakaze* sank in a sizzling, steamy blaze, to be joined twenty minutes later by its two sister ships. Only the *Shigure* escaped. Hundreds of helpless troops intended to bolster the defenses on Kolombangara were left flailing in the uninviting gulf water.

At 1:15 A.M., the USS *Lang* glided through the area where the ships went down and saw a seascape of Japanese, some living and some dead, as far as could be seen. Bodies were being plowed up in the ship's phosphorescent wake. While they continued through the area, the *Lang*'s skipper heard a droning sound that he thought was his crew jeering at the enemy as they passed them by. At one point he reached for the megaphone and ordered his men to stop the harassment and return to their stations. Then he discovered that the sound was coming from the Japanese. A chorus arose from the water like some preternatural funeral strain, the sound of hundreds of voices chanting something in unison—perhaps a plaintive cry to their ancestors or a plea to the spirit world. It was as though the ship was sailing across the ceiling of hell, with the groaning souls of the doomed crying out in misery below them. There was an eerie silence on board as the destroyer turned to sail through the watery charnel house again to pick up survivors. There were no takers. Whenever an offer of help was made, someone in the water would blow a whistle, the chanting would stop, and the Japanese would swim away from the ship.

Some 1,520 of the 1,810 soldiers and sailors on the three ships drowned in the choppy waters five miles off Kolombangara's west coast. It was the single worst loss of life at sea for the Japanese since the Battle of Midway. More importantly, it was the first time American surface forces got the better of their adversaries in an exchange of torpedoes at night, where the enemy had consistently displayed a marked preeminence.

The captain of the *Shigure* reported the sinkings to his superiors at Rabaul and requested a rescue effort be mounted, but none ever came. Perhaps the Japanese brass believed that it was too dangerous to do so or too late to make a difference. Nevertheless, it is inconceivable that the Allies would have refused such a mission, regardless of its potential danger. Nor would there have been a shortage of volunteers to carry it out. The three hundred or so Japanese who survived the battle apparently made it to Kolombangara, but coastwatcher reports indicated that many of the ragged, unarmed Japanese who washed ashore were either ambushed and killed or taken prisoner by the island's fierce natives.[83]

• • •

Although the airfield was in Allied hands, Bairoko yet remained under Japanese control, with hundreds of enemy soldiers still unwilling to concede defeat. Planes struck the installation daily, and Colonel Liversedge's patrols out of Enogai confined the escaping troops to the harbor area.

On August 5, General Griswold sent the 25th Infantry Division's 27th and 161st Regiments, supported by four tanks, to the village of Zieta, located about three and a half miles south of Bairoko and four miles northwest of Bibilo Hill. Intelligence reports indicated that this village, like Bairoko, was becoming a springboard for the enemy's escape from the island. The reports were accurate. Sasaki had ordered the remnants of the 229th Infantry and the two other rifle battalions that had survived the assault on Munda to move to Zieta and cross the narrow channel to the neighboring island of Baanga with two 120mm naval guns.[84] There they were to defend themselves and shell Munda. The 25th Division GIs, slowed by diligent enemy trail blocks, persistent rain and mud, and supply problems—many of the same gadflies that had plagued the troops before them—did not take Zieta until the fifteenth. By that time, most of the Japanese had made it to tiny Baanga, although those who remained fought like bulldogs before submitting. Once Zieta was subdued, the 27th Infantry continued west and eight days later secured the Piru plantation on the New Georgia coast. The 9th Marine Defense Battalion then moved there with its 155mm artillery to shell Vila and other targets of opportunity.

Meanwhile, the 161st Infantry continued north to Bairoko and, together with the NLG's 3rd Battalion, 145th Infantry, occupied Bairoko on the twenty-fifth. This time the village fell with hardly a fight, save for a few snipers. Three of them had been knocked out of a tree by the concussion from artillery fire and lay on the ground stunned. A veteran marine approached the trio, took out his knife, and said: "This is the way we used to do it in Nicaragua." With no more emotion than a fish peddler preparing the day's catch for his customers, he nonchalantly thrust the blade into the throat of one, the chest of the second, and, while holding down the third squirming victim with one hand, stabbed him in the stomach.[85]

Nineteen barge loads of Bairoko's men and supplies slipped through a rather suspect PT boat blockade to Vila, the last leaving a few hours before the Americans stormed in. Sasaki and the remnants of the 13th Infantry and 6th Kure SNLF were now safely ensconced on Kolombangara, where the general made his new headquarters. New Georgia was finally under American control, almost two full months after the initial landings, but a sizable number of Japanese troops had made their escape across the Kula Gulf. This was Sasaki's only route of retreat, given that all trails out of Bairoko were sealed. Why a squadron of destroyers was not there to intercept the barges has never been answered. It was Guadalcanal all over again.

8 "Death Is Lighter Than a Feather"

In 1904, a thesis titled *Nippon Shindo Ron* ("The Way of the Japanese Subject") was published in an attempt to promote nationalism. Its theme was glorification of the emperor and absolute obedience to him. The thesis's popularity was such that it was regarded by some as an expression of the very soul of Japan—the equivalent of the Bible, Mao's "little red book," or Thomas Paine's *Common Sense*.

During the war, Japanese servicemen carried with them a collection of epigrams taken largely from *Nippon Shindo Ron*. Much like Paine's pamphlet was to Washington's Continental Army during the American Revolution, the proverbs were meant to motivate and inspire them to fight on for the emperor despite hardship. "Loyalty is the very life and spinal nerve of the Japanese subject," said one. The Japanese fighting man's devotion was to be so pure that he should be willing to die to defend his honor. "To offer our lives to the Emperor in order that our foes may be defeated and subdued," one maxim instructed, "is our *highest privilege*" (emphasis added). Death, whether self or enemy inflicted, thus became desirable in the absence of victory. The Japanese trained to destroy the enemy, the "worm-like foreign reptiles that dare insult the dignity of the Emperor or pollute his virtuous name." However, it was more important to subscribe to the "blood pact" each soldier and sailor made to "die at his [the emperor's] command." This was the mysteriously revered concept of *gyokusai*—the desire to seek death rather than dishonor.

Consider another adage: "When the true flag is unfurled and the loyal troops advance, what soldier is there that lacks in gallantry or in courage? Careless of the corpses of the fallen piled in heaps, heedless of rivers of blood flowing on every hand, we concentrate only upon the fulfillment of the Emperor's commands and the duty of sacrificing ourselves in the realization of his designs."[1]

The same theme surfaces in the most influential of all samurai treatises, *Hagakure:* "Tranquillize your mind every morning, and imagine the moment when you may be torn and mangled by arrows, guns, lances, and swords, swept away by great waves, thrown into a fire, struck down by thunderbolts, shaken by earthquakes, falling from a precipice. . . . Die every morning in your mind, and then you will not fear death."[2]

An ancient poem used by soldiers awaiting movement to the front prescribes:

> Across the sea, corpses soaking in water,
> Across the mountains, corpses heaped upon the grass,
> We shall die by the side of the lord.
> We shall never look back.

This verse was set to music in 1937, and after 1943 the song was played over the radio before news of battles was reported.[3] This alone says much about the enormous cultural differences between the Japanese and their enemies, for it would be unthinkable for such morbid lyrics to be broadcast in the West during the war.

The exhausted Japanese soldiers who fled to Kolombangara and Baanga were certainly among the emperor's worthy subjects. Malnourished, lacking in medical care, and completely depleted both physically and mentally, they nevertheless continued to fight with courage and skill. Many had been on New Georgia since November 1942, ravaged by the interminable bombings and shellings and unhinged by having to live in the midst of horror and death.

Yet they persisted: "Our morale is very high. Will die in honor if necessary—like Admiral of the Fleet Yamamoto. Will follow the heroes of Attu."[4]

An unidentified diarist recorded the following in his journal, which was discovered at Munda after its fall: "Scores of planes attacked our bivouac area. They strafed and bombed us continuously. I was so terrified, I hugged a tree. . . . For about 20 minutes bullets rained as in a squall. Tracers exploded directly at our eyes and we decided we were about to die. . . . For a moment we were completely stunned. It was like a blizzard that hit us and suddenly stopped, leaving both sky and earth quiet again. It gives you the feeling of having seen life and death before your eyes."[5]

There was no radar at Munda, so the defenders' only means of observation was through field glasses. Consequently, there was hardly time to seek shelter when Allied planes approached. Lookouts rang gongs and a siren screamed the warning as men scrambled for safety. Another diary found in the rubble on one of the overlooking hills provides a glimpse of the suffering: "Last night's shelling was terrific. This concentration of fire is just above our dugout, which is on the northeast side of the slope. The shrapnel is failing into the dugout. Since it has only one entrance, the air is stuffy and the sound of the explosions causes ringing in my ears. . . . It is really more than I can bear."[6]

One of the most curious phenomena of the war was the universal acceptance by the "Yamoto race" of the Bushido code—the samurai warrior's standard of conduct pledging unswerving devotion and service to the emperor and strict moral behavior. Once reserved only for this small, selective class of men, all Japan was expected to subscribe to its extreme philosophy. During the concluding days of the New Georgia campaign, however, there is evidence that some of the Imperial Army's best dishonored their ancestors.

Private First Class Yokichi Iwase, a disgruntled rifleman with the 229th Infantry who was captured at Munda, explained that his company's officers were evacuated as early as 18 July and that NCOs were forced to assume command for the final stand. Morale plummeted. Then something else happened that further angered the men. Immediately after the departure of the officers, presumably for Kolombangara, the NCOs pilfered the unit's food supplies. When the Americans closed in on the airstrip on 4 August, several men from the 6th Kure SNLF deserted their positions and fled from Munda in barges.[7] A POW captured during the retreat from Kolombangara claimed that many of the men at Munda pretended to be ill so they could be evacuated from the front. According to him, a sympathetic medical officer took their word for it and approved their requests. He him-

self was despondent the entire time he was stationed at Munda because defeat "seemed inevitable."[8]

Both men—one a wounded soldier who was denied medical attention from his unit, the other a disgruntled civilian engineer—had
good reason to make uncomplimentary statements about their former comrades. Still, prisoners commonly say things to ingratiate
themselves with their captors, so their disparaging reports might be
read with some skepticism. Even if these men's stories are entirely
true, such behavior was not the norm. The majority of Japanese servicemen conducted themselves in the manner expected of them.

Only twenty-eight Japanese POWs were taken from 16 July to 5 August, and most of them were unable to resist because of serious
wounds.[9] They had been conditioned to feel irredeemable disgrace,
even if they were unconscious when captured. Once they were physically able to talk they were interrogated by Japanese-American interpreters, who generally gave them a cigarette or something to
drink, made them feel relaxed, and then asked a series of standard
questions. Surprisingly, all talked freely about anything the interrogators asked. They apparently saw nothing wrong with sharing
valuable intelligence information with their captors. This was another curiosity that the Americans found difficult to comprehend
about their strange enemy. A complete metamorphosis occurred.
One day they were prepared to die rather than surrender, and the
next they were cooperating meekly with their enemy.

A sailor from the 6th Kure SNLF said that he would have been
better off dead. Only then, he lamented, would he have been en-
shrined forever. He had no hope for a postwar life in Japan, for he
was sure he would be banished if he attempted to return home. He
never wanted to see or even communicate with his wife or family
again.[10] Another soldier expressed a similar wish, such was the hu-
miliation and dishonor of his capture. He was admittedly happy to
be alive and appreciated the medical attention he was receiving, but
he said he would have preferred death with his brothers on the glorious field of combat. He feared being mistreated if he returned
home after the war.[11] Still another prisoner, a young rifleman suffering from two bullet wounds and malaria when he was captured
at Munda, said he would like to see his children again, but knew he

could not because of the disgrace he had caused his family. Moreover, he was convinced that if he returned to his homeland he would be executed.[12]

While the mop-up on New Georgia was in progress, the 169th Infantry was ordered to clear tiny Baanga Island of the enemy who had escaped there and silence the two 120mm guns they had taken with them. It did not appear to be too difficult an assignment since the enemy forces were scattered and beaten. A twenty-five-man reconnaissance patrol was dispatched on 11 August, and a rifle company soon followed. When this force was unable to get beyond the beach, another company was sent over. Before long, the entire regiment faced an estimated four hundred enemy troops in a fierce jungle battle as mean as any they had experienced during the previous month. Finally, the 172nd Infantry (less one battalion) had to be sent in to assist in the increasingly ugly struggle. The last enemy forces slipped away for Arundel on 21 August, and Baanga was declared secure—but not before fifty-two more 43rd Division troops were killed in action, most from the 169th. It made more than a few of the men angry. Frank Giliberto, a squad leader in the 2nd Battalion, spoke for most of his regiment:

Our morale is at rock bottom. Our losses are quite high. The men in my squad would look at me with reproach in their eyes, as if to say, "Why are we the point squad again? Are we the only unit around?" I knew how frustrated they feel. How much longer will our luck last? What the hell are we doing on this two-bit island? Why, when the Japanese started shelling Munda Field from Baanga Island was no attempt made to engage the Japanese 120-mm gun positions, with all of those artillery guns we had at our disposal? Where was the navy with their big guns? Where were our bombers? From my point of view, here in the middle of Baanga Island, I felt strongly that everything that's happened thus far is one big screw-up by all the top brass, and we are left to suffer because of their screw-ups. The navy for not being able to control the sea around us. The G-2s and S-2s with their intelligence reports. And our army, navy, and marine air support that we seldom got. With all the artillery that is available to us, you would have thought that all these small islands would have been shelled before we would land on them.[13]

General Griswold sent the 172nd Infantry to Arundel on 27 August. After five days, the Americans finally collided with enemy troops. At first there were only a couple of hundred, but, strengthened by infantry sent over from Kolombangara, they began to push the regiment back. Two more battalions from the 27th Infantry, along with thirteen tanks and heavy artillery, had to be sent in to smother Sasaki's men. The enemy fled Arundel for Kolombangara on 21 September, leaving the GIs to bury forty-four more of their comrades. A total of 256 men were wounded. These were exceedingly high casualty figures for what were supposed to be mop-up operations.

Despite his backpedaling, General Sasaki was still not ready to throw in the towel. In fact, he planned to use the emaciated 13th Infantry on Kolombangara to lead a new assault against New Georgia. Before he could do so, though, he had to send his naval liaison officer to Rabaul to again seek support from the Eighth Fleet.[14] However, the loss of more than fifteen hundred men and three destroyers in the 7–8 August Battle of Vella Gulf was enough to convince Imperial General Headquarters of the futility of any further offensive activity there. Sasaki's request was flatly denied. The focus would be on defending Kolombangara, the next logical step in Halsey's approach to Rabaul.

The original plan for Operation Cartwheel called for the capture of New Georgia, then Vila on Kolombangara, the Shortland Islands, and finally the crucial Japanese airfield at Kahili on Bougainville in the Allies' step-by-step drive to Rabaul. That was before the ordeal on New Georgia, however. By the end of the operation, Admiral Halsey had poured 29,000 men onto the island and spent twice as long as he and his staff had estimated it would take to seize Munda from a force of no more than 4,000–5,000 scattered defenders. Kolombangara, the next rung up the Solomons ladder, had even more enemy troops than New Georgia (about 10,000) and roughly the same implacable terrain. If the ratio of U.S. to Japanese troops on New Georgia were applied to Kolombangara, seizing the island would require about 60,000 men. Those numbers even made the aggressive Bull Halsey balk. In his own words, he was "wary of another slugging match." Besides, another protracted encounter would allow the enemy more time to strengthen Bougainville.[15] Consequently, his staff suggested what would become standard procedure for the Allies in the Pacific. Heavily defended Kolombangara would simply be bypassed in favor of landings on virtually unoccupied Vella Lavella, located fourteen miles to the northwest and that much closer to Bougainville. The Americans had employed this island-hopping technique in the Aleutians with success. It ought to work equally well in the Solomons. The SPA commander enthusiastically sent the proposal to Admiral Nimitz, who quickly approved it. Halsey's boss had himself recommended as much as early as 11 July.[16]

"Hit 'em where they ain't," baseball Hall of Famer "Wee Willie" Keeler once said was his key to success. It was an attractive alternative to what almost certainly would be a terribly bloody affair on Kolombangara. Moreover, once an airstrip was built on Vella Lavella, Vila would be outflanked, with a base for hostile aircraft between it and Rabaul, cutting it off from supplies and reinforcements. Kolombangara and its ten thousand defenders thus would be left to wither on the vine, sealed off by sea and air and pounded by daily artillery barrages from New Georgia and Arundel. Hopelessly ineffective, they would eventually have to abandon the island altogether.

The strategy worked perfectly. As soon as word reached Rabaul that six thousand Americans had landed on Vella Lavella on 15 August (where another airfield would soon be constructed), Sasaki was ordered to prepare to withdraw from Kolombangara. Destroyers, PT boats, and PBY patrol bombers operating at night were expected to make it difficult for the enemy to escape the trap. In deference to the enormous assistance given by the native islanders, however, the Americans took great care to avoid attacking canoes during this operation, even if occupied by Japanese. Indiscriminate bombing or strafing of beaches was also strictly prohibited.[17] All else was fair game.

The retirement began in earnest in late September. Attempts to interdict the barges and destroyers, operating at night under moonless skies, were mostly unsuccessful. The Japanese claimed that 80 percent of the thirteen hundred remaining defenders safely reached Bougainville.[18] They had slipped through the noose. Vila's airfield was subsequently occupied by U.S. troops on 6 October. General Sasaki was gone from the central Solomons for good. In November, he joined General Imamura's staff at Eighth Area Army headquarters, an assignment that could not have delighted him. Sasaki was much more comfortable commanding troops in the field. He at least could be proud of his remarkable defense of Munda. His outnumbered forces hung on to the airfield for four weeks and forced his adversaries to employ the better part of three infantry divisions. The men under his command performed with exceptional courage and skill against a force over six times their number.

Seven months after the Japanese surrender, Admiral Samejima shared his own view about why the defense of Munda failed. He confessed that it was his fault for failing to dispatch the appropriate orders, although he stopped short of specifics. The admiral explained that he allowed Sasaki the latitude to make most of the crucial decisions himself, for he understood the "folly of placing a naval commander like myself in charge of land operations involving army and navy units." Still, he reiterated his office's responsibility for the debacle.[19]

When one takes into account the overwhelming firepower of Halsey's air and ground forces, the Japanese casualty rate was low. Only 1,671 Japanese are known to have died in the campaign for the airfield.[20] Enemy air losses were much worse: 358 aircraft, including 259 fighters, 60 heavy bombers, 23 dive-bombers, and 16 floatplanes. When compared to the 93 Allied planes destroyed—71 fighters and 22 bombers—a little over a third the number of Japanese losses—Halsey's victory was impressive.[21] The "Butchers of Munda," as Tokyo Rose nicknamed the men of XIV Corps, lost 1,195 killed roughly half from the 43rd Division. In comparison, the epic Guadalcanal campaign lasted three times as long with only about 400 more dead. Four thousand Americans were also wounded, with nearly 2,200 coming from the 43rd Division.[22]

With the fall of the New Georgia group, Halsey's growing force began preparations for the invasion of Bougainville, with its sixty thousand defenders and five enemy airfields. Securing the island would complete Operation Cartwheel's first stage. Fighters launched from Bougainville would then be in range to escort heavy bombers flying out of Munda and New Guinea on missions over the huge Japanese base at Rabaul. On 1 November 1943 the Americans landed at Empress Augusta Bay. What is notable is how totally U.S. strategy had been transmuted since the bitter experience on New Georgia just four months before. The beachhead selected for the invasion of Bougainville was, like New Georgia's, miles from the nearest enemy base. The difference was that there would be no order to claw from the beachhead through the island's cluttered interior to capture Japanese installations. Instead, engineers built airfields near the landing sites and AirSols pulverized and eventually nullified the Japanese bases on the island. Lessons are learned quickly within the deep recesses of combat, but sometimes not quickly enough.

Halsey embraced the strategy of leapfrogging to Vella Lavella and on to Bougainville not only because it sped the drive across the Solomons chain, but also because it saved lives. This, then, begs an important question: Why did the SPA commander not bypass Munda as well? In January 1943, when the fighting on Guadalcanal was in its last few weeks, plans were being made for the next step up the Solomons. At the time, Halsey's and Nimitz's staffs seriously considered bypassing both Munda and Vila.[23] However, an offensive to seize Bougainville, the most important island in the northern Solomons, would require the use of an airfield to support such an invasion, and they decided Munda was the one they needed. They believed it was simply too valuable to bypass. But was it?

Both Munda and Vila were neutralized almost immediately by daily bombing missions from Guadalcanal. Moreover, after they first received planes in late December 1942, artillery positioned on the adjacent barrier islands pummeled them. Clearly, the airfields posed no threat to American forces as long as the skies belonged to the Allies. The Seabees built an air base in the Russells in February 1943, and in July the thirty-three-hundred-foot runway at Segi provided another base for AirSols planes. Segi, just over forty miles farther east than Munda, was well within fighter range of Bougainville and could have provided the necessary aircraft needed to support the invasion of that island. In addition, TBFs and SBDs from as far away as Guadalcanal began flying regular missions against Bougainville's bases at Ballale and Kahili well before the New Georgia landings. True, Munda's runway was enlarged after its capture to accommodate heavy bombers for use against Bougainville and Rabaul, but a longer runway could also have been built at Segi for that purpose. Rendova could still have been seized and used as a platform for heavy artillery to fire on Munda. Then, instead of fighting a costly offensive through a nasty labyrinth of bunkers and pillboxes from Zanana beach, the 43rd Division could have been used to defend Segi, forcing the enemy to assume the offensive if he wanted to dislodge the Americans. Interestingly, this is exactly the strategy Halsey later used for the capture of Bougainville.

Why, then, did Halsey insist on a large-scale assault to seize Munda? Did he not believe that his men would have such a rough go of it? If that is the case, he certainly had not paid much notice to the 32nd Infantry Division and the Australian 7th Infantry Division on New Guinea. Both units suffered terribly in the December 1942 Buna-Gona offensive, where they encountered a well-designed network of machine-gun emplacements in unyielding jungle much like that found on New Georgia. MacArthur relieved the 32nd Division commander, Maj. Gen. Edwin F. Harding, because of dissatisfaction with the National Guard unit's progress, a move that presaged Halsey's relief of General Hester. Later, the SPA commander's own marine Raiders, a fast-strike commando outfit, struggled to keep more than a sluggish pace through the choking jungle in the Viru Harbor operation. These models notwithstanding, Halsey remained unmoved.

Perhaps the hard-charging admiral simply had not yet fully appreciated the level of air supremacy that his air arm had attained by the time D day arrived on 30 June. This advantage would later provide both him and MacArthur more latitude in their decision making during the methodical march toward Rabaul. Yet Halsey the gambler chose to play conservatively. Leapfrogging over Munda, he believed, would be too risky, causing his logistical train to be too thin. That would repeat the mistake the Japanese made early in the war.

Whether or not the assault on Munda should have taken place is debatable. However, another decision Halsey made was not as uncertain. It has been proposed that Halsey underestimated his opponents. The effortless seizure of both the Russell Islands and Rendova, the theory goes, may have misled the SPA commander into thinking that New Georgia would be another cakewalk. This explanation is difficult to accept, however, given that those two places were virtually free of enemy troops when the Americans landed. Nevertheless, once the commitment was made to traverse occupied New Georgia and capture Munda, Halsey should certainly have insured the operation's success by ordering a sufficient force into the fray. Instead, only two regiments were given the mission to directly assault the airfield, and both were untested National Guard units with little preparation for jungle warfare. Lacking experience and training, the green GIs stumbled until they had a few weeks in the festering jungle under their belts. Halsey and Harmon must bear the responsibility for not having the foresight to team them with an experienced unit from the 25th Division on Guadalcanal. Such a move at the very least would have helped minimize the number of war neurosis casualties that so debilitated and embarrassed the 43rd Division. At best it could have speeded the operation and saved lives.

Halsey hoped that the operation would not develop into a major engagement.[24] Consequently, even after the offensive stalled, he, Admiral Turner, and General Harmon were too parsimonious and too slow with reinforcements. Ironically, this piecemeal augmentation of troop strength was all too reminiscent of the mistakes made by the Japanese on Guadalcanal.

By March 1944, the major fighting on Bougainville was over and MacArthur's troops had landed on New Britain, the island on which Rabaul is located. Meanwhile, his men had also seized key islands in the Admiralties in a bold thrust northwest of the huge Japanese base. Rabaul was outflanked, isolated, and ready for the inevitable Allied attack. But it never came. Seven months before, just days after Munda fell in August 1943, the Anglo-American Combined Chiefs of Staff met in Quebec at the so-called Quadrant Conference. There the decision was made to neutralize Rabaul from the air rather than to assault it. The bastion of Japanese air and sea power, like Kolombangara before, would also be bypassed. "Island hopping" had become a central tenet in Pacific operational planning—six weeks too late for XIV Corps's soldiers and the marines of the 1st and 4th Raider Battalions. These same men carried memories of their horrific experience in New Georgia's malevolent interior to New Guinea, the Philippines, and Okinawa. Two years later, their pilgrimage to Tokyo was over. For many, however, nightmares of the crucible they endured in the central Solomons would continue to shadow them.

Notes

Introduction

1. General Douglas MacArthur, commander in chief, Southwest Pacific Area, with whom Admiral Nimitz shared command in the vast Pacific theater, at first claimed that he could take Rabaul in three weeks if he were given just one marine division and two carriers. But the navy was nervous about exposing its precious carriers in an area buzzing with Japanese planes, so Gen. George C. Marshall, the army chief of staff, approved King's proposal for a more gradual approach.

2. Ronald Spector, *Eagle Against the Sun* (New York: Free Press, 1985), 198.

3. John Ellis, *Brute Force: Allied Strategy and Tactics in the Second World War* (New York: Viking, 1990), 464.

4. Masatake Okumiya and Jiro Horikoshi, *Zero!* (New York: E. P. Dutton, 1956), 465.

5. Ibid.

6. John Prados, *Combined Fleet Decoded: The Secret History of American Intelligence and the Japanese Navy in World War II* (New York: Random House, 1995), 447.

7. Quoted in Ellis, *Brute Force*, 465.

8. Prados, *Combined Fleet Decoded*, 447–48.

9. Ibid.

Chapter 1. Blood Against Fire

1. Dan van der Vat, *The Pacific Campaign: The U.S.-Japanese Naval War, 1941–1945* (New York: Simon and Schuster, 1991), 210.

2. Mark Honan and David Harcombe, *Solomon Islands*, 3rd ed. (Hawthorne, Australia: Lonely Planet Publications, 1997), 14. This

travel handbook provides an excellent overview of the islands, particularly their history and culture.

3. Given the islanders' reputation as headhunters, it is surprising that Kennedy risked nurturing such a relationship. Tradition had it that if a soldier cast an eye toward a native woman, her relatives and boyfriends would cut her up into small pieces and deliver them to the offender as souvenirs.

4. Maj. Donald Kennedy, "Keeping Watch Over the Japs," *Pacific Islands Monthly* (Sept. 1945), 43–45.

5. "Planning: New Georgia Operations," 22 Nov. 1942–7 Oct. 1943, United States Armed Forces in the South Pacific Area (USAFISPA) files, Southern Pacific Base Command, Record Group (RG) 338, National Archives and Records Administration, College Park, Md. (hereafter NARA), 7. Emphasis added.

6. Eric Hammel, *Aces Against Japan: The American Aces Speak* (Novato, Ca.: Presidio Press, 1992), 1:78–79.

7. Hiroshi Ito, diary, 43rd Infantry Div. G2 Intelligence File, Item no. 848, RG 338, NARA.

8. Robert Sherrod, *History of Marine Corps Aviation in World War II* (Washington: Combat Forces Press, 1952), 144.

9. Richard Frank, *Guadalcanal: The Definitive Account of the Landmark Battle* (New York: Penguin Books, 1990), 548.

10. Ibid.

11. Foster Hailey, "Night Raid on Vila," *U.S. Naval Institute Proceedings* 70 (Sept. 1944): 1111.

12. Quoted in Henry T. Shaw and Maj. Douglas T. Kane, *The Isolation of Rabaul,* History of the U.S. Marine Corps in World War II, vol. 2 (Washington: Marine Corps Historical Branch, 1963), 30.

13. Frank, *Guadalcanal,* 526.

14. Rafael Steinberg, *Island Fighting* (Alexandria, Va.: Time-Life Books, 1978), 35.

15. Adm. William F. Halsey and Lt. Comdr. Joseph Bryan III, *Admiral Halsey's Story* (New York: Whittlesey House, 1947), 152–53. The last sentence in the message became popular with the American pilots. If one of them was assigned an especially repellent task, another was certain to remind him in pidgin: "These are the instructions of the government, and you must obey them."

16. Hammel, *Aces Against Japan*, 2:137–39.

17. Steinberg, *Island Fighting*, 77.

18. D. C. Horton, *Fire Over the Islands: The Coast Watchers of the Solomons* (Sydney: A. H. and A.W. Reed, 1970), 192.

19. Andrèe Quin, *The Solomons: Strategic Stepping Stones in the Pacific* (Sydney: Les Editions du Courrier Australien, n.d.), 15.

20. 2nd Class Petty Officer Morita, diary, Allied Translator and Interpreter Section (ATIS) Reports, 1942–46, 10-IRR 71, NARA.

21. Jim Lucas, quoted in S. E. Smith, ed., *The U.S. Marine Corps in World War II* (New York: Random House, 1969), 362.

22. Lamont Lindstrom and Geoffrey M. White, eds., *The Pacific Theater: Island Representations of World War II* (Honolulu: Center for Pacific Island Studies,University of Hawaii, 1989), 364.

23. Janet Kent, *The Solomon Islands* (Harrisburg, Pa.: Stackpole, 1972), 144.

24. Roy Struben, *Coral and the Colour of Gold* (London: Faber and Faber, 1961), 38.

25. Charles E. Fox, *The Story of the Solomons* (Sydney: Pacific Publications, 1967), 63.

26. David W. Gegeo, Geoffrey M. White, et al., eds., *The Big Death: Solomon Islanders Remember World War II* (Suva: Fiji Institute of Pacific Studies, 1988), 188.

27. Ibid., 178.

28. "Analysis of the New Georgia Campaign," 103rd Infantry, June-July, 1943, RG 338, NARA.

29. Smith, ed., *U.S. Marine Corps in WWII*, 391.

30. Gegeo and White, eds., *Big Death*, 134.

31. Lindstrom and White, *Pacific Theater*, photo caption, n.p.

32. Honan and Harcombe, *Solomon Islands*, 88.

33. XIV Corps G2 Daily Intelligence Summary, 4 July 1943, RG 338, NARA; and Lt. Col. Marvin D. Girardeau, *Dragons Peninsula* (New York: Vantage Press, 1967), 27.

34. Gegeo and White, eds., *Big Death*, 141.

35. Col. S. B. Griffith, "Corry's Boys," *Marine Corps Gazette*, May, 1949, 47.

36. Lindstrom and White, *Pacific Theater*, 341.

37. Horton, *Fire Over the Islands*, 132.

38. Harold Cooper, "Kennedy's Boys Go-a-Feudin," *Pacific Islands Monthly*, July 1943, n.p.

39. "Planning: New Georgia Operations."

40. Hqs., USAFISPA, G2 Daily Summary, 9 Jan. 1943, RG 338, NARA.

41. 43rd Division Miscellaneous Communication File, n.d., RG 338, NARA.

42. John Miller Jr., *Cartwheel: The Reduction of Rabaul*, U.S. Army in World War II, vol. 8 (Washington: Office of the Chief of Military History, Department of the Army, 1959), 47.

43. Pfc. Takeo Masuda, POW Interrogation Report no. 140, Combat Intelligence Center, South Pacific Forces (hereafter CIC, SoPacFor), RG 338, NARA.

44. Japanese monograph no. 99, Southeast Area Naval Operations, pt. II, ATIS, General Headquarters, Far Eastern Command, 1948, NARA, 33.

45. "Vice Admiral Samejima's Observations," Doc. no. 16638A, ATIS, 16 Apr. 1946, Naval Historical Center Archives, Washington Navy Yard, Washington, D.C. (hereafter NHC).

46. Quoted in Shaw and Kane, *Isolation of Rabaul*, 89–90.

47. "Planning: New Georgia Operations."

48. Ibid.

49. Ibid.

50. Horton, *Fire Over the Islands*, 195.

51. Both accounts are found in the James N. Cupp Papers (hereafter Cupp Papers), archives, Marine Corps Historical Center, Washington Navy Yard, Washington, D.C. (hereafter MCHC).

52. Quoted in Smith, ed., *U.S. Marine Corps in WWII*, 375–76.

53. Diary, unknown Japanese author, XIV Corps G2 files, SoPacFor, RG 338, NARA.

54. Maj. Edna L. Smith, untitled correspondent's report, PC no. 326, Col. Harry Liversedge Papers, MCHC.

55. Translation of Captured Japanese Document, Item no. 1082, CIC, SoPacFor.

56. *Combat Narratives—Solomon Islands Campaign: Operations in New Georgia Area, 21 June–5 August 1943* (Washington: Office of Naval Intelligence, 1943), 56.

57. Quoted in Walter Lord, *Lonely Vigil: Coastwatchers of the Solomons* (New York: Viking, 1977), 185.

58. XIV Corps Weekly Intelligence Summary, 23 Apr.–8 July 1943, RG 338, NARA.

59. "Navy Catalinas Known as 'Black Cats' of Guadalcanal," *Aeropinion,* 25 May 1944, n.p.

60. Eric Hammel, *Munda Trail* (New York: Avon, 1989), 41. Hammel's account of the battle is incomplete in that he fails to tell the story of the Northern Landing Group's campaign against Enogai and Bairoko. This operation was one claw of the pincers applied against Munda. Nonetheless, it is a valuable source of information on the main (southern) drive to the airstrip.

61. Lindstrom and White, *Pacific Theater,* 331–32.

62. Ibid., 342.

63. Gegeo and White, eds., *Big Death,* 135.

64. Lindstrom and White, *Pacific Theater,* 348.

65. Horton, *Fire Over the Islands,* 148.

66. Kennedy, "Keeping Watch Over the Japs," 44–45.

67. Horton, *Fire Over the Islands,* 131–32.

68. Lord, *Lonely Vigil,* 174; and Maj. Donald Kennedy, "Battle of Morovo Lagoon," *Pacific Islands Monthly,* Mar. 1944, 34–35.

69. Lindstrom and White, *Pacific Theater,* 349.

70. Russell Sydnor Crenshaw Jr., *South Pacific Destroyer: The Battle for the Solomons from Savo to Vella Gulf* (Annapolis, Md.: Naval Institute Press, 1998), 81–82.

71. Louis Burton, interview with author, Jan. 1997.

72. Sal Lamagna, unpublished memoir, Ocala, Fla.

73. Crenshaw, *South Pacific Destroyer,* 85.

74. Quoted in Bob Conrad, "169th's Prelude to Jungle Warfare," *Hartford (Conn.) Courant,* 21 Feb. 1993, 1.

75. Quoted in Smith, ed., *U.S. Marines in WWII,* 360–61.

76. Capt. John DeChant, "Devil Birds," *Marine Corps Gazette,* Apr. 1947, 32.

77. Charles Henne, interview with author, July 1997.

78. Cupp Papers.

79. Quoted in Smith, ed., *U.S. Marines in WWII,* 365.

80. Quoted in Conrad, "169th's Prelude to Jungle Warfare," 1; and Ray Winialski, interview with author, Oct. 1996.

81. James Chase, interview with author, Feb. 1999.

82. Conrad, "A Call to Arms for Connecticut Regiment," *Hartford [Conn.] Courant,* 1 Oct. 1992, 10.

Chapter 2. First Communion

1. Crenshaw, *South Pacific Destroyer,* 109–10; and Prados, *Combined Fleet Decoded,* 489–90.

2. E. B. Potter, *Bull Halsey* (Annapolis, Md.: Naval Institute Press, 1985), 150.

3. Quoted in William Manchester, *American Caesar: Douglas MacArthur, 1880–1964* (New York: Dell, 1978), 385.

4. Potter, *Bull Halsey,* 160.

5. E. B. Potter, *Nimitz* (Norwalk, Conn.: Easton Press, 1976), 218.

6. Gerald F. Linderman, *The World Within War: America's Combat Experience in World War II* (New York: Free Press, 1997), 178.

7. Potter, Bull Halsey, 346.

8. Ibid., 348.

9. Lt. Col. Frederick P. Henderson, "Naval Gunfire Support in the Solomon Islands Campaign," 1954, archives, NHC, 43.

10. Sgt. Frank Tolbert, "Advance Man," *Leatherneck,* Mar. 1945, 15.

11. Hammel, *Munda Trail,* 28.

12. John McCormick, *The Right Kind of War* (Annapolis: Naval Institute Press, 1992), 56.

13. Ibid., 65–66.

14. Jorn Rentz, *Marines in the Central Solomons* (Nashville: The Battery Press, 1952), 25, 27.

15. Lord, *Lonely Vigil,* 179.

16. Frank Guidone, unpublished memoir, Las Vegas, Nev.

17. Prados, *Combined Fleet Decoded,* 500.

18. D. O. W. Hall, *Coastwatchers* (Wellington, N.Z.: War History Branch, Department of Internal Affairs, 1951), 29.

19. William B. Huie, "Seabees and Mud at Munda," in *The 100 Best True Stories of World War II* (New York: William H. Wise, 1945), 183.

20. Maj. Jon T. Hoffman, *From Makin to Bougainville: Marine Raiders in the Pacific War* (Washington: Marine Corps Historical Center, 1995), 3.

21. Maj. Roy D. Batterton, "You Fight by the Book," *Marine Corps Gazette,* July 1949, 17. Batterton's account draws heavily from Clay Gowran's superb series in the *Chicago Tribune* written six years before.

22. Henry Berry, *Semper Fi, Mac* (New York: Arbor House, 1982), 185.

23. Lowell Bulger, "Editor's Note," *Raider Patch,* Nov. 1979, 20.

24. Clay Gowran, "We Storm Viru," *Chicago Sunday Tribune,* 7 Nov. 1943, 25. The story was carried in the "Graphic Section" in three installments.

25. Maj. Gen. Oscar F. Peatross, *Bless 'em All: The Marine Raiders of World War II* (Irvine, Calif.: Review Publications, 1995), 200. This is the most detailed account of the marine Raiders on New Georgia to date.

26. Rentz, *Marines in the Central Solomons* 41 n 51

27. Sgt. Anthony P. Coulis, "The March to Viru Harbor," in Smith, ed., *U.S. Marine Corps in World War II,* 387.

28. Earl Lambert, interview with author, July 1999.

29. Coulis, "March to Viru Harbor," 387.

30. Howard Biggerstaff, "Marine Writers Describe Attacks on Munda, Vila," *Chevron,* 11 Sept. 1943, 3.

31. "Memorial to the Men of C/P Company, 4th Marine Raider Battalion, 50th Anniversary of the Formation of the Company, 1942–1992," n.p. This is another unpolished but most helpful publication that assembled stories from survivors of New Georgia a half-century later.

32. Batterton, "You Fight by the Book," 18.

33. Gowran, "We Storm Viru," 14 Nov. 1943, 8.

34. Peatross, *Bless 'em All,* 202.

35. Gowran, "We Storm Viru," 14 Nov. 1943, 8.

36. Batterton, "You Fight by the Book," 19.

37. Ibid.

38. Coulis, "March to Viru Harbor," 387.

39. Hoffman, *From Makin to Bougainville,* 29.

40. "Observer's Report," Hqs, 103rd Combat Team, 5 July 1943, RG 338, NARA.

41. Biggerstaff, "Marine Writers," 3.

42. "Memorial to the Men of C/P Company," n.p.

43. "Observer's Report."

44. Batterton, "You Fight by the Book," 20.

45. Gowran, "We Storm Viru," 21 Nov. 1943, 4.

46. Ibid.

47. Ibid.

48. Ibid., 5.

49. 43rd Division G2 Daily Summary, 1 July–31 Oct. 1943, RG 338, NARA.

50. "Editor's Note," *Raider Patch,* July 1977, 5.

51. Peatross, *Bless 'em All,* 197.

52. "Observer's Report."

53. Japanese monograph no. 99, 35.

54. Peatross, *Bless 'em All,* 204.

55. R. G. Rosenquist, Martin J. Sexton, and Robert Buerlein, eds., *Our Kind of War* (Richmond, Va.: American Historical Foundation, 1990), 88.

56. Lowell Bulger, "Editor's Note," *Raider Patch,* July 1976, 12.

57. Rentz, *Marines in the Central Solomons,* 46.

58. Shaw and Kane, *Isolation of Rabaul,* 78 n 20.

Chapter 3. Rising Shadows

1. Francis T. Miller, *The Complete History of World War II* (Chicago: Progress Research, 1950), 637.

2. Between 30 June and 31 July, 28,748 personnel and 21,471 tons of ammunition, fuel, vehicles, and other supplies were unloaded on the island (*Combat Narratives—Solomon Islands Campaign,* 14).

3. Samuel Eliot Morison, *Breaking the Bismarcks Barrier: 22 July 1942–1 May 1944,* History of U.S. Naval Operations in World War II, vol. 6 (Boston: Little, Brown, 1950), 150.

4. On 30 June the Allies had 455 tactical aircraft in the combat zone, including 213 fighters, 170 light and medium bombers, and 72 heavy bombers. Even with help from Rabaul and Truk, the Japanese were outgunned nearly two to one (Harnmel, *Munda Trail,* 31).

5. Stanley A. Frankel, *The 37th Infantry Division in WWII* (Washington: Infantry Journal Press, 1948), 79. Frankel was a member of the 37th Division. It was the unit's good fortune, for his account is easily one of the best unit histories written. The Japanese soldier is not identified.

6. Lord, *Lonely Vigil,* 184.

7. Leslie Gill, "Landing on Rendova," *Pacific Islands Monthly,* Apr. 1944, 8.

8. D. C. Horton, *New Georgia: Pattern for Victory* (New York: Ballantine Books, 1971), 55.

9. Horton, *Fire Over the Islands,* 216.

10. Lt. Comdr. F. A. Rhoades, *Diary of a Coastwatcher in the Solomons* (Fredericksburg, Tex.: Nimitz Foundation, 1982), 35.

11. Jisuke Kogima, POW Interrogation Report no. 117; Kyoichi Totsuka, POW Interrogation Report no. 105, CIC, SoPacFor. There were about twenty Japanese soldiers near the beach where the Americans landed. Most tried to escape to Munda using makeshift rafts or logs. The others, including nonswimmers Kogima and Totsuka, fled into the woods. They lived for a month on stolen GI rations and roots, but their strength was failing rapidly and four of them decided to build a raft and try for Munda. But at daybreak they were sighted by a PT boat and picked up.

12. Rhoades, *Diary of a Coastwatcher,* 39–40.

13. Rhoades passed the dead Japanese officer that he first shot and noticed that a souvenir hunter in the patrol had already beaten him to the man's sword. Later, at the plantation, he saw a soldier displaying it to his buddies. That night, Rhoades stole it from him. "I killed its owner and reckoned that it was legitimately mine." (Ibid., 41).

14. Ibid., 40.

15. Quoted in Eric Bergerud, *Touched with Fire: The Land War in the South Pacific* (New York: Viking, 1996), 65.

16. Shaw and Kane, *Isolation of Rabaul,* 87.

17. Fletcher Pratt, *The Marines' War* (New York: William Sloan, 1948), 126.

18. The PT boat reported that they had struck an enemy transport, so the 43rd Division's commander believed that the Japanese were landing troops on the island and ordered a "Condition Black" to prepare for an assault. "I hate to think what might have happened if the enemy had been able to stage a powerful counterattack," said Rhoades (Rhoades, *Diary of a Coastwatcher,* 33).

19. Miller, *Cartwheel,* 90.

20. Quoted in William B. Huie, "Men and Mud," in Smith, ed.,

The U.S. Navy in World War II (New York: Ballantine Books, 1967), 478–79.

21. Hammel, *Munda Trail,* 86.

22. Quoted in Huie, "Men and Mud," 479.

23. David Slater memoirs, archives, MCHC.

24. Sam LaMagna memoir.

25. Louis Burton interview.

26. Leslie Gill, "Lambeti: How a Solomon Island Planter Returned Home," *Pacific Islands Monthly,* Mar. 1944, 8.

27. VAdm. George Dyer, *The Amphibians Came to Conquer: The Story of Admiral Richmond Kelly Turner* (Washington: U.S. Government Printing Office, 1969), 554–55.

28. Edwin P. Hoyt, *The Glory of the Solomons* (New York: Stein an Day, 1983), 110.

29. Japanese monograph no. 99, 30.

30. War Diary, Strike Command, 2 Apr.–25 July 1943, NARA.

31. *Combat Narratives—Solomon Islands Campaign,* 14.

32. Wesley Frank Craven and James Lea Cate, eds., *The Pacific: Guadalcanal to Saipan,* The Army Air Forces in World War II, vol. 2 (Chicago: University of Chicago Press, 1950), 222.

33. Miller, *Cartwheel,* 98.

34. Quoted in Andrew J. Wilde, "The USS *Strong* (DD467) in World War II," Andrew J. Wilde Collection, Needham, Mass., n.p.

35. C. W. Kilpatrick, *The Night Battles in the Solomons* (Pampano Beach Exposition Press of Florida, 1987), 83.

36. Lt. Comdr. Joseph H. Wellings, "The Night the *Strong* was Sunk," *Shipmate,* July–Aug. 1977, 24.

37. Ibid., 25.

38. Comdr. Eph McLean, "Shore Bombardment, Kula Gulf Area, Night of 4–5 July 1943," RG 38, NARA, 4.

39. Ibid., 5.

40. O. Milton Hackett, "The *Strong* is Sunk," Lt. Comdr. Joseph H. Wellings Papers, Naval Historical Collection, Naval War College, Newport, R.I. (hereafter Wellings Papers), 1.

41. Wellings, "Night the *Strong* was Sunk," 25.

42. Lt. Donald A. Regan, "Miscellaneous Lessons Learned from Torpedoing and Sinking of the USS *Strong,* 4–5 July 1943," Wellings Papers, n.p.

43. Hugh B. Miller, "Report of Activities While Missing," Wellings Papers, 1. A similar account of Miller's ordeal is told by Frank Tremaine in "The Castaway of Arundel Island" in *The Best 100 True Stories of World War II*, 219–25.

44. Regan, "Miscellaneous Lessons Learned," n.p.

45. Ibid.

46. Wellings, "Night the *Strong* was Sunk," 25–26.

47. "Berkley County Boy Tells Thrilling Adventure Tale," *Charleston (S.C.) News and Courier,* 1 Nov. 1943, 6.

48. Ibid.

49. lbid.

50. Miller, "Activities While Missing," 3–4.

51. Ibid.

52. Ibid., 5.

53. Ibid., 6.

54. Ibid.

55. Photo caption in Wilde, "USS *Strong.*"

56. *Combat Narratives—Solomon Islands Campaign,* 23.

57. Prados, *Combined Fleet Decoded,* 492.

58. E. E. Lajeunesse, journal, www.geocities.com/CapeCanaveral/Hangar/5115/Gene.html.

59. Japanese monograph no. 99, 32.

60. Lt. A. W. Borne (New Zealand Army), interview by G2, US-AFISPA, Mar. 1943, RG 338, NARA.

61. Horton, *Fire Over the Islands,* 221.

62. Ibid., 222.

63. Lord, *Lonely Vigil,* 194–212.

64. Hammel, *Munda Trail,* 98.

65. Prados, *Combined Fleet Decoded,* 494.

66. Miller, *Cartwheel,* 99.

67. "Vice Admiral Samejima's Observations."

68. Japanese monograph no. 99, 27.

Chapter 4. Dragons Peninsula

1. Lt. Comdr. James F. Regan, diary, 5 July 1943, copy in author's collection.

2. USS *Waters,* War Diary, 24 July 1943, RG 38, NARA; "Editor's Note," *Raider Patch,* Nov. 1989, 20.

3. Maj. David Marshall, "The Operations of Company I, 3/145th Infantry (37th Inf. Div.) on New Georgia Island, 4–12 July 1943," 1950, Donovan Technical Library, Fort Benning, Ga. (hereafter DTL), n.p. The author wrote this as a course requirement while a student at the Infantry School.

4. Charles Henne, unpublished memoir, Archives, U. S. Army Military History Institute, Carlisle Barracks, Pa. (hereafter MHI), 38.

5. Quoted in Prados, *Combined Fleet Decoded,* 582.

6. Frank Guidone memoir, n.p.

7. Regan diary, 5 July 1943.

8. Peatross, *Bless 'em All,* 212.

9. Ibid., 208.

10. Unfortunately, without the experience of Currin and his Viru Harbor expedition, the NLG was going into the green abyss blindly. Currin's 4th Raiders were penciled in to land at Rice Anchorage with Liversedge, but because of delays in their assault on Viru, they had to be replaced by the army's 3rd Battlion, 148th Infantry.

11. Shaw and Kane, *Isolation of Rabaul,* 123.

12. TSgt. Frank McDevitt and TSgt. Murray Marder, "The Capture of Enogai," *Marine Corps Gazette,* Sept. 1943, 7.

13. TSgt. Frank McDevitt, unpublished navy news release.

14. Frank Guidone to author, Dec. 1998.

15. Lt. Col. Samuel B. Griffith, "Action at Enogi," Marine Corps Gazette, Mar. 1944, 15.

16. Quoted in Bergerud, *Touched With Fire,* 74.

17. Dr. Lee N. Miner, "The Ridge," *Raider Dope Sheet,* Jan. 1989, 8.

18. Griffith, "Action at Enogai," 16.

19. McDevitt and Marder, "Capture of Enogai," 8.

20. Peatross, *Bless 'em All,* 214.

21. Regan diary, 10 July 1943.

22. Ibid., 7 July 1943.

23. Lt. Col. Marvin D. Girardeau, Dragons Peninsula, (New York: Vantage Press, 1967), 43.

24. Jim Lucas, Combat Correspondent (Cornwall, N.Y.: Cornwall Press, 1944), 138.

25. lbid.

26. Griffith, "Action at Enogai," 18.

27. Regan diary, 10 July 1943.

28. Peatross, *Bless 'em All*, 218.

29. Ibid., 217.

30. "Meet the Marines Who Took Enogai," *Leatherneck*, Nov. 1943, 71.

31. Guidone memoir.

32. Regan diary, 10 July 1943.

33. Ibid.

34. Tatsuo Miyantani, POW Interrogation Report no. 166, CIC, SoPacFor.

35. Regan diary, 18 July 1943.

36. "Editor's Note," *Raider Patch*, Sept. 1979, 11.

37. Frankel, *37th Division in WWII*, 76.

38. Henne memoir, 82.

39. Ibid., 83.

40. Ibid., 85.

41. Ibid., 86.

42. Frankel, *37th Division in WWII*, 76.

43. Henne memoir, 77–78.

44. Miller, Cartwheel, 104.

45. Rentz, Marines in the Central Solomons, 109.

46. Henne memoir, 72.

47. Miller, *Cartwheel*, 105.

48. Morison, *Breaking the Bismarcks Barrier*, 184; Kilpatrick, *Naval Night Battles*, 202.

49. Prados, Combined Fleet Decoded, 493.

50. One of the ships on its way to Vella Lavella to retrieve survivors of the *Helena* spotted a whaleboat from the sunken *Gwin*. Inside were two sailors from the *Jintsu* who were happy to be rescued (Morison, *Breaking the Bismarcks Barrier*, 193–94).

51. Ibid., 190.

52. "Vice Admiral Samejima's Observations."

53. Girardeau, *Dragons Peninsula*, 49–50.

54. Henne memoir, 37.

55. Francis Hepburn, *Raider Patch*, Apr. 1995, 17.

56. Hoyt, *Glory of the Solomons*, 120.

57. Miller, *Cartwheel*, 128.

58. Apparently the standard operating procedure (SOP) at Air-Sols was to accept requests for next-day air missions only if received

before 4 P.M. Unaware of this policy, Liversedge made his request after the deadline and was therefore ignored (Rentz, *Marines in the Central Solomons*, 111). As inconceivable as this may seem, such things happened all too often during the war.

59. "Memorial to the Men of C/P Company," n.p.

60. Lucas, *Combat Correspondent*, 150.

61. Capt. Royal F. Munger, "Munda Jungle Nasty Foe, But Yanks Whip It," *Chicago Daily News*, 17 Jan. 1944, 11.

62. Bergerud, *Touched with Fire*, 285.

63. Peatross, *Bless 'em All*, 225.

64. Ibid., 226.

65. Richard Maurer, letter, *Raider Patch*, Nov. 1990, 15.

66. "Memorial to the Men of C/P Company," n.p.

67. Ibid.

68. Ibid.

69. McCormick, *Right Kind of War*, 74.

70. Rosenquist et al., eds., *Our Kind of War*, 85.

71. "Memorial to the Men of C/P Company," n.p.

72. Ibid.

73. Guidone memoir.

74. McCormick, *Right Kind of War*, 78.

75. Peatross, *Bless 'em All*, 227.

76. It is interesting to note that in the jungle, officers were called by their first names. Griffith was "Sam" or "Griff," and Colonel Liversedge was called "Harry" or "Horse." It was also recommended that no rank be worn—even by sergeants. Medical personnel did not wear Red Cross armbands. Pointing was also discouraged. These things identified men as leaders, therefore making them more lucrative targets (Girardeau, *Dragons Peninsula*, 23).

77. Dr. Lee N. Miner, "The Ridge," *Raider Dope Sheet*, Mar. 1989, 12.

78. Ken Haney, *U.S. Navy Medical Personnel in Marine Parachute and Raider Battalions* (Jackson, Tenn.: Ken Haney, 1989), 37–39.

79. Olin Gray, letter, *Raider Patch*, May 1992, 10.

80. Lucas, *Combat Correspondent*, 151.

81. Regan diary, 21 July 1943.

82. Rentz, *Marines in the Central Solomons*, 117.

83. Guidone memoir,

84. Henne memoir, 110.

85. Guidone memoir.

86. Martin Clemens, letter, *Raider Patch*, July 1985, 1.

87. Father Paul Redmond, letter, *Raider Patch*, May 1976, 18.

88. Guidone memoir.

89. Henne memoir, 94.

90. Shaw and Kane, *Isolation of Rabaul*, 145.

91. Charles Henne, "New Georgia Campaign—The First to Fight, The First to Die," *Buckeye Star News*, 1 July 1997, 8.

92. The marine Raider battalions were disbanded in early 1944. Most of the Raiders who served in the NLG were reassigned to the newly formed 5th Marine Division, which participated in the invasion of Iwo Jima in 1945.

93. Quoted in Rentz, *Marines in the Central Solomons*, 119.

94. Rosenquist et al., eds., *Our Kind of War,* 89.

Chapter 5. Terra Incognita

1. Hammel, *Munda Trail*, 104.

2. Conrad, "Soldiers Fought Confusion in Jungle," *Hartford [Conn.] Courant*, 26 July 1993, A-1.

3. Ibid., A-5.

4. Miller, *Cartwheel*, 108.

5. Hammel, *Munda Trail*, 106.

6. Conrad, "A Desperate Battle Up a Dark Jungle Trail," *Hartford (Conn.) Courant*, 3 July 1993, A-6.

7. Sal LaMagna memoir.

8. Norvil Wilson, interview with author, June 1997.

9. Hammel, *Munda Trail*, 184.

10. Miller, *Cartwheel*, 109.

11. Capt. Eugene A. Wright and Lt. Michael Mitchell, "Battle Facts for Your Outfit," *Infantry Journal*, Dec. 1943, 12–15.

12. Statement taken from Lt. Col. John M. Barry on 169th Infantry, 19 July 1943, 57th Field Hospital G2 files, RG 338, NARA.

13. Hammel, *Munda Trail*, 185–186.

14. Conrad, "Desperate Battle," A-1.

15. Shaw and Kane, *Isolation of Rabaul*, 93.

16. Barry statement.

17. LaMagna memoir.

18. Raymond Winialski, interview with author, Nov. 1997.

19. Wilson interview.

20. Franklin F. Phelps, "Memories of Munda," RG 407, NARA, 16.

21. Capt. Joseph Risman, "Medic on Munda," RG 407, NARA.

22. Capt. Arthur Davis, questionnaire, archives, MHI.

23. Quoted in Miller, Cartwheel, 121.

24. Joseph O'Hara, interview with author, Oct. 1996.

25. Norman Q. Brill and Gilbert Beebe, *A Follow-up Study of War Neurosis* (Washington: Veterans Administration, 1955), 26.

26. Accurate casualty statistics are not available for the New Georgia campaign, mostly because in the first two weeks of the battle many evacuees did not go through medical channels. Not until mid-July was this problem corrected. The 43rd Division sustained more than 4,400 casualties of all types during the course of the five-week operation—according to one source, 1,764 were psychiatric cases, or about 40 percent. (See Maj. William H. Kelly, "War Neurosis," *Infantry Journal*, Aug. 1946, 20, and Col. Frank T. Hallam, "Medical Service in the New Georgia Campaign.")

27. Albert E. Cowdrey, *Fighting for Life* (New York: Free Press, 1994), 84.

28. 118th Medical Battalion Unit History, RG 338, NARA.

29. Operations Report, Company A, 118th Medical Battalion, 22–29 July 1943, RG 338, NARA.

30. Hallam, "Medical Service in the New Georgia Campaign," NARA, 33–34.

31. Robert Schwolsky, interview with author, Oct. 1996.

32. Memo from Brig. Gen. A. J. Barnett to Maj. Gen. Millard Harmon, deputy commander, SPA, 30 Aug. 1943, RG 338, NARA.

33. Bergerud, *Touched with Fire*, 210.

34. Phelps, "Memories of Munda," 14.

35. Sgt. Arthur O'Connell, questionnaire, archives, MHI.

36. Cpl. Maurice Laplant, questionnaire, archives, MHI.

37. XIV Corps G2 Intelligence Report, 29 Aug. 1943, RG 338, NARA.

38. Burton interview.

39. James J. Fahey, *Pacific War Diary* (New York: Kensington, 1962), 45–46.

40. Carl Grotton, interview with author, Nov. 1996.

41. Bergerud, *Touched with Fire*, 446.

42. Burton interview.

43. Phelps, "Memories of Munda," 42.

44. John Hersey, "Experience by Battle," *Life,* 27 Dec. 1943, 48.

45. Gen. J. Lawton Collins, excerpt from interview by Lt. Col. Charles C. Sperow, 1972, vol. 1, Gen. J. Lawton Collins Papers, archives, MHI (hereafter Collins Papers).

46. Halsey and Bryan, *Admiral Halsey's Story,* 161.

47. Collins interview.

48. Mary Ellen Condon-Rall and Albert E. Cowdrey, *Medical Service in the War Against Japan,* U.S. Army in World War II (Washington: Center of Military History, 1998), 189–90.

49. Hallam, "Medical Service," 35.

50. Col. William Mullins, ed., *Neuropsychiatry in WWII,* vol. 2, *Overseas Theaters* (Washington: Office of the Surgeon General, Department of the Army, 1973), 476.

51. "Col. Holland C. Temple, Conference Presented by Ft. Benning, Ga.," n.d., DTL, 4. There is no date here, but the conference was probably held shortly after the war. Essentially a debriefing of the campaign, it is in question-and-answer format with the questions coming from instructors at the Infantry School.

52. Barry statement.

53. Roger Spiller, "Shell Shock," American Heritage, May-June, 1990, 85–86.

54. Kelly, "War Neurosis," 21.

55. Jeter A. Isely and Philip A. Crowl, *The U.S. Marines and Amphibious War: Its Theory and Its Practice in the Pacific* (Princeton, N.J.: Princeton University Press, 1951), 172.

56. Ruth Rothstein, "Two Servicemen Home from Pacific Prefer Bombings to Night in Foxhole," *Hartford (Conn.) Courant,* n.d.

57. 36th Field Artillery Battalion History, RG 338, NARA, 5.

58. Miller, *Cartwheel,* 111.

59. Operations Report, 43rd Division Artillery, 30 June–5 Aug. 1943, RG 338, NARA.

60. Ibid.

61. Ibid.

62. Lt. Col. Robery C. Gildart, "Artillery on New Georgia," *Field Artillery Journal,* Feb. 1944, 89.

63. War diary, Strike Command, 2 Apr.–25 July 1943.

64. Risman, "Medic on Munda," n.p.

65. Henne memoir, 74.

66. Phelps, "Memories of Munda," 7.

67. Ibid., 8.

68. Hammel, *Munda Trail,* 115.

69. Ibid., 120.

70. Ibid., 116.

71. Operations Report, 37th Division G3, 22 July–6 Aug. 1943, RG 338, NARA.

72. Capt. Joseph Lieberman, "Road Construction on New Georgia," *Military Engineer,* Mar. 1944, 78.

73. Quoted in Conrad, "Soldiers Fought Confusion," A-5.

74. Jack Wilcox, interview with author, Oct. 1996.

75. Craven and Cate, *Pacific: Guadalcanal to Saipan,* 225.

76. 136th Field Artillery Battalion History, 6–7.

77. Ralph Martin, *The G.I. War, 1941–1945* (Boston: Little, Brown, 1969), 269.

78. LaMagna memoir.

79. Conrad, "A Desperate Battle," A-6.

80. Martin, *G.I. War,* 268.

81. Leonard G. Hall, *Brothers of the Fox* (Orange, Tex.: Leonard Hall, 1986), 24.

82. Holland conference, 70.

83. Miller, *Cartwheel,* 116.

84. Hammel, *Munda Trail,* 129.

85. Shaw and Kane, *Isolation of Rabaul,* 97.

86. Phelps, "Memories of Munda," 13.

87. Holland conference, 6, 9; 37th Division Chemical Officer's report, 21 Aug. 1943, RG 338, NARA.

88. Holland conference, 11.

89. Phelps, "Memories of Munda," 9.

90. Holland conference, 37.

91. Ibid., 7.

92. Robert Casko, diary, Putnam, Conn.

93. Phelps, "Memories of Munda," 18.

94. Schwolsky interview.

95. Holland conference, 7.

96. Hammel, *Munda Trail,* 134.

97. Conrad, "Soldiers Fought Confusion, " A-5. Eric Hammel states that the order for the bayonet charge was battalionwide and came from Major Zimmer, the battalion commander, who was "urged" by Holland to issue it. Later, he was ordered to rescind it (Hammel, *Munda Trail,* 135–36).

98. Risman, "Medic on Munda."

99. Hammel, *Munda Trail,* 139.

100. Holland, 7.

101. Risman, "Medic on Munda."

102. Phelps, "Memories of Munda," 20.

103. Holland conference, 37.

104. Capt. Bennett F. Avery, ed., *The History of the Medical Department of the U.S. Navy in World War II,* vol. 2 (Washington: U.S. Government Printing Office, 1953), 76.

105. Hammel, *Munda Trail,* 138–39.

106. Condon-Ralland Cowdrey, *Medical Service,* 184–90.

107. Holland conference, 34.

108. Phelps, "Memories of Munda," 27.

109. Holland conference, 36.

110. Risman, "Medic on Munda."

111. Phelps, "Memories of Munda," 19. At least one unit captured a loudspeaker system that played a variety of recordings of humans screaming (ibid., 20).

112. Ibid., 22, 29.

113. Risman, "Medic on Munda."

114. Phelps, "Memories of Munda," 31.

115. Ibid., 33–34.

116. Alvin P. Stauffer, *The Quartermaster Corps,* vol. 3, *Operations in the War Against Japan,* (Washington: Office of the Chief of Military History, Department of the Army, 1956), 277–78.

117. Capt. Robert W. Blake, "Death on the Munda Trail," in Smith, ed., *U.S. Marine Corps in World War II,* 422.

118. Robert Gilman, interview with author, Nov. 1996.

119. Capt. Robert W. Blake, "The Battle Without a Name," in *The 100 Best True Stories Of World War II,* 199–201.

120. Shaw and Kane, *Isolation of Rabaul,* 103.

121. Hoyt, *Glory of the Solomons,* 124.

Chapter 6. A Dark Coner of Hell

1. Quoted in Miller, *Cartwheel,* 124.

2. Spector, *Eagle Against the Sun,* 236.

3. Adm. William F. Halsey Jr. to Adm. Chester W. Nimitz, 19 Aug. 1943, Adm. William F. Halsey Jr. Papers, Manuscript Division, Library of Congress (hereafter LOC), Washington, D.C.

4. In an apparently unrelated move that same day, Admiral Turner was replaced as commander of the amphibious and attack forces. He was to assume a similar post in the upcoming central Pacific invasions. RAdm. Theodore S. Wilkinson was his replacement.

5. Quoted in Rentz, *Marines in the Central Solomons,* 71; Hammel, *Munda Trail,* 192.

6. van der Vat, *Pacific Campaign,* 243–44.

7. Henne interview.

8. Hoyt, *Glory of the Solomons,* 139.

9. Hammel, *Munda Trail,* 160.

10. Rentz, *Marines in the Central Solomons,* 84; Shaw and Kane, *Isolation of Rabaul,* 105.

11. Jack Mahon, "The Terror Begins at Twilight," 30 Jan. 1963, copy in author's collection.

12. Ibid.

13. Frankel, *37th Division in WWII,* 83.

14. "Record of Trial Proper in the Case of Kliebert, 2nd Lt. Nicholas T.," Clerk of Court Office, U.S. Army Judiciary, Falls Church, Va.

15. Ibid.

16. Ibid.

17. Ibid.

18. lbid.

19. Phelps, "Memories of Munda," 35.

20. Col. John J. Higgins, *A History of the 1st Connecticut Regiment, 1672–1963* (Hartford, Conn.: John Higgins, 1963), 27.

21. "Record of the Trial Proper." This statement, however difficult it may be to believe, was made under oath. Then again, under the stress of combat, reality and illusion are often blurred.

22. Ibid.

23. Ibid.

24. Ibid.

25. Ibid.

26. Carmen Kliebert Collection, Mount Clemens, Mich.

27. Mrs. N. T. Kliebert to author, May 1999.

28. Lt. Gen. Oscar Griswold, diary, 18 July 1943, archives, MHI.

29. Shaw and Kane, Isolation of Rabaul, 104.

30. "Vice Admiral Samejima's Observations."

Chapter 7. The Final Torment

1. Air Solomons pilots could point with greater pride to their record against rival Japanese aircraft. During the period from 30 June to the start of the corps offensive on 25 July, 428 enemy fighters and 136 bombers were reported destroyed with the loss of only 80 planes of their own (Shaw and Kane, *Isolation of Rabaul*, 107).

2. Ibid., 108.

3. Frankel, *37th Division in World War II*, 83.

4. 1st Battalion, 145th Infantry History, RG 338, NARA.

5. Wilson interview.

6. Phelps, "Memories of Munda," 38.

7. Capt. Robert Howard, diary, 25 July 1943, archives, MHI.

8. Miller, Cartwheel, 139.

9. Griswold diary, 24 July 1943.

10. *Combat Narratives—Solomon Islands Campaign*, 54.

11. Chase interview.

12. Blake, "Battle Without a Name," 202–203.

13. Ibid., 203.

14. Martin, *G.I. War*, 269.

15. *South Sea Reveille*, n.d., copy in author's collection. This publication was printed by the 37th Division in the islands for local distribution among the men.

16. Griswold diary, 25 July 1943.

17. 37th Division Chemical Officer's report; Brooks Kleber and Dale Birdsell, *The Chemical Warfare Service*, vol. 3, *Chemicals in Combat*, U.S. Army in World War II (Washington: Office of the Chief of Military History, 1966), 538–40, 558–59.

18. Miller, *Cartwheel*, 148.

19. Maj. Charles E. McArdle, "The Operations of the 103rd Infantry Regiment, 12 July–25 Sept. 1943," 1948, DTL, 12, Hammel, *Munda Trail*, 215.

20. Rentz, *Marines in the Central Solomons*, 88–92.

21. Chase interview.

22. Capt. Robert S. Scott, "The Operations of the 3rd Platoon, Company C, 172nd Infantry Regiment (43rd Division) at Morrison-Johnson Hill, Approaching Munda Airstrip, New Georgia, British Solomon Islands, 28 July 1943," 1949, DTL, 9.

23. Ibid., 15–20.

24. Ichiro Kato, POW Interrogation Report no. 142, CIC, SoPac-For.

25. Elson Matson, "The Story of the 161st Infantry Regiment," archives, MHI, 60; Rentz, *Marines in the Central Solomons*, 87.

26. Matson, "Story of the 161st," 61.

27. Halsey to Nimitz, 19 Aug. 1943. For reasons unexplained, Halsey did not advise Admiral Nimitz of his decision to relieve General Hester, an error that earned Halsey a mild reprimand from his commander.

28. Griswold diary, 12–13 July 1943.

29. Quoted in Dyer, Amphibians Came to Conquer, 586.

30. Maj. Gen. Oscar W. Griswold to Lt. Gen. Lesley J. McNair, 29 Aug. 1943, RG 338, NARA.

31. Griswold diary, 25 July 1943.

32. 2nd Battalion, 145th Infantry History, 20 July–25 Aug. 1943, RG 338, NARA.

33. Howard diary, 25 July 1943.

34. Company F, 2nd Battalion, 145th Infantry, commander's diary, 28 July 1943, copy in author's collection.

35. Holland conference, 9.

36. The problem of the enemy reoccupying defeated pillboxes was so acute that it prompted the 37th Division's operations officer to emphasize it in his after-action report. See Lt. Col. Russell Ramsey, G3, 37th Infantry Division, "Jungle Tactics and Operations," RG 338, NARA.

37. Matson, "Story of the 161st," 65–66.

38. 1st Battalion, 145th Infantry History, 8–12.

39. Holland conference, 9.

40. Hodge to Halsey, "Action of the 169th Infantry during the period 29 July to 6 Aug., 1943," 14 Aug. 1943.

41. Hodge to Brig. Gen. A. J. Barnett, 30 Aug. 1943.

42. Company F, 2nd Battalion, 145th Infantry, commander's diary, 31 July 1943.

43. Biggerstaff, "Marine Writers," 2–3.

44. Craven and Cate, *Pacific: Guadalcanal to Saipan,* 233.

45. Hall, *Brothers of the Fox,* 21.

46. Miller, *Cartwheel,* 159.

47. Japanese monograph no. 99, 38.

48. Rentz, *Marines in the Central Solomons,* 122.

49. Quoted in Bergerud, *Touched With Fire,* 376.

50. Matson, "Story of the 161st," 73.

51. Henne, "Norvil Wilson Was There," 8.

52. Risman, "Medic on Munda."

53. Ibid.

54. Wilson interview.

55. Biggerstaff, "Marine Writers," 2–3.

56. Phelps, "Memories of Munda," 47–8.

57. John Fairfax, "Blasted By War," *Pacific Islands Monthly,* Mar. 1944, 36.

58. Wilson interview.

59. 43rd Division G3 Journal, 5 Aug. 1943, RG 338, NARA.

60. Quoted in Miller, *Cartwheel,* 164.

61. Stanley A. Frankel, *World War II in the South Pacific* (Scarsdale, N.Y.: Stanley Frankel, 1992), 64.

62. Commander, Air New Georgia Intel Summary, 7 Aug. 1943, RG 338, NARA.

63. Hugh Finkle, interview with author, Oct. 1996.

64. Phelps, "Memories of Munda," 45.

65. Frankel, *37th Infantry Division,* 107.

66. 37th Division G2 Daily Summary, 31 July 1943, RG 338, NARA.

67. Arthur Miller, *Situation Normal . . .* (New York: Reynal and Hitchcock, 1944), 150.

68. Prados, *Combined Fleet Decoded,* 500.

69. Risman, "Medic on Munda."

70. Matson, "Story of the 161st," 76.

71. Wilson interview.

72. Casko diary, 6 Aug. 1943.

73. Rentz, *Marines in the Central Solomons,* 146.

74. 13th Air Force Operations, Analysis Section, "Report on Study of Non- Combat Accidents," 15 Nov. 1943, RG 338, NARA.

75. Capt. T. Ohmae and Comdr. M. Yamaguchi, POW Interrogation Report no. 495, U.S. Strategic Bombing Survey files, Manuscripts Division, LOC.

76. Craven and Cate, *Pacific: Guadalcanal to Saipan,* 236–37.

77. 40th Field Artillery Battalion, Narrative History, RG 338, NARA.

78. Capt. Robert Bulkley, *At Close Quarters: PT Boats in the U.S. Navy* (Washington: U.S. Government Printing Office, 1961), 128.

79. Robert J. Donovan, *PT 109* (New York: McGraw-Hill, 1961), 143.

80. Ibid., 203.

81. Bulkley, *At Close Quarters,* 124–28; Morison, *Breaking the Bismarcks Barrier,* 212.

82. Morison, *Breaking the Bismarcks Barrier,* 219.

83. Kilpatrick, *Naval Night Battles,* 19–23; Hoyt, *Glory of the Solomons,* 167–69.

84. Hqs., New Georgia Occupation Force, G2 Daily Summary, 4–5 Aug. 1943, RG 338, NARA.

85. Otis Cary, ed., *War-Wasted Asia, Letters, 1945–46* (Tokyo: Kodansha International, 1975), 37.

Chapter 8. "Death Is Lighter Than a Feather"

1. Brig. Gen. Bonner Fellers, G2, SWPA, "The Psychology of the Japanese Soldier," in "Pacific War Notes," 1945. RG 338, NARA.

2. Ivan Morris, *The Nobility of Failure: Tragic Heroes in the History of Japan* (New York: Holt, Rinehart, and Winston, 1975).

3. Haruko Tara Cook and Theodore F. Cook, *Japan at War: An Oral History* (New York: New Press, 1992), 259.

4. "Translation of Captured Japanese Document," CIC, SoPacFor.

5. 43rd Division G2 Intel files, n.d., RG 338, NARA.

6. 37th Division G2 reports, 2 Jan.–24 Oct. 1943, New Georgia Operation, RG 338, NARA.

7. Yokishi Iwase, POW Interrogation Report no. 138, CIC SoPacFor.

8. Kinsaku Shimada, POW Interrogation Report no. 199, CIC SoPacFor.

9. Hqs., New Georgia Occupation Force, G2 Daily Summary, 4–5 Aug. 1943, RG 338, NARA.

10. Gengi Uchimura, POW Interrogation Report no. 212, CIC SoPacFor.

11. Yoshio Kitazato, POW Interrogation Report no. 217., CIC SoPacFor.

12. Pfc. Katsumi Shimano, POW Interrogation Report no. 205, CIC SoPacFor.

13. Frank D. Giliberto, unpublished memoir, Las Vegas, Nev., 154–55.

14. Miller, *Cartwheel*, 172.

15. Halsey and Bryan, *Admiral Halsey's Story*, 170.

16. Rentz, *Marines in the Central Solomons*, 131.

17. War Diary, Strike Command, 28 Aug. 1943, RG 338, NARA.

18. Shaw and Kane, *Isolation of Rabaul*, 161; Hoyt, *Glory of the Solomons*, 165, 171.

19. "Vice Admiral Samejima's Observations."

20. Dyer, *Amphibians Came to Conquer*, 592.

21. Robert Sherrod, *History of Marine Corps Aviation in World War II* (Washington: Marine Corps Historical Branch, 1963), 153.

22. Hallam, "Medical Service," 42–43.

23. van der Vat, *Pacific Campaign*, 283.

24. Miller, *Cartwheel*, 18.

Bibliography

Unpublished Sources

Manuscripts, Diaries, Papers, Monographs, Histories, and Memoirs: Allied Forces

These primary sources represent the most important collection of material used for this work. Without these, the story of the New Georgia Campaign would amount to little more than another rather routine narrative. A few—like those of Frank Giliberto, Charles Henne, and Sal LaMagna—were kindly shared with me by their authors. Others are located in the National Archives and Records Administration (NARA) in College Park, Md., and in the archives of the U.S. Army Military History Institute at Carlisle Barracks, Carlisle, Pa. The latter houses the personal diary of General Griswold, whose remarks concerning the relief of General Hester ran counter to the conventional wisdom. The manuscripts by Sgt. Franklin F. Phelps and Capt. Joseph Risman retained in the NARA are especially noteworthy for their poignant description of jungle warfare and war neurosis. Finally, the Library of Congress; the Marine Corps and Naval Historical Centers at the Washington Navy Yard, Washington, D.C.; the Donovan Technical Library, Fort Benning, Ga.; and the Naval Historical Collection at the Naval War College in Newport, R.I., were also helpful.

Donovan Technical Library, Fort Benning, Ga.

Holland, Col. Temple C. Conference presented by Ft. Benning, Ga., n.d.

Marshall, Maj. David. "The Operations of Company I, 3/145th Infantry (37th Inf. Div.) On New Georgia Island, 4–12 July 1943." 1950.

McArdle, Maj. Charles E. "The Operations of the 103rd Infantry Regiment, 30 June–5 August." 1943.

Scott, Capt. Robert S. "The Operations of the 3rd Platoon, Company C, 172nd Infantry Regiment (43rd Infantry Division) at Morrison-Johnson Hill, Approaching Munda Airstrip, New Georgia, British Solomon Islands, 28 July 1943." 1949.

Manuscript Division, Library of Congress, Washington, D.C.
Adm. William F. Halsey Papers.

Marine Corps Historical Center Archives, Washington Navy Yard, Washington, D.C.
James N. Cupp Papers.
Col. Harry Liversedge Papers.
David Slater Memoirs.

National Archives and Records Administration, College Park, Md.
RG 38, Records of the Chief of Naval Operations.
RG 338, Records of the Army Commands.
RG 407, Records of the Adjutant General's Office.

Naval Historical Center Archives, Washington Navy Yard, Washington, D.C.
Henderson, Lt. Col. Frederick. "Naval Gunfire Support in the Solomon Islands Campaign." 1954.

Naval Historical Collection, Naval War College, Newport, R.I.
Lt. Comdr. Joseph H. Wellings Papers.

U.S. Military History Institute, Carlisle Barracks, Pa.
Gen. J. Lawton Collins Papers.
Lt. Gen. Oscar W. Griswold Diary.
Capt. Robert Howard Diary.
Pfc. Elson Matson. "The Story of the 161st Infantry Regiment."
Col. Jay D. Vanderpool Papers.

Private Collections
Casko, Robert. Putman, Conn.

Giliberto, Frank D. Las Vegas, Nev.

Guidone, Frank. Las Vegas, Nev.

Henne, Charles. Gilbert, Ariz.

Kliebert, Carmen. Mount Clemens, Mich.

LaMagna, Sal. Ocala, Fla.

Lambert, Earl. Metairie, La.

Mahon, Jack. "The Terror Begins at Twilight. " 30 Jan. 1963. Author's collection.

Regan, Lt. Comdr. James F. Diary. Author's collection.

Wilde, Andrew J. "The USS *Strong* (DD467) in World War II." Needham, Mass.

Japanese Interrogation Reports, Diaries, and Monographs

Given the scarcity of translated Japanese material, the POW interrogation reports that I found in several different archival locations proved most beneficial. Conducted by military intelligence branch interrogators and interpreters, the reports include details of the prisoner's capture, his training and operations, unit strength, and morale. Most Japanese were cooperative and loquacious.

U.S. Army Military History Institute, Carlisle Barracks, Pa.

Allied Translator and Interpreter Section (ATIS), General Headquarters, Far Eastern Command, Japanese monographs no. 35 and no. 99, Southeast Area Naval Operations, pt. II, 1948.

Naval Historical Center, Washington Navy Yard, Washington, D.C.

Samejima, VAdm. Tomoshige. "Vice Admiral Samejima's Observations," ATIS Doc. no. 16638A, 16 Apr. 1946.

Combat Intelligence Center, South Pacific Forces, G2 Files.

Fujino, Mamoru. POW Interrogation Report no. 121

Ishikawa, Shigeo. POW Interrogation Report no. 106.

Kawabata, Shigeo. POW Interrogation Report no. unk.

Kitazato, Yoshio. POW Interrogation Report no. 217.

Kogima, Jisuke. POW Interrogation Report no. 117.

Kozutsumi, Kiyoyasu. POW Interrogation Report no. 122.

Matsushita, Isao. POW Interrogation Report no. 115.

Miyantini, Tatsuo. POW Interrogation Report no. 166.

Nagama, Mitsuto. POW Interrogation Report no. 120.

Shimano, Katsumi. POW Interrogation Report no. 205.
Tokugawa, Yoshio. POW Interrogation Report no. unk.
Uchimura, Gengi. POW Interrogation Report no. 212.
Yokoyama, Kazuyoshi. POW Interrogation Report no. 158.

RG 338, National Archives and Records Administration, College Park, Md.
ATIS Reports, 1942–46.
Morita, 2nd Class Petty Officer. Diary.
Combat Intelligence Center, South Pacific Forces, G2 Files.
Iwase, Yokichi. POW Interrogation Report no. 138.
Kato, Ichiro. POW Interrogation Report no. 142.
Masuda, Takeo. POW Interrogation Report no. 140.
Shimada, Kinsaku. POW Interrogation Report no. 199.
Totsuka, Kyoichi. POW Interrogation Report no. 105.
37th Infantry Division G2 Reports, 2 Jan.–24 Oct. 1943.
Oura, Toshishiro. Diary.
43rd Infantry Division G2 Intelligence File
Ito, Hiroshi. Diary. Item no. 848.

Manuscript Division, Library of Congress, Washington, D.C.
United States Strategic Bombing Survey Files
Ohmae, Capt. T. and Comdr. A Yamaguchi. Interrogation Report no. 495, 6 Dec. 1945.
Yunoki, Lt. Comdr. S.

Questionnaires/Interviews with Allied Servicemen
The U.S. Army Military History Institute houses a collection of questionnaires that were mailed to thousands of combat veterans. None are dated. Several afford important anecdotal information about such issues as war neurosis on New Georgia. Some respondents included longer unpublished documents with their questionnaires.

Archives, U.S. Army Military History Institute, Carlisle Barracks, Pa.
Baker, Capt. Arthur.
Baldwin, Sgt. Bryan.
Davis, Capt. Arthur.
Friedburg, Capt. Isadore.

Henne, Capt. Charles.
Laplant, Cpl. Maurice.
O'Connell, Sgt. Arthur.

Interviews by Author
Bradley, Jesse. San Diego, Calif. Sept. 1999.
Brown, Harold. Glastonbury, Conn. Oct. 1996.
Burton, Louis. Slidell, La. Jan. 1997.
Chase, James. Cape Cod, Mass. Feb. 1999.
DiMauro, Sam. Glastonbury, Conn. Oct. 1996.
Emmons, Vernon. San Antonio, Tex. June 1997.
Finkle, Hugh. Glastonbury, Conn. Oct. 1996.
Gilman, Robert. Baton Rouge, La. Nov. 1996.
Grady, Robert. Glastonbury, Conn. Oct. 1996.
Grotton, Carl. Baton Rouge, La. Nov. 1996.
Guidone, Frank. Correspondence. Las Vegas, Nev. Dec. 1998.
Henne, Charles. Interview and correspondence. Gilbert, Ariz. July 1997.
Kean, William. Glastonbury, Conn. Oct. 1996.
Kliebert, Mrs. N. T. Correspondence. Cypress, Calif. May 1999.
Lambert, Earl. Metairie, La. July 1999.
Odett, Fred. San Diego, Calif. Sept. 1999.
O'Hara, Joseph. Glastonbury, Conn. Oct. 1996.
Schwolsky, Robert. Glastonbury, Conn. Oct. 1996.
Wilcox, Jack. Glastonbury, Conn. Oct. 1996.
Wilson, Norvil. San Antonio, Tex. June 1997.
Winialski, Raymond. Glastonbury, Conn. Oct. 1996.

Published Sources

Books

Despite their age, the official military histories of the Pacific War remain dependable references for researchers to consult. They are thorough, heavily documented, and objective. John Miller Jr.'s *Cartwheel: The Reduction of Rabaul* provides a solid framework for the New Georgia story with particular respect to the army. For a detailed account of the Marine Corps's role, Maj. John N. Rentz's *Marines in the Central Solomons* and Henry T. Shaw's and Maj. Douglas T.

Kane's *The Isolation of Rabaul* should not be overlooked. Samuel Eliot Morison's *Breaking the Bismarcks Barrier* in his series on the U.S. Navy in World War II provides an excellent analysis of the most important sea engagements of the operation. The air war is adequately described in Wesley Frank Craven's and James Lea Cate's *The Pacific: Guadalcanal to Saipan,* part of their seven-volume history of the U.S. Army Air Forces in World War II. The very best source of information on the coastwatchers is Walter Lord's well-researched *Lonely Vigil: The Coast Watchers of the Solomons,* which should be required reading for any scholarly assessment of combat operations in the Solomons.

Abney, Capt. John. "We Are Going to Ditch." In *The U.S. Marine Corps in World War II,* ed. S. E. Smith. New York: Random House, 1969.

Avery, Capt. Bennett F., ed. *The History of the Medical Department of the U.S. Navy in WWII.* Vol. 2. Washington: U.S. Government Printing Office, 1953.

Bennett, Judith A. *Wealth of the Solomons: A History of the Archipelago, 1800–1978.* Honolulu: University of Hawaii Press, 1987.

Bergerud, Eric. *Touched with Fire: The Land War in the South Pacific.* New York: Viking, 1996.

Berry, Henry. *Semper Fi, Mac.* New York: Arbor House, 1982.

Blake, Capt. Robert W. "The Battle Without a Name." In *The 100 Best True Stories of World War II.* New York: William H. Wise, 1945.

———. "Death on the Munda Trail." In *The U.S. Marine Corps in World War II,* ed. S. E. Smith. New York: Random House, 1969.

Breuer, William. *Devil Boats: The PT War Against Japan.* Novato, Calif: Presidio Press, 1987.

Brill, Norman Q., and Gilbert Beebe. *A Follow-Up Study of War Neurosis.* Washington: Veterans Administration, 1955.

Bulkley, Capt. Robert. *At Close Quarters: PT Boats in the U.S. Navy.* Washington: U.S. Government Printing Office, 1961.

Cary, Otis, ed. *War-Wasted Asia: Letters, 1945–46.* Tokyo: Kodansha International, 1975.

Clemens, Martin. *Alone on Guadalcanal: A Coastwatcher's Story.* Annapolis, Md.: Naval Institute Press, 1998.

Combat Narratives—Solomon Islands Campaign: Operations in the New Georgia Area, 21 June–5 Aug. 1943. Washington: Office of Naval Intelligence, 1943.

Condon-Rall, Mary Ellen, and Albert E. Cowdrey. *Medical Service in the War Against Japan.* U.S. Army in World War II. Washington: Center of Military History, 1998.

Congdon, Don, ed. *Combat WWII.* New York: Arbor House, 1993.

Cook, Haruko Taya, and Theodore F. Cook. *Japan at War: An Oral History.* New York: New Press, 1992.

Coulis, Sgt. Anthony P. "The March to Viru Harbor." In *The U.S. Marine Corps in World War II,* ed. S. E. Smith. New York: Random House, 1969.

Cowdrey, Albert E. *Fighting for Life.* New York: Free Press, 1994.

Craven, Wesley F. and James L. Cate, eds. *The Pacific: Guadalcanal to Saipan.* The Army Air Forces in World War II, vol. 2. Chicago: University of Chicago Press, 1950.

Crenshaw, Russell Sydnor Jr. *South Pacific Destroyer: The Battle for the Solomons from Savo Island to Vella Gulf.* Annapolis, Md.: Naval Institute Press, 1998.

Davis, John H. *The Kennedys: Dynasty and Disaster, 1848–1984.* New York: McGraw-Hill, 1985.

Dod, Karl C. *The Corps of Engineers.* Vol. 2, *The War Against Japan.* U. S. Army in World War II. Washington: Office of the Chief of Military History, Department of the Army, 1966.

Donovan, Robert J. *PT 109.* New York: McGraw-Hill, 1961.

Dull, Paul L. *A Battle History of the Imperial Japanese Navy, 1941–45.* Annapolis, Md.: U.S. Naval Institute, 1978.

Dyer, Vice Adm. George. *The Amphibians Came to Conquer: The Story of Admiral Richmond Kelly Turner.* Washington: U.S. Government Printing Office, 1969.

Ellis, John. *Brute Force: Allied Strategy and Tactics in the Second World War.* New York: Viking, 1990.

Fahey, James J. *Pacific War Diary.* New York: Kensington, 1962.

Forty, George. *U.S. Army Handbook, 1939–1945.* New York: Charles Scribner and Sons, 1979.

Fox, Charles E. *The Story of the Solomons.* Sydney: Pacific Publications, 1967.

Frank, Richard. *Guadalcanal: The Definitive Account of the Landmark Battle.* New York: Penguin, 1990.

Frankel, Stanley A. *The 37th Infantry Division in WWII.* Washington: Infantry Journal Press, 1948.

―――. *World War II in the South Pacific.* Scarsdale, N.Y.: Stanley Frankel, 1992.

Gegeo, David W., Geoffrey M. White et al., eds. *The Big Death: Solomon Islanders Remember World War II.* Suva, Fiji: Institute of Pacific Studies, 1988.

Girardeau, Lt. Col. Marvin D. *Dragons Peninsula.* New York: Vantage Press, 1967.

Greenfield, Kent R., ed. *Command Decisions.* Washington: Office of the Chief of Military History, Department of the Army, 1960.

Grinker, Lt. Col. Roy R., and Maj. John P. Spiegel. *War Neurosis.* Philadelphia: Blakiston, 1945.

Guppy, H. B. *The Solomon Islands and Their Neighbors.* London: Swan, Sonnenschein, Lowray, 1887.

Hall, D. O. W. *Coastwatchers.* Wellington, N.Z.: War History Branch, Department of Internal Affairs, 1951.

Hall, Leonard G. *Brothers of the Fox.* Orange, Tex.: Leonard Hall, 1986.

Halsey, Adm. William F., and Lt. Comdr. Joseph Bryan III. *Admiral Halsey's Story.* New York: Whittlesey House, 1947.

Hammel, Eric. *Munda Trail.* New York: Avon, 1989.

―――. *Aces Against Japan: The American Aces Speak.* Vol. 1. Novato, Calif: Presidio Press, 1992.

―――. *Aces Against Japan: The American Aces Speak.* Vol. 2. Pacifica, Calif: Pacifica Press, 1996.

Haney, Ken. *U.S. Navy Medical Personnel in Marine Parachute and Raider Battalions.* Jackson, Tenn.: Ken Haney, 1989.

Hata, Ikuhiko, and Yasuho Izawa. *Japanese Naval Aces and Fighter Units in World War II.* Annapolis, Md.: Naval Institute Press, 1989.

Hayashi, Saburo, and Alvin D. Coox. *Kogun: The Japanese Army in the Pacific War.* Quantico, Va.: Marine Corps Association, 1959.

Hepburn, Francis, ed. *Thank You Father Redmond.* San Diego: U.S. Marine Raider Association, 1993.

Higgins, Col. John. *A History of the 1st Connecticut Regiment, 1672–1963.* Hartford, Conn.: John Higgins, 1963.

Hoffman, Maj. Jon T. *From Makin to Bougainville: Marine Raiders in the Pacific War.* Washington: Marine Corps Historical Center, 1995.

Honan, Mark, and David Harcombe. *Solomon Islands.* 3rd ed. Hawthorne, Aus.: Lonely Planet, 1997.

Horton, D. C. Fire *Over the Islands: The Coast Watchers of the Solomons.* Sydney: A. H. and A.W. Reed, 1970.

———. *New Georgia: Pattern for Victory.* New York: Ballantine, 1971.

Howlett, R. A. *The History of the Fiji Military Forces, 1939–1945.* London: Crown Agents of the Colonies, 1948.

Hoyt, Edwin P. *The Glory of the Solomons.* New York: Stein and Day, 1983.

———. *Marine Raiders.* New York: Pocket Books, 1989.

Huie, William B. "Seabees and Mud at Munda." In *The 100 Best True Stories of World War II.* New York: William H. Wise, 1945.

———. "Men and Mud." In *The U.S. Navy in World War II,* ed. S. E. Smith. New York: Ballantine, 1967.

Ienaga, Saburo. *The Pacific War, 1931–1945.* New York: Pantheon, 1978.

Isely, Jeter, and Phillip A. Crowl. *The U.S. Marines and Amphibious War: Its Theory and Its Practice in the Pacific.* Princeton, N.J.: Princeton University Press, 1951.

Kent, Janet. *The Solomon Islands.* Harrisburg, Pa.: Stackpole, 1972.

Kilpatrick, C. W. *The Naval Night Battles in the Solomons.* Pampano Beach: Exposition Press of Florida, 1987.

Kleber, Brooks, and Dale Birdsell. *The Chemical Warfare Service.* Vol. 3, *Chemicals in Combat.* U.S. Army in World War II. Washington: Office of the Chief of Military History, Department of the Army, 1966.

Koburger, Charles W. Jr. *Pacific Turning Point: The Solomons Campaign, 1942–43.* Westport, Conn.: Praeger, 1995.

Leckie, Robert. *Strong Men Armed: The U.S. Marines Against Japan.* New York: Bonanza, 1962.

Linderman, Gerald F. *The World Within War: America's Combat Experience in World War II.* New York: Free Press, 1997.

Lindstrom, Lamont, and Geoffrey A. White, eds. *The Pacific Theater: Island Representations of World War II.* Honolulu: Center for Pacific Island Studies, University of Hawaii, 1989.

Lord, Walter. *Lonely Vigil: Coastwatchers of the Solomons.* New York: Viking, 1977.

Lucas, Jim. *Combat Correspondent*. Cornwall, N.Y.: Cornwall Press, 1944.

————. "Occupation of the Russells." In *The U.S. Marine Corps in World War II*, ed. S. E. Smith. New York: Random House, 1969.

Manchester, William. *American Caesar: Douglas MacArthur, 1880–1964*. New York: Dell, 1978.

Maroon, Capt. Thomas J. *War in the South Pacific: A Soldier's Journal*. Winslow, Me.: Tom Maroon, 1995.

Martin, Ralph G. *The G.I. War, 1941–1945*. Boston: Little, Brown, 1969.

McCormick, John. *The Right Kind of War*. Annapolis, Md.: Naval Institute Press, 1992.

McManus, John C. *The Deadly Brotherhood: The American Combat Soldier in World War II*. Novato, Calif: Presidio Press, 1998.

Mesky, Peter. *Time of the Aces: Marine Pilots in the Solomon Islands, 1942–1944*. Washington: Marine Corps Historical Center, 1993.

Miller, Arthur. *Situation Normal . . .* New York: Reynal and Hitchcock, 1944.

Miller, Francis T. *The Complete History of World War II*. Chicago: Progress Research, 1950.

Miller, Hugh B. "The Castaway of Arundel Island." In *The 100 Best True Stories of World War II*. New York: William H. Wise, 1945.

Miller, John Jr. *Cartwheel: The Reduction of Rabaul*. U.S. Army in World War II. Washington: Office of the Chief of Military History, Department of the Army, 1959.

Morison, Samuel E. *Breaking the Bismarcks Barrier: 22 July 1942–1 May 1944*. History of U.S. Naval Operations in World War II, vol. 6. Boston: Little, Brown, 1950.

Morris, Ivan. *The Nobility of Failure: Tropic Heroes in the History of Japan*. New York: Holt, Rienhart and Winston, 1975.

Morriss, Sgt. Mack. "The Five Day Attack on Hastings Ridge." In *The Best from Yank, the Army Weekly*. New York: E. P. Hutton, 1945.

————. "Infantry Battle in New Georgia." In *The Best from Yank, the Army Weekly*. New York: E. P. Hutton, 1945.

Morton, Louis. *The War in the Pacific: Strategy and Command, The First Two Years*. U.S. Army in World War II. Washington: Office of the Chief of Military History, Department of the Army, 1962.

Mullins, Col. William, ed. *Neuropsychiatry in World War II*. Vol. 2, *Overseas Theaters*. Washington: Office of the Surgeon General, Department of the Army, 1973.

Mytinger, Caroline. *Headhunting in the Solomon Islands Around the Coral Sea*. New York: Macmillan, 1942.

Okumiya, Masatake, and Jiro Horikoshi. *Zero!* New York: E. P. Dutton, 1956.

Peatross, Maj. Gen. Oscar F. *Bless 'em All: The Marine Raiders of World War II*. Irvine, Calif.: Review Publications, 1995.

Porter, Col. R. Bruce. *Ace! A Marine Night-Fighter Pilot in World War II*. Pacifica, Calif.: Pacifica Press, 1985.

Potter, E. B. *Nimitz*. Norwalk, Conn.: Easton Press, 1976.

———. *Bull Halsey*. Annapolis, Md.: Naval Institute Press, 1985.

Prados, John. *Combined Fleet Decoded: The Secret History of American Intelligence and the Japanese Navy in World War II*. New York: Random House, 1995.

Pratt, Fletcher. *The Marines' War*. New York: William Sloan, 1948.

Quin, Andreè. *The Solomons: Strategic Stepping Stones in the Pacific*. Sydney: Les Editions du Courrier Australien, n.d.

Rentz, Maj. John N. *Marines in the Central Solomons*. Nashville: Battery Press, 1952.

Rhoades, Lt. Comdr. F. A. *Diary of a Coastwatcher in the Solomons*. Fredericksburg, Tex.: Nimitz Foundation, 1982.

Rosenquist, R. G., Martin I. Sexton, and Robert Buerlein, eds. *Our Kind of War*. Richmond: American Historical Foundation, 1990.

Shaw, Henry T. Jr., and Maj. Douglas Kane. *The Isolation of Rabaul*. History of the U.S. Marine Corps in World War II. Vol. 2. Washington: Marine Corps Historical Branch, 1963.

Sherrod, Robert. *History of Marine Corps Aviation in World War II*. Washington: Combat Forces Press, 1952.

Smith, S. E., ed. *The U.S. Navy in World War II*. New York: Ballantine Books, 1967.

———. ed. *The U.S. Marine Corps in World War II*. New York: Random House, 1969.

Spector, Ronald. *Eagle Against the Sun*. New York: Vintage Books, 1985.

Stauffer, Alvin P. *The Quartermaster Corps*. Vol. 3, *Operations in the*

War Against Japan. U. S. Army in World War II. Washington: Office of the Chief of Military History, Department of the Army, 1956.

Steinberg, Rafael. *Island Fighting.* Alexandria, Va.: Time-Life Books, 1978.

Struben, Roy. *Coral and Colour of Gold.* London: Faber and Faber, 1961.

The Soldier's Guide to the Japanese Army. Washington: War Department, 1944.

United States Strategic Bombing Survey. *Interrogations of Japanese Officials,* vols. 1 and 2. Washington: U.S. Government Printing Office, 1946.

van der Vat, Dan. *The Pacific Campaign: The U.S.–Japanese Naval War, 1941–1945.* New York: Simon and Schuster, 1991.

Zimmer, Joseph E. *The History of the 43rd Division, 1941–1945.* Baton Rouge, La.: Army and Navy, n.d.

Zimmerman, J. L. *The Guadalcanal Campaign.* Washington: Headquarters, Marine Corps, Historical Division, 1949.

Periodicals

The *Raider Patch* is the official newsletter of the U.S. Marine Raider Association (Irvine, Calif.), It is a valuable source of anecdotal information on Raider activities and personalities during the war. Unfortunately, they exist only in private collections as of this printing. The *Buckeye Star News* (Gilbert, Ariz.) is the newsletter of the Lone Star Chapter of the 37th Infantry Division Veterans Association and is valuable in that its editor and publisher, a New Georgia veteran, provides an excellent history of his division in each edition. Bob Conrad's excellent series on the 169th Infantry Regiment in the *Hartford [Conn.] Courant* is based on his collection of oral histories and diaries. It delivers a superb grunt's–eye view of the New Georgia campaign. Clay Gowran, who walked with the 4th Raiders at Viru, wrote an indispensable account of that operation in the *Chicago Tribune.*

"A Guide to the Solomon Islands." *Pacific Islands Monthly,* Dec. 1942, 22.

Bachmann, Capt. Lawrence P. "Blocking Rabaul By Air." *Air Force,* May 1944, 49–54.

Batterton, Maj. Roy D. "You Fight by the Book." *Marine Corps Gazette,* July 1949, 14–21.

Biggerstaff, Howard. "Marine Writers Describe Attacks on Munda, Vila." *Chevron,* 1943, 2–3.

Bulger, Lowell. "Editor's Note." *Raider Patch,* July 1976, 12.

———. "Editor's Note." *Raider Patch,* July 1977, 5.

———. "Editor's Note." *Raider Patch,* Sept. 1979, 3, 11.

———. "Editor's Note." *Raider Patch,* Nov. 1979, 20.

"Berkley County Boy Tells Thrilling Adventure Tale." *Charleston (S.C.) News and Courier,* 1 Nov. 1943, 6.

"Campaign by Air." *Flying,* Oct. 1944, 46–47, 310.

Clemens, Martin. Letter. *Raider Patch,* July 1985, 1.

Conrad, Bob. "169th's Prelude to Jungle Warfare." *Hartford [Conn.] Courant,* A-8. 21 Feb. 1993.

———."A Call to Arms for Connecticut Regiment." *Hartford [Conn.] Courant,* 1 Oct. 1992, A-10.

———. "A Desperate Battle up a Dark Jungle Trail." *Hartford [Conn.] Courant,* 3 July 1993, A-6.

———. "Soldiers Fought Confusion in Jungle" *Hartford (Conn.) Courant,* 26 July 1993, A-1–A-5.

Cooper, Harold. "Kennedy's Boys Go-a-Feudin." *Pacific Islands Monthly,* July 1943.

DeChant, Capt. John. "Devil Birds." *Marine Corps Gazette,* Apr. 1947, 32–39.

———. "Milk Run to Munda." *Leatherneck,* July 1944, 22–23.

Dupuy, Col. Ernest. "Bibilo Hill—and Beyond," *Infantry Journal,* Jan. 1944, 21–26.

Eller, Byron. Letter. *Raider Patch,* Sept. 1983, 18.

Fairfax, John. "Blasted by War." *Pacific Islands Monthly,* Aug. 1943, 36.

Ferrin, Harold. Letter. *Raider Patch,* Mar. 1987, 24–25.

Gildart, Lt. Col. Robert C. "Artillery on New Georgia." *Field Artillery Journal,* Feb. 1944, 89.

Gill, Leslie. "Lambeti: How a Solomon Planter Returned Home." *Pacific Islands Monthly,* Mar. 1944, 8.

———. "Landing on Rendova." *Pacific Islands Monthly,* Apr. 1944, 8.

Gowran, Clay. "We Storm Viru." *Chicago Sunday Tribune,* 7 Nov. 1943, Graphic Section, 4; 14 Nov. 1943, 8–9; and 21 Nov. 1943, 4–5.

Gray, Olin. Letter. *Raider Patch,* May 1992, 10.

Griffith, Col. S. B. "Corry's Boys," *Marine Corps Gazette,* May 1949, 43–47.

Griffth, Col. S. B. "Action at Enogi," *Marine Corps Gazette,* Mar. 1944.

Hailey, Foster. "Night Raid on Vila." *U.S. Naval Institute Proceedings* 70 (Sept. 1944): 1111.

Hepburn, Francis. "Mortars." *Raider Patch,* Nov. 1989, 2.

———. *Raider Dope Sheet,* Apr. 1995, 17.

Henne, Charles. "Norvil Wilson Was There." *Buckeye Star News,* 1 Oct. 1997, 8–9.

Henne, Charles. "New Georgia Campaign—The First to Fight, the First to Die." Buckley Star News, 1 July 1997, 8.

Hersey, John. "Experience by Battle." *Life,* 27 Dec. 27, 48.

———. "Rendova, the Jungle." *Life,* 27 Dec. 1943: 71–73.

"Japs Gleeful as They Hack Wounded Yanks in Litters." *The Tribune,* 1 Feb. 1944.

Kelly, Maj. William H. "War Neurosis." *Infantry Journal,* Aug. 1946, 20–21.

Kennedy, Donald. "This Is the Solomon Islands in Peace." *Pacific Islands Monthly,* Sept. 1944, 24–26.

———. "Keeping Watch Over the Japs," *Pacific Islands Monthly,* Sept. 1945, 43–45.

———. "Battle of Morovo Lagoon." *Pacific Islands Monthly,* Mar. 1944, 34–35.

Lieberman, Capt. Joseph. "Road Construction on New Georgia." *Military Engineer,* Mar. 1944, 78.

Lodge, J. Norman. "Detroiter Tells of Massacre of American Wounded." *Detroit Free Press,* 9 Aug. 1943, 1, 20.

Mathieu, Capt. Charles Jr. "The Capture of Munda." *Marine Corps Gazette,* Nov. 1943, 31–32.

Maurer, Richard. Letter. *Raider Patch,* Nov. 1990, 15.

McDevitt, TSgt. Frank, and TSgt. Murray Marder. "The Capture of Enogai. " *Marine Corps Gazette,* Sept. 1943, 7–8.

"Meet the Marine Raiders Who Took Enogai Inlet." *Leatherneck,* Nov. 1943, 71.

Miner, Dr. Lee N. "The Ridge." *Raider Dope Sheet,* Jan. 1989, 8.

———. "The Ridge." *Raider Dope Sheet,* Mar. 1989, 12.

Mullener, Elizabeth. "Above and Beyond." *New Orleans Times-Picayune,* 25 July 1999, 10–11.

"Munda Airfield." *Life,* 6 Sept. 1943, 36–44.

Munger, Capt. Royal F. "Munda Jungle Nasty Foe, but Yanks Whip It." *Chicago Daily News,* 17 Jan. 1944, 11.

"Navy Catalinas Known as 'Black Cats' of Guadalcanal." *Aeropinion,* 25 May 1944.

"New Georgia Offensive." *Life,* 26 July 1943, 36–38.

"Plain Story of a Solomons Native." *Pacific Islands Monthly,* Mar. 1943, 27.

Redmond, Father Paul. Letter. *Raider Patch,* May 1976, 18.

Rothstein, Ruth. "Two Servicemen Home From Pacific Prefer Bombing to Night in Foxhole." *Hartford (Conn.) Courant,* n.d.

South Sea Reveille. 37th Infantry Division newsletter. n.d.

Spaulding, Roger. Letter. *Raider Patch,* May 1990, 22.

Spiller, Roger J. "Shell Shock." *American Heritage,* May-June 1990, 85–86.

Tolbert, Sgt. Frank. "Advance Man." *Leatherneck,* Mar. 1945, 15.

Van Deurs, George. "The Segi Man." *U.S. Naval Institute Proceedings* 84 (Oct. 1958): 56–61.

Wellings, Lt. Comdr. Joseph. 26. "The Night the *Strong* Was Sunk." *Shipmate,* July-Aug. 1977, 23–26.

Wells, Col. James B. "The Team on New Georgia." *Field Artillery Journal,* Nov. 1943, 843–45.

Wright, Capt. Eugene A., and Lt. Michael Mitchell. "Battle Facts for Your Outfit." *Infantry Journal,* Dec. 1943, 12–15.

Internet Sites

"Journal of E. E. Lajeunesse." www.geocities.com/CapeCanaveral/Hangar/5115/Gene.html

"Navy Medicine—July to August, 1943." www.nmimc-web1.med.navy.mil/bumed/med-09/med-09h/chron/file11.htm.

Index